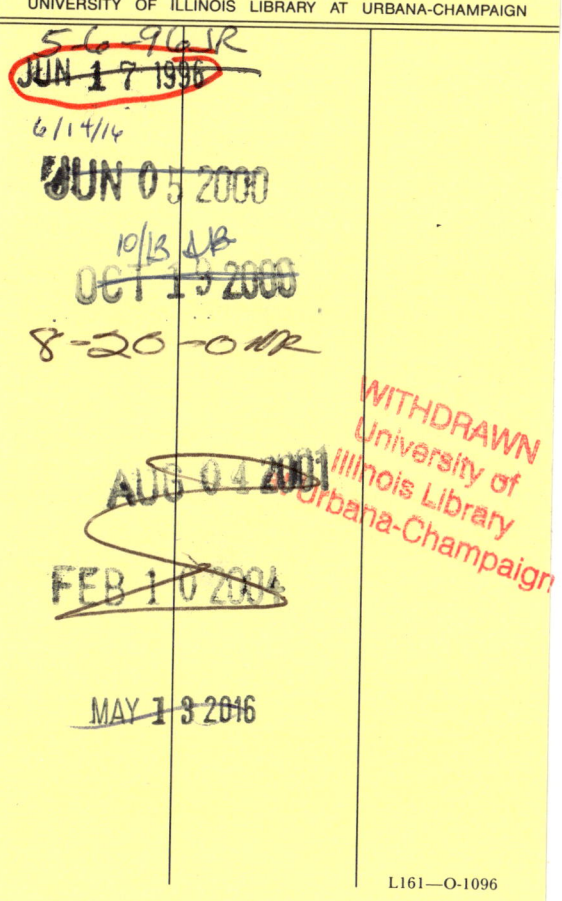

BENJAMIN BORETZ

META-
VARIATIONS

STUDIES IN THE FOUNDATIONS OF MUSICAL THOUGHT

J. K. RANDALL

COMPOSE
YOURSELF

A MANUAL FOR THE YOUNG

VOLUME 1: META-VARIATIONS

OPEN SPACE

This publication is made possible in part by a grant from the Princeton University Music Department, which is gratefully acknowledged.

Managing Editor for Open Space printbooks and audio-visual productions is Noel Bush. Published 1995 by Open Space, R.D. 2, Box 45E, Red Hook, N.Y. 12571.

ML 3880
B67M4
v.1

some background notes

In 1972–73, we were having intense, almost daily, discussions of issues which had been crystallizing out of, first, *Meta-Variations* (1968–69) and *Compose Yourself* (1970); and then, later, my "Nelson Goodman's *Languages of Art*" (1970) and "In Quest of the Rhythmic Genius" (1971), and Jim's *Depth of Surface* (1972) (on the Minuet of Beethoven's Op. 22, following on his earlier analysis of the slow movement of the *Ghost* Trio, which metamorphosed into *Compose Yourself*'s Revelstoke (Stimulating Speculation No. 3)). And then two texts, written almost simultaneously in the summer of 1973 ("a soundscroll" (JKR), "A World of Times" (BAB)), captured the drift of the process and opened it anew.

Our issues, the ones we returned to over and over, were, first, how to capture and represent, accurately and believably, our musical experience; and, second, how to extend and intensify it. We didn't spend much time discussing issues of philosophy, method, logic, or rhetorical style as such—the problem was always how best to get at what we so strenuously were struggling to get at: a satisfactory external interface with what we internally knew and intuited as 'music'. And the fundamental ontological claim of *Meta-Variations,* that the very being of music is created by cognitive attributions made by individual perceiving or conceiving imaginers, in individual acts of perceiving or conceiving—that, in fact, the only real music 'theory' *is* the creative-intellectual transaction which ontologizes music itself—was a primary conceptual environment for these discussions, and lent to them some of their particular urgency.

But also, we found ourselves trying to reclaim our issues, on our own ground, from what had already, even at that time, become a labyrinth of what we perceived as misconstruals—of intents, of preoccupations, of the implicated or desired effects of our work. The incompatibility of our sense of music, of our reason for doing it, with authoritarian, prescriptive, hegemonic constructions, was an overt text of our discourse, as far as we were concerned; the location of the identity of music in the volition of self-determining individual acts of music-cognizing or music-imagining made it theoretically absurd, as well as conceptually objectionable, to assert any sort of prescriptive closure for musical possibilities. Music theory, under our analysis, would have to be non-prescriptive even to *be* music theory,—rather than the theory of something else, or just an intellectual-looking cover for some kind of power-asserting operation. And it was obvious to us too that we did not want to 'logicize' or 'scientize' music, on similar grounds; what we could do and wanted to do was represent how our musical intuitions could be externalized and specified with the assistance of logic, 'scientific' models, or any other appropriately rigorous language as literalizing notations and sense-analytic (or nonsense-diagnostic) tools. But even some very attentive, even some very sympathetic, readers and onlisteners seemed to miss these crucial—to us it felt radical—turns our discourse was taking relative to a whole universe of long-standing givens—our own long-standing givens too—about the natures of music, of thinking, of discourse.* It may be that the epistemological gap thus exposed crystallized in that moment to become a defining feature of the music-intellectual culture we have inhabited since then.

A word about this publication:

These volumes are the first integral and complete publication of *Meta-Variations* and *Compose Yourself*. Both appeared serially in *Perspectives of New Music* between 1969 and 1974. The present version of *Meta-Variations* integrates its two previous versions, and incorporates a number of error corrections, non-substantive rewordings, newly added footnotes, and minor excisions; the text has been completely reset for this edition. The original publication of *Compose Yourself* paused after Part II, No. 4—in anticipation of the composition of Part II, No. 5, whose non-materialization is addressed on the title page of Part II, No. 6 in this edition. The text of *Compose Yourself* Part I and Part II Nos. 1–4 is reproduced directly from the pages of *Perspectives*. Part II, No. 6 was composed as a graphic (with artwork by Naomi Boretz) and is reproduced from the original pasted-up sheets. In that form, it was also printed in *News of Music* No. 11 (1990).

—B.A.B., 1995

---

*For example: in distinguishing 'reference' from 'surface', and thereby liberating both, *Meta-Variations* makes it coherent to imagine a neological (even a non-developmental, non-'teleological') music without sacrificing syntactical depth or determinacy.

META-VARIATIONS

STUDIES IN THE FOUNDATIONS OF MUSICAL THOUGHT

Benjamin Boretz
1969

OPEN SPACE

Meta-Variations was first published serially in *Perspectives of New Music*, Vol. 8 No. 1 (Fall–Winter 1969) [Preface, Introduction, Part I]; Vol. 8, No. 2 (Spring–Summer 1970) [Part II]; Vol. 9, No. 1 (Fall–Winter 1970) [Part III (1)]; Vol. 9, No. 2/10, No. 1 (1971) [Part III (2)]; Vol. 11, No. 1 (Fall–Winter 1972) [Part IV (1)]; Vol. 11, No. 2 (Spring–Summer 1973) [Part IV (2), Compositional Postscript]. For the present publication, all logical definitions were reviewed and re-inscribed (1993) by Keith Eisenbrey. Typography, layout, and graphics were done (1995) by Noel Bush.

Meta-Variations
Studies in the Foundations of Musical Thought

I. Preface: Normatives and Objectives 1

II. Introduction: Varieties of Musical
Thought and Confusion 11

III. Part I: Models and Metaphors in Musical Discourse

   INTRODUCTION 25

   THE THEORETICAL CHARACTER OF MUSICAL ENTITIES

   Music as thought:
   the cognitive status of "musical experience" 26

   Cognitive consequences of a "nonrational" model 29

   THE DESIGNATA OF MUSIC

   Music as "Given in Nature":
   the problem of apriorism 35

   Music as a "human-communicative"
   manifestation: the problem of universalism 41

   Music as a "uniformly qualified entity-class":
   the problem of noncontextual theoretical
   transference 43

   EXPLANATORY ADEQUACY

   Preconditions, applications, and
   limitations of music-explanatory power 49

   Model constructability as a general
   criterion of explanatory cognitivity 53

   LINGUISTIC MODELS AS MUSICAL MODELS 61

   CONCLUDING REMARKS 83

IV.   Part II: Sketch Of A Musical System..........................86
      MUSIC THEORY, EPISTEMOLOGY,
      AND CONSTRUCTIONAL SYSTEMS 88
      THE NOTION OF DEFINITION 90
      THE NOTIONS OF STRUCTURE
      AND MUSICAL COHERENCE..............................94
      THE EXTRALOGICAL BASES
      OF CONSTRUCTIONAL SYSTEMS 97
      THE EXTRALOGICAL BASIS
      OF THE SYSTEM TO BE SKETCHED 98
      THE ROLE OF SOUNDS IN MUSIC.....................100
      MUSIC-THEORETICAL SYSTEMS,
      AESTHETICS, AND EAR TRAINING....................102
      SOME CONCEPTUAL CONSEQUENCES
      OF A MUSIC-CONSTRUCTIONAL SYSTEM 111
      THE BEGINNING OF THE SYSTEM....................113
      OUTLINE OF THE CONSTRUCTION....................115
      PRIMITIVE SYMBOLS AND OPERATORS..........128
      PITCHES, PITCH FUNCTIONS,
      AND PITCH RELATIONS..................................129
         Syntactical operations on pitch-class intervals..............152
      TIME-ORDER PRIMITIVES,
      ORDER CLASSES, AND ORDER RELATIONS....................159
      CONCLUSION OF THE ALL-MUSICAL SYSTEM..............172

V.   Part III: Systematic and Extrasystematic
      Preconditions for the Construction
      of Musical Syntax
      THE NOTION OF REFERENCE..........................174

	CONTENT-CENTRICITY AND ORDER-DETERMINACY 177
	APPENDIX 189
	MUSICAL SYSTEMS: SOME PRELIMINARY REMARKS 196
	STRUCTURAL LEVELS 197
	POLYPHONY 208
	LINEARITY AND ADJACENCY 215
	STRUCTURAL COHERENCE IN "ORDER" AND "CONTENT" MUSIC 220
	OUTLINE OF A TONAL-SYNTACTICAL SYSTEM 224
VI.	**Part IV: Analytic Fallout (I)**
	ANALYSIS AND COMPOSITION 240
	ANALYTIC SIMPLICITY AND SYSTEMATIC GENERALITY 246
	THE *TRISTAN* PRELUDE 253
	WEBERN: OP.5, NO. 4 313
VII.	**Part IV: Analytic Fallout (II)**
	ABOUT COMPARISON 320
	THE FIRST EIGHTEEN MEASURES OF BRAHMS'S FOURTH SYMPHONY 325
	PETROUCHKA: FIRST SCENE 332
	SCHOENBERG: OP. 15, NO. 1, mm. 1–7 342
	CONCLUDING REMARKS 355
VIII.	**Compositional Postscript** 357
	References 373

I.
Preface:
Normatives and Objectives

This study originated in a compositionally induced aspiration to find ways of thinking *about* music that would accurately reflect and explicate the content, and ultimately feed back to the advantage, of that thinking *in* music which is the essential content of every musical activity, compositional, analytic, theoretical, or merely auditional. What this led to was an attempt to discover conditions and principles at least minimally adequate to account for the conceptual richness we ascribe to music, in terms of the cognitive foundation on which that ascription rests. In the course of inquiry, many issues that seemed crucial were turned up and inspected. This essay is essentially a report of the results of that inspection. In it, concepts that seemed underanalyzed in the traditional literature are tentatively re-explicated, and only those that stubbornly resisted microscopic scrutiny for glimmers of possible cognitivity or rational purpose in their use are dismissed. On the other hand, concepts that seemed to present promising candidacy for membership in a foundational basis for all musical thought are placed herein in defined orderings intended to extrude a maximum degree of interrelation in the hope of providing a radically simplified map of what is generally understood about music in order to facilitate inquiry into what isn't. Moreover, the possibility of such an extreme simplification at the very base of musical thought, where maximal complexity had previously seemed unavoidable, raises the hopeful expectancy of perceptions and realizations of unprecedented degrees of subtlety and complexity at the higher levels of musical structure and relation.

The fear—or rather certainty—of the non-ultimacy of any of the formulations arrived at in the course of this study I have taken not as an inhibiting but rather as a motivating consideration: for only by having available formulated questions, answers, and theories to refute is it possible for a discipline to develop and sharpen the tools with which to discover deeper answers to subtler questions. And not only is the encouragement of further investigation itself a prime and worthy objective of research in any discipline, but the very fact of subsequent falsification is, if not the most gratifying, surely the most valuable (and manifestly the sincerest) form of emulation. Thus, like Nelson Goodman, I too, look forward to the time when rational thinkers "will be known by the topics they study rather than by the views they hold."[1]

At the same time, it is easier to rationalize the motivations of such a formidable undertaking than it is to defend the mode or adequacy of its realization. For I do find myself still in a very primitive state, conceptually and methodologically speaking, with respect to the inexhaustibly tricky and ramified questions engaged herein, many of which are near the very center of today's extraordinary Quinean/Goodmanian implosion in empiricist epistemology and its linguistic origins and consequences. And there is little direct help available from the literature of either musical or philosophical thought. Why, then, should a musician, specifically a composer, elect or presume to intrude on ground so evidently more properly, or at least ultimately, the domain of the professional technical philosopher? The answer may be found in the confluence of the urgent music-intellectual needs expressed above and the awareness of the demonstrable benefits that accrue to scientific enterprises from cognitive analyses of their methods and concepts such as are undertaken by philosophers of science. And since, in our area, such analyses have either not been undertaken by philosophers, or their efforts have failed to engage the relevant issues (in the sense of asking or answering questions that musicians themselves consider significant), there seems to be obvious potential value in a practitioner's own attempt to find correlates for his field of the insights into cognitive concepts and methods developed in connection with other fields. At the very least, such an attempt might be useful in persuading philosophers of the appropriateness of one's field as a domain for their discourse, so that the benefits of philosophical thought might be enlisted directly for music as they have been for science and language.

But how, in advance of this utopian eventuality, can philosophical considerations relevant to empirical science be made useful or valuable to music? Here a declaration of normative bias is a conscientious requirement: I do think of music, composition as

---

[1]Goodman [53], p. xviii.

well as explanation, as actually constituting an "empirical science" in an important sense, a sense that bears directly on the confrontation with *traditional* questions in both musical domains. Thus it might be useful to begin by showing, in a more than heuristic or analogical way, how I believe this identification (or at least association) can be asserted and used.

The issue itself has much to do with a deep conviction that, whereas "aesthetics" deals with what it calls "works of art", rational metamusical discourse might better concern itself with "works of thought", for the emotive "values" dealt with in aesthetics are evidently not a necessary, nor a customary (not perhaps even, ultimately, a possible) concern in the investigation of the cognitive aspects of musical *composition* and *understanding*. But such a conviction (perhaps counterintuitively for some readers) equally entails the rejection of a trivialized notion of musical structure as pure "design", as inadequate to account for the intellectual significance we wish to attribute, and feel justified in attributing, to "works of thought" in music as well as in the other "arts". Thus our "scientific attitude" resists purely descriptive characterizations or pure "formalization" just as much as it does pure attitudinal aesthetics. We might, for analogy, locate the "scientific" position toward music in that of Goodman toward philosophy, as "...having the function of clearing away perplexity and confusion on the most humble as well as the most exalted levels of thought...in philosophy as in science, the microscopic attitude has its own fascinations and rewards".[2]

In adopting such an attitude, we obviously would not mean to "equate" musical thought with that of any actual science; especially, we do not rely on results of physical research, and do not invoke such "correlative" measurements as those of "frequency" to "explain" perceptual phenomena such as "pitch relations" any more than we would use "wave lengths" to explain "color relations".[3] These senses of the "scientific" are, in fact, quite as external to our concerns as are the "abstractly formal" or "aesthetic" notions mentioned above; but research conducted in any of the areas mentioned may be interesting insofar as the correlations produced with results in, e.g., physics, psychoacoustics, sociopsychology, and combinatory theory, are revealing or suggestive.

---

[2] [53], p. xviii.
[3] A different music-science dichotomy is discussed in Part IV.

Moreover, since mathematics and other uninterpreted calculi are merely schemata on which "meaning" is conferred only by "semantic interpretation", and since, as languages of pure relation, symbolic logic and mathematics (taken as wholes or as fragments) are trivially capable of being regarded in inexhaustible ways as characterizing any relations whatever, and only through a system of correlates can any *particular* such characterization be judged preferable to any other, so questions of the *formal* niceties of logicization or arithmeticization are equally irrelevant to our specifically musical pursuits.

These strictures may or may not correspond in spirit, effect, or detail to Babbitt's by now famous (or notorious) dictum of 1961 regarding the use of "scientific language" and "scientific method".[4] For it should be evident that I do not (though I cannot of course speak for Babbitt) equate the notion of "music as a scientific discipline" with any further notion that it is thus a mere tributary of existing scientific disciplines, of whatever sort.[5] On the contrary, I mean to insist that the statements made about music by its practitioners are at least potentially capable of cognitive explication, whatever their evident deficiencies in rigor or coherence, and that this cognitive potential is independently supported by principles of thought developed with unique reference to the element- and relation-concepts particular to music. And any correlation like the "musical-scientific" one proposed here, involving a juxtaposition of two disparate domains, is, moreover, always necessarily regarded as preeminently metalinguistic and partial;[6] for in the present instance it is just the evidence of the potential of music for positive cognitivity and independence that justifies the application to it of the "scientific" epithet. One could, in fact, make the point just as well by invoking some metaterminological fabrication applicable equally to "sciences", "arts", and other "thoughts"—such as,

---

[4] In *Proceedings of the International Musicological Congress*, 1961.

[5] As, e.g., Arthur Berger seems to do (cf. his [6], pp 2–3). For otherwise his distinction of rigor from "system-building" and "scientific method" is unintelligible although the appearance of the term "musicology" as an apparently persuasive term of opprobrious implication may provide a clue to the rationale involved.

[6] This consideration is closely related to those involved in the "thought-language" analogy proposed in Sellars [69] and in the discussion of "cognitive synonomy" in Quine, esp. [66].

say, "cognitive language", "cognitive method", and "cognitive discipline".[7]

Of course, one might also just as well take the converse tack, as J. K. Randall does in the first lecture of [32], and be at pains to warn against the confusion of musical thought with that of any separate science by demonstrating that some of the crucial issues being engaged in supposedly other-scientific research (as, e.g., experiments in "psychoacoustics") are properly understandable only as music-cognitive ones. By asserting the possibility of the distinction of course, Randall actually makes the same point as mine, but my emphasis on the nature of the musical discipline as cognitive in principle, however ruggedly independent its internal postulates and modes of observation are at the same time admitted to be, is intended in part to make visible the possibility of usefully employing for our musical purposes methods, appropriately translated (and again, *that* is only possible where one's discipline does have a cognitive basis), that have been developed to deal with problems in other fields, as well as the equally valuable possibility of acquiring frameworks for the judgment of the adequacy of our methods to accomplish just those internal purposes we have intended them to serve. The latter in particular may be accomplished by "plugging in" (again through appropriate correspondence rules) a musical "method" not only to methods in "other fields", but also to general epistemological-methodological systems developed by the "scientists" of cognition itself, i.e., philosophers.

But these methodological considerations should not be construed as suggesting that expertise as a physicist, logician, philosopher, psychologist, or mathematician confers any *a priori* authority with respect to musical methods or results. It is only the judgment by musicians of the adequacy of their own results, the degree to which their methods provide them with answers that they regard as satisfactory to questions they regard as significant, that is considered to be at issue in this essay. If the methods of cognitive analysis, criticism, and construction show that they are capable of producing better answers (that is, ones closer to what musicians want), or further ranges of unexpected possibility, than are available in the existing music-conceptual arsenal, or if the ap-

---

[7]Thus, in school curricula, it would no longer be necessary or appropriate to distinguish the Arts from the Sciences, but only the Thoughts from the Acts.

plication of such methods shows that the answers traditionally arrived at are actually not as clear or applicable or operationally distinct as had been supposed, then we may feel amply well served by the invocation of these methods for our own purposes just to the extent that we care about whether our own thought and discovery are under control and freed from the inhibition of the possible, the hypothetical, and the speculative, by the local, the conventional, or the superficial. Nor does the "theory-practice" relation, as here conceived, contain any "imperatives" either: The theorist, in producing "theoretical discourse" is under no absolute *obligation* to acknowledge as such the musical "theorizing" that *may* be inferred from what is compositionally unfolded; the point is, that he *can*. Nor *must* any composer make only considered, or maximally considered, choices in doing composition. But taken in its most general sense, "theory" liberates "practice", interpreting musical "specifics" in terms that make them usable to inform progressively more unlike-appearing things. The more "defined" are the more "dimensions" of a musical "syntax", the more the ways that can be conceived for compositions "therein" to be deeply and uniquely expressive of their determining relationships. And in the same sense that practice is no more than what theory makes of it, so there is no theory distinct from the discoverable cognitive content of a given use of the phrase, "this piece".

But there is a further aspect of the "music as science" analogy envisioned here that may actually best be suggested by a purely heuristic explication: The physical scientist "constructs" the world, then tests the viability of "his" structure against the measurable "facts" of observation. An experiment is a specific delimitation of a field of observation within a finite segment of the physical world taken as "the" significant "universe" under consideration, the orderings of observations within which field are scaled according to the magnitudes relevant to the properties being tested for. Thus the special universe and the measuring devices applied against it are so constructed as to isolate and project specific relations as functions of underlying structural properties for which there exist (or are created) concepts; the experimental complex is designed as the optimum medium through which the variable operations of these properties may be inferred. In physical science, then, the "resistant element" is the "behavior" of physical phenomena in producing "physical measurements".

In music, on the other hand, the "resistant elements" are the psycho-physiological limitations of auditory response and cognition; and although musicians are, by the nature of their "universe", much better able than physical scientists to construct "universal complexes" which actually exhibit the "order" imputed to them, "surprises" do happen constantly at thresholds of human capacity in these domains.[8] In this context, composition may be described as the definition and creation of a relational universe of elements in whose interrelations are embedded hypothetical (along with previously, empirically validated) properties of "relational behavior", a hypothesis, that is, of "what can be learned to be heard" on the basis of what has already, by "appropriate receptors", *been* "learned to be heard".[9] And what is "heard", in this sense, is only to begin with the pure "data" of the composition; ultimately, it is the reasonable possibility that from this data the relational properties embedded might be the "most favorably" inferable things that "justifies" the composer's "experiment". For just so, the data of a physical experiment have no imperative interpretation either, but—at least in its objective of construction—its selections of data should reasonably be expected to make particular slicings thereof particularly plausible. And just as the "experiment" is like the "composition", so its interpretations in terms of local structures and general principles of structure are comparable to the musical activities of analyzing and theorizing about individual compositions and classes thereof.

In music, of course, all the "measuring instruments" are perceptual, not physical; but their measurements, on the quantizational scales needed to infer all the significatively embedded properties, are equivalently precise and unambiguous (which should not be surprising in view of the fact that the data were to begin with arranged so that their significant attributes would lie in a range where such precision on the part of such a non-mechanical measuring device as the human auditory mechanism would be feasible). And it is just this possibility of precision in music, understood as the perception of precisely definable functions among precisely delimitable elements, that makes also possible the extraordinary devel-

---

[8]E.g., experiments publicly reported by Babbitt in as yet (1969) unpublished lectures; but see also the *caveats* in Randall [31] and [32].

[9]This formulation is indebted to Babbitt.

opment of works of music as complex structures of cognitive thought, and thus as participants—whose significance as such has perhaps been overlooked—in the contemporary intellectual effort to extend maximal rational control over phenomena and situations of maximal structural complexity.

From the foregoing, it follows that, in contrast to the tendencies of some recent "philosophical" approaches to musical structure, my concerns here are first of all with *epistemic* matters (in keeping with my interest in the elucidation and resolution of *traditional* musical puzzles, in which of course are included any uniquely contemporary ones arising directly from the practice of musical thought *qua* musical thought). And hereby, too, arises my initially noted conviction that the aptness of the motivation for an essay of this kind in this context is relatively defensible: since the "technical" characteristics of a composition are completely available from a study of the score, it seems appropriate that a composer's verbal endeavors be addressed to the considerations that provide the *rationale* for the engagement, development, use, and belief in the efficacy and compositional relevance of, those techniques.

In the elucidation of such a rationale, these studies range over a rather ambitiously broad field of subjects, from the variant categories of musical discourse and the explanatory adequacy of means employed therein, to questions of "foundation theory", and specific analytic and compositional matters. None of these issues is engaged in great depth in itself; such depth is not only beyond the least modest construction placed on the appropriate scope of such an essay as this, but is not really its objective. The idea is rather to sketch a conceptual progression, from the most general "what-is-music" considerations to the most particular issues arising in individual compositions, with the idea of, first, indicating a conviction that they can (and by implication really *need* to) be continuously interlinked, and, second, indicating one such path of linkage in the conceptual scheme of, at least, one composer .

This, too, is the place for acknowledgments, which as always are offered as assignments of indispensability rather than responsibility. They seem especially crucial in this essay since no amount of citation, however conscientious, could account even minimally for the extent of its indebtedness. Above all, the myriad influences of the ideas, methods and insights of Milton Babbitt are manifest on every page, beyond any hope of explicit acknowledgment, though they will be unmistakable to knowledgeable readers. Indeed, any original contribution ascribable to the contents hereof is, in essence, a rearrangement of the furniture in a music-conceptual world first conceived, constructed, and inhabited as an integral musical and intellectual "total environment" by Babbitt. The lines along which the particular rearrangement is proposed have themselves been envisaged and developed in largest part in the course of a long and close intellectual friendship with J. K. Randall, whose participation in the genesis and, in its final stages, the realization of this essay has frequently crossed the boundary of collaboration. Indeed, what communicative lucidity is attained herein is due largely to his inexhaustible patience and persistence; the residual opacities, as well as the views expressed, are of course my own responsibility.

Special mention should be made, too, of the fertile intellectual presence and example of Godfrey Winham, who has given attention to many of the questions dealt with herein, though along significantly different lines. Since most of his work remains, unhappily, publicly inaccessible, I am especially glad of an occasion to call to it the serious awareness it merits.

To my teacher Arthur Berger is due my first explicit realization of the possibility, scope, and nature of musical intellection, and an impressive exemplification of the "examined traditionalism" that still seems to me the heart of my music-intellectual concerns; but I am aware that he may regard the present manifestation of these concerns as divergences from rather than projections of his example.

I am indebted, too, to the work, counsel, and attention of Edward T. Cone, with whom I share many preoccupations if perhaps fewer conclusions; but his criticism and encouragement have both been of significant value in the course of this study. I have benefited, also, from discussion with Peter Westergaard, as well as from his writings. And David Burrows has long been a faithful, conscientious, skeptical, and perceptive critic and lucid advocate of divergent positions on many issues, in many intense and important discussions. Murray Gould performed the valuable and difficult service of testing the formulations and definitions in Parts II and III.* The illumination I have found in conversations with colleagues and friends engaged in the practice of philosophy is (except in the case of Mary Gibson) too indirect to make explicit recognition practical; but it has been no less vital therefor.

Finally, acknowledgment is due to those organizations and responsible individuals who helped in the development of these ideas by making available a public forum for their exposure. The papers that most directly formed the basis for this essay were read at Denison University in March, 1967; before the Hunter College Philosophy Society in November, 1967; at the national conference of the American Musicological Society in Santa Barbara in December, 1967; before the New England Chapter of the American Musicological Society (Leo Treitler, chairman) in March, 1968; and at the Third Annual Conference of the American Society of University Composers in April, 1968.**

---

*(1993): Keith Eisenbrey is responsible for verifying and reassembling the logical definitions in Part II for the benefit of this publication.

**(1993): The Princeton Music Department, by inviting me to submit one of the initial dissertations for its new Ph.D. in musical composition, provided a probably irreplaceable occasion for the integral writing of this text.

II.
Introduction:
Varieties of Musical Thought and Confusion

> ...a discourse is regarded as intelligible not only if it is formulated wholly in observational language, but also if it is formulated in theoretical or mixed language, if only the theoretical terms in it are connected via theoretical postulates and rules of correspondence with the observation terms...nevertheless, [though] the analytic philosopher may be willing to regard the specifically metaphysical terms used by his colleagues as theoretical terms of which he is quite ready not to require more than partial or indirect interpretation...he will continue to ask his colleague to supply him this interpretation at least in sufficient outline...most analytic philosophers are today aware ...that the line of demarcation between theoretical and observational terms is blurred, elastic, and even to a certain extent arbitrary, and will therefore be rather careful with their use of the epithets 'meaningless', 'nonsensical', or 'unintelligible'. But... if an analytic philosopher finds that a certain...text is *underinterpreted,* [he] will still know no more rational reaction than to count himself out....
>
> —Y. Bar-Hillel, "A Prerequisite for Rational Philosophical Discussion" ([43])

Since so much of this essay is devoted to the examination of other people's discourse, a good question to start with might be, Why so? What, that is, does one hope to gain by talking about talk about music when even just talking about music uses a language that is itself "metamusical"? Might not one, rather, be spending one's time better by doing actual musical thinking, in or about music itself, using whatever mode of discourse or medium of communication seemed handiest? The answer depends mostly on the degree of awareness of the extramusical contemporary intellectual world included in and regarded as a significant part of the metamusical equipment of the questionee. For in the world of, say, Carnap's

Aufbau (and not less in the later, physicalist Carnapian worlds) one learned that there are no *essences* of things to talk about, only structures of relations, languages in various senses. And in the Quinean world of the present, we realize that, further, the very selection of a theory, or a mode of theoretical discourse, involves a significant prior bias toward an ontology (the variables quantified over as individuals), a bias which cannot be detached as a way of looking at the world from the structural and descriptive resources and biases of the language itself (which thus limits the "external-internal" dichotomy between metaphysical and empirical discourse maintained by Carnap et al,[1] but does so by *relativizing* it to the language-metalanguage "layer" being considered rather than by disallowing it in an "absolute" sense that may not be in the Quinean spirit in any case—but see Harman, "Quine on Meaning and Existence", *Review of Metaphysics,* January 1967, for a radical interpretation).

This inseparability of the "fact" from its relational description is perhaps the principal contribution of twentieth-century philosophy to all fields whose domains consist of phenomena of experience of any kind, and its recognition makes it impossible to sustain an intellectual attitude that ignores conditions, standards, or characteristics of discourse in confronting "objects of thought".[2]

---

[1] See Carnap [47], but also Quine [67].

[2] But this makes it especially essential not to overlook the distinction between what, *within a language, is cognitively designable* and what is not. Thus, in [35] and [36], Leo Treitler's proposed criticism of "neo-Positivism" in musical discourse is seriously flawed by just such an oversight; for in his rejection of an "objectivity" based on an elusive empirical Given, he seems unaware of any middle ground worth considering short of a complete retreat into "subjectivity". What he declines to take account of is the possibility of *intersubjectivity,* linguistically dependent to be sure but cognitive in the only sense that word has. Yet, of course, the assumption of such intersubjectivity must underlie any effort at explicit communication such as Treitler's own essay. The trouble appears to be that Treitler, along with many other writers, is so overwhelmed by the sins of Positivism that he is blinded to the residual virtues of empiricism, and, in advocating a restriction of the function of rational discourse to the merely *persuasive,* he is evidently, and in my view unnecessarily, throwing the cognitive baby out with the dogmatic bathwater. For while he accounts for intellectual activity as "constructing" rather than "discovering truth", his radical subjectivism would hardly permit him to know what it is that has been constructed, or whether the "constructed things" can be scrutinized (in thought, observation, or both) or only regarded as verbal place-holders without cognitive content. By the same token,

Thus, when something called "music" is the ostensible object of thought referred to in a discourse, various "facts" of many kinds are invoked to support diverse claims, most often framed as "properties truly predicable of 'music'", of the forms "M(x)" ("x is music"), or "∀x(M(x) ⊃ P(x))" ("if it's music, it has melody"), or even "∀x (M(x) ~ P(x))" ("if it has melody, it's music, but it's not if it doesn't"). Now among the problems that arise in trying to understand the extraordinarily diverse, apparently professionally acceptable ways to discourse about "music" is that both the denotative extension and the conceptual intension associated with the basic term indicating the "object-of-thought" domain itself seem to be taken overly for granted as "factually" self-evident, without consideration of the circumstance that linguistic-relative dependency extends right down to that core concept itself. This is undoubtedly the origin of many fruitless disputes that take place over the more or less undeclared issue "What is Music?", and many equally heated ones over the epithetical rather than extension-definitional use of the phrase "That's not music!". Moreover, the status of the predicates used in musical discourses is quite frequently taken to be "truth" or "falsity" in a sense whose confusions resemble the extension-intension confusion just noted; namely, these "properties" are often invoked as though they were "truly predicable" in a directly observational sense,[3] rather than being, as they most often

---

Treitler's position would make it impossible to suppose that any argument, even if purely persuasive, could be reasonably insured to extrude a *particular persuasive content;* for persuasive discourse is not "less cognitive" than other discourse, but merely locates its relevant "field of cognitivity" elsewhere (this, of course, is the core of the linguistic relativist's argument against the "emotive" theory of meaning and of ethical discourse in, e.g., C. L. Stevenson's explication thereof). So Treitler's effort to attain a radical relativism actually reverts, because of his failure to recognize some vital distinctions, to a metaphysical solipsism, as impossible of realization as the "objectivity" it purports to supplant. And since his articles also contain valuable attempts to clear away dogmatic confusion, empiricist as well as deterministic, from music-historical discourse, and many penetrating critical and constructive observations, the ultimate inconsistency that his "meta-position" imposes on the structure of his argument as a whole is all the more regrettable.

[3]As, i.e., parts of a pure "observation-language" in which all properties or relations are observable, definable, or conditionally reducible, where the values of variables are always concrete or observable entities, where there is for the language at least one finite model, and such that for every value of a variable there is a designating expression, and that only truth-functional connectives are used,

are, *theoretical* terms invoking particular interpretive conceptualizations on particular groupings of observation-data. Since most *explanatory* discourse purports to use these terms nontrivially, i.e., as predications that involve an at least implicit claim that they "explain" or "interpret" beyond what is *taken, for the purposes of the discourse,* as more or less "trivially descriptive" (in the sense of "purely observational" or, systematically speaking, "undefined")—and the authors of most such discourse would be discontent with a lesser attribution—most of the significant uses of the terms are indeed as *theoretical* ones requiring interpretation to be explanatorily functional. And, of course, their use as if they were simple observation predicates automatically frustrates this functionality, and probably conceals the necessity or possibility of interpretation from their users as well as many of their readers.

A related problem in the use of predicating terms is the frequent equation of their relations in the language (the "natural language") in which the discourse is taking place with those in the domain about which it is taking place without consideration of the basis, or often even of the need, for specified correlation. This problem arises from a fundamental, and classic, failure to observe the distinction between a metalanguage and an object-language; a typical difficulty is the invocation of some heuristic metaphor ("gravity", say) to explain some musical phenomenon suggestively, followed by the invocation of all the deductive and inductive consequences of the metalinguistic term as it is used in the metalanguage as though it were consequentially explanatory, or analogously significative, in the object-linguistic domain,[4] without further justification.

A major and frequent consequence of such uncritical use of terms is that the domains of appropriate verification for various theoretical statements produced thereby are often quite different despite the apparently common "terminology" of such statements (which in this case constitutes mere homonymy). As we shall see in the sequel, in different instances of talk all supposedly "equally" about "music", statements are made the determinations of whose truth or falsity require tests of quite different natures, a fact which

---

excluding logical or causal modalities such as necessity, possibility, etc. (See Carnap [48].)

[4]See the Sellars passage cited above (Preface, n. 6), and the discussion below.

often fails to emerge due to the underanalyzed condition of the concepts involved. Thus, to take a simple case, the statements "This is beautiful" and "This is in C major", whatever their comparative "factual" content, would depend for their verification on different sorts of tests: it is as absurd to use an audience poll as a demonstration of the truth or falsity of "This is in C major" as it would be to use a set of "facts" of the musical-data-descriptive sort, and generalizations therefrom, to determine the truth value of "This is beautiful". In other words, the relevant *observation fields* for the two sentences in question are wholly different (one might even say that their *referents* are different too): in the "This is beautiful" case, the intersubjectively cognitive aspects of people's behavior that we observe are independent of the cognitive intersubjectivity of the musical data as construed in a given audition; in the "This is in C major" case, the latter is the referential domain, independent of the former. But in which case are we making a statement "about music"? To come forth boldly at this point with an answer to this question would only be to adjudicate the issue on the basis of some *third* category, a normative one which would enable us to decide which of the explanatory objectives and domains of the other two were most "legitimately about music". Thus each of these assertions necessarily involves a separate theory that includes a delimiting criterion for the "range" of its field. Our concern, then, is not really to choose among them on any absolutistic normative basis, for that simply involves us in an infinite regress of "defined bases of choice" within our metatheory; rather, it is relevant to notice that they do not in fact bear upon the same matters or even the same subject. For even though a certain category of "things" is involved in both sentences, those "things" are as differently involved as "books" are, and are as different as "facts" about "books" are, according to whether typographers or critics are the discoursers. So our choice in each instance will depend simply on whether we happen to be interested in facts about beauty or facts about C major; their common involvement with something called "music" is more red herring than reference.

A further respect in which we want to observe an attitude of critical scrutiny involves considerations *internal* to the distinct domains of musical discourse themselves; namely, what are the "standards of explanation" in terms of which claims and assertions are advanced as being either cognitive or demonstrable? What are the "standards of evidence" and formulation involved? And how is the relation between the explanatory claims and the thing explained determinable from the characteristics of the discourse? Thus we would have great difficulty making use of a predicated "beauty" which depended as a "necessary condition" on "being in C major", or used "musical data" as its crucial intersubjectively cognitive observation field.

In the sequel, we shall be considering discourse in which the object language/metalanguage confusion is a central problem. But here our effort is to distinguish, rather more generally, conceptual problems that hinder the communicative capacity of musical discourse. Thus we turn for the moment away from problems of "expository" writing, that which puts forth proposals for true or useful predications, and turn to "critical" discourse, that which attempts to explicate or otherwise adjudicate musical issues by confronting other discourse. Of course, all the same confusions arise, but a particular one that seems to cause the widest range of problems is the familiar procession from the descriptive to the normative, from "is" to "ought", as, from "I cannot determine how this can be cognized as being in C major, so I don't know what to make of it as a musical structure" to *"this isn't in C major* and hence *is musically incoherent"*, in which latter not only the compounded material implication but each of the italicized propositional components is a normative assertion disguised by grammar as an observational fact. More confusing still is the situation in which the definitionally crucial criterion is left unstated, as: "You may have shown how the piece *is organized,* but not how it *makes musical sense"*. Here, the conditions under which the latter reservation would be withdrawn are unstated and seemingly inscrutable, and those justifying the affirmation of the antecedent seem equally elusive. A more subtle problem emerges from the obverse of this tendency: the *assumption* that all theoretical language *as used by others is purely normative,* and is thus to be understood as beyond all else *persuasive* in its implicit claim of coercive authority. The validity of such an assumption seems especially obvious to some critics when the surface of the discourse involved has a "scientific" aroma. Whatever the justification of the charge on many occasions (and the equation of "scientific" with "scientistic", and "formal" with "numerological" is just as prevalent in the "object" as in the "meta"-literature), it has not often been substantiated by an account of the failure of any considerable effort on the critic's part to discover the possibly theoretical or otherwise cognitive—as distinct from polemical—advantages the particular instance of the use of such language might entail.

Even further off target are the intense controversies over the appropriateness of the *names introduced* for particular properties, which usually arise as manifestations of either or both of two vices of inadequate critical perception: Vice No. 1 is the non-awareness of the degree to which "neutrality" may be attained by effective definition; and Vice No. 2 is the non-recognition of the possibility that a useful conceptual distinction or insight might be embedded in such a definition. The oddity here is that the criticism of terminology and methodology along these lines often appears to invoke the very notion of the dependence of "meaning" (factual or relational) on "language" (the characteristics of discourse) on which much of our own present discussion itself is dependent. But the way the notion is invoked is idiosyncratic, even perverse; what is essentially involved is an implicit denial of the very possibility of intersubjectivity, while the latter is, in fact, the phenomenon that the "linguistic-dependence" notion itself specifically explicates, in a fashion that emphasizes the degree to which it is even more *necessary* to specify the terms on which discourse can be taken as intersubjectively intelligible. Some critics, in regarding terminological and methodological choice as primarily persuasive in content, seem to exchange the old "aesthetics-as-fact" fallacy for a "facts-as-aesthetics" one that is naively solipsistic in its "logic". For one of the principal implications of the "linguistic model of cognition" involves a view of intellectual discipline as, in large part, an effort to maximize the degree to which we can interpret the content of utterances with maximum independence from the local terms of their utterance (personal "tone of voice", "polemical style", etc.) which of course are part of their "cognitive content" as well, but a part distinguishable through the distinction of separable domains of behavior associated in linguistic utterance through isomorphisms observed within them at the appropriate moments (as in our "domains of discourse" discussion above). And in particular, this interpretation itself takes the linguistic form of language maximally "neutralized" by its accompanying qualifications and restriction to relatively unambiguous parts of language, in lexical and truth-functional respects.

In particular, both Cone [12] and Krenek [23] seem to undervalue the object-language/metalanguage distinction in their worry over whether terms introduced with all due definiential care are the "intuitively right" ones, metalinguistically, for the phenomena defined. This might be an important consideration in cases where the word used had another possible—or, especially, an actual—application in the same discourse-field; but its "stylistic" awkwardness, according to some metalinguistic criterion of stylistic grace, its similarly offensive "unintentionally humorous overtones", or its supposed "illogic" as part of an externally normative criterion of "logical ordering", are hardly major *theoretical* issues, however significant as matters of taste.

Thus the first of the critical vices seems largely to arise as the result of insufficient common agreement about the degree to which the *degree of interpretation* of a theoretical term or language in musical discourse confers intersubjective cognitivity regardless of its "logic" or atmosphere in some metadomain.

In [6],[5] Arthur Berger, who elsewhere appears to harbor warm feelings toward Vice No. 1, strikes attitudes that seem to reveal a still deeper affinity for No. 2. For, he in effect asks, why does anyone *need* to introduce new terms for old concepts when the good old terms "mean" the same thing anyhow, and all that is gained apart from a neologistic-scientific "kick" that perhaps shakes us out of our complacency but that at the same time replaces it with hopeless lexical confusion is an imputation of rigor that is illegitimate and questionably come by in any case. This criticism, however, fails to take adequate account of the problems associated with cognitive synonymy in any language. And it appears to ignore the motivation underlying much introduction of new terminology in any evolving explanatory field: the desire to minimize the uninterpreted theoretical content of every term by an analysis which results in its association, wherever possible, with a term that can be, relatively to a given discourse, regarded as in the "observation-linguistic" direction (that is, with respect to others in the theory regarded as being either "theoretical-linguistic" or, if their degree of interpretation is at the vanishing point, "metaphysical"—it is terms of the latter type that are most often used persuasive-normatively). In short, a serious effort has often been made

---

[5]See especially pp. 8–9 and note 9, p. 9.

precisely to *minimize,* for the terms used in a discourse, the amount of their pure linguistic dependence (here again, correlated with a relatively weaker degree of interpretation). The extent to which such "non-dependence" is achieved can be determined by examining the degree of isomorphism exhibited in use by the different term-names involved to establish *within what portion of language* any pair of them may be considered cognitively synonymous, and where cognitively distinct. Thus both terms in such pairs as "chord" and "simultaneity"; "major second" and "2"; "triad" and "(0 4 7) trichord" will all have *identical extensions* within particular domains—which is obviously why the "traditional terms" did serve as virtually "observational" without evident strain as long as those domains were regarded as universal for music. But even as correlated with, say, the domain of tonal music alone, the second term of each of the pairs above has extensions not shared with the first one, although the converse does not hold: every chord is a simultaneity, but not every simultaneity is necessarily a chord; every major second is an interval of size 2, but not every interval of 2 semitones is a major second, etc. Thus is discriminated a class of terms with greater generality than their traditional "counterparts", terms that require significantly fewer theoretical constructs for their interpretation, to the extent that they may be considered virtually "observational" relative to most music-theoretical discourse. In this respect they may be considered to designate properties at a level of thought that forms a conceptual substructure on which the other, partially interpreted and semantically biased theoretical terms, depend. Now this kind of analysis, it should be clear, neither denies cognitive status to nor confers it on either the "traditional" or the "new" terms (although it more usually improves than impairs their cognitivity in use); that still depends on the quality of the surrounding discourse. What it does accomplish is to distinguish a particular systematic interpretation of a concept that has a more general observational form in terms of that more general form. And this greater generality is useful not only in satisfying some of our nobler concept-analytic normatives, but, primarily, because it enables transference to other interpreted systems of discriminables like "simultaneity" without also requiring the transportation of all the baggage attendant on "chords". To clarify this point, I offer an arrangement of some familiar terms, old and new, on a "more-to-less-observational" scale, whose polar extremes (which themselves are not instantiable but rather designable in principle as "directional limits") are, at one end, "fully observational" terms, and, at the other extreme, "totally metaphysical" terms useful primarily in persuasive discourse, with intermediate degrees of "theoreticalness" lying in between, wherein the less the "observational" the more the "theoretical" content:

Observation Language	Theoretical Language	Metaphysical Language
"simultaneity"	"chord"-"triad"-"tonic triad"	"chord of nature"
"simultaneity succession"	"harmony", "progression"	"harmonic propulsion"
"pitch contour"	"span"-"register"-"phrase"-structure	"logical form"
"pitches"	"pitch classes"-"A♭"	"musical sounds"
"pitch-dyad identity"	"interval"-"pitch-class interval"-"scale-degree interval"-"interval of simultaneity (consonance) and of succession (dissonance)"	"harmonious/inharmonious sounds"-"dissonance/ consonance" (as intrinsic properties of "sounds")
"duration contour"	"rhythmic structure"	"rhythmic music"
"pattern-of-repetition structure"	"Sonata Form"-"Baroque"	"baroque"

Again, it should be stressed that the criterion of name-formulation for new terms is not primarily intuitivity, however much one may approve of the "plain-English" bias that many "new term"-names manifest (they mean the same in music as in the dictionary, which of course *is* to some extent related to their more nearly "observational" character),[6] but the fact that they name concepts which

---

[6] A misinterpretation of a remark of mine to this effect is the evident subject of Berger's note 9 (p. 9 [6]). Misunderstood as an assertion that new terms "need no explication because they are intuitively obvious", my remark is indeed obnoxious as charged; but Berger's subsequent example precisely overlooks the observation-theoretical aspect of the relation between "new" and "old" terms,

apply more generally and with fewer intervening theoretical constructs than do the term-names they supplement and support.

[A comparative explication of the notions of "simultaneity" and "chord" is roughly sketched here to illustrate the cognitive distinction noted above; in the sketch, all lower-case Roman variables are to be understood as designating "pitch-instances":

Df. 0.0: "a and b are *partially simultaneous*."

$$PS(a, b) \equiv_{df} \{[Ti(a) < Tt(b)] \wedge [Tt(a) > Ti(b)]\}.$$

where Ti(a) = "the time of initiation of a"
Tt(a) = "the time of termination of a"
< = "earlier than"
> = "later than"

Df. 0.1: "X is a *simultaneity*."

$$Sim(X) \equiv_{df} \forall a \, (a \in X) \, \exists b \, [(b \in X) \wedge PS(a, b)].$$

Df. 0.2: "X is an *arpeggio*."

$$Arp(X) \equiv_{df} \forall a \, (a \in X) \, \exists b \, [b \in X \wedge \neg(PS(a, b)) \wedge$$
$$\forall c \, [(Ti(a) < Ti(c) < Ti(b)) \vee (Ti(b) < Ti(c) < Ti(a)) \supset c \in X]].$$

("X is a simultaneity if, for all a's that are members of X, there is at least one b such that b is a member of X and a and b are partially simultaneous". "X is an arpeggio if, for all a such that a is a member of X, there is at least one b not partially simultaneous with a that is also a member of X, and for all c whose time of initiation is between that of a and that of b, c is also a member of X".) Note the relative absence of theoretical terms in these definitions; except for those terms specifically introduced as primitive, everything is "fully interpreted".

Now, while "X is a chord only if X is a simultaneity or an arpeggio":

0.0: $Ch(X) \supset (Sim(X) \vee Arp(X))$,

the conditions under which "X is a chord are considerably more complicated:

---

through which the new also *explicate* the old, an oversight which reinforces the general aura of Vice No. 1.

Df. 0.3:

$$Ch(X) \underset{df}{\equiv} (Arp(X) \vee Sim(X)) \wedge (X = \{x_a, x_b, \ldots, x_k\}) \supset$$
$$(\{x_a, x_b, \ldots, x_k\} \in SU)).$$

("X is a chord if X is an arpeggio, or X is a simultaneity; and if the set of all members of X is a member of a (defined) *pitch-syntactical unit set*".)

Df. 0.3, then, is a "rule for the introduction of Ch(X), interpreted as 'X is a chord'". Note the essential function in the definition of the (here uninterpreted) theoretical term "pitch-syntactical unit", whose interpretation is of course an essential prerequisite for the implementation of the definition. And since "pitch-syntactical unit" is necessarily a term of the "theoretical language", this gives the notion of "chord" a considerably lower degree of "observationality" than "simultaneity" (and even, incidentally, than "pitch-syntactical unit", since "chord" is defined in terms of it), the conditions for whose introduction are thus significantly less complex.]

A major resource in the attempt to maximize intersubjectivity in music-theoretical discourse by minimizing linguistic ambiguity is the construction of *models,* understood as particular interpretations of theories correlated with sets of empirical data; in Suppes's description, "a theory is a linguistic entity consisting of a set of sentences, and models are nonlinguistic entities in which the theory is satisfied...[a model is] a certain kind of ordered tuple consisting of a set of objects and relations and operations on these objects...the physical model may be simply taken to define the set of objects in the set-theoretical model".[7] In this light, and that of the usual mathematical-logical sense of the word, a model may be regarded as either a "model of the theory" or a "model of the data";[8] the two senses merely reflect different emphases, and despite appearances, are definably interchangeable. What is important about their use is just that (to quote Suppes again) "in the exact statement of the theory or in the exact analysis of the data the notion of model in the sense of logicians provides the appropriate intellectual tool for making the analysis both precise and clear".[9] Thus the possibility of constructing an explanatory model will be

---

[7] In [70].
[8] Cf Tarski as quoted in Suppes [70].
[9] *Op. cit.,* p. 171.

regarded as one of the prime determinants of the cognitiveness of a domain, an instance, a fragment, or a term of discourse. It can also help to analyze the structure of argument in such discourse, with particular respect to claims made about answers given to, and prescribed for, questions of similar verbal appearance raised in disparate music-intellectual domains. In particular, we can distinguish by the model-enabling criterion the persuasive-emotive from the cognitive content of a discourse, by the observation of operational superfluity. And perhaps most significantly, we can show that the model of "questions asked—answers given" is not only fundamental to the consideration of frankly explanatory, theoretical, and analytic activity, but also to that of compositional thought. *Historical* explanation asks questions about macro-successions of "musical facts", the answers to which are sometimes derivable from observations on musical data, sometimes on sociocultural or chronological or "theoretical-discursive" data. *Theoretical* explanation asks basic music-epistemological questions (having to do with the notions underlying the use of terms like "music", etc.) whose answers lie in particular orderings of empirical data, both "perceptual data" and "conceptual data" (the concepts governing the slicing of perceptual data into "musical structures") in more or less formally articulated language. *Analytic* discourse asks questions about the particular respect in which the notion of "musical structure" is inferable from a particular set of data, whose answers are to be found in the *respects in which* a "model of the data" is also a "model of the theory" (not the *fact that* it is, for that is trivial). And *compositional* questions relate to the possibility of producing "musical structures" through variant degrees of "reordering" (I hope the reason for the quotes is obvious), "reinterpreting", and "extending" the elements, relations, and operations of existing data-model-theory complexes, the answers to which lie in the domain of experiential confirmation and cognitive insight. The interrelation of the latter three of these domains is, I think, evident, although their connection with the first is difficult to establish with precision, owing both to the highly variable and informal nature of most "historical" discourse in music (which insofar as it *is* "historical", has quite as different a relevant domain of intersubjective observation from that shared by theory, analysis and composition, as do aesthetics and physics).

Complementary to the notion of model-constructability as determining the "degree of determinacy" of a discourse is the use of models in the scrutiny of highly formalized discourses to determine their *degrees of interpretation,* on which in turn is dependent their status as contributions to *music-explanatory* thought, quite apart from their internal structures as *uninterpreted calculi* or schemata. Again, we seek to discover to what extent such formalized discourses may be considered to represent theories of music, with what partiality or generality they do so, and thus to what extent they are capable of offering answers to musical questions in terms acknowledgeable as *musically interpretable*—that is, we shall be interested in their *epistemic depth* and, correspondingly, in their music-explanatory power.

These matters occupy Part I of this essay. Part II sketches a constructional path which is intended to clarify many of the notions discovered to be underexplicated, both as formalisms and informalisms, in Part I. This is done partly through logical-definitional constructs which attempt to order and interrelate basic "foundational" concepts, and partly through metadiscursive explications of what appear to be the "logics" of essential concepts in various music-structural domains. Part III extends the formal and informal discussions to matters of "syntactical systems", and concludes with an outline of an interpreted theoretical model whose particular orderings and interpretations of the previously defined relations and operations constitute a possible "preliminary" basis for "tonal syntax" on a "post-Schenkerian" model. Part IV then considers how music-analytic problems may be fruitfully approached in terms of such a "background theory", from the point of view both of the possible simplification of existing analytic methods, and the projection of possible new domains for inter- and intracompositional understanding. Finally, Part V discloses how the considerations arising in the preceding sections are related to the germination and realization of a particular composition (my *Group Variations*), and how they are manifest in some of its presented content.

III.
Part I:
Models and Metaphors in Musical Discourse

> A question is an expression of intellectual anxiety and an answer is an attempt at resolution of that anxiety...a formal question carries with it the form of its answer...it asks for the matter of its answer but provides the form; an informal question asks for both...a question does not have to be precise in order to express a genuine anxiety and thus be a genuine question.
>
> —John Myhill, "On the Ontological Significance of the Löwenheim-Skolem Theorem"[1]

INTRODUCTION

0. Musical discourses, as we have noted, ask questions of various kinds, and seek to find answers of various kinds for them. We, in turn, ask our own questions about their questions as well as about the answers they imply or offer, and about the relation between the questions and the answers. And we tend to value a discourse more because it answers *our* questions satisfyingly, or gives answers we approve of to those of its own questions we care about or are led to care about by the discourse, than because of the adequacy of its answers to its questions, or the efficacy with which both questions and answers support its explanatory or cognitive claims. Thus the danger that our judgment of the discourse of others is colored by our own "intellectual anxieties" is more than a danger; it is a virtual certainty. So a critique of other people's discourse is always primarily self-serving, and will be interesting to other readers, as well as the authors criticized, on exactly the same grounds as the original discourse might be: that it gives satisfying answers to engaging questions. Nevertheless, if self-service is conceived to consist, in a given instance, of finding out as much as pos-

---

[1] [65].

sible about the ways in which it is possible to be cognitive about something (call it "music"), and about the ways in which "music" is something about which one can be cognitive, and the relations among the ways to be cognitive and the things to be cognitive about, then one will try to formulate one's metadiscursive questions so as to minimize the "coloration of judgment" they impose at the *object-discursive* level, while accounting for the biases they manifest at their own level as fully and frankly as possible. This, in effect, will be the program of the examination of problems of music-explanatory discourse to which this part is devoted.

A. THE THEORETICAL CHARACTER OF MUSICAL ENTITIES

1. Music as thought: the cognitive status of "a musical experience"

The first question that we want to ask of a musical discourse, then, is: "In what respects are musical compositions regarded in it as 'objects of thought'?". And the variance of the answers that appear to be given to this question in the literature constitutes one of the most vexing problems that we confront in this chapter. But an effective approach to the problem is perhaps not feasible without a preliminary consideration which reveals some of its particular complexity. For music is among those domains in which the "objects" of consideration *are* objects (i.e., *have* "shape" and "identity") only by special virtue of a singular disposition and observation of "real" events by, respectively, an author and a perceiver. And thus the further question (or, really, prior question) arises concerning the respects in which these "objects of thought" are also *instances of thought.* In other words, we are confronted with an experiential domain that is not only *thought about* but also, apparently, *thought in.*

For verbal and symbolic languages, this characterization is relatively uncontroversial; but even some of those who most seriously propose a linguistic-analogical explication of music locate that analogy in the purely emotive, rather than the cognitive aspects of language, often, in fact, disregarding the dependence of the sense of the former on the form of the latter:[2] once more the question is

---

[2]That is, whatever "meaning" is conferred on an emotive predicate is by virtue of its modeling on the form of a cognitive predicate: "x is beautiful"/"x is blue". And of course, the "x" in both *is* necessarily presumed to be a cognitively designable entity. Thus it may be said that an emotive predicate can be predicated

not one of "meaningful-meaningless" but of the proper location of a relevant intersubjective confirmation-field. The view I propose is that when someone does not regard music as thought he is not regarding it as "music" either—just in the sense that the relevant evidence for confirmation or disconfirmation of any of his assertions cannot come from observations of musical data or how it is perceived, but must come from other aspects of behavior, however associated with "being in the presence of some particular set of perceivable musical data"[3] they may be. And this is, of course, not to assert any "imperatives" about the *necessity* of regarding music as thought or, for that matter, as music. Thus a corollary of my proposal is that anyone who does make the musical data-field his pasture,[4] but still maintains a view of musical "being" as something other than a form of cognitive communication is actually not in a position to carry out such a program cognitively (by which I mean to distinguish between the "object-linguistic" cognitiveness attributable to music itself and the cognitiveness attributable to the explicative "metalinguistic" discourse). Now one of the most characteristic ways in which music's cognitiveness is denied is by the denial that principles and criteria of cognitiveness—"laws of thought"—operative in other domains of (linguistic and nonlinguistic) experience are applicable to musical experience. But no one ever really seems to mean that music is experientially "autonomous" in the way that this view would seem to imply. Instead, the invocation of the language of "noncognitive autonomy" usually

---

only of something of which an empirical predicate can also be (except for "metaphysical" entities or terms, of which of course anything is predicable without truth-value implications since their linguistic position is rather like that of "proper names" for uninterpreted variables in a sentence-*schema,* i.e., placeholders for any other metaphysical entity or uninterpreted predicate whatever). And also that the model for emotive discourse is cognitive discourse in a way essential to its communicative capacity (see note 2, p. 12 above). Hence offering an explication of music according to just the emotive segment of language without providing a corresponding cognitive substructure seems bound to result in *empty* statements.

[3]But it might even be necessary to qualify this condition (because of the difference between "musical" data and physical-object data) still further as "being in a 'perceptual field-space' where some sounds occur (or some marks on paper are visible) that are perceived by at least one person therein *as* constituting some particular musical data".

[4]See Randall [32].

appears in discourse which in other respects appears to make use of the usual processes of reasoning and cognitive observation of empirical objects and events in terms familiar and "factual" enough to musicians. The "special" vocabulary, in fact, usually appears to be "autonomous" just in its referential opacity, and not in any ascriptions inferable from it: thus it may be said to be "autonomously expressive" rather than "expressive of autonomy". And what manifestations of such vocabulary actually appear to do is simply to present rather vague characterizations of "facts" observable at some particular event- or data-discriminative level, as a way to "connect" various "events" without specifying a perceptually cognitive way to distinguish the relevant process of relation or the critical characteristic(s) of relatedness involved. It is just in the requirement that he supply these, completely cognitive, aspects for himself that the reader is asked to be "intuitive"; but be it noted that the terms of the discourse itself, and their relation to the musical observables, are still the only things available for him to be intuitive *about*—not, in any sense, the musical data itself, or the contents of his particular slices of it, which are either just "factual", or remain unnoticed and therefore effectively nonexistent. So what ends up happening is not that we encounter cognitive discourse about a more or less "noncognitive object", as is in effect advertised by some discourses, but rather discourse which itself has more or less noncognitive aspects, to the extent of which it cannot securely be said to be "about" anything—and it can in fact only be said to be about something just to the extent that it does treat musical data-arrays and their slices as intersubjectively cognitive objects.

But if no one can seriously be said to regard music as "autonomous", in the sense of being empirically anomalous and thus beyond the scope of normal conceptualization, then, if music is still not regarded as cognitive in the sense of "thought", what are the alternatives? And if they are not proposed explicitly, what proposals along these lines can we infer from the language and logic of the discourses? In fact, the introduction of "emotive" or other "impressionistic" terms to characterize musical structures appears most typically to signalize just that point at which a writer has chosen to abandon the effort of making anything *particular* out of a composition and has resorted, instead, to the issuance of slogans. Technically, this may be considered equivalent to a switch from the use of defined observational or theoretical predicates to that of undefined proper names. Thus it seems to me that the points at which musical events and relations are described by terms like "struggle", "tension and release", "sensory images", "emotional effects", et al., are not those where a discourse diverges to make some special observation of or some special sense of a piece, but just where it has ceased trying to make any very specific sense of that piece at all, whatever else it may be engaged in communicating. In this connection it is particularly revealing that the sloganizing terms chosen to "illuminate" music from without usually come from domains of discourse whose contemporary cognitive condition is far more opaque and analytically refractory than that of music itself: among the domains typically invoked—as, for example, the behavior and nature of "organisms", of "human emotions", of "forces of history", of "society", or of "dispositions of nature"—none is supported by a theoretical or conceptual development nearly as advanced or secure as that of music.

2. Cognitive consequences of a "nonrational" model

Let us now, for illustration, scrutinize as carefully as we can (that is, far more carefully than we would in any normal "reasonable" reading) a passage from the professional literature which appears to embrace a view of musical objects and their experiencing as nonrational. This passage appears in an article otherwise devoted to a clear and cogent presentation of microdata for the construction of certain new pitch-vocabulary domains for composition by correlating pitch-tunings with various physical frequency ratios:

> ...If a system of scalar order can be grasped intuitively, patterns easy to remember can be composed by rearranging it. The psychological tension between a particular scalar order and the pattern imposed on it by composition stimulates memory, attention, and interest. The interrelation of many such patterns stimulates associations, memories, and images having similar patterns. Whether I experience these associations as sensory images, as emotional affects, or as abstract patterns, the music has meaning because of them.[5]

---

[5]Johnston [17], p. 58.

Here the earnest attempt to circumvent the "music-as-thought" model leads to a curious "deterministic psychologism", which involves the grafting of nonempirical predicates onto empirical or theoretical variables, and substitutes "automatistic" predicates in the places where "cognitivistic" ones would normally appear. Thus observe the coupling of a theoretical concept such as "system of scalar order" with the theoretically indeterminate predicates "can be grasped intuitively" and "easy to remember". But "a system of scalar order" cannot be "grasped" *in vacuo*, but only from either something that instantiates it or something that explains it; Johnston does not specify which he means, but it seems reasonable to suppose that he is thinking of the former. A still greater problem arises in the connections of terms in the second sentence of the passage. To speak of "composition" as the "rearrangement" of a reference ordering or of "a particular scalar order and the pattern imposed on it by composition" is to treat an abstraction—as, "English grammar"—as if it were one of the concreta from which it was derived—as, "English utterances". (Actually, the "scalar order" presented in Johnston's article is more precisely a vocabulary usable in the interpretation of unspecified systems, than a grammar of such use, and it is not described as correlated with or generated in terms of any particular music-syntactical system.)

But further, the assertion of "psychological tension between" (the last word of which I take to signify "resulting in a human being from the observation (recognition, contemplation) of the relations between" rather than as implying an attribution of feelings of mutual aggression between a set of object-tokens and the domain of object types inferred therefrom) again throws the matter into another court than that whose jurisdiction is the assertible content within, and the assertible relations among, data-sets. The same is true for such attributions of "lawlike" connections as are implied by the universal form of "stimulates" and the various dispositional predicates that follow.

Later, what "similar" signifies is critically in need of explication, and "experience" seems to be just another preferred substitution for a hidden verb of cognition; for "experience" cannot, in this context, properly team with "as" if it is to be distinguished from "identify as". Thus we can say we "experience" a "feeling of warmth" or that we "*identified* an experience *as* a 'feeling of warmth'", which refer to two different activities, however simultaneous their motivating data. On the other hand, I find "experiencing associations" a virtually inscrutable conjunction.[6] And the presented parallelism of "sensory image" (how is this different from a "sound-event" or simply "something perceived"?) which is, probably, the "awareness of something that has been presented to perception"; "emotional affects", which seems simply to signify "succession of feelings experienced while in the perceptual-field-space where a 'piece' was audible"; and "abstract patterns" (what would "non-abstract patterns" be like?), which are, undoubtedly, the "contours of characteristic-variation among the things associated", does not seem to propose alternative ways of noticing the same things but rather alternative ways to behave while in the audible presence of the performance of a piece; and thus, insofar as the passage is "about" something, it is about people's behavior in respects other than *what they can notice music as*—in other words, respects in which the actual "musical data" are peripheral.

The root of much of this cognitive uncertainty may be located in a transference to the *language* used in the passage of the notion of "meaning" that is apparently attributed to *music*. This use of "meaning" seems essentially "emotive", and perhaps exemption from cognitive strictures might therefore be claimed for it. But it is, in fact, a use of "meaning" that is not even limited to being just an existential *ascription* of the presence of some *intension* or

---

[6]Note in this connection Sellars's contention rejecting the notion of "objective fact...which though a relational fact involving a perceiver, is...logically independent of the beliefs and the conceptual framework of the believer" in favor of a notion that experiences contain propositional claims and statements endorse them. Here is a selection from the relevant passage: "Evidence for the proposition 'this necktie is green' is *ipso facto* evidence for the proposition that the experience in question is seeing that the necktie is green" (p. 272). Thus, consider a similar interpretation of "There is an A♭ in that simultaneity", whose factual falsification depends on a set of circumstances distinct from that on which its experiential emptiness might rest. For factual denial would be relevant under circumstances where the entity "A♭" was an admissible value of the variable "pitch", but where "not-A♭" was actually the case. But the experiential question arises where "A♭-or-not-A♭" is not an issue (where, e.g., quantization of pitch is either cruder or finer than "semitones" and hence involves a different pitch-identificational "system" and attendant nomenclature, or where "nothing-but-A♭" is the case, etc.), but where in principle it might be possible that someone subjected to the same perceptual environment whose concurrent conceptual scheme included choosing to hear it that way could report truthfully his (correct or incorrect!) observation of "an A♭".

other (whose identity is unstated), which (though problematically enough) might be signaled by a locution such as "has a meaning"; this, however, would be simply redundant following a list of things that *constitute* just that very meaning (as "is in C major and thus has a meaning"; see n. 2, pp. 26–27). But Johnston's article uses "meaning" as a simple *qualification:* "has meaning"/"has pneumonia"/"has red hair"/"has money". This seems just to be a case, then, of an "is red"-"is beautiful" mis-identification, and again the problem is grammatical, in that the position of the word "because" implies that evidence of a certain type would influence the determination of an appropriate truth-value assignment of a given use of the predicate, when in fact such could not be the case. On the other hand, if there is an "intensional" attribution to be inferred, it would seem to be the claim that successions of musical events derive their meanings by their similarity to successions of introspected experiences, which is rather like the "meaning as reference" (correspondence) theory of language in which words "refer" to objects, concepts, or qualities as "things in the world". Aside from the absurdity of the claim that this would appear to make, that music is "about" things in the same way that language is, it also represents an old and discarded linguistic notion whose reappearance here probably reflects a failure to take into account the difficulty of distinguishing "things in the world" from their supposed linguistic co-referents. For words have significations only by virtue of their structural interrelations as parts of complete language-behavior systems; this is their only "real world", whose further correlation with a physical "real world" "out there" depends on the internal isomorphism of linguistic behavior with the rest of the behavior of the world. Hence such "significance" cannot escape the context of the language itself.

Thus even if this "nonrational" model of musical experience were stated nonimperatively, in grammatically unambiguous form, and even if some rules of correlation were given to relate normative to descriptive predicates, and to correlate descriptive predicates in nonintersecting domains, the degree to which such correlations, which would necessarily be correlations with observations external to those of the "behavior of musical data", would offer answers to questions about "the nature of musical structure" that would *make a difference* beyond what is already known from purely music-cognitive observations, is severely limited. And when, later in the same article, there appears the remark "To establish the connection between the known and the rational and the familiar...and the unknown and irrational and unpredictable...requires subjecting them to the same measure", it seems less a proposal for literal experimentation than an ideologically driven image of a transcendental idea of "measurement" which Johnston is struggling to express.

But the point of engaging in such microscrutiny is hardly just to call into question the rational fastidiousness of a single, mostly unexceptional writing; rather such scrutiny represents a requisite amount of care in examining a seriously proposed epistemic attitude to musical experience that—at such a fundamental level—runs counter to the cognitive view embraced here. Yet the conclusion that emerges from the examination is not so much of the "irrationality" as of the "futility" of such a counterproposal, in the sense that all the descriptions of musical objects that purport to characterize them as instances of something other than cognitive communication actually fail to do so, insofar as they engage the observational domains relevant to regarding such objects as *"particular* instances of *music"*. And to the extent that they engage these domains in an *interpretable* way, these descriptions cannot be understood to be even *proposing* to regard musical objects as anything but "instances of cognitive communication", whatever unawareness of this fact they display, or however much they may attempt to ignore or circumvent it. For all of the ascriptions they explicitly *do* propose are in fact intelligible only as things ascribable to something to which *prior* recognition has been given as just such an instance of cognitive communication, a recognition which, because unstated, must be supplied as a postulate of the discourse by the reader. And the only discernible *alternative* proposal is that we turn our attention to *other domains of observation* than those of the "musical data" themselves (our "inner states" during the time of audition, for instance*), in order to make significative statements *about music*; this seems to be the case even where the statements made in the name of the alternative in question do purport to be *about* musical data. For when we do interpret such

---

*(1995:) This is, in fact, a line of inquiry which I have recently pursued and articulated in a series of texts which explicitly eschew the attempt to account for the cognitive expressive content of music and the cognitive material content of music within a single ontological system.

statements as though they were about musical data, what appears is not, as implicitly claimed, an "anti-cognitive" approach to the same data, but simply a *relatively incomplete cognitive approach,* in which heuristic "proper names" (the "metaphysical predicates" discussed above) replace precise characterizations of data-relations beyond some particular level of description.[7] This is about equivalent to the sudden introduction of undefined terms, relations, and assumptions at a point near the terminus of a logical proof-structure, as a final strategy. Similarly, claims for the cognitiveness of predicates like "chaos" or "irrationality" or "indeterminacy" applied to musical data-arrays (whether in advocacy or denunciation) as "attributes" thereof simply demand recognition as a "property" name for what actually just denotes the *low degree of determinacy* of those arrays with respect to some set of coherence-conferring properties. We have no mechanism through which to understand, much less to effectuate, a notion of "organizing negatively", or "de-organizing"; the maximal "chaos" we have is simply "zero-deter-

---

[7]The appearance of proper names in a discourse may also be considered a symptom that the observational focus on the data of a composition has been restricted to the "gross-reactive" level rather than extended to a level of maximum specificity (through maximal individuation of discriminables and construction of a maximum multiplicity of data-exhaustive element-complex successions). The passage from Sellars quoted above (n. 6, p. 31) and the subsequent commentary bear upon this question, as does even more particularly the following later passage in Sellars's article (p. 274):

> ...a necktie, for example, can look red to S at t, without looking scarlet or crimson or any other determinate shade of red. In short...things can have a *merely generic* look, a fact which would be puzzling indeed if looking red were a *natural* as opposed to an *epistemic* fact about objects [see below— B.B.]. The core of the explanation, of course, is that the propositional claim involved in such an experience may be, for example, either the more determinable claim "This is red" or the more determinate claim "This is crimson". [Compare "Passage A is higher than passage B" to "Passage A's pitch-successional content presents the contour characteristic X, and is in the transformation-transposition relation P to the pitch-successional content of passage B" as a similar progression from a "more determinable" to a "more determinate" discriminative act.] ...we can note the resemblance between the fact that x can look red to S, without its being true of some specific shade of red that x looks to S to be of that shade, and the fact that S can believe that Cleopatra's Needle is tall, without its being true of some determinate number of feet that S believes it to be that number of feet tall. [Thus also, S may identify two sounds as "having the same pitch component" without its being true of, say, C♯ that S identifies it as *the* pitch component in question.]

minable inter-event influence", and there is no way to assert a *minus* degree thereof (or, thus, the existence of *more than one* "variety" of "chaos" or "randomness").

In short, there is no way for a way of thinking about musical data to be a non-theory, or for a musical succession to be a non-event. The former can only succeed in being a relatively weak or incomplete theory, one that accounts less determinately, less comprehensively, and less unambiguously, for fewer relations among fewer things than some other theories do; and the latter can only, at weakest in a weakest such theory, be a thing with a relatively low degree of internal specificity, hence a low degree of *particular* identity, or "characteristicness". And even discourse which does not acknowledge "musical coherence" as "intellectual communication" does not in fact succeed in treating it as anything else; it is only by locating their concerns in domains where the "musical" aspects of music are peripherally or not at all involved that musical discourses can circumvent the fact that when the "object of thought" consists of the contents of a musical composition, just the recognition of the *identities* of any of these contents (or even of the undivided single identity of them taken all together as a "unit") involves (to varying degrees) the same considerations that are involved in a discourse that explicitly—and hence with a better chance of cognitive particularity—regards such a composition as an instance of communicative thought.

B. THE DESIGNATA OF "MUSIC"

> The conception of the necessary unity of all that is resolves itself into the poverty of imagination, and a freer logic emancipates us from the straitwaistcoated benevolent institution which idealism palms off as the totality of being.
>
> —Bertrand Russell,
> *Our Knowledge of the External World*

3. Music as "Given in Nature": the problem of apriorism

But how does it happen to occur to people in the first place to wish or to think it appropriate to regard music otherwise than as the expression of ideas of relation, evolving in time? (What makes "ideas of relation, evolving in time" seem to some people like something experientially inferior to express by comparison with other communicable experiences is, however, still another question.) Disregarding the purely sociocultural-historical aspects of this question, one might consider the conceptual fulcrum on which such an attitude might turn. For illustration here, let us consider an analogy in the "behavior" of numbers in mathematics to that of musical "elements" in compositions: Numbers are invented, and given certain properties (used according to certain rules that determine whether any given use is appropriate or inappropriate, correct or incorrect). These properties are correlated with the observable world in different ways (with, e.g., *numerals*), and sometimes exhibit in their operation peculiar "behavior" which tempts the belief that they "exist" in some prior, metaphysical sense. What this "behavior" amounts to is a demonstration that a system of relations invented to display certain properties humanly intuitive, may also possess the capacity to exhibit, even when the same rules are followed, quite other results—initially unforeseen, unintuitive, counter-intuitive, or even wholly unwanted. These results may make it necessary to accept as *uninterpreted* certain theoretical terms (e.g., "set membership") and as *assumptions* certain propositions necessary to the part of the system regarded as essential; but that this in turn necessitates belief in the existence of such "things" as "numbers" in a naturalistic sense is out of the question. At most numbers need to be recognized as special "abstract entities", a view that differs only in metaphysical particulars from the notion of accepting them as uninterpreted. Thus, even the promulgation of the notion that numbers do "exist" is not commonly accompanied by a turnabout of the whole process by assertions like: "Since numbers exist, as we now have been forced to believe by behavior of theirs beyond our predictive control, they mustn't be permitted to behave in any respect like things that don't exist".

But is not this last, obviously absurd, assertion closely analogous to what is often quite seriously asserted in discourse that commits itself to the musical correlate of such an ontological reification? For although people evidently invented music, some people appear to want to find in it a manifestation of nature, and speak about it with a kind of idealism that assumes a predetermined, inherent "natural" model of the course and shape of musical phenomena, both external and internal to the human auditory mechanism. The pragmatics of this musical ontology consist in an appeal to supposedly "natural" properties of sound, and "natural" dispositions toward the hierarchical primacy of certain relations of auditory phenomena, framed as an appeal to the "ear" in the sense of "psychoacoustic" behavior external to the musical context.

Now if one were to accept such an ontology, and these as its necessary implications, it would indeed be possible to say "what music is" when it is being regarded as a "phenomenon of nature". Moreover, by selecting and listing those properties which one decides to consider preeminently "natural", and by defining correlations of these properties to definable measurements of musical data, one could indeed assert which music was more "natural" than which other, whether by virtue of comparison to some ideal tuning, the conformity in the object to some auditory response curve selected as "optimum", or whatever one would wish and could implement with some semblance of intersubjective realism. (That is, if I knew what you meant by "natural", I too could perform tests whose results would enable me to make a list ordering a group of pieces from "more" to "less" "natural" with some confidence in the probability that it would look like your list and that I would be able to explain my choices in language that would sound like yours.)

But to invoke such criteria to justify the assertion that some musical characteristic is inherently more natural than some others in an aprioristic sense, or simply to assert such "greater naturalness" without indicating the necessary prior assumptions, is to produce discourse in which the word "natural" appears as no more than a metaphor for a personal valuation of the characteristic in question.

On the other hand, the admission that such prior assumptions have been made, or the admission that they *are* assumptions, would often amount to an admission that the discourse involved was powerless to substantiate its major claims. For to make such admissions is at the same time to renounce any claims regarding the demonstrability of such an assertion as, e.g., "Music based on intervals (or tunings) assumed to be more naturally hearable is thereby *more coherent than* music that isn't", for this simply defines a rule for the introduction of the predicate "more coherent than" in terms of a "condition" and a truth-functional connective that merely rephrase what has already been assumed. Hence the *conceptual content* of the assertion is, at most, an emotive nuance. The logic of the situation may be rendered as follows:

Definitions: Let $M(x)$ = "x is a composition"

$I(x)$ = "x is an interval"

$I_m(x)$ = "x is the principal interval of m"

$\vec{N}(x, y)$ = "x is more natural than y"

$\vec{C}(x, y)$ = "x is more coherent than y"

Then, let

1. $a =_{df} (\imath x)(M(x) \wedge I_x(y))$.
2. $b =_{df} (\imath z)(I(z) \wedge \vec{N}(y, z))$.
3. $c =_{df} (\imath q)[M(q) \wedge \exists r (I(r) \wedge I_q(r))]$.

Assumptions: Then, if

4. $r = b$

and

5. $\forall x \forall y \forall z \forall q \{[M(x) \wedge I_x(y)] \wedge [M(z) \wedge I_z(q)] \supset [\vec{N}(y, q) \supset \vec{N}(x, z)]\}$.

and

6. $\forall x \forall y \{M(x) \wedge M(y) \supset [\vec{N}(x, y) \supset \vec{C}(x, y)]\}$.

Conclusion: Then,

7. $\vec{C}(a, c)$.

Since this entire sequence is based on definitions, assumptions, and postulates, and none of the predicates has an observational referent, and, indeed, none (*except* $\vec{C}$) is defined in terms of any other (No. 5 is just a rule that $\vec{N}$ is *expansive*), the "demonstration" is seen to be nothing more than an affirmation of the assumptions.

Such problems militate seriously against the possibility of any demonstration that it "explained more about music" to regard it as this kind of "natural phenomenon" than to regard it from some other point of view. The problem is simply that of the impossibility of *testing* or *demonstrating* the truth of a *universal assumption* within the discourse in which it is assumed. Thus, if we asserted, "All Dutchmen wear wooden shoes", as though it were an informative observation, but rejected all demonstration that people not wearing wooden shoes were Dutchmen by other criteria, such as holding a Dutch passport, having been born in Holland, etc., on the grounds that if they were *really* Dutchmen they would be wearing wooden shoes, it would soon become evident that what we have asserted is *not* an empirical proposition after all but a universal assumption not open to disconfirmation by observation or argument.

By the same token, empirically based arguments of the following kind could have no suasive force against assumptions about "what is a priori natural": let us say there *were* such things as "natural dispositions" that, for example, made it *initially* (prior to any actual post-natal experience) easier to discriminate certain pitch relations as individuals than to so discriminate some others—among, say, all the pitch relations likely to be encountered by individuals in a certain sociocultural environment; and let us agree that one could find an empirical test to determine the identities of the relations having such a property and the relative degrees to which different relations had it; even then, the notion that the *receptor of music is,* and is likely to remain, in an unsullied "state of nature" auditorially is still hardly plausible in view of what we know of developmental psychology and—especially—of what people have in fact learned to perceive in musical audition. One line of evidence that would bear on this would be the observation of patterns of facial-muscular dispositions in the production of phonemes in different languages, to determine the relative "naturalness" of such production to native speakers and to newly arrived foreigners. The perceptual *recognition* of phonemes under similar conditions would offer similar evidence; and so would the relative immediacy of recognitional response to "triads" by members of Western and those of Eastern musical cultures. Thus, too, I don't know of any musician, however "naturalistically" biased, who claims that *he finds it harder to perceive that something is a tritone than that it is a perfect fifth,* although complexes of either that are less familiar to him might pose recognition problems of varying degree.

In this connection, too, it might be evidentially relevant to notice that it has been the "conditioned" extension of such interval-associational and other capacities "learned" through the developing contextual characteristics of compositions, that has always accompanied successive "reforms" of instrument tuning—down to the present-day consideration of appropriate "electronic" tunings for certain compositional objectives—all of which have increasingly contravened the supposed "natural" constraints thereon. But this has not been because such tunings have ever been produced in the disregard of empirical constraints; quite the contrary, their production has clearly seemed to result from an "intellectually" motivated development of the capacity to hear "what was wanted to be heard"—the development, that is, of a truly music-empirical basis that progressively replaced, to whatever extent was compositionally relevant at each time, any supposedly "authoritative" but extramusical criteria of "naturalness". And such music-conceptual hearing is invariably the critical determinant for which physical correlates of musical relations produce appropriate sonic identities, or other empirical correlates of those relations that satisfy the "intellectually intuitive" notions that guide choice.

Nevertheless, no rational argument, nor any historical or empirical evidence of these kinds, however imposingly it mounts, ever has the power to shake the "natural" idealist's faith—which he typically believes he has arrived at inductively and rationally—that music has become, in a meaningful sense, "less natural" and therefore (by the intervention of some further hidden assumptions) less "universally valid".

The difficulty, a deep one in much musical discourse, and not restricted to its naturalistically biased instances, is just that the human desire to solve problems relating to matters of "fundamental" significance is powerful but that at the same time, as Archimedes's lever can only be operated from a standpoint outside the world, an intellectual standpoint independent of its own conceptual scheme is manifestly unavailable. For cognitive discourse cannot justify in the same sense that it can describe or explain. But in the aspiration to confer "objective" authority on a musical attitude sincerely held and deeply cherished, people have frequently substituted persuasive discourse for cognitive discourse; and this substitution, whatever its virtues in communicating attitudes and dispositions, has tended to weaken the descriptive and explanatory value of their texts. In attempting to realize the impossible program of a cognitive establishment of a metaphysical position, they have thus robbed even what actually could be cognitive or evocative in their thought of its power to communicate and thus to contribute to musical understanding.

4. Music as a "human-communicative" manifestation: the problem of universalism

Although I cannot see what possible cognitive questions do remain askable under the "naturalistic" or other sweepingly aprioristic frameworks, there are other conceptual frameworks, within which attempts at musical explanation have been made, that share some of the same problematic characteristics but which are not as obviously vacuous in the same sense with respect to musical manifestations. The discourse that most closely resembles that produced by "natural idealism", but walks a slightly less absolute line, takes place within the framework in which music is regarded as a cultural manifestation, particularly insofar as this involves an attempt to infer *universals* about all musical manifestations on the basis of inferences from observations made within some *particular* culture or group of cultures. Again, the conceptual problem is the notion that it is possible (or even desirable) to assert authoritative universals for the definition and admission of any given manifestation as "music". For "music" as a gross world phenomenon, I believe, can best be regarded as an object-type extension, consisting of any collection, of whatever size and historical, geographical, or "presentational" range, of "manifested sound objects" whose macrogrouping within such a class seems particularly favorable to the reciprocal individuation of its subject members (by assertion of boundary conditions for group membership) and for making "theoretical" inferences about these group members that "explain" various levels of correspondences among them (that we care about) by correlating these correspondences with progressive "partitionings" of the group into subgroups. And the nature of the boundary conditions most favorable to a given discourse will vary *depending on* the conceptual framework within which that discourse is in a *prior* sense formulated.

Now people possess, as part of their psychophysiological constitutions,[8] discriminative capacities of certain kinds with respect to auditory phenomena. These capacities are then universally available for utilization in intelligible communication, through the medium of human-made "perceptual objects" created by the defined structuring of differentiation and similitude in the various dimensions of auditory discrimination.

Some human (if not also some extrahuman) cultures manifest activities which take advantage of these capacities in ways that do not qualify as "speech". Some people want to call *all* these activities "music", and they attempt to discover "what music is" by inferring common characteristics of every culture's "music". Sometimes a characteristic from a given culture's music is taken as a potential basis for explaining a phenomenon observed in another's. Perhaps this might be called the "music is a universal language" fallacy.

For in order that this program be realized, it must be *assumed* that the "cultural" and communicative implications of "music" are (somehow) "the same" in all the different cultures, even though the only things they *necessarily* share are the *means* through which their "contents" are projected and discriminated. The implications of such discrimination are determined only by the constructions placed upon the patterns of differentiation by members of the culture, and by the particular ways in which these patterns are seen—or rather heard—to cohere.[9]

This assumption, however, is frequently made, and seems to underlie what are perhaps the most persistent metaphorical effusions in musical discourse; namely, those deriving in various ways from some analogy between "music" and "language". Now auditory signals other than speech may, of course—and apparently actually do in some cultures—function in a way precisely describable as language. Drum signals and telegraphic codes are the most obvious instances (but dial tones, busy signals, radio signatures—the NBC chimes, or even a "theme song"—automobile horns, doorbells, may also be instances; but note the distinction between them as

---

[8]In the light of Sellars, *op. cit,* this should perhaps be emended as "...people who share in common the experience of verbal language possess, as part of their so-conditioned psychophysiological mechanisms...".

[9]Cf. n. 6, p. 31, above.

"evidences of presence" and as "assertions of presence", "warnings", etc.). No such literally linguistic imputation is normally made, of course, especially with respect to what we call "western music". Nor is it necessary, I hope, to take into account here those who mean by a "universal language" anything so patently noncognitive as "'expressive' in a universally apprehensible way". But much musical explanation has rested on metaphorical transferences of such words as "phrase", "sentence", etc., which are plainly intended to derive their musical meanings by implicit conferral from an analogy with language. At best, however, these terms, in the absence of explicit and independent musical definition, can only represent heuristic imagery about *kinds* of things having certain functions in language that are being associated with kinds of things and functions in music. And which way "explanation" lies is thus hard to determine, since the respects in which music and language are "behaving" analogously in the chosen areas of correspondence is, at least, extremely unclear.

5. Music as a "uniformly qualified entity-class": the problem of noncontextual theoretical transference

In contradistinction to those discourses which extend the class-term "music" over phenomena without taking account of the considerable theoretical baggage necessarily transported thereby (because the contents of such baggage are regarded, if recognized at all, as pre-ordained or universal, and hence *non-theoretical,* which makes the very applicability of the class-term itself declarative of—and dependent on—*self-evidence* rather than *choice*), there are other discourses in which such a class-term extension is regarded as always carrying with it *all* the theoretical baggage associated with some particular members of the class. In such cases it would seem as though that baggage-array were regarded as an indivisible unit from top to bottom, whose components must be equally—and equivalently—applicable to all members of the class, and—hence—as though the (however admittedly) theoretical decision enabling the act of extension automatically incorporates the authorization for (and prescribes the superior utility of) such wholesale commensuration. This is tantamount to the replacement of implication by equivalence, the notion that the conferral of some attribute of one entity onto another confers *all* the other attributes of the first onto the second at the same time. Carried to this logical extreme, the notion reduces to absurdity the concept of "relationship" altogether, and this absurdity much resembles the cognitive effects of the "runaway analogies" in metaphorical discourse that were described on pp. 14–15, above. For just as the effect of the latter kind of transference is to confer all the *categories of behavior* of objects in one domain onto those of another on the authority of a single (and merely suggestive) relation among particular aspects of behavior, so the present kind of transference confers *attributions* uniformly. Thus, for example, a "runaway analogy" that uses "organism" as its operative metaphor (on the grounds, perhaps, of some notion of the presence of "coherence" and "development") also assumes the presence of "growth" and "decay", "fulfillment" and "frustration", "inner mechanism" and "surface appearance", and whatever other joys and ills organisms are heirs to. And a wholesale attribute-transference might entail, for example, that for everything over which it was convenient to extend the class-name "vehicle" it would also be equally relevant, possible, or worthwhile to describe its wheelbase, its rigging, its ceiling altitude, its thrust, its lead dog, or its cadenza. (I hope the distinction of this notion of the *uniformity* of a predication from the assumption that all relevant predications [and even their *values*] are *given in,* or *universally entailed* by a given class-term extension, is evident.)

Now this kind of metaphorical unclarity is one that particularly tends to go undetected in, and thus to poison the cognitive well of, otherwise rigorous discourses, in particular some that are ostensibly devoted to strictly "contextual" analyses of musical structures. Here, the problem frequently manifests itself in the transference of terms (whether already transferred from elsewhere or not) that are in fact defined for particular music-structural contexts (at least extensionally, by denotation alone) piecemeal (and again often just extensionally) to other analytic contexts where no evident one-to-one correlation exists (and where no principles are asserted according to which to infer such correlations) among the observable-functional aspects of structures arising in the different contexts. In this connection, words like "phrase", "cadence", "dissonance", "melody", "harmony", drawn from tonal contexts, when used to describe, say, events in twelve-tone music, lack even whatever explanatory value they have in tonal-structural discourse unless explicitly so correlated. Often, in such cases, the best inferable bases for the attributions (silences, for example, as delineators of "phrase" articulations) are insufficient as critical discriminants; they would hardly be regarded (even by the same writers) as primary determinants in their parent contexts, but would at most be considered to be in correspondence with other dimensions that, in a particular composition, would happen always to vary in invariant conjunction with the function in question. Thus, for example, silences, the limits of pitch-contour curves, etc., may all coincide in a given tonal piece with all its "cadences"; but our definiential criterion for the introduction of the term "cadence" to describe any one of those instances is independent of those coincidences. That is why it is intelligible to speak of a cadence-occurrence without an accompanying inflection-occurrence in melodic curve or textural continuity. And therefore it is inconsistent to assert, with respect to nontonal music, that the presence of such inflections justifies the introduction of the term "cadence" with cross-explanatory value (and to wish to introduce it without cross-explanatory value would seem an inexplicable *courtship* of confusion). Rather, however, a hidden metaphor*, of dubious heuristic value, will have been offered, not a conjunction of parallel associations on which a metatheory could be based. At best, such observations might delineate promising fields of observation where evidence might be sought to enable more cognitive transferences of concepts through the assertion of functional correlates or even through analogies of a less formal nature.

The depth to which the problem of un- or under-interpreted theoretical-term transference pervades musical discourse may be illustrated by taking as an example an article of otherwise exemplary rigor, Westergaard [38]. For even though Westergaard is a notably elegant and parsimonious writer, whose standards of analytic cognitivity are fiercely "pure", he nevertheless seems to place considerable analytic weight on questionable devices of the sort under discussion here. Normally, the theoretical position Westergaard represents is a salutary one that may be characterized as analogous to that of a practicing scientist, who, on the one hand, tends not to question traditional methodology on what seem to

---

*(1993:) It is probably worth pointing out, with exquisite (and somewhat defensive) hindsight, that the ensuing critiques of "metaphors" are directed toward metaphors masquerading and trying to function as operationally defined terms rather than frankly evocative imagery in explicitly metaphysical texts.

him merely formalistic grounds when that methodology has yielded satisfactory practical results and has presented no evident operational problems, but who, on the other hand, is even less charitable than the "foundation" theorist toward purely speculative hypostatizations and introductions of theoretical terms for which no correlations to any observables are defined. So it seems surprising that, in his discussion of possible approaches to the analysis of the rhythmic structure of Webern's Op. 27, III, one encounters the following rule for the introduction of the term "phrase"—a quite operational one, to be sure, but (as noted above) one that seems quite out of accord with the conditions under which a term of the same name would be introduced in a description of tonal music; and yet it does seem to be the analogical, "functional" sense of the concept that Westergaard hopes to capture:

1. Phrase

Phrases are demarcated by the traditional means of (a) silence and (b) dynamics. With one exception...there are no silences within phrases...(p. 185)

Now the language here, which seems to be *about* phrases rather than *definitional of* them ("demarcated" rather than "defined"; "no silences within phrases"), may suggest that a functional definition of "phrase" distinct from the manner in which phrases appear in a given piece is offered or referred to elsewhere, but this is not the case; and if such a definition is being assumed, it is not evident from any characteristic of the discourse. So the various "demarcative" criteria are the only *stated* basis we are given for the identification of both where "phrases" happen and of what phrases are in Webern's Op. 27, although it seems doubtful that a similar limitation would satisfy Westergaard were his subject tonal music. (A similar problem regarding "structural voices" as referred to in Westergaard's article is discussed in Part III.) But even with respect to tonal pieces, the "concept" underlying the term-name "phrase" seems so poorly explicated that the introduction of the term in any musical discourse without clear directions for the way in which the operations of its supposed referents are to be considered "structurally significant" seems dubious. I have a still greater difficulty with the cognitive status of "structural downbeat", which, as used by Westergaard, appears to be a wholly undefined term; that it is used as though defined suggests the influence of some hidden assumptions (as does the similar invocation of "finality", "rhyming effect of the isorhythm", "expectation"—as, "unexpected shortness of the third phrase", "expected downbeat", "shorter than expected", "too early", "too late", "too final", "destroys", "sense of delay", etc.—all of which appear on p. 187). (I also question the prescriptive "it couldn't be otherwise" type of locution apparently preferred to the "it can be so regarded" type, which latter seems to me rather more *conceptually* defensible for music; but at least in this area there is no question of a barrier presented to cognitive application, as in the other cases cited.) For the structural meaning of "structural downbeat", and the necessary and sufficient conditions for its identification among phenomena, and its explanatory value—i.e., what it accounts for that is not *equivalently* accounted for in an ontologically sparser descriptive discourse in which it does not appear—are badly in need of explication before the useful introduction of the term is possible. Meanwhile, the fact that these matters remain unexplicated renders the concept and its associated term cognitively inscrutable and referentially opaque. As for "expectation", which appears usually to be used to account for the sense of time-dependency in presented musical structures, it is unclear *how* it actually does so, or why this musical characteristic is not better accounted for by a "total-structure" model in which time succession is understood not as an added-on, separably domained "experiential process", but rather as just the time-dependent dimension among the totality of information-producing dimensions relationally observable from (or *as*) the "data". Thus the observation that one pitch-complex slice is shorter, or longer, than all the others we have decided to integrate it to just creates a particular relational phenomenon, and our "surprise" upon encountering it during an actual audition is no more or less determinate of it as an aspect of musical structure than are the reactions of any of our neighbor-auditors who happen just at the same moment to fall asleep.[10]

---

[10]With respect to theoretical terms, of whatever degree of interpretation from "phrase" to "structural downbeat" to "expectation" to "organic forces of pitch attraction", or whatever, this "What difference does it make?" question is perhaps even more troubling than the purely interpretational one, since in principle any of the terms could be rendered literally "intelligible", or at least more fully interpreted. In this connection, the following remark of Sellars (*op. cit.,* pp. 316–317) seems particularly apposite in its distinction of two dimensions of the logic of

One final issue that I find raised by Westergaard's approach to Webern analysis may be generalized as the problem engendered by applications of the idea that maintaining maximal simplicity in the construction of local, foreground evidence is a prime analytic principle for the sake of which the necessity of having a theoretical background of sufficient complexity to account for all the nuances is accepted. The question here is whether it is preferable to have such a more complicated theoretical explanation to permit a simpler "perceptual" activity at the foreground level (which also entails a maximal dependence on "conventional" conditioning for effective audition), or whether a more complex construal of the foreground as a particular nuancing of orderings of the predicates of a simpler, more comprehensive, and more economical background reference (even if it is the background of only one piece), would be preferable. Cognitive thought has traditionally inclined toward the latter (as I do also, on fundamental grounds of music-experiential preference), but much music-explanatory discourse seems firmly rooted in the ideology of the former. In Westergaard, I regard the passages on "Meter" on p. 186 as especially exemplifying the former approach. Further consideration of this question in connection with other analytic problems is relegated to Part IV, where the question of simplicity as a normative and as a realizable analytic principle is engaged.

---

theoretical terms, as "a) their role in explaining the selected phenomena of which the theory is a theory; and b) their role as candidates for integration into...the 'total picture'. These roles are equally part of the logic, and hence the 'meaning', of theoretical terms. Thus, at any one time, the terms in a theory will carry with them as part of their logical force that which it is reasonable to envisage—whether schematically or determinately—as the manner of their integration...the less a scientist is in a position to conjecture about the way in which a certain theory can be expected to integrate with other specialties, the more the concepts of his theory approximate to the state of pure theoretical concepts"—which latter I have been calling, perhaps too polemically, "metaphors". Sellars's criterion, of course, applies both externally and internally, *between* musical and *other* discourses (in terms of, e.g., criteria of cognitivity and general-epistemological considerations), *between* musical discourses *of different kinds* ("analytic"/ "historical"/"cultural"/"normative", etc.) and *among* different *areas* of discourses *within* the domain of *one* such kind ("Eastern-Western"/"twelve-tone-tonal"/ "modal", etc.). Thus the invocation of this criterion might be considered a central methodological concern of this part of this essay, stated in its most general form.

C. EXPLANATORY ADEQUACY

6. Preconditions, applications, and limitations of music-explanatory power

Here we consider what actually *constitutes explanatoriness* in a theory or a discourse, what this explanatoriness *depends on*, what kinds of *cognitive claims* it *can* support, and what kinds it *cannot*. To assist this consideration, we bring back into view the issue of "music as a phenomenon of culture" earlier introduced. In connection with "cultural explanations", we have seen that it is only by making universal assumptions with respect to a given set of cultural (or other) conditions that anyone can assert absolutistically "what music is", which turns out to be merely a tautologous restatement of those assumptions under those particular conditions. But by isolating a set of such conditions as a framework for saying "what music is *with respect to*" that set, "what", e.g., "music is *as* a cultural phenomenon in this (that, these) culture(s)", he is in a much better position to produce cognitively explanatory discourse, but shorn of the prescriptive, normative claims that seem so vital to many writers. This relativistic analysis, it seems to me, holds for every theory in every domain of discourse: if it is an adequate theory, we *should* be able to say what every relevant observable object (not, e.g., a "sight" in the case of a theory of "auditory" objects) "is" as an instance of the domain over which that theory ranges. But for such a theory to be workable, to produce genuinely explanatory results, not only must its theoretical terms be interpretable, but they and their associated observation-disposition terms must lie in the same "domain" of cognition, and the rules of correspondence interpreting the former in terms of the latter must not "cross" domains either. In short, it must be possible for us to know what observations we are to make to corroborate an explanatory predication, and in turn, we must be able to see how *that* evidence is relevant to the explanatory claims made by the discourse. Thus, we have seen that the "evidence" for "this interval is more naturally hearable than that" cannot be used as confirming evidence for "this music is more coherent than that", since no empirically significant correlation can be established for the two predicates *within the same observational domain*. Similarly, "music is language in culture X" is not evidence for "music is language", however disguised, or for "music is language in culture Y" for that matter, unless it be shown how "language in culture Y" relates to "language in culture X" and how "music in culture Y" can be related to "language in culture Y" in a way correlative with the way "music in culture X" is related to "language in culture X"; or, perhaps, how "music" in each culture is correlative with some "universal" sense of "language". And, especially, it would be important to know whether we were comparing the "syntactical-semantical structures" of the musics as *we* interpret them, or as we infer that the members of cultures X and Y interpret them; or if we were comparing them to language as we regard it (or them, if what we mean is "the languages of those cultures"), or as we infer that the members of cultures X and Y regard it (or them, if those cultures have concepts of "other languages"). In most of these cases, we are producing observations about music in a way that reflects on our knowledge of its role in various cultures in the sense that is normally regarded as *anthropological*. At another extreme, we may be explaining "what the structure of an instance of the music of culture X is as an instance of the music of our own culture". Somewhere in between, we may be considering what the structure of an instance of the music of culture X is, in some terms derived either from our own way of understanding music or what we can infer of theirs, with respect to structures of other instances of that music interpreted along similar lines. The only way any of these categories of observation could bear upon "the structure of the music of X as compared with that of our music" is by either regarding our music *as* X's music, or X's music as our music, which however would still reveal nothing at all about the relation of X's music as X's music to our music as our music. Again, the investigation of this latter question could be accomplished only anthropologically, it seems to me, and would have no more general-musical repercussions except in the unlikely event that it could be determined that "X's music to X-natives" = "X's music to us" and that this equation be extensible so that each of its components is equatable both with "our music to us" and with "our music to X-natives". For otherwise, the degree to which explanatory remarks in one domain could explain anything in the others seems nonexistent.

      Similar comments could be made with respect to the musical manifestations within a single culture at different times. To begin with, successions of "technical" observations of different such literatures might be correlated with successions of "what the cultural meaning of music was at the time", but it would hardly be possible to *explain* one in terms of the other (especially when terms like "difficulty", "complexity", etc., that are often used in such transactions, have such utterly different applications and referents in the hands of different users—even within the *same* historical period—and can never be used cognitively as undefined terms or supposedly observational-dispositional predicates (because of their heavy theoretical burden), but only as explicitly interpreted theoretical terms). Here, of course, we are speaking of discourse in the *music-historical* explanatory domain, and of some of the problems encountered therein in correlating observed data with explanations offered of that data. The most difficult area here, perhaps, is that associated with the notion of "style", which is often treated as though it signified "the presentational-surface characteristics that are assertible of a given composition by regarding it as an instance of a fixed type of music taken a priori as universally referential for all music, as they associate with the meanings such characteristics would be taken to have in a composition of the 'referential' type". (So, e.g., a given acoustic phenomenon occurring anywhere in music "is" always, say, "C-E-G", or "a triad" or even "a tonic triad", and a certain succession of similar phenomena "is" always a "cadence" or a "V-I progression", or a "fifth-relation", etc., regardless of—or rather without consideration or apparent awareness of—contextual considerations.) However well this notion of "style" works for music *of* the referential kind (and because of the notion's conceptual deficiencies it would seem just as likely to work *against* that music as well), to regard its application as a universal implementation of the notion of "musical style" seems questionable at best. But such an application may, in fact, be performed with varying degrees of rigor (I have purposely stated the idea in its most cognitively realizable form), and its implementation actually does form the basis of many music-historical discourses that stray beyond associated biography, chronology, and uncontextualized sociocultural mythohistory. And were the meanings of the descriptions and interpretations of the theoretical terms (usually left unstated in any form) offered understood in the above sense, then the decision as to the relative interest of the resultant findings (even if they seemed no more interpretable than as reports of the author's dispositions: Leo Treitler's "persuasion") would be up to the reader, but they would be as immune from the reproach of "absolutism" as any "absolute" application would be beyond their reach. The only dangerous application of this notion of "style" would be in the commission of a rather gross form of the uniform-transference malpractice described in Section 5; this, unfortunately, is its most familiar application in the music-historical literature.

But perhaps the notion of "style" might be explicated in a more general, and perhaps conceptually deeper, sense, as "the particular relation in a given composition between the particulars of presentation and the syntactical functions inferred from them". Thus one might consider a "literature" of musical manifestations as evidencing a "repertory" of diverse presentational characteristics and one of diverse syntactical functions; then, the way any composition projects the sense of the latter by means of the selection from and disposition of the former may be considered its "style"; the area of correspondence among such relations in all the works, or groups of works, by the same composer, "his style"; the correspondences among the members of a literature, the "style of a period"; and the account of the contours of change in these relations among successive literatures, the "history of style". But the correlation of "style" in this sense to "cultural history" would always remain at an "explanatory remove", in the sense that the presence of invariances of correlation among diverse activities within a culture might be interesting or revealing, but could never *explain* anything in either the "stylistic" or the "cultural" domain as such. So the correlation of the history of style with the history of culture cannot by itself explain anything about either style or culture, except how they happen to coincide chronometrically. In particular, the correction of texts (production of "authentic editions") and the explication of "later than/because of" relations are encumbered by difficulties of this type.[11]

---

[11]"Style" in the sense explicated here may be regarded as a very important notion indeed, as in fact the link between the *contextual* domain of musical discourse—that which is concerned with the "formal" representation of works of music as *relational structures* of various kinds—and the *perceptual* or *phenomenal* domains—those where music is considered as the representation of structures of perceptual "data" perceptually "measured" by psychological "instruments". This link consists of a set of inferences that determines the "data" to be selected as relevant information in reconstructing the "musical structure", the quantizational scales for the degree-measurement of different data-dimensions

52

7. Model-constructability as a general criterion of explanatory cognitivity

Before proceeding to further direct confrontations with domains in which "musical explanation" is rumored to take place, we should find it advantageous to generalize from the varied methodological resources employed in the foregoing to a broader explanatory concept against which to place the circumstances, claims, and methods of any particular discourse, and in terms of which to project a comprehensive image of the structure of the domain of musical explanation as a whole, with the hope that it may attain some cohesion and plausibility, and hence cognitive functionality. Now the various problems of discourse we have been observing may be considered to center on two key issues: the question of the cognitive value of analogies of various kinds employed therein; and the question of the degree of operational interpretability that can be ascribed to descriptively employed theoretical terms of various kinds. We have used these as our principal metrics of cognitivity in distinguishing various levels of explanatory power, degrees of fulfillment of claims of explanatory relevance, and degrees of interpretability of explanatory terms in the practices, domains, and instances of discourse examined. And we have observed that some discourses are "emotive" statements of metaphysical positions, some others are statements of personal disposition, some others involve the purely heuristic linking of interpreted terms from one domain with another domain in which they are either nonanalogously interpreted or entirely uninterpreted; others define and use terms whose names are the same as those of other terms used elsewhere in the same or associated discourses with different referents and extensions, and still others use chains of observational and theoretical discourse that are genuinely cognitive in one domain to support claims in another domain whose relevant observational and theoretical terms seem wholly distinct. And we have concluded that discourses of any one kind of these "explain" different "things about music" from those of any

---

and, correspondingly, the syntactical functions which are being ordered by particular interpretations in particular aspects of the presented, perceptual, data. In short, "style" in this explication is nothing less than the whole set of correlations between a syntactic structure and its semantic interpretation (in the sense of Church [50]); and this is just the whole of the "epistemic" domain of music-structural thought.

of the other kinds, that what they explain appears often to differ from their own declarations of explanatory intent, and that all of them are "explanatory" in a sense different from that ascribable to discourses of less equivocal nature.

Now the criteria of applicability that we have been using in a rather *ad hoc* fashion to ferret out individual cognitive problems on specifically "music-meaningful" grounds may be placed in a more coherent structure and given a more general application by virtue of their evident correspondence with the principal considerations customarily involved in the construction of *explanatory models*. Such models may be informally characterized as "working analogies", the determinability of whose efficacy depends on the structure of interpretation of a collection of theoretical terms.

To see how explanatory models can be helpful in resolving explicitly musical problems, let us generalize further some of the cognitive standards invoked above to distinguish what we have decided to regard as a cognitive problem in the first place in its most general possible form. Specifically, we may regard what we have been involved in as the distinction between questions raised in terms of and directed toward issues *within* a given operational framework, and questions asked, more or less *in vacuo, about* the framework itself.[12]

Another way to characterize the same distinction is in terms of what C. G. Hempel[13] calls "explanation-seeking why questions", the answers to which seek to assert the non-anomalous nature of a distinguishable datum, and "reason-seeking why questions", which question the "true existence" of such a datum and ask for evidence therefor. In music, an "explanation-seeking" question

---

[12]This formulation is an attempt to relativize the "internal-external question" dichotomy utilized by Carnap in e.g., [47] and [48], along lines that account for the objections to Carnap's formulations by Quine, e.g., [67], from which it may be inferred that every language, however "formalized", is biased with respect to a metalanguage, including all metalanguages with respect to possible meta-meta-languages. My invocation of the notion here, however, depends for effectiveness only on the possibility of deciding, with respect to a given discourse, whether, with respect to some plausible demarcation inferred for its conceptual sub-framework, any passage in it is best regarded as "object-" or "meta-linguistic" *relative to the discourse*. Thus every such "metalinguistic" question may be regarded as an "external" one *with respect to* the "object-linguistic" questions *in the same discourse*.

[13]In [58].

may take the form, "Why (i.e., from the point of view of what [empirically and deductively] reasonable structure of elements and relations) is it reasonable for this 'thing' to be here in this 'place' in this 'piece'?" An alternative way of putting the same question is, "What does it mean for this to be here in this place, etc.?" As to what basis exists for asserting that the "thing" is "there", or even to distinguish "it" as a "thing", a rigorous relativism requires one to admit that all musical "things" more complex than the single "atomic sound-element" are, precisely, inferred complexes of such "sound-elements" interpreted by individual perceivers as significative "events". But even the decision as to the sizes of the "degree-slices" in the various perceptual-dimension continua that will determine what counts as a "simple" (or rather what will be the least degree of discernible difference among sound-events that will also be considered to represent a "syntactical" distinction), is ultimately an "interpretative" matter as well, part of the primitive-assumptive basis of the underlying theory guiding perception, and thus not open to "objective" disconfirmation (within psychophysical thresholds), although always subject in principle to revision (and in practice as well, if the results yielded are found insufficiently satisfying).[14] Thus the reason-seeking question that demands proof that the datum is "really there" is essentially unanswerable.

In the domain of explanation, the questions asked are, in the most formal sense, susceptible of formulation and response in terms of the explanatory-predictive model called (by Hempel in particular) "deductive-nomological". Here, observation sentences are conjoined with "laws", the totality presumably constituting sufficient (though never, in any ascertainable sense, *necessary*) conditions to account for the occurrence of some event, to confirm

---

[14]The epistemic status of this "data-discriminative" activity may be understood in terms of Sellars's explication of the similar status of "thoughts" (*op. cit.,* pp. 317–320): "...these [inner episodes] are 'in' language-using animals as molecular impacts are 'in' gases, not as 'ghosts' are in 'machines'...[But they are non-empirical in that they, like theoretical entities, are not definable in observational terms.]...Nor does the fact that they are, as introduced, unobserved entities imply that Jones could not have good reason for supposing them to exist. Their 'purity' is not...metaphysical...but...methodological...the concept of thoughts is primarily *intersubjective,* as intersubjective as the concept of a position, and...the reporting role of these concepts—the fact that each of us has a privileged access to his own thoughts—constitutes a dimension of the use of these concepts which is built on and presupposes their intersubjective status".

that "it was to be expected". This differs, of course, from a *purely deductive* model, in which inferences are made directly from observation sentences, without intervening laws framed as "rules of inductive inference", in the form of universal conditionals:

A purely deductive model (after Hempel [58]):

$$\frac{ab}{\therefore a} \text{ (observation sentences)}$$

The "D-N" model (after Hempel, *op. cit.*):

$$\frac{C_1, C_2, \ldots, C_k \quad \text{(observation sentences)}}{L_1, L_2, \ldots, L_k \quad \text{(laws)}} \supset$$
$$E \quad \text{(explanandum-sentence)}$$

Each law itself is framed as $\forall x (F(x) \supset G(x))$. Thus a "musical" explanation of this form might run as follows:

Where a, b, c, d are *pitches*, and P(x) = "x is a pitch",

I(x, y) = "(x, y) is the *interval* determined by x and y where x and y are pitches",

IE((x, y), (z, t)) = "(x, y) is *interval-equivalent* to (z, t)", and

PS(x, y) = "(x, y) is a *presented simultaneity* where x and y are pitches",

then, if

$C_1 = (PS(a, b) \wedge PS(c, d))$ and $C_2 = (a + t = c \wedge b + t = d)$

and, if

$L_1 = \forall x \forall y \forall z \forall w \forall t [P(x) \wedge P(y) \wedge P(z) \wedge P(w) \wedge (x + t = z \wedge y + t = w) \supset IE((x, y), (z, w))]$

then it follows that

IE((a, b), (c, d)).

The "truth" of this "explanandum" can be *tested* by whether it corresponds to the "intuitive" truth-value assignment we would make for the sentence "IE ((a, b), (c, d))". It is in this sense that "structure-descriptions" are "predictions", for our "law" simply "predicts" that every time a certain set of defined conditions holds for some entities, it will be "true of them" (i.e., "truly predicable" of them) that a certain *further* condition *also* holds.*

Such post-diction, under musical interpretation, describes a theoretical-empirical "structure" (perhaps a unique one) within which such an occurrence "could be expected to happen". The absence of such a covering structure would render an event "incoherent"—a "surprise", in the terminology of some recent music-theoretical discourse. The structure thus asserted, therefore, has no *prior* ontological status, but is merely a particular ordering of the elements and relations that constitute a particular conceptual framework, an ordering that corresponds to a *descriptive interpretation* (i.e., explanation) of a particular musical manifestation (*ascribing* characteristics to it, and *defining, denoting, dimensioning,* and *proportioning* its elements and their quantized relations).

Correspondence between a complex of observation-disposition and theoretical terms, on the one hand, and a phenomenal manifestation on the other, is what constitutes the "modeling" aspect of this explanatory procedure. And while other explanatory procedures may differ in degree of presented or possible formality, this *cognitive correspondence* and *comprehensiveness of coverage* are the operative determinants, relatively speaking, of the distinction between what I have called a "metaphor", or a "metaphorical" discourse, and a "model", or a "cognitively explanatory" discourse.[15]

---

*(1993:) This is the basic sense in which the sequences of definitions in Part II have music-cognitive content.

[15] The relation between the operation in this regard of informally presented discourses to more formal renderings of their "content" may be considered in terms of the critique of pure "logicism" in Sellars (*op. cit.,* p. 313): "...fundamental assumptions are...developed not by constructing uninterpreted calculi which might correlate in the desired manner with observational discourse, but rather by attempting to find a *model,* i.e., to describe a domain of familiar objects, behaving in familiar ways [but, of course, they need not be "familiar" so long as they can be intersubjectively denoted or defined: see Hempel [58]. pp. 430–33 —B.B.] such that we can see how the phenomena to be explained would arise if they consisted of that sort of thing. The essential thing about a model is that it is accompanied, so to speak, by a commentary which *qualifies* or *limits*—but not precisely or in all respects—the analogy between the familiar objects and the entities which are being introduced by the theory. It is the descriptions of the fundamental ways in which the objects in the model domain, thus qualified, behave,

Thus, it should be evident that we can regard the mode of discourse—especially its specific verbal or symbological surface, its formality, "density", or whatever—as *relatively* immaterial; immaterial, that is, just to the degree that its terms are interpretable as relatively clearly correlated to observational quantifications of variables that can be observed to be or not to be, to do or not do, the things the discourse claims they are and are doing. On the other hand, to try to establish an absolute criterion for intersubjectivity is just as futile as any attempt to establish absolutes rationally; for, pragmatically, the notion that a discourse is "acceptable" as "explanation" if and only if it is "intersubjectively intelligible" begs the question of "intelligible to how many individuals, to which individuals or collections of individuals in particular, and with respect to what?". For what rejoinder is possible when a writer or a reader of an apparently "incoherent" explanation assures us that "it's meaningful to him"? Here we are in exactly the same predicament as, e.g., we are with respect to a piece whose coherence we can't discover: I may never permit myself the assertion that it "is incoherent", but only that "I am incoherent about it", or that "I find no way in which to find this coherent that I can cognize as an adequate way for something of this sort to be coherent". But someone else's claim that "it's coherent to him" cannot be *denied,* first, in the case that the assertion is merely the report of a belief, and, second, in the case where an unacceptable or seemingly inscrutable basis for coherence is offered; for the fact that such a basis may not seem evidenceable or adequate or otherwise acceptable by one's own standards of explanatoriness or cognitivity, does not entail that those standards are also those of our friend or of the universe.

Thus, all we could do in such a case would be to articulate those principles we do hold that are violated by the piece or discourse as we find it, and how they are violated; then we can only hope for agreement on the acceptability of the asserted principles.

---

which, transferred to the theoretical entities, correspond to the postulates of the logistical picture of theory construction.

"...the logistical picture obscures the most important thing of all, namely that the process of devising "theoretical explanations" of observable phenomena did not spring full-blown from the head of science.... [It is mistaken] to suppose that "hypothetico-deductive" explanation is *limited* to the sophisticated stages of science" (italics mine; see especially the remarks made above, regarding the difficulty of a "nontheoretical" basis for any musical experiencing or understanding—B.B.).

If these principles themselves are denied, we may try further to demonstrate that the "substitute" set of principles affirmed (presumably in the course of the denial) are, in operation, isomorphic with our own in that behavior under them is indistinguishable from behavior under ours, so that whatever violates ours, violates them. If this doesn't work either, we must resign the attempt, for then the criteria of what constitutes "intersubjective communication" in any sense are probably also beyond redemption for us with respect to him, in any case.

Another problem that has arisen in the application of the D-N model has more to do with misunderstanding than inherency; this is the confusion of its formulation in terms of universal-conditional "laws" with a *causal* bias. That the claim of causality in the metaphysical sense is not something that the D-N model requires for its efficacy should, I believe, be clear from the foregoing; and the special interpretation offered above of the notion of *prediction* in this context is equally extensible to *causation,* regarded as merely a hypostatization of the conjunctions of antecedents in sentences of universal-conditional form. On the other hand, of course, any causal explanation is translatable into a D-N explanation—this is in fact one of the greatest advantages of that model, in its removal of the "causal-dependent" metaphysical sting from explanations of that form; but to use this as an indicator of the "causal bias" of the D-N model itself is to commit a classic affirmation of the consequent.[16] Hempel offers "operational" translations of several "metaphysical predicates": "determinism" becomes the principle that the state of a system at any given point *gives* its state at any other specifiable point by operations of the D-N model (p. 351); the causal type is in any case not the only "intuitive" category for D-N explanations of general laws by deductive subsumption under theoretical principles, for the relationships expressed in a law (e.g., the time for a pendulum swing) are not generally *causal*

---

[16]This ascription, however, is fundamental to Treitler's dismissal of the D-N model as appropriate for historical explanation in [35] and [36]; his point could still be made, however, simply by affirming and evidencing a conviction that of the possible models available, the D-N one does not most prominently *extrude* the structures and processes which the historian or the critic of historical discourse desires to be regarded as most significant; (1995:) Some such consideration was in fact operative in determining the descriptive paths chosen in the present essay.

when the factors are *internal* (quantitative dispositional characteristics, etc.) (p. 352). Also, "laws of coexistence", and "laws of succession" (with respect to temporal changes within a system), often involve explanation by reference to *later* occurrences and can thus hardly be regarded as causal. Moreover, putting the matter conversely, *not* all *predictions* are *explanations,* as in cases of apriori probability, pure empirical inference, statistical preponderance of conjunctions (note the resemblance of this latter to the methods employed in "lawless" harmony-texts), etc. We may add to this, for music history and theory, "explanation" in terms of "practice", which just reports and collates data gathered from some more or less unspecified point of view, and uses this as "evidence" for post- or pre-diction. Thus, a prediction of high probability with respect to some music, such as, "chord x will follow chord y" may or may not be used as an *explanation* to guide, e.g., compositional practice; for not only may it be derived from a mere statistical preponderance, it may also be one of those "explanations" some of whose hypotheses are supported only by the fact that the event did in fact occur (which most often seems to underlie historical "it was to be"s).

Another consideration for the explanatory adequacy of a "modellable" theoretical discourse is the relative "degree of approximation" with which, as part of a larger theory, such a discourse accounts for its chosen segment of the case-range. Consider, e.g., a theory of harmony consisting entirely of "laws" about "chord progression" compared with theories in which such phenomena are explained as local, particular instances of larger processes of "progression" in whatever sense of "consequential succession". The "explanatory" sentences arising in both theories may equivalently coincide with the same observable facts, but in a way that the "propositional content" of the sentences of one may be considered subsumed within that of those of the other, so that various instances that are explained indistinguishably in the former theory may emerge as quite *distinct* entities (while the similitude in some respects is also accounted for) in the latter, thus more comprehensive, theory (and of course everything that is *distinct* in the former is also distinct in the latter). Thus "chord-identity" analysis is contained as a subdomain within "total-structure" analysis, which distinguishes between "function in general" and "function in particular" as "chord-identity" description alone cannot.

D. LINGUISTIC MODELS AS MUSICAL MODELS

> The true function of logic,...as applied to matters of experience,...is analytic rather than constructive; taken a priori, it shows the possibility of hitherto unsuspected alternatives more often than the impossibility of alternatives which seemed prima facie possible. Thus, while it liberates imagination as to what the world *may* be, it refuses to legislate as to what the world *is*.
>
> —Bertrand Russell,
> *Our Knowledge of the External World*

8. Earlier (Section 4) I noted the persistence of language-derived analogies among the metaphorical conceits in musical discourses. But on a more seriously explanatory level as well, the association of music with language is a frequent, even a predominant, tendency in discourses from almost every domain of "musical" explanation, with widely varying degrees of explicitness, and in widely varying senses. So here we turn our attention, fortified with the analytic tools with which we have provided ourselves in the foregoing, to discourses that propose to find genuine explanatory value in a "model of language as a model of music" analogy (to put the proposal in a form appropriate to our discussion). Here, the situation, being first of all metamusical, and second of all tied to the question of whether someone's intuitions about the "appropriateness" of an analogization of functions in two apparently non-commensurable domains are likely to resemble anyone else's, is highly complex. In particular, we are confronted with the "metamusical" remove from "explanation" involved in the notion that a *model* derived—more or less well—to explain one empirical domain is an adequate model of another *model,* derived more or less well from the musical domain. Put in terms of *explanation,* the process is something like this: from a model of a theory of language, either *terms* or *relations* or both are extracted (wholly or in part) which are then presumed to constitute an interpretation of an explanatory theory of music. From here, the ramifications are formidable: in different discourses (and sometimes, at different places in the same discourses), we may find that what is *supposed* to be *explanatory* and *how* it is supposed to be so varies among the following schemes, at least:

1. It is simply asserted as a position of the discourse that music *is* (or is going to be regarded as some kind of) a language; in the "cultural" domain, this appears to be done often just as a kind of "reduction to the familiar", a heuristic metaphor not offered as any more explicitly explanatory than by the appropriateness of the "aura" of the term-name, "language". But elsewhere its use is more assertive.

2. It is a method of producing theoretical terms just to transfer *names* of terms from some linguistic theory(ies) to musical entities, thereby conveying a heuristic "sense" of their correspondence, not otherwise explicated ("phrase", "period", etc., whose *musical use* may be explicated but whose transference from language rarely is).

3. Criteria for the application of linguistic terms in language are given music-theoretical interpretations as justifications for their introductions into musical discourse, showing how the "musical" functions may be regarded as *instances* of the linguistic functions.

4. An entire syntactic-structural model of language is interpreted by a system of music-theoretical entities and relations, showing how the "deep structure" of linguistic utterance corresponds with the "deep structure" of musical events.

5. The principles of theory formation and model construction developed in connection with linguistic-typical domains are invoked, in ways deemed empirically and intuitively appropriate to the intelligible rendering of musical concepts, to produce a contextual-theoretical model for a *given* musical structure (or a more or less extensive class of such structures; the more extended, the less comprehensively explanatory for each one any theoretical model that *explains them all to the same degree*).

6. The principles for the formation of uninterpreted formal-linguistic calculi are invoked to construct a logistical system which is offered, with a greater or lesser degree of interpretation, as a "measure" for the "admissibility" of individual musical instances as "members of a literature" defined in terms of the "language" of which the model is a model. Or, alternatively, the model is regarded simply as a model for some or all musical manifestations, whose "goodness of fit" under interpretation with respect to that model is regarded as an explanatory "fact" either about the composition or the model in question.

Obviously, what constitutes adequacy for each of these types varies with its "inherent" explanatory claim and its domain of relevance, in application and confirmation. Thus, in case No. 1, there is no true explanatory claim discernible beyond the "rightness of feel" of the metaphor, which demands no particular further cognitive validation. Case No. 2 is only slightly at a more cognitive remove; and since the "definitions" are simply name-conferring conventions, their rightness-of-feel aspects are quite separate from the cognitivity of their applications. Yet, if it were to be claimed that the names used transfer some correspondences with their "parent" terms in language, and that these transferences carry explanatory messages, this claim is not supportable under the conditions designated.

In the third and fourth cases, linguistic models as, in varying degrees, *actual models of actual linguistic theories,* are given the status of serious candidacy for the role of cognitive "models for music". Here the operative criterion should be the condition that Hempel calls[17] "syntactic isomorphism". What this entails is that a *uniformity* in the structure of the governing laws of the two theories can be asserted; that empirical terms (those not purely formal) be matched, one by one, in such a way that if in laws of the first context each term is replaced by its counterpart, a law of the second set is obtained, and vice versa. The final question is how far— that is, into how many dimensions—the analogies will actually carry.[18] For in transferring from one model to another, mere "appearances of similarity" (such as between articulation-breaks among the outer-end-words of adjacent uttered sentences, and those at data-flow junctures in music; or, within music alone, the simple appearance of a "major triad" or a "C major cadence" in a

---

[17] *Op. cit.,* p. 436.

[18] Thus Sellars *(op. cit., p.* 318) remarks: "...all theories formulated in terms of a model...[include] a *commentary* on the model, a commentary which places more or less sharply drawn restrictions on the analogy between the theoretical entities and the entities of the model. Thus, while [Jones's] theory talks of 'inner speech,' the commentary hastens to add that, of course, the episodes in question are not the wagging of a hidden tongue, nor are any sounds produced by this 'inner speech'."

Similarly, where we are not given the commentary on a transferred term, we have no way of knowing which of the myriad of its assertible aspects are being regarded as transferred, and hence the location and confirmation of the supposed explanatory claims are quite seriously obstructed.

piece otherwise understood as "twelve-tone" or otherwise "non-tonally") are not, in general, adequate as bases for decision independently of total-contextual considerations that require at least the conditions of Case No. 4. But "organic" analogies, anthropomorphisms, etc., which may function as supposed "explications of correspondence" (metaphors "once removed") at the level of any one of the four cases, usually lack both correlative and explanatory force because they fail to specify any basis for nomic or syntactic isomorphism.

Now all four cases depend on the intuitive acceptance of the notion that music and language have something pretty directly to do with one another, from bottom to top of their presented structures. It is, in fact, this "bottom-to-top" aspect which is most problematic—the Sellars remark on limiting an analogy comes to mind here—for without some criterion for discernment of a level at which music and language *detach,* a theorist may find himself in the rather awkward position of appearing to claim that they are literally *interchangeable,* or at any rate of having failed to assert or demonstrate *that* and *how* they are not.

But to find the place to detach one from the other, one must first have confidence that the levels of structure at which they remain undetached are "high" enough epistemologically that the analogy has some discernible advantages over just "anything"—say, sexual experience (which has, of course, been seriously and plausibly proposed as a musical model), life-cycles of organisms (also proposed as a metaphor, at least, for music), molecular patterns in gases, or actuarial tables. What are the strikes *against* the privileged status of the language/music model, then? To begin with, the notion that *all* structures are *linguistic* reduces the speciality of the idea to near zero, because then "musical things" would be no *more* "linguistic" than "physical things". This notion may even represent a confusion between the "language modeled" and "the language of the model" (metalanguage/object language confusion again); or, conversely, confusion may arise from the fact that we speak of "linguistic entities" by which, however, we must mean to say that language *has* "things" in it, in some more or less delimited sense, and *is* a particular "thing" (assuming a certain explication of the extension and intension of "thing" which I believe to be standard), but none of this can entail that *things are* also *languages, ipso facto.* Further, any exhaustive image of language includes a fundamental pragmatic aspect not shared by music in any evident way, however remotely analogical; the behavior *occasioned* by music that would be considered "contextually relevant" is massively incommensurable with that range of overt physical and verbal responses pragmatically associated with language. In fact, music-pragmatic behavior, insofar as we could speak of it at all, is entirely an activity of thought (of "inner episodes"), the *reports* of which may indeed be literally verbal-linguistically pragmatic in interpretation.*

Moreover, the status of *lexical* or *conventional* considerations in the explanation of musical structures casts a heavy constraint on the limits to the "semantic" and "syntactic" connections assertible between music and language.[19] For the transference of *semantics* in its natural-linguistic sense, as the relation between linguistic expressions and their designata or denotata would involve the presence of such notions as "meaning-unit", or "sound-function relation", or "aboutness", in music. Now obviously, the respect in which sounds in music "refer" to physical events or objects (onomatopoeically, that is), is in the domain of the "conceit", and hardly needs to be taken as a serious issue in the explanation of musical structures as such. But functional "meanings" of "sounds", for which "significative" (or "well-formed") "sound-meaning units" need to be derived, may be more relevant to music, even in purely structural terms. Yet the criterion for "meanings", whatever "meaning" may further signify, is essentially determined for verbal languages by *lexical* considerations; but such considerations are absent as *essentials* from music, where "meaning"—again, whatever that means—*can* always be determined *contextually* down to

---

*(1993:) I obviously was excluding dances, marches, ritual processions, etc., as constituting "second-order" responses to musical identities, or, perhaps, "first-order" responses to "second-order" musical identities (that is, to social-contextual identities of musical phenomena pursuant to, and consequent on, their music-contextual identities). (See p. 70, below.)

[19] This "pragmatic"-"semantic"-"syntactic" categorization represents the tripartite divisions of the domain of semiotic proposed by C. W. Morris (in [64]), sustained by Carnap (in [47] and [48] and elsewhere), and seriously questioned by several linguistic philosophers recently (notably Gilbert Harman), though such other authors as, e.g., R. M. Martin (in, for example, [63]), find its applicability unblemished. Again, our use of it is so trivial as to be well below the battle; but in every case, regarding the "distinction" as merely directional, relative to a discourse rather than absolute, seems a useful relativistic "way out".

a far more basic level of structure. Similarly, the criteria of "well-formation" for what constitutes a "complete meaning-unit" among sonic or symbolic strings, are *essentially* conventionally determined in language, but not in music, which can be contextually determined at the corresponding levels.

Also, the *syntactics* of verbal language, the matter of the signs and expressions and their interrelations, "descriptive" in the case of "natural" language and "pure" in that of formalized languages, is also essentially conventional at levels where music may be contextually described. Thus, for example, the criterion for "completion" of a "unit of syntactic structure" is and must be external with respect to any individual utterance in language; in music, such units of "completion" may again be contextually determined on the basis of single instances from "internally", or "implicitly" defined criteria. Thus, beyond the conventional ("assumptive") definition ("denotation") of a *single* sound-datum, what is inferred in a composition as a complex "unit of structure" in the sense of "meaning-element" or "syntactical unit" is, if analogous at all, based on a theory of that composition's structural foundations—surely one reason why the perceptual and conceptual difficulty of instant cognition of musical structures from single encounters with their embodying presentations is so much greater than the analogous activity in verbal-linguistic contexts. At this level, the frequently proffered analogies to linguistic units like "phrase", "sentence", etc. appear weakest, since in language they are always names for units whose formative completeness is determinable, and determinable only, by prior information, in the absence of associated behavior (such as pointing, speaking loudly, etc.). We have also hinted here at what may be another fundamental problem with the linguistic model for music: that the "focus of discourse" for language (especially for natural languages) is always the totality of possible utterances, whereas in music, it is always the particular structure of a particular composition (see the discussion of this question at the beginning of Part II). Thus it would surely seem that, if there were such a thing, a theory of poetry, as a study of relations among and within individual (closed) structures or orderings of linguistic entities and their syntactical and semantic relations, would provide a more reasonable model for a model of a theory of music than a theory of language as such possibly can.

But one demurrer at least is called for: in case it has not been evident from the choice of language in the above, it is not the intention here to deny that musical "semantics" and "syntax" *could* be explained as conventional—up to a complete "structural" or even a "detail" description, for that matter. Some aspects (more often than all) have been preponderantly so described in the literature; and I have already indicated how some supposed explanations are, in fact, mere restatements of assumptions, which to be applied must be taken precisely as "conventions of the discourse". Thus, anything that can be inferred *can* also be assumed; the question is whether one prefers to if one doesn't have to, for the quest for the fewest requisite assumptions is one of the most characteristic features of cognitive activity, motivated by the sense that minimal assumptions result in maximal cognitive yields from the same entities. The relevant operator here, however, goes the converse way: *not* everything which *can* be assumed *can also* be derived by inference in any discourse or structure. Thus, where "$D(x)$" means "x is derivable" and "$A(x)$" means "x is assumable", "$D(x) \supset A(x)$" always holds, but not "$A(x) \supset D(x)$". And where "x" is a "rule, definition, or denotation of the discourse", "$\forall x\, A(x)$", which is of course the extreme boundary of the condition that leads us to prefer, as more "explanatory", theories where the *fewest* "x's" *need* to be assumed (which may be considered a rough explication of the notion of "cognitive yield" invoked above).

9. Now, in asserting semantic and syntactic contextuality on all but the most basic levels of musical structure, one is saying just that the syntactical rules for every composition are uniquely inferable from that composition beyond some minimal primitive basis, whatever their degree of correspondence or intersection with other sets of rules derived for other compositions. As I have indicated, such rules could (perhaps on the basis of transference from such a pool of generally occurrent rules) be regarded as *assumed* syntactical-semantical conventions for any composition. But since the possibility for more unique determination exists, this means that the possibility also exists for each composition to exhibit significant variability and hence uniqueness of relational structure on many more, and more fundamental, levels. This may be considered the *musical* significance of the notion of "greater cognitive yield". And one consequence of this fact is the far greater degree to which, in music, it is realistic to regard "musical structure" (meaning the to-

tality of systematically ordered interpretations of data-complexes, relational paths, and their resultant concatenations) as "in the ear of the perceiver", and as to a virtually "total" degree variable for any given hearer, with respect to any given composition. Thus I can "hear" any piece just about any way I decide to, or am asked to, as long as that way is empirically realistic. The consequences of any such decision or compliance will, of course, be more or less interesting to me according to my own "normative criteria" about what constitutes a satisfying relation of musical data to musical structure, and what constitutes a satisfying musical structure. But I *can* decide to hear a "tonal" piece *as* a "twelve-tone" one, or vice versa. What I *cannot* do is hear in a way that cannot be cognitively delimited. Thus I cannot comply with a request to hear a piece as one whose events and elements are only vaguely specified*, since the way an event has been specified is not one of the aspects of information about it available from audition (i.e., "*as* music"), and since I can only hear *particular,* not "general" events in any given performance. And at another performance I may conclude that I am hearing a piece so similar to the first that it seems worthwhile to regard it as a "variant"—which is just a way of noting the fact that they *are* distinct pieces, but have more aspects of similitude than pieces I call "different" from each other generally share. But this is not in any sense a factor that could affect anything concerning the specificity of the piece I hear at either performance. Look at the score, I am told; but I simply conclude that the score is so much less specific than the scores I am accustomed to that it seems inadequate to furnish a secure predictive basis from which to infer what piece I am actually likely to hear on any occasion when the names on the score correspond to those on a concert program, although I may infer to varying degrees what "kind" of piece I am likely to hear. But what happened, or will happen, at some other historical moment cannot in any way I know be made an aspect of the way I *hear* (or what I hear as) particulars of relation and data on a given occasion.

    At the other end of the music-conceptual spectrum, what E. T. Cone says in [13] about the "indifference" of certain kinds of musical explanation to the actual composition they explain is true enough just where, and only where, a given model of the piece is

---

*(1995:) as, music aspiring to attribution of "indeterminacy" or "randomness".

understood as determining the *entire* structure of the piece, to the extent that there exists a completely determinate relation between every theoretical term and observational terms. But a determinacy of such absoluteness can *never* be the case, or be asserted to hold, in empirical theories or models thereof. Every interpretation is thus necessarily a *partial* interpretation, which not only makes essential the associated "rules of correlation" and the "commentary on the model", but also entails that what is considered *as the* musical structure is, and is only, the *entire* complex of *theory, model,* and perceptual-conceptual *interpretation,* as well as any and all connective links among their parts.

Showing *that* something is a model, then, can be seen to be actually just the relativistic activity of showing *how* it is one, under some particular interpretation, and thus, showing to what degree it specifies the observable aspects of its referents (the sound-concreta to which the model entities refer under the given interpretation). Thus, if time-dependency and other aspects essential to the "perceptual identity" of Schoenberg's Op. 33a (Cone's example) are not specified in any given model of the work, they may still be regarded by any observer using that model as essentials (however weakly determined) of the "structure", as we have explicated it here.

10. So now one may suppose that the question we have come down to is, Is there *any* respect in which the language-music analogy is salvageable, or worth salvaging? On the basis of the above considerations, I would answer, Not much that will give comfort to the promulgators of Cases 1 through 4. But perhaps one could propose a deeper level of community, an epistemic-categorical one that would incorporate *both* music and language into what might be called a domain of "things by virtue of second-order cognition". The notion may be considered to correspond to something that would enable us to designate fields of empirical observation and structure-making as "language-typical" in different ways. And this is precisely the one sense retained by, involved in, and required by our Case No. 5, which thus avoids the formidable pitfalls confronting the cognitive realization of the programs of Nos. 3 and 4 while also capturing an epistemically significant aspect of the underlying analogy itself, well short of the virtually complete retrenchment represented by Case No. 6.

This "second-order" cognition may be distinguished as follows: the "things" called "languages" are not "directly perceivable" in the sense that physical "things" are. They are, in fact, inferred concretions "mentally" constructed by selective observations of particular aspects of physical objects and events considered as their "media", whose orderings (the assertions of conjunctions of those objects) constitute their "messages". The "physical objects" and "events" associated with verbal languages are thus "seen" symbols and "heard" sounds. These are "things" in the same way that physical objects are, and can be regarded simply as such by any non-cognizer of their linguistic import; indeed, since all "sounds" have the same perceptual-discriminative dimensions, a "vocal emission" *heard as* a "sentence" by one receptor may be heard as a "tune" or simply a "noise" by another. Now even the discrimination of a physical concretum may be considered a "first-level interpretive act", which distinguishes the *perception* of a "thing" or an "event" as an act in which a seen color area, touched surface, or heard sound are "interpreted" as *effects* of physical objects and events, from that "zeroth", "raw-feel" level of acts of "pure perception" whose supposed further intervention can nowhere be cognitively isolated, nor even distinguished within the conceptual framework of our language (as much of Wittgenstein's *Philosophical Investigations* is at pains to point out). By what means, then, are the "concreta" that actually *are* language-things constructed from the orderings of physical objects and events that supposedly collectively—potentially, that is—"embody" them? First, there is the necessity of inferring what the relevant data are.[20] These inferences include, in particular, decisions about what the aspects and extent of the data are that determine the nature and boundaries of the macro-"thing" of which they are being

---

[20]Some analyses of "physical-object perception" include this step as well, but this raises the question of what Sellars and others call the "myth of the given"; see [67], especially see. 61–62, which offers a radically divergent perspective on the implications of such analyses, and distinguishes "languages", where such "interpretations" are *essential,* and "things", where they are *possible* as "micro-analyses" that actually add new dimensions to our perception of objects rather than explicating our customary way of perceiving, dimensions that seem, epistemically, strikingly "linguistic" in the sense advocated here—i.e., as "things" by virtue of selective inferences ("quasi-analysis" in the language of Carnap [45]) from *distinguishable aspects* (the qualia of Goodman's *The Structure of Appearance* and of our Sketch in Part II) of *concrete individuals.*

construed as generating components. Thus, we need to "decide" what part of the perceptual field we are going to use in constructing a "piece of music": first, which perceptual domains; second, assuming restriction in the first step to the auditory, which distinguishable subset of all concurrent auditory experience is going to be regarded as "part of the piece"—this may or may not eliminate bow-scratches, subway rumbles, audience coughs, surface noise, or conversation as belonging among the "data of the piece"; third, what temporal expanse of such data constitutes "the piece". Further, assuming we pay no attention to "applause" noise, which may after all "interrupt" a piece as well as articulate the "breaks" between pieces, we must decide where "the piece" begins and where it leaves off.[21] What we are going to regard as an "internal articulation", a "section", a "movement", a "piece", a "concert", or a "concert season", must also be decided; and the practical necessity of doing so is well illustrated by the exigencies of many music-auditory situations, from the performance of an assorted collection of individual Lieder to the multi-Sitzung performance of the *Ring*. This stage of cognition, as a whole, seems to be just where the community of identity among instances of music and those of language would dissolve. For it is through these choices that we decide whether to hear individual sounds and successions as, first, "uninterpreted sound-experiences", then "effects of physical objects"— as, e.g., hearing "speech" uninterpreted as particular utterances in a particular language could still be taken by a perceiver as "evidence for the existence, presence, and location of a human individual", in the same sense as a lion's or an automobile's roar, a bird-call, or a footstep—then "language-type things", then "tunes" (rather than "sentences"), then "a piece" (rather than "a collection of musical events"), then "a twelve-tone piece" (rather than "a tonal piece"), and finally, "this piece" (rather than "any other piece"). The last three of these discriminations involve, of course, further inferences from the selected aspects of the data than simply whether they are "musical" or "linguistic". These include, first, comparative measurement of data-aspect instances according to various scales

---

[21]Here we engage the "picture-frame" relationship mentioned by Cone in [9] (see especially pp. 13–16); but I do not assume apriori certainty with respect to *any* given piece in this decision, nor does it seem possible to speak of "a piece" without making it, two points on which I am not entirely certain of the implications of Cone's argument.

whose quantizations of "unit-size slices" and kinds of comparative information yielded (element relations, fixed-quantity relations, proportions, nominal-scale relations, etc.) are also decision-requiring matters, and, second, the ordering of these measurement-entities into tuples that singly or multiply exhaust the data.

The ascending "epistemic order" of these cognitive acts may be schematized roughly as below, with the category-boundaries to be understood as relative directions ("more x-like", or "more y-like", for any given act), thresholds relative to a discourse rather than absolute demarcations:

1. "the stream of experience"
2. "the stream of auditory experience"
3. "the articulation of auditory experience into individual sounds"
4. "the separation into 'domains of relevance' of individual sounds (e.g., as evidences of presences of physical objects, or as evidence for potential 'readability' as language)".
5. "the identity of language-types involved" (what *aspects* of the data and "possible" relational information about them are to be noticed, and how: as "music", or as "speech"; then between this step and the next, the decision among alternatives like "a piece", "an utterance", "a poem", etc.).
6. "the identity of the relevant semantic-syntactic domain" (Alternatives here: "English or German"; "tonal or twelve-tone". How the analogy suggested by the parallelism of these two pairs *is not* to be taken should be evident from the foregoing, but by indicating the cognitive *aspect* of this parallelism—similar position on a shared "epistemic level"— we are presumably pulling the teeth of an "overdetermined" analogical bias. That is, we can see where the analogy is relevant and how it is, and will still have all the intersubjectively relevant information we had before even if we don't admit the analogy or even if we regard it as counterintuitive with respect to the "concepts" involved.)
7. "the identity of the particular individual" ("*this* utterance"; "*this poem*; "*this* piece" become cognitive designations at this level.)

With respect to our relativistic scruples, note particularly the phrasing of the ascriptions under our Nos. 6 and 7. This relativism will itself be very much relative to whether, and by how much, a discourse (or the "noticing" act potentially reportable in such a discourse) is more concerned with those things that *associate* a given piece with more or fewer other pieces, or more concerned with distinguishing that piece "as itself". But also, a progression from "more syntactical" or "more particularized", asserted of a discourse, may be equated with "more definitional for all relations within the structure" and "more descriptive of particular relations", and so forth.

11. Having halted the precipitous decline of the music-language analogy at Case No. 5, we now have the problem of what to make of and/or do with Case No. 6. How does it fit, if at all, into our model-building-strategic scheme? As described, it does not seem to fit at all unless we add to our "seven epistemic stages" an eighth which, so to speak, impinges on the very frontiers of epistemic content-bearing. For Case No. 6 represents the most radical possible retrenchment from the initial, naive, "music *is* language" notion (which shades over the epistemic cliff-edge at the other extreme) that still can be considered to retain any shred at all of the "music *as* language" notion. Here the only epistemic connection to language itself is that of "formal syntax" and "formalized language"; a connection which depends on the presumption that the truth-connective operators and functions—and, in fact, the meaning of the "0/1"-values of a two-valued "formal truth" system—of uninterpreted logistical or mathematical calculi are "inherently"—epistemically—equivalent to their "semantic" counterparts, rather than just "partially interpreted" by them as the terms of a model are interpreted by entities of data. The question of whether even "syntax" and "language" are being used in a cognitive or only a heuristic way when conjoined with "formal" is thus the principal epistemic issue involved. For otherwise, uninterpreted calculi are simply neutral means for the representation of structures, such that without interpretation, no logistical schema may be said to "represent" any empirical structure—or, better, any logistical schema may be said to potentially represent any or all empirical structures. And it can also be said that, before interpretation, and given appropriate rules of correlation, it can always be shown how (in fact in infinite numbers of hows) any logistical schema "represents" any structure. At this level, logistical structures are "linguistic" in a sense as independent of actual, verbal language as musical struc-

tures are at a similar level, but such logistical structures are equally resistant to any imputation of correspondence to music in any explicit way.

So, to be part of our scheme at all, Case No. 6 must consist not only of an uninterpreted calculus, a "formal syntax", but must also provide explicit "semantical rules" which specify observational or theoretical entities as referents for its terms and operations. Then, and only then, can it be regarded as a "model" of a *musical* theory or of a musical structure constructed in terms of such a theory.

But note that the adduction of "semantical rules" to give "epistemic content" to a formal model actually converts Case No. 6 into a special, more explicitly formalized, instance of Case No. 5. In fact, the procedures outlined for No. 5 might very well terminate—perhaps even most favorably—in the construction of just such a formalized model;[22] and the fact that Case No. 6 *starts* life with one can be regarded as a merely biographical coincidence, for the decision as to "goodness" of the model as theoretical explanation is still controlled by the way it is tied to the empirical "model of the data", the degree to which its principal operations correlate with critical discriminants of "most significant" aspects of the theoretical structure, rather than by "formalistic" criteria of pure logistic "elegance" or "ingenuity" as a *Gedankending-an-sich*. Now this model-evaluative issue is obviously quite different from that of whether some such particular calculus or schema explicitly devised for its usefulness under interpretation as an explication or model of some segment of some actual *verbal* language would also be useful as a schema for a *musical* interpretation, or whether there was any illuminating correspondence that could be made between a set of semantical rules tying it to a musical theory or structure and a set tying it to a verbal-linguistic theory or structure. The answers to these questions lie considerably "higher up" the epistemic scale, and perhaps have already been given at least implicitly in our discussion.

By invoking the notion of "height on the epistemic scale", we raise, in turn, the issue of the "ordering" of the six music-as-language "cases" given above, the rationale for which has not yet been

---

[22]The advantages that might accrue in this case may be inferred from the explication in Suppes [71].

supplied, whatever intuitive plausibility it may have been granted by the reader's principle of charity. What, then, is the nature of the progression involved? This question may be approached by considering the notions of "conceptual scope" and "cognitive scope" as constituting "complementary epistemic directions", in which the former may be measured as "degree of *subsumption* of divergent particulars under the explanatory cover of the theoretical terms of a theory", and the latter, as "degree of *individuation* of identity and function of the discernible particulars presented in the concrete interpretations of the theoretical entities of a theory". A greater "conceptual claim" is thus a more universal one, the more implicitly approaching the ascription of "essences" the less interpretable observationally, and the fewer discriminables accounted for differentially at the same levels of differentiation. Thus also an account having greater "cognitive scope" can always account for any particular accounted for in one belonging to the same "chain" that exhibits greater "conceptual scope", and for at least one subclass more of particulars as well. On the other hand, an account of greater "conceptual scope" can subsume every theoretical term or class-term of one of greater cognitive scope, adding at least one more such term in so doing. On this model, it should be evident that every lower-numbered "case" of our chain depends on a theory of greater conceptual scope than does any higher-numbered one, but that every case has greater cognitive scope than its lower-numbered predecessors. The extremes are *universal* conceptual scope, whose cognitive scope is zero, and universal cognitive scope, where no conceptual claim at all can be inferred. "Music is language", naively asserted, is virtually a case of an account at the furthest remove toward the first polarity, and a proper name, or a calculus with no semantical rules, even if it is labeled "Music", is a case at the other polarity. (Logistically, one could represent the universal condition in the form of a "universal assumption", "$\forall x\, P(x)$", where "$P(x)$" is not a "formal truth" (such as "$x = x$") or an axiom of the system, and the condition at the other extreme as the trivially tautologous "law of thought" "$\forall x \{\neg[P(x) \wedge \neg P(x))]\}$".

What we strive for, then, is an account having the maximum conceptual scope compatible with a cognitive scope that enables us to account for every observable and inferable difference we notice or care about. The suggestion here is that, of our cases, only No. 5 stands a good chance of accomplishing this in terms of an analogy between "music" and "language", and that, to do likewise, No. 6 must include an interpretation as complete and consistent as would be required under No. 5 as well.

12. In the light of the foregoing, let us consider a "No. 6-type" model offered as an explication of "twelve-note-class music" by Michael Kassler (without prejudice to the question of how or in what order, biographically, the particular choices of calculi and interpretations were made), to determine to what degree it also qualifies as a good candidate for a "No. 5-type" model. That is, we will want to see how fully it explicates the relation of the *discernibly particular* to the *conceptually general,* and thus to what degree it gives answers to questions that musicians regard as crucial ones regarding musical structures. Thus we would hope that, for every "musical concept", the theory under consideration would either *interpret* it as an essential aspect of the scheme of relations, or *eliminate* it as redundant (show how it could be replaced in full operational extensionality by a term or conjunction of terms already in the theory).[23]

So we will want to be as critical of a "top-light" theory which fails to account for concepts that we do believe "make a difference" as of a "top-heavy" one that gives us plenty of names for

---

[23]Thus might a theory proceed through some intervening steps from, say, "simultaneity" and "succession" to "presented triadic construct" and "presented linear succession", eliminating "chord" and "melody" as conceptually inessential and cognitively redundant, or might omit "Sonata Form" as the final, most embracing "class-term" of a structure description on the grounds that its definition at best offered no distinction that had not already been otherwise accounted for, and hence the term had no cognitive meaning that an explanation identical except for its omission did not also have. Obviously, an infinite number of inessential, extraneous class-terms can be added to any (maximal or lesser) class, and be defined as such without actually adding to the individuals contained in the "universe" in question (although my objection here resembles the nominalistic scruple, it really appeals for an "Occam's razor"-like parsimony in the construction of classes rather than for their abandonment): (The class of all "works of music") $\subseteq$ (The class of all "pieces") $\subseteq$ (The class of all "compositions") $\subseteq$ (The class of all musical compositions involving sound) $\subseteq$ (The class of all compositions involving sounds having a pitch and a duration component), and so forth. Since the sign of equivalence could have been used rather than that of inclusion, the "classes" named having (presumably) identical extensions, no cognitive-explanatory use could be made of all these names together to distinguish anything from any other thing that could not also be accomplished by any one of them alone.

the same things but enables us to discriminate too few distinct things.[24] Now the account offered by Kassler in [20] is a model of what a model should be insofar as its purely cognitive scope is concerned. The models offered therein do indeed provide one-to-one correlations between discernible atomic elements and their formal representations, and give operational definitions in terms of which formulas can be effectively decided, and empirical predicates "tested" for truth-value assignment. Four independent, but inter-defined, mutually consistent, and hierarchically ordered syntactical systems are described: "R_1" is a model for determining, for monolynearly presented pitch arrays, *whether* they represent the "assertion" of a single "twelve-note-class row", as defined by criteria of admissibility framed as "rules of formation" and "rules of transformation" (here, simply, one determinably unique ordering of the twelve-element vocabulary of primitives), which so determine for any such presented array whether a sequence of applications of the rules reduces the string to one axiom of the system, as evidenced by the substitutability of its element-tokens in the single given axiom schema to produce such an axiom.

"R_2" gives criteria for the admission of more complicated strings that reduce to one or more axioms (with reference to just one axiom-schema) by adding rules of transformation to those of "R_1", rules that correspond in their "results" to the operation of "inversion", "retrogression", and "transposition", although "transposition" and "inversion" are "defined" purely by correspondence to the contents of "lexical lists", and "retrogression" simply as "order reversal". An interesting discussion of conditions under which the "basic set" (not the "basic tnc row") is ambiguously de-

---

[24]Obviously, a theory that had maximum cognitive scope, included all the relevant concepts, but also multiplied "conceptual terms" to excess could not be actually faulted except on grounds of terminological gluttony. And where that "extra term" is added with a twitch of evident self-satisfaction as though it were *the* illuminating nuance, a suspicion of verbal prestidigitation of the sloganizing variety might also arise. When the name of the term sounds fancy enough, it may correspond to the hypostatization of which the best-known instance is the Bourgeois Gentleman's discovery of his customary use of "prose"; a few musicological writers use this as a basic tactic to generate an "ideational"-sounding surface for an otherwise wholly factual discourse, a technique I believe they borrow from historians. The strategy goes (collection of facts) → ("general principles") which is a "theoretical"-looking schema, but in the absence of intervening rules, is really just a way of giving a fancy package-name to the "collection of facts".

terminate (pp. 22–23) reveals in its approach some of the underlying conceptual characteristics of the entire account.

"R_3" deals with *simultaneously* presented sets, in terms of "depth" (number of concurrent set forms) and "simultaneity subformulae", out of which such inferences are made; these account mostly for "note-against-note" characteristics, a limitation which leads to what are affirmed by Kassler to be identificational problems in application, notably that a passage from Chopin is "explicable" as an "instance of R_3".

To compensate for this difficulty, "R_4" is offered as a candidate for "the tnc system". In particular, this system allows for the decision of passages of non-note-against-note compositionally presented counterpoint in determining set-unfolding boundaries and other characteristics. Again, the procedure consists of the most immediate possible procession from the "musical surface" to the most "background" possible "generating set", by means of rules for:

1. "tie-breaking", which allows for inferences of "repetition" over a span containing discrete "attack-points" during which a note is "held".

2. "tying", which simply allows the inference as a wff of "R_1" of something which differs from such a wff as described under "R_1" itself only by the presence of tied notes.

3. "attack-suppression", which allows for the inference of "tying" where notes are re-attacked (which in turn allows a single attack to be interpreted as "belonging" to *two different* basic wffs).

"R_4" is then considered the most promising current candidate for identification as "the tnc system", and some analytic results are presented that demonstrate the difficulty of regarding *all* of Schoenberg's Fourth Quartet as admissible instantiation of the system. The introduction of various "stylistic rules", more or less "ad hoc", is suggested to overcome such anomalous findings, the continuing resistance of some more of the Schoenberg Fourth Quartet is demonstrated, and some "literary" evidence is introduced to indicate "[that] for much of Schoenberg's music the twelve-note-class system seems a point of departure, and that discovery of transformations capable of regenerating these departures is a central remaining task required for an understanding of the style or styles in which Schoenberg composed [tnc] music. So neither the musical nor the literary evidence that we have cited seems to disqualify the candidacy of R_4". The final portions of the article are occupied with rather populistically biased discourse about "appreciation" of tnc music, accompanied by suggestions of the possible explicative relation of such appreciation to the "empirical aspects" of the system itself.

Throughout, the "primary principal interpretation" specified is *notational,* the "secondary" one is "physical", and the "tertiary" one is "perceptual" as an "interpretation" of "logged waveforms" on an audio tape. An explanation of the intersubjective validity of this interpretation is offered by Kassler on pp. 12–13.

All this is handled, and rather fully developed, in true and classic logistical style, and in clear and unambiguous verbal formulation; and no one that has attempted to verify the effectiveness of Kassler's procedures or the correctness of his proofs has, to my knowledge, reported failure. As with any good logistical system, one is confident that its implementation as a computer program will enable examination of any relevant set of data with decisive results, as expounded. And thus the various systems offered are, it seems to me, optimally operational models as we have defined them here and as they are described in the classical literature.

Still, there remain serious questions about the adequacy of these models as explanatory for "the twelve-tone system"; indeed, there is a strong case to be made for the notion that the respects in which they are "models for music" in any sense is quite unexplicated. The first doubts that arise have to do with the strict "operationism" exhibited; the model *works,* but does not seem to *explain* very much (whereas "music is language" "explains" *all* but doesn't even *begin* to work!). For some of the "musical" questions mentioned above have to do with questions of how the *theory* of which the model is a model—or on the basis of which the model interprets the data—explicates, orders, and determines the discriminative status of functional concepts like "inversion", "simultaneity", "transformation", etc. These concepts are *operationally* defined in Kassler's model but there is no commentary which correlates each operational definition with a *particular* "conceptualization" of the "intuitive" notion involved as a component of a "musical structure".

In particular, many of our fundamental musical questions are short-circuited in Kassler's models by its substitution of "yes-no" criteria of "admissibility" for criteria of overlapping "music-structural predications", and thus they rank musical compositions into just two discrete groups, "Kassler (R_n)-admissible" and "Kassler (R_n)-inadmissible". In fact, any kind of "background-structural" determination we might wish to make, to discover just how to *order* individual "Kassler (R_n)-admissible" pieces with respect to one another, would be severely limited in depth by the dispatch with which the model transfers surface observations to final decisions, with the intervention only of "conventional" lists of "admissible" operations. Thus it would seem that what we have here is an uninterpretability that is the "inverse" of that of naive metaphorical discourse; in short, we have a "model of the data" in terms of a theory which is inscrutable in large part in the model as well as the associated commentary. In this sense, Kassler's models remain at the furthest remove from theoretical or conceptual interpretability, and thus sacrifice "epistemic depth" for formal concision.[25]

In the absence of such a background theory, in fact, there exists no cognitive basis on which to determine whether a "Kassler (R_n)-admissible" piece is also a "Kassler-coherent" piece; but even if we assume that it is, we cannot ascertain that it is also a "twelve-tone coherent piece", and, thus having no explicit "special theory", we are equally unable to infer a "general theory", and hence have no way of determining whether (or, rather more crucially, how) any "Kassler-coherent" piece is also a "musically coherent" one,

---

[25]Here, too, the use of *notation* as the primary interpretation is an interesting aspect of this epistemic shyness. For while the "phenomenal" aspect of music is indeed "subjective" as Kassler's note explains, it is also "intersubjective" as he also points out, and is the single *controlling* domain in which the *appropriate* interpretation of any given concept of relation or "entification" is determined, in terms of which the correctness of correlation in all others is *decided*. And notation, in particular, is itself a "model of the data" of a purely conventional (and, indeed, rather partial) kind, which makes Kassler's model a "model of a model" of the data. But this indirectness seems consistent with his strict avoidance of epistemic problems to concentrate on the construction of "effective procedures". My remarks, therefore, should not be taken as directed toward the invalidation of this enterprise, but only to the enjoinder that any use of these models as explanatory models of "musical structures" awaits their supplementation—not necessarily by Michael Kassler—by a background theory for their interpretation as structures of music-structural entities. That there are other, more contextual, problems involved in the particular sequencing of operations in Kassler's models will emerge in a different sense from Part III.

and hence an instance of a "musical structure", which amounts to the same thing. So we may entertain serious doubt that Kassler's models show how any set of presented sound-tokens is to be regarded as an instance of music at all, for we do not know "what music is" in his theory from the evidence available at any level of his account of it.

This is particularly evident in Kassler's operational substitution of "admissibility" for "coherence" (the general "conceptual category", or "metaclass", of "music-structural predicates"). Consider, in this light, the "difficulties" presented by the "excessive permissiveness" of "R_3" in "admitting" a fragment of Chopin. For with an adequate theoretical structure, we can *always* show *what* a given sound-array *is as* an instance of a particular music-syntactical framework, and ultimately of a particular music-structural model. Here, the "langue/parole" analogy with language that Kassler invokes is also questionable, as is his remark (p. 61) that some "stylistic rules" are "unfortunately ad hoc". For what is residually "unique" about a particular composition will usually emerge, given an adequate background theory and a sufficiently general "common model" for a number of conveniently associated compositions, as "ad hoc" in the sense of the *particular differences* between a *complete* model of *that* composition and the necessarily *incomplete* "general" model.[26] For a composition is the *whole* of "its language" in any relevant epistemological sense, and is thus not analogous, as we have pointed out above, to an "utterance".

Thus, if we are in the possession of a background theory rooted in a theory of "musical" coherence, we are not likely to be interested in questions of "admissibility" at all, since in principle we can show how any pitch-successional array "is an instance" of some "special" theory-model; and thus, since we can show how any piece is a "tnc piece", our concern is restricted to those that we *care to* so describe. Therefore, we needn't trouble to show

---

[26]How much the "general" model leaves interpretively "open", and how much it binds interpretively, is largely a matter of convenience dictated by the generality desired and the nature of the literature in question—a model of "tonality" will probably usefully bind more of its interpretation than will one of "twelve-tonality", for example, a difference which reflects what we already know about the greater degree of *unique* "precompositionality" involved in twelve-tone pieces; thus this issue is not of profound conceptual, theoretical, or methodological importance.

"how" a fragment of Chopin "is a tnc composition", since we never doubted that it "was" one, in some assertible but not particularly interesting sense. And an assertion such as "Schoenberg's Fourth Quartet is really in d minor" is, in fact, *empty* unless and until it is accompanied by an explication of just *how* it is to be so regarded. And since unlimited numbers of demonstrations may answer to this description, with whatever intuitivity, each *assertion* of this kind needs a *qualification* such as, e.g., "Schoenberg's Fourth Quartet (is in d minor$_1$) or (is in d minor$_2$), etc". The same, of course, holds for pieces we *normally* want to describe as "in ——"; namely, that even within that already narrow circumscription both the "metaquestion", What does it mean for a piece to be "in X"?, and the question, In a particular sense of what it means for a piece to be "in X", how is this piece "in X"? have multiple possible answers, among which choice is dictated by normative standards of explanatory adequacy, preferences about "neatness" or other considerations with respect to the "structure-data" relation for "musical structures" as well as by the particular explanatory objectives for which the discourse has been undertaken and which the model has been designed to extrude.[27] The remarks made earlier (pp. 68–69ff.) about demands for "analytic completeness" apply here very particularly, and should at this point be further understood in terms of the connection of any single piece with a collective "total-musical metatheory"; for the availability at every level of a "range of theory-satisfying interpretations" means that the program of absolute completeness of structure description ("analysis") is *always* unrealizable in principle, and in this sense, "metaphysical".

So it seems, epistemically speaking, that what we have in Kassler's calculus is actually an *operationally interpreted,* yet *musically underdeterminate* model (i.e., its interpretation is not ade-

---

[27]Equally, there is no "necessary" reason for using only one set-class as "the basic set" of a given composition; it is just that our notion of what "twelve-tone syntax" involves makes it unlikely that we would want to use more than one in the same explanation (or, at least, that we would want to use more than the fewest we found we had to). Thus, we could say what a given composition "is as based in a given way on a given set", as well as "what it is as based in another way on another set"—and the recognition of such options might very well inhibit the transference to twelve-tone theory and analysis of at least one of the most unfruitful controversy-types plaguing "traditional" analysis: "but what key is it *really* in?"

quately understandable as a *musical* one). And if we should want to render it conceptually operational as a model *within* "music", we would have to supply virtually all its "music-epistemic depth" ourselves, by constructing a regressive series of subsumptions, applying theoretical terms and theoretical constructs until we reached a point where we could "plug in" to an underlying "theory of music" embodying a still further underlying "theory of music-structural coherence". And a theoretical ladder that would rest on such a basis would be one that we could regard as a candidate for a general "model of music", which would branch out into particular "syntax-typical" models, particular "syntaxes", and finally models of particular "structures", thus making use of the formidable cognitive advantages of formalism to help explicate both the concepts and the logic by which we decide to include everything we choose to under the class-term "music", as well as the conceptual and syntactical respects in which each "musical structure" can be regarded as unique. It is in this way that we can use the techniques employed by Case No. 6 to maximize the cognitive scope of, without sacrificing the conceptual scope envisaged for, instances of Case No. 5.

E. CONCLUDING REMARKS

13. Thus we have come, by a rather serpentine road, over virtually the entire conceptual and methodological gamut of a substantial segment of existing music-explicative discourse. But where, in fact, have we got to? The answer to this, our final question, is given as much hopefully as assertively. But I believe that it has been reasonably demonstrated, first, that even the most *emotive* view of music has to *be* emotive *about something distinct,* which necessarily involves having a *theory* about it, for better or worse, in awareness or unawareness, and that a *musical* something distinct can be cognitively understood as an "emotional experience" only insofar as it is first cognitively understood as a human-communicative manifestation, as an "instance of thought". As such, then, it can still be variably construed as a peculiarity of particular cultures, as a phenomenon occurring in and even having its own history, as a purely empirical-phenomenal sound-object, as a contextual "pure structure", or as a "language" in the sense of a conjunction of the latter two. In connection with other, frequently offered, "music-language" analogies, we have discriminated among the kinds of ques-

tions asked and the kinds of answers given in several explicative domains, establishing, first, that "true explanation" *can* take place in any one of them, but just in terms of its own internally defined contexts, and given the observance of adequate standards of cognitive discourse. But no explanation offered in any one domain can ever bear upon the relevance of that domain itself or of any of its fellow-domains as *the* appropriate or determinant domain for all "musical explanation". Nor can any such explanation bear on the relevance or accuracy of any *statement* made in any other domain on its own terms.

Finally, we may acknowledge the depth of the desire that also underlies the activity of musical explanation, to offer a "model of music" that somehow asserts for music as high a place in the spectrum of human intellectual activity as every dedicated musician would like to assign to it. It is just here that the "scientific" metaphor of our Preface, and the "microanalytic" method of our scrutiny, may seem most incongruent to some professional observers. And so they may commit acts of aggressive humanism, equating "scientific method" and "scientific language" with "scientism", imputing to all discourse having such an appearance a normative equation of music with "science", as a necessary condition for regarding it as a "good thing". Now it does need to be acknowledged that offenses against cognition just as problematic—in fact, equivalently problematic—as those we have analyzed here often do display such a scientistic surface. But that this is so demonstrates only that metaphorical statements can be made quite as uninformatively through the use of the names of and symbols for mathematical and scientific terms as through emotive, cultural, historical, or analytic ones; the synesthesia involved can be equally opaque to cognition, and equally transparent to detection under the illumination of such epistemically guided rational scrutiny as is attempted and advocated here.

But insofar as a "noble" vision of musical endeavor is still desired, there hardly seems anything inferior about one that regards the activity of every musical thinker, as observer or performer or composer, as a participation in the invention and propagation of man-made "possible worlds", perceivable and palpable, and yet unconstrained by the exigencies and contradictions of the physical, but only by the bounds of human perceptual and intellectual capacities, whose horizons are thus at the same time both revealed and expanded.

It is, then, to a consideration of some of the fundamental groundwork on which such worlds have been and are being constructed and projected that Parts II and III of this essay are devoted.

IV.
Part II:
Sketch Of A Musical System

> "...one assumes a grave responsibility in setting out to apply symbolic logic to any subject matter; for even so promising a method can easily be discredited by a plague of overelaborate systems that do not repay the effort required to master them....Systems of logical philosophy...I call "constructional" to distinguish them from uninterpreted formal systems and from amorphous philosophical discourses...A passionate effort at construction is needed and is wholly compatible with the dispassionate appraisal of results."
>
> "Such advantages as a system of one sort may have over a system of the other sort are to be found...by examining their consequences rather than their foundations."
>
> —Nelson Goodman, *The Structure of Appearance*

The study of musical structure is quite unlike that of the structure of the physical world, or of language, and rather more like that of poetry, or human personality. For it is the distinct individual itself that is the relevant "world" of musical interest, for whose sake alone are constructed more general "worlds" as its extensions, to facilitate understanding of it and other "worlds" susceptible of understanding under some of the same considerations. Individuals in the physical world, on the other hand, like utterances in the linguistic world, are interesting to students of physical and linguistic structure just insofar as they instantiate, confirm, articulate, suggest, or demonstrate "lawlike" conditionals for the world as a whole, a model of the structure of which is the essential operational objective. However various, the physical and social sciences, and the branches of linguistics, regard the single instance as the *least* significant aspect of their concern, while the student of musical, poetic, pictorial, and perhaps even philosophical structures must regard those instances as the most important such aspect.

Thus the construction of a "model of music" is always best understood as the construction of a model of an individual composition, or, at most, that of a *multiple* model which incorporates and distinguishes among a community of relevant considerations, and ultimately produces a "tree" into which everything regarded as a "musical structure" is "plugged", and whose "extremities" represent just the unique characteristics of the individual structures themselves. Thus, there is no question of the "structure *of*" a piece; the piece *is* its structure, and its structure *is* just the interpretive-synthetic-intellectual-perceptual construct in the mind's ear of some beholder(s).

Therefore, to the extent that knowing or even just having music is important to anyone, he will wish to penetrate as deeply as possible into what can be asserted as the *shared* basis of musical structures; it is thus that one can most completely individuate each particular such structure, for the depth and breadth to which every assertible relational phenomenon within a structure can be multiply determinable is just the extent to which that structure can exhibit individuality and interrelational profundity; and these are surely what constitute "creativity" in the musical world as they do in science, linguistics, or philosophy. Thus, the more *generally* every musical concept is defined, the "further away" its definition from the particulars of a given interpretation in a given instance of literature, then the more that instance or literature can be observed as "uniquely itself" rather than as "musically general". And, on the other hand, the more securely we can regard manifestations of widely different individual appearances as resting on the same or cognitively analogous conceptual-perceptual-theoretical bases, the more confidently we can call them all "music",[1] and the more widely and daringly the creative projection of musical worlds can extend hypothetical images of new relational multiplicities and depths on the foundation of a broadly interpretable, because deeply understood, "tradition".

---

[1] What we wish to call "music" is just the group, of whatever size or range, of "objects in the world" that is thought to be usefully so grouped for mutual characterization (assertion of boundary conditions by which the group may be inferred to have been delimited) and explanatory inference on various macro- ("whole-group") or micro- ("sub-group") levels.

2. MUSIC THEORY, EPISTEMOLOGY, AND CONSTRUCTIONAL SYSTEMS

Thus every theory of music must stem from a fundamental notion of "musical structure" that guides the definition and formation of other concepts, selections of elements, and ordering of relations, a notion that stems, in turn, from a prior notion of "linguistic structure" which in its turn stems from a general notion of "structure" that connects any special study with the general theory of knowledge and cognition itself. And thus it is that the *conceptual* reconstruction of musical systems "from the ground up" proposed here models itself on the constructions developed for the phenomenal world as a whole in Carnap's *Aufbau* and, especially, in its considerably more fully realized and less problematic successor, Nelson Goodman's *The Structure of Appearance*. Through these works, too, music's connection with "general epistemology" as, ultimately, both "a part of the phenomenal world" and "dependent on the phenomenal world" will be realizable; by the same token, the characteristics particular to music, as, first, being in a domain of "linguistic-type" structures and, then, *"as music"*, occasion methodological and conceptual divergences from Carnap's and Goodman's systems, divergences which one can only hope will be regarded as illuminating rather than evasive or abusive.

What this method consists of essentially is the explication of the cognitive conceptual basis on which the construction of coherent structures rests, through a chain of interconnecting "formal" definitions. Each such definition introduces, entirely by means of terms introduced earlier, along with elements, operations, and predicates taken as undefined primitives of the system, a "theoretical construct" which asserts the empirical validity (and, implicitly, the "musical relevance") of a given "relational property". By virtue of this definition, the property is considered, in realizations that are asserted to be its *interpretations* in terms of particular observables, to be, first, *decidable in conjunction with observations* (as well as to be logistically "connected"), and, second, to constitute an *explication* in cognitive terms of an "intuitive" musical concept, whose traditional (or neologistic) name is used to designate the "theoretical term" interpreted by the instances of the defined "situation".

In our sketch, as in Goodman's and Carnap's systems, the interpretation of each variable is specified just to the extent considered necessary to explicate the concept and to project the associated property in question. The notion here is that under every possible "auditory" interpretation left "open" by a given definition, the property involved *will hold* as long as the defined specifications are observed; that is, essentially, what the definition claims. This produces, for every concept, a maximum degree of generality (as well as explicating it in its "deepest" sense) and, hence, renders it operative under the widest range of divergent actual interpretations in, first, syntactic domains and, then, individual compositions. Realized this way, too, a consequential succession of such definitions is also an index of, and an implicit *commentary* on, the relative degree of generality assertable for every relation-concept. And since all the terms are at least partially interpreted, and the specifications logistically particularized, the definitions are *usable* as a *model* of a theory, and ultimately, as a syntactical guide for the experientially significant "models of the data" we call "analyses".

It is this "modeling" function that constitutes the total extent of "formalization" herein, the exclusive use to which logistical methods and definitions are put. Actual demonstrations of theoremhood are avoided, except in isolated instances, although any of the definitions or any complex of them could of course be (and "by definition" *must* be able to be) a basis, along with the formal apparatus of the calculi involved (here, the first-order predicate calculus with equality and set and class membership), on which theorems could be proved regarding, e.g., the "logical properties" of the defined relations, the necessity and sufficiency of the specified conditions for the decision of any given wff, and, especially, any unsuspected, unintuitive, or perhaps even counterintuitive and unwanted consequences ensuing from the asserted conditions in non-standard situations.

The standards of cognitiveness for definitions, and the logistical apparatus used, are just those given in Goodman [53], in Chapters I and II (a reading of which would much facilitate the understanding of what follows here), with the principal difference that the calculus of classes is used here rather than the exclusively nominalistic calculus of individuals. There are several defensible reasons for this deviation (such as the wish to distinguish between "model-of-the-theory" and "model-of-the-data" constructs) but essentially, the conceptual attractions of the nominalistic basis were outweighed by the difficulties involved in its manipulation (Goodman himself reverts, apparently for convenience, to classes in his recent *Languages of Art*).

3. THE NOTION OF DEFINITION

Here follows, in some detail, an outline of some of the definiential criteria mentioned above, relying principally on selective quotation of passages from Goodman's text. Readers familiar with the latter may omit this section altogether.

1. The notion of "constructional definition", and its distinction from "pure formalism": "The definitions of an uninterpreted symbolic system serve as mere conventions of notational interchangeability, permitting the replacement of longer and less convenient definientia wherever they may occur by shorter or more convenient definienda. These conventions are theoretically unnecessary because the elimination of definitions and defined terms would affect the system only by making its sentences much longer and more cumbersome. Furthermore, notational conventions are of course arbitrary and cannot be disputed so long as certain formal requirements are satisfied...."

"In a *constructional* system, however, most of the definitions are introduced for explanatory purposes. They may be arbitrary in the sense that they represent a choice among certain alternative definientia; but whatever the choice, *the definiens is a complex of interpreted terms, and the definiendum a familiar meaningful term, and the accuracy of the definition depends on the relation between the two* [italics mine—B.B.]. In a formal system considered apart from its interpretation, any such definition has the formal status of a convention of notational interchangeability once it is adopted; but the terms employed are ordinarily selected according to their usage, and the correctness of the interpreted definition is legitimately testable by examination of that usage." (pp. 3–4)

2. The criteria for correctness of a constructional definition are purely extensional: "A constructional definition is correct...if the range of application of its definiens is the same as that of its definiendum. Nothing more is required than that the two expressions have identical extensions...our willingness to accept a proposed definition will be measured by our confidence that the definiendum and the definiens apply to exactly the same things, regardless of how that confidence is acquired or sustained....We do not require that the definiendum and the definiens agree with respect to all cases that "might have been" as well as to all cases that actually "are"." (p. 4)

"Extensional identity may or may not be a sufficient guarantee of sameness of meaning . . . but . . . extensional identity is the most that is required for, or implied by, the definitions...." (p. 5)

"[O]ften we cannot demand even that the extension of the definiens be exactly identical with that of the familiar term being defined; for ordinary usage is often ambiguous and scientifically inept, while a constructional language must be precise...common usage is indeterminate with respect to certain entities...we demand of a constructional definition only that it accord with common usage insofar as that usage is determinate...[where] the popular concept is inappropriate for scientific purposes,...again we have to modify the demand for *strict* extensional identity in order to make possible the construction of an adequate systematic language....In most constructional systems there are at least a few legitimate and indispensable definitions which, if they are taken to imply extensional identity, seem diametrically opposed to common sense....And it is clear that extensional identity is *not* demanded of the terms conjoined as definiendum and definiens...such a demand would be inconsistent with the fact that a single definiendum may be quite properly so conjoined with any of several extensionally nonidentical terms." (pp. 5–7)

3. The criterion substituted for strict extensional identity is not *substitutability*,[2] but "extensional isomorphism": "About the best we seem to be able to do toward a criterion along the lines [of substitutability] is this: a definition must be such that every sentence we care about that can be translated into the system shall have the same truth value as its translation. But this is no criterion at all without some specification of what sentences we "care about". It is rather a criterion of criteria—a condition that must be met by definitions satisfying any acceptable criterion. And while the sentences we care about will vary somewhat with our purposes, what we want in a criterion is at least an approximately general characterization of at least a minimum class of sentences that we care about preserving in any constructional system" (p. 12).

"If we now look more closely at the very divergent definitions of a given concept that were equally legitimate, we find that they possess in common one feature that every illegitimate definition lacks; namely, that in each legitimate definition, the extension of the definiens is isomorphic to the extension of the definiendum. The necessary and sufficient condition for the accuracy of a constructional definition seems to be that...*the set of all the definientia of a system must be extensionally isomorphic to the set of all the definienda.*" (p. 13)

---

[2] The criterion used by Carnap in the *Aufbau*. [B.B.]

"We may think of the extensions of the definienda and definientia in question as relations—that is, as classes of...[tuples] of any uniform length...if we progressively dissolve each component that is a sequence into its components [the n tuples, as, from ((a, b), c), (d, e), the components are the two couples ((a, b), c) and (d, e)], and every component that is a class into its members, and continue this until we reach elements that have no further members or components, we have...the *ultimate factors* of the sequence....An ultimate factor is always either an individual or the null class.

"A relation R is isomorphic to a relation S in the sense here intended if R can be obtained by consistently replacing the ultimate factors in S...this sort of isomorphism is not symmetric...[it is trivially reflexive]....Also every class having the same number of members as a given class of *individuals* is isomorphic to it; but a class is not necessarily isomorphic to every class having the same number of members or of ultimate factors." (pp. 13–14)

4. The correlation of a definition with elements of an interpreting system may or may not be uniquely determinable: "The fact that so many ways of replacement would give the required class reminds us emphatically that our definition of the class of points as the class of pairs of intersecting lines does not define any given point as any given pair of intersecting lines; the matter of determining a particular correlation is left open...[T]his is generally true of the definition of classes....For example, to define triangles as three-sided polygons is not to define a given triangle A as consisting of the three lines that actually constitute A. The definition of triangles sets up no unique correlation by itself; it would be equally consistent with the correlation of A with three other lines that actually constitute a different triangle, B. We may be thinking of, or intending, the normal correlation; but apart from other definitions such an intention is given no expression within the system and imposes no restriction on its interpretation"[3] (p. 16).

"...It must always be borne in mind that isomorphism of the whole is demanded by our criterion. Without this demand there would be no safeguard against...the identical definition of several different but isomorphic classes...relationships below the level at which isomorphism is determined provide...the very means for defining a relation without using additional primitives, and so aid in the construction of a comprehensive system upon an economical foundation." (p. 21)

5. Consequences of isomorphism:

   a) Truth-value preservation: "...since extensional identity is no longer required, a given term may alternatively be defined by any of

---

[3]See pp. 88–89, above.

several others that are not extensionally identical with one another...a system is serviceable if its translations of such sentences as we care about are truth-value preserving. The demand that its translations of *all* sentences be truth-value preserving is incompatible with the...flexibility that we have been seeking...in...a criterion of definition. That there are some statements we do not care about is immediately evident from the fact that in actual practice we accept alternative extensionally nonidentical expressions as equally good definientia for the same term. Exactly what...latitude we want and allow indicates which statements do not much concern us." (p. 23)

b) Adequacy of the system: "Naturally isomorphism does not guarantee the *adequacy* of a system but only its *accuracy*....An adequate system would have to provide...a translation for *every* sentence we care about.

"Now it is clear that to adopt a criterion for constructional definition is to make a decision concerning the significance of these definitions and indeed of any use in a system of a constructionally defined term." (p. 23)

c) Naturalness: "...the degree of naturalness [of correlations] while it does not affect the legitimacy of any system that satisfies the criterion, may well affect our efforts to determine whether a system does satisfy the criterion...the correlations we consider the most natural are in general just those that most readily engage our confidence.... Furthermore, the most natural and uniform correlation often serves technical as well as psychological convenience....Nevertheless, naturalness and technical efficiency alike are imprecise and entirely subsidiary considerations." (pp. 25–27)

d) Identity or nonidentity of correlated entities: "Acceptance of a constructional system...involves no commitment to the nonidentity, any more than to the identity, of the correlated entities. Since every relation and every system is self-isomorphic, nothing in any definition or system implies that the definiens relation or set of definiens relations is being correlated with anything but itself...the nonidentity of the correlates [may be] evident on extrasystematic grounds; but the system itself is nevertheless uncommitted....in other words, the reductive force of a constructional system consists not in showing that a given entity is identical with a complex of other entities but in showing that no commitment to the contrary is necessary." (pp. 28–29)

We return here to the main discourse. The relevance of the strategic considerations outlined above to the evaluation of the definitions offered in this essay will be, I believe, self-evident.

4. THE NOTIONS OF STRUCTURE AND MUSICAL COHERENCE

A significant by-product of the construction of a system that anything we want to call "music" can "plug in" to, is that it also provides a basis for discovering *how* any given piece in any given system "is music", and thus a basis for *comparison* between, or "intercommunication" among, musical structures regarded as "instances" of even maximally divergent discrete musical syntaxes,[4] as well as, of course, hierarchical interconnection of the whole range of musical terms.

But in order for such a system to account for all these things adequately, it must not only extend upward to a maximally articulated degree, but must begin with fundamental underlying notions and primitive elements, operations, relations, and predicates sufficiently "universal" as the principal bases for all musical structure as to fulfill their role without encountering epistemic weaknesses (such as defining principal relations in terms of subsidiary ones, etc.) and methodological awkwardnesses.

We have declared, then, that every musical theory involves a notion of music-structural coherence, as a particular instance of linguistic-type structural coherence, in terms of a notion of empirical-structural coherence and an ultimate "pure" notion of "structural coherence". Without specifically suggesting any of the lower levels of this "conceptual chain", I consider that whatever the "essential" meaning of "structure", a cognitive, though of course informal and extrasystematic, concept of it involves a "polarity" of two factors, which we may call "coherence" and "complexity". We may define "significant coherence" as the relation between these two factors, as individually defined in each cognitive case and domain. In music, however, we may "place" the notion of complexity in terms of the *number of inferred "event-levels"*, or "structural levels" (a concept explicated in Part III of this essay) and "individual"- (or "event"-) types. "Coherence", on the other hand, may be described as *inverse* to the *number* of *distinguishably distinct individuals* enclosed within *single* level-generative steps, including the

---

[4]An approach to the practical implementation of this resource is the subject of Part IV.

step from "zero" to the "primitive-basis"-level[5] (how 'much' *has* to be taken as 'given', and how 'much' must each particular level 'take in' to arrive at the next minimally distinguishable higher level of 'event-extension'?).

> Examples: 1) If what I can hypothesize for some musical structure (by virtue of perception) as a "perceptual atomic unit" turns out to be "smaller" than the "smallest" individual I find usable as a total basis for relatedness (where, i.e., explanation cannot proceed "up from"—or "down to", depending on the chosen explanatory path—any and all single pitch-pitch relations), I must "retreat" to the use of a "larger" individual—one I actually can perceive as a *complex*—as the structural "atom", treating it as an indivisible, or at least undivided, unit, from which relations extend.
>
> 2) And if, for *some* of a composition (i.e., some segments, or structural layers) I am able to proceed continuously from "simple" atomic elements, but for some segment (in some layer, or consisting of it), this degree of particularity cannot be sustained, then my explanatory model is *relatively opaque* with respect to this passage or its associated layer.

Thus, one might informally characterize a hypothetical index of "significant musical coherence" as varying with, 1) the complexity of the structure (with varying criteria, of course, for what *constitutes* "a level" and variable *weighting* of levels of differing "orders of significance" within the total structure), 2) the *simplicity of the primitives,* and 3) the *inverse* of the *relative opacity* (which is equivalent to the "simple coherence" designated above).

But still another factor can, I believe, be discerned as relevant to this complex; namely, what might be termed an "intensive-extensive" disjunction with respect to compositional elaboration, in which "intensivity" is determined by the *function-multiplicity* associated with single individuals at given structural levels (or relative expanses), and "extensivity" by the *individual-multiplicity* associated with single "event-types" or "relation-types" (or "schemata"), which we may call "musical functions" by analogy with the "propositional functions" of formal syntax. Thus, the "observation

---

[5] See Goodman [54], pp. 66–117 for an exhaustive discussion of the cognitive status of this question.

field" here is that from which can be inferred the relation between the numbers of functions associated with individual events, and the numbers of events and event-types associated with individual instances of individual functions.

Examples: 1) Thus, in tonal music, *extensive* elaboration is exemplified by such expansion-phenomena as the elaboration of a *neighbor-note* inflection through a complete triadicization thereof, or a "linearization" of an arpeggiation of a triadic interval (such arpeggiation being itself an "extensive" elaboration out of the triad), such as produces a "passing 7th" in the succession:

```
       C | C              C ‖ C                    C ‖ C
1.     A | A        2.    A |     A         3.    A |   B♭ A
       F | F              F | G | F                F | G    F
       F | F              F | E | C                F | E    C
                          ‖ C | F                    C |   F
```

out of which the "V₇" arises. And, to use the latter example, an "intensive" elaboration is just the kind of "contraction-phenomenon" that *reduces* the succession:

```
       C   C | B♭ | A              C ‖ B♭ | A                   ‖ B♭ | A
3.     A   G | G  | F      to 4.   A | G  | F   and then to 5.  | G  | F
       F   E | E  | C              F | E  | C                   | E  | C
       F   C | C  | F              F ‖ C  | F                   ‖ C  | F
```
,

where the "dissonant" (B♭, C) simultaneity occurs without "preparation". Note that in a *complete* level-derivation, the *contraction* appears as a contraction of a *previous expansion,* and thus a given event-span may have *more prolongation-tokens* at a "more background" level than the same event-span has at some "more foreground" level. And *every* intensive elaboration will necessarily be preceded by an extensive one (except in the unlikely event that it is performed directly on an *Ursatz*). It is, manifestly, in the complex mixture of extensive and intensive elaborations that advanced tonal music produces its high individuation of particular structures.

2) One could consider this intensive-extensive factor to underlie the peculiar respect in which "simplistic" music is often analytically "difficult", and "complex" music often "simple".

Such "simplistic" music is "difficult" just in that so much needs to be regarded as given in order to find a relevant level of "functioning", but then the functions themselves are often of such a gross nature that they are trivially "hearable at first encounter"; but any subsequent attempt to go "deeper" than what is initially noticeable is to encounter an impenetrable "cognitive opacity" that contrasts drastically with the "obviousness" at the surface.

"Complex" music, on the other hand, is often multiply ramified from the "simplest" elements in "structurally relevant" ways, that is, ways that meaningfully affect our sense of "what the piece is".

3) Historically, one might also regard "musical development" as typically characterized by drastic intensivity at the beginning of a "stylistic revolution", which concentrates previously "extensialized" relations into new multiplicities of syntactic dimensions, so that the increased structural complexity is accompanied by, even to a certain extent *enabled* by (though this requires more explanation than I can offer here), a greater simplicity of the *presented* surface; typically, this is then followed by a new development through "extensive" elaborations as well as new intensivities.[6]

5. THE EXTRALOGICAL BASES OF CONSTRUCTIONAL SYSTEMS (FROM GOODMAN [53])[7]

"The extralogical basis of a system consists of all its primitives that are not in our list of basic 'logical terms'. It thus may include, in addition to primitives peculiar to the system, primitives...which are common to many systems.

"To adopt a term as primitive is to introduce it into the system without defining it. In so far as its interpretation is not clear from ordinary usage, an explanation—which is not part of the formal system—must be provided. Familiar terms in familiar contexts...may need little explanation. The interpretation of newly invented words or symbols, on the other hand, depends entirely upon the unofficial explanation in terms of words whose usage is familiar. Often, the interpretation of a

---

[6]Cf. Westergaard [40], pp. 90–92.

[7]It is possible that readers familiar with Goodman's work may wish to skip this section.

primitive is given partly by ordinary usage, partly by an explanation designed to resolve any ambiguities in that usage." (p. 63)

"But what, now, are the implications of choosing one term rather than another as primitive? It is not because a term is indefinable that it is a primitive; rather, it is because a term has been chosen as primitive for a system that it is indefinable in that system. No term is absolutely indefinable. And if indefinability is taken to mean incomprehensibility, incomprehensible terms have no place at all in a system. In general, the terms adopted as primitives of a given system are readily definable in some other system. There is no absolute primitive, no one correct selection of primitives. Attention is therefore directed to the factors that affect the choice of primitives for systems." (p. 64)

[Inapplicable ('circular and non-circular'), obscure ('predisposed to telepathic communication with supernatural aid'), paradoxical in normal use ('denoted') cases are dismissed. *Clarity* is regarded as significant for enabling ease of construction and comprehension, and for minimizing the risk of fundamental error; but terms obscure in normal, presystematic usage *may* be clarified for the system at hand by explanation. *Limitations* derived from the nature of the problem principally operate to circumscribe a 'sphere of eligible primitives.'] "The primitives chosen must, of course, form an *adequate* basis for all the definitions required; but adequacy, in so far as it is attainable at all, could readily be insured by adopting as primitive all predicates not excluded by the conditions of the problems at hand. Not merely an adequate basis but the minimum of a *simplest* adequate basis is wanted." (p. 66)

6. THE EXTRALOGICAL BASIS OF THE SYSTEM TO BE SKETCHED

Rather than continuing to quote Goodman *in extenso*, I relate, in the following, observations made in connection with the sketch contained herein to those passages in Goodman where the relevant considerations are noted and where similar conditions are under scrutiny. We choose for our system, first, a *phenomenalistic basis,* on the same non-normative grounds as Goodman (p. 140), but we, additionally, are focusing on "things" whose "reality" is manifestly phenomenal and thus manifestly "non-physical", although they could be *described,* by means of a cumbersome apparatus such as is employed in Kassler [20], in terms of purely physicalistic predicates. So I take "some perceptible phenomenal individuals" as basic units. As noted, I differ from Goodman in using classes (in the manner of Carnap in the *Aufbau*—see Sections

33–37 of that work especially), so this system is "ontologically platonistic"; but, for those concerned about such things, the translation into a purely nominalistic system should pose no insuperable obstacles. Similarly, following Goodman rather than Carnap, individuals are constructed out of repeatable qualities rather than particulars (Goodman, pp. 142–145). These "repeatable qualities" are understood in the sense of the *qualia* of Goodman's system (pp. 127–135). The two qualities I use for construction are *pitch qualia* and *time-order qualia;* other qualia relevant to musical structures await a more fully developed system. The *basic units* chosen as *atoms* for the system are just such *single qualia,* pitch qualia alone for the first definitions, then order qualia for later stages. The pitch qualia chosen as atoms are "minimal distinguished (commonly called 'least-discernible') qualia" (p. 198), which seemed to hold out a basis for being regarded as foreseeably potential (if not presently actual) discriminants in a functional relation. (See Goodman, pp. 198–199 for a fuller discussion. Note especially the remark that "while some of these qualities [the single phenomenal qualia to be taken as atoms] may be presystematically divisible into *components,* none is presystematically divisible into other phenomenal [qualities]. As atoms of a system, they are of course not divisible at all in that system and are thus systematically discrete from one another. As finite parts of a finite stream of experience, they are finite in number". Note the relevance of this remark to our choice of "least-discriminated" pitches under a given interpretation; where "noises" [in the ordinary sense] are the interpreting sound-concreta, their relative pitch *characteristics* constitute the interpreting pitch qualia of the system, even though in some other context the same sounds would be considered as having a pitch aspect distinguished as "indeterminately multi-pitched within a registral band" or some such thing; and, also, in a system whose only sound-individual is a "major triad", such a "complex" would constitute the individual of the system whose total invariant pitch-content conjunction interprets the term "a pitch quale", and all the asserted properties are assumed to hold [there may be other properties that arise in both these sample cases not arising in "standard" musical cases, such as the "registral overlap" of two "atomic elements" where the "atomic elements" are triads, but their occurrence would at most modify the system without falsifying or weakening the operationality of any of its definitions, such as that, say, every pitch quale is "higher", "lower", or "equivalent to" every other pitch quale].)

The basic presystematic notion here is that "there exists a pitch domain within auditory experience whose characteristics are specifiable as independently variable with respect to all other so-specifiable domains involved in that experience". The primitive predicate chosen, then, is $P(x)$, which means, "x is a pitch quale". The later predicate used is $T(x)$, which means "the time of x"[8].

The basic relation taken as primitive is $Pm(x, y)$, which translates as "x and y are matching pitch qualia". This is equivalent to Goodman's M ("matches") with the interpretation restricted explicitly to pitch qualia. One of the principal features of this predicate is that although reflexive and symmetric, it is not transitive, so that two pitch qualia may both match a third but not each other; the creation of unambiguous "syntactic units" out of this situation is a task of our definitions, one that corresponds to Goodman's effort to define "linear arrays" and "color boundaries" through his predicate M. Further discussion of Pm is deferred to the sequel.

7. THE ROLE OF SOUNDS IN MUSIC

"A concretum is a fully concrete entity in that it has among its qualities at least one member of every category within some sense realm. It is a minimal concrete entity in that it contains nothing more than one quale from each such category" (p. 204). "Sounds" are the concreta associated with music. But we are here limiting our system to the description of relations among *pitch* and *time-order* qualia, or at most pitch-time-order quale complexes as (at least *partial*) "musical structures", rather than relations among the associated sounds themselves. This is why the members of our relation-classes, which may at first resemble particulars as, for example, "instances of the presentation of a particular pitch", are actually just the qualia themselves without regard to any "sounds" in which they may actually occur. We are thus occupied in constructing "music" without "sound", which may seem paradoxical, but is not. For a "musical structure" "exists" in the mind's ear of someone *thinking of* it (while looking at a score, for example), as explicitly and experientially as it exists by virtue of the perception of its

---

[8] See Goodman, *op. cit.*, pp. 200–217.

concrete embodiment, in a sense quite different from that in which a physical object may be "thought about" or remembered. That is, it is possible to "experience" a composition mentally (as it is possible so to experience an instance of *language*), *fully* in terms of just those *aspects of relation* among sound-successions which function as dimensions of variability in creating the "musical structure". So a composition may be considered to be constructed out of complexes rather than out of concreta: "...qualia are qualities but never instances. Complexes that are neither qualia nor concreta, then, are both instances (of their complex *proper* parts) and qualities (of more comprehensive complexes that contain them)" (Goodman, *op. cit.*, p. 233). So however completely the information with which to construct a musical structure is inferred from observations on sounds, of differentia among qualia within given "categories" of the auditory domain, that structure itself *is* the totality of these relations, not of those sounds. This explains why we can think of compositions, with varying adequacy, just in terms of *some* of their observable categories; for each category is a "potential" area of significant differentiation, but there are many compositions whose structures are significantly determined by the quale-relations in only some categories. These actually "function", while the others are present as "media" which are of course essential to the existence of every sound concretum, or presented sound, but which are *not part of the musical structure.* Such "media" are, e.g., "timbre" in a piano piece, "dynamics" in a piece for one-keyboard, stopless harpsichord, "register" in a Baroque trio sonata, or "duration" in St. Martial organum. Minimally, a "musical structure" to be usefully characterizable as such, needs only "pitch" and "time-order" (time-position just as "earlier than", "later than", "simultaneous with", *minimally*). In performance, of course, *something* has to be done about the non-functional categories, but what that needs to be is just an articulative assistance (or at least non-contradiction) in the projection of the other-categorical relations. If this "assistance" is pushed to the point where the "performed" differentia begin to take on such large "degrees of difference" as to be likely to be taken to be parts of the structural quale-complexes, a radically different *kind* of musical structure is likely to be inferred. This is really the key consideration in the "authentic-performance" issue: not to assure that performances of "old music" "duplicate" antique performance conditions, as "playing without dynamics" (which seems a highly unlikely "antique condition" in any event), or just "playing what is notated" (impossible in any case, since particular loudnesses, etc., have to be produced even where none are notated), but rather that, relative to a given context, the production in such performances of differentia in those "other" (whether notationally specified or not—the decision is analytic not conventional) non-functional dimensions be non-independent with respect to the functional ones, and that those differentia be produced below (in context) the perceptual threshold of "significant degrees of differentiation", however they are determined.[9] So that, in the end, we need not *ever* construct sounds to construct music, regardless of their indispensability in its transmission, for once we have extracted their full burden of significant relational information (as uniquely determined, indeed, in terms of *audible* characteristics) we have no further *musical* use to put them to.

8. MUSIC-THEORETICAL SYSTEMS, AESTHETICS, AND EAR TRAINING

Sections 1 through 7 deal with methodological and conceptual considerations involved in the formulation of music-constructional systems. The present section is concerned with the *practical* musical applications of such systems, and their consequences for musical thought and experience.

---

[9]Could a deaf man who had never heard understand music? Probably not, since we could never convey (or tell if we were conveying) the relevant relational information, for that is based on the intersubjectivity of auditory perception. And his world would be altogether so different where, especially, events prominently involving auditory aspects are concerned, that the problem of determination would be insurmountable: imagine that we take him to an orchestral concert, the advance information having been given that he was about to experience "music". Then he *sees* a succession of events associated with discriminable objects, including people, instruments, batons, etc. "How did you like the music?" we ask. "It was beautiful" is his answer. Our enthusiasm at thus having created yet another music-lover against what appeared to be insuperable odds so overwhelms us that we offer to take our friend to yet another concert, this time involving only a string quartet. He accepts with pleasure, and in the event observes a subset of what he has already become familiar with from his previous encounter with "music". "How charmingly intimate, what graceful and elegant music" is his report this time. But then we take him to an organ recital, with no familiar instruments in view. At the end he turns to us in unconcealed irritation: "You call *that* music?"

In the foregoing it has been asserted that musical entities, insofar as they can be distinguished (conceptually or perceptually), are composed of *qualia,* such qualia being *in* successions of concreta; but musical entities are not themselves concreta. What they *are,* rather, are *structures of relations* (by which we amplify remarks on p. 87, above), determined by patterns of relative quantity of perceptual qualities. These qualities are quantitatively articulated by scales of measurement *chosen* by a *perceiver.*

Thus the "psychological" dependency of music need not be relegated to any a posteriori "metaperception", emotively or otherwise oriented. The very *identification* of something *as* a musical entity is, by virtue of the characteristics noted above, necessarily a psychologically dependent activity, in a sense decidedly beyond that of physical-object perception, and perhaps, because of the relative "contextuality" of musical entities, in a sense somewhat beyond the activity of language-entity perception as well.

From the notion that musical entities are constructed by means of a quantitative interpretation of discriminated successions of quality-instances, it follows that a conceptually and operationally hierarchized set of definitions which under interpretation specify at least one determinate relational function for each discriminated quale-element in a musical work may be called an *exhaustive determinate syntax* for that work, *minimal,* if it contains just one possible such specification, and *maximal,* if it contains the most possible. And the particular orderings determined as being imposed on those relations by *observed* orderings of the interpreting quale-elements may be called a *structure* of that work. The relation between the functional elements of the syntax and the particular quale-elements (in terms of type and "bandwidth") which interpret them semantically may be called the *style* of the work under that particular syntactic-semantic interpretation.

Now the imposition of "scales of measurement" on the perception of qualities is just what distinguishes a "musical" from an "aesthetic" experience of any given slice of "auditory" experience. For "aesthetic" experience is what results from noticing the quale-aspects of a thing as the content of that observation of that thing, as distinct from an observation in which the identification of these quale-aspects is subsidiary and even possibly subliminal, if essential, to the "pragmatic" identification of the thing which they "determine". Thus, "pragmatically" noticing a red, translucent spheroid *as* a balloon is distinct from "aesthetically" noticing something also designable as "that balloon" *as* a particular conjunction of a given color over a given spacial expanse with a certain curvature, reflective surface, texture, etc. "Art" works, on the other hand, are things *constructed* out of the "aesthetically perceived" qualities, *using* them as the *functional* elements of a *relational language*.[10]

In "aesthetic experience" the qualities noticed are not given determinate measured interpretations. They are, so to speak, "continuously variable" down to the degree of least-discriminability, and the appropriateness of any degree of determinateness with which any perceiver chooses to notice them, as against any other which he might on another occasion choose, or against that which any other observer happens to choose, is not determinable by any familiar criterion, nor does there seem any special desirability or need for the existence of such a criterion. In the usual course of such "aesthetic perception", however, such qualities tend to be rather crudely determined; as, for example, pitch would be likely to be quantized in the perception of "wind in the trees" as "high" ("whistling"), "middle" ("sighing"), and "low" ("moaning"). But there is no clear assigned uniqueness of function, even in these coarse terms, in any given context. In general, then, "aesthetic" qualities are measured largely in an analog sense, on a continuous undifferentiated scale of measurement—as on a pressure gauge without demarcations of degree or specifications of scale.[11]

In "musical perception", the same qualities are ordered into a finite functional vocabulary: a regularly articulated face and a scale are introduced under the dial of the pressure gauge; and this face and scale are interchangeable with any others such that thresholds between adjacent degree-articulations are not narrower than the least perceptible movement-span of the indicator dial. Thus a "digital system" is superimposed on the "analog" one to create a vocabulary whose relative quantities provide the relational material that is ordered into coherent music-structural entities. This vocabulary is, as Goodman prescribes (in [56]), "discontinuous but differentiated throughout, syntactically and semantically": the *syntactic*

---

[10]These considerations are more fully characterized, and generalized to art-typical domains of all kinds, in Boretz [8a].

[11]See Goodman [56] and Boretz [8a].

discontinuity and differentiation are associated with the entity-*types* specified by the primitives and definitions of a music-constructional system. The *semantic* discontinuity and differentiation are associated with the interpreting quantized entities in the given presented instance.

Thus, for example, the *pitch qualia* that are, as the "least-discriminable" pitch entities, taken as universally "atomic" for music, are syntactically regarded as members of a finite set of discrete *pitch-functions*,[12] which latter are the "discrete pitches" that make up the *functional* pitch vocabulary of a musical structure. All "pitch relations" in music, such as "intervals", "chords", and "tunes", are constructed from relations among these functional particles: this is the syntactical matter. But what *interprets* "a pitch", or "a pitch function", semantically, may vary from instance to instance, so that what counts as "a pitch" for one music-perceptual instance may count as "a band of pitch" (or "of noise") for another (with greater or lesser music-structural appropriateness), just as what counts as "a color interval" in one painting may be a "color inflection" in another, depending on the perceiver's decisions, predispositions, and capacities. And the "requisite fineness of discrimination"[13] regarded as appropriate to a given work does in practice vary widely from instance to instance and, especially, from literature to literature (the case of "dynamics" is perhaps more intuitive in this regard than that of "pitch").

So a perceiver of any musical work must have at least an *internalized* referential system in order to perceive the component entities of that work as determining any sort of coherence, or identity. The more internalized, and the less generalized, of course, the less able such a reference is likely to be able to interpret *as* coherent, or as having any particular "musical identity", an unfamiliar disposition of entities even where these are recognized as entities of the relevant kind. And in the case of music, the contextual determinability of a "requisite fineness of discrimination" and of the other characteristics of a syntax from quale-information alone—and hence its variability at quite basic levels from instance to instance—is at the same time one of the richest resources of the art and one of the principal reasons for its pervasive inscrutability to casual re-

---

[12]See Sections 11B and 13C, below.
[13]See [56].

ceptors. For such variability deprives the would-be cognizer of musical entities of any *prior* assurance of success at the syntactical level comparable to that which he can count on, for example, in deciding, in approaching an encounter with something he was going to regard as a literary work, that he was about to contemplate, say, *English* sentences.

Thus a listener to music who supposes that he "understands" Beethoven but who asserts that he "doesn't understand Schoenberg" is simply reporting thereby the limitations of his internalized theory which, however capable of enabling some auditory data to be put together as "a Beethoven tune", is simply unable to account at all for the scanning of the data of "a piece by Schoenberg", so that the latter simply emerges as "noise". The matter here is one of threshold rather than category: let us imagine that this background theory is simply an internalized model of some melodic-harmonic-timbral-dynamic details of a particular Beethoven piece. Plainly, the theory will have more success determining how another Beethoven piece is an "instance" of the internalized one than it will trying to do the same with the Schoenberg piece, with the resultant reports as noted. And a perceiver without *any* background theory of musical structure is, at most, an "aesthetic" perceiver, in just the same condition with respect to music as would be a scientist with respect to physical phenomena if he tried to measure fluctuations using a gauge with an unarticulated face.

On this account, then, the *externalization* of his theory of musical structure is a significant *experiential* matter for anyone seriously interested in perceiving, reflecting on, or inventing music. And the experiential consequences of a music-constructional system are thus also the principal measure of its value, and the principal justification for its undertaking. But what, exactly, is the relation of the process of formal definition to the musical entities such definition is regarded as interpreting, or constructing? And how does formal definition contribute to musical experience, or to the perceptual apprehension of musical entities and identities? The remainder of this section attempts answers to these questions, through a description of how the processes of formal definition and musical perception may actually be conjoined to produce musical cognition, and how particular cognition arises as a resultant of each stage of the construction-definiential procedure.

At the bottom layer of our system, for instance, we choose to "possess", as our "total musical vocabulary", just all discriminable values of the variable "pitch". "Pitch" itself is taken as *undefined;* it designates a "quale-category" of "aesthetic sound-experience". At this stage then, this vocabulary, its (extrasystematic, metalinguistic) description, and its admissible semantic interpretations (for any given observer) are the "whole" of our "theory of musical structure". This theory gives us a "view" of the identity of any presented, contemplated, or conceived music-structural entity (in the sense of "a piece") as a trivial one, consisting simply of a certain *set* of distinct things (i.e., pitch-quale elements, a distinct one for each presented pitch instance—for we have no relations at this level, not even that of identity outside of *self-identity*). But except in this trivial sense we have no *characteristic of coherence assertible for* that "musical structure".

Now when, on the definiential side, we say "assertible for", that entails a commitment to our being able to say, on the experiential side "*observable in* under just the stipulated conditions"; for it is only by passing such an experiential-correlative test that our definition qualifies as *music-theoretical,* that is, assertive of something about (read: within) music. The matter is a practical one, as every theoretical matter must be to be intelligible as a theoretical one in a specific sense. This practicality is experientially demonstrable, moreover, in the voluntary activity of *listening to,* or *thinking* **of** (*not* **about**), any "instance of music" in terms of what can be perceived solely by means of the stipulated observables. This voluntary reduction of one's accustomed perceptual acuity may be a difficult trick to perform, especially at the very most fundamental levels of musical coherence. But its accomplishment is an essential, and productive, ear-training task for every musician, however otherwise facile or sophisticated he may be. For it is just *this* sort of ear training that engenders the externalization of internalized music-theoretical baggage, and makes that baggage available for purposive use in the service of its possessor's musical undertakings. The principal work of "music theory", pedagogically speaking, is thus clearly not so much to *proliferate* musical capacities, by *adding* new capacities *on to* existing ones (using the existing ones as a "basis"), but rather to reconstruct ("reconstitute") those existing capacities, eventually arriving at, as complex resultants, the "same" musical-entity perceptions and conceptions which had been taken, under the "internalized" conditions, as "simple".

As noted, the *extent* to which such music-theoretical baggage is externalized determines (*uniquely*) the extent to which its possessor is able to observe a *particular* identity (i.e., a *cognitive coherence*) as characteristic of a musical entity. And for this extent to be maximal, ear training must start at the level of the most minimal possible primitive basis. Conversely, the more that remains internalized, whether because ear training has taken place beginning only from more complex levels, or because possible distinguishable levels intervening between the primitive basis and the musical-data "foreground" have been "subsumed" without being distinguished, the more limited the musical experience, and the smaller the capacity for musical experience, both in depth and in breadth. That is, what are limited are both the *degree* to which any single entity can be experienced as a determinate musical *individual* ("depth"), and the *number* of things that can be experienced as determinate *musical* individuals ("breadth").

To continue our ear-training exercise: to our primitive initial "structure" of "as many distinct pitches as there are discernible pitch instances", we now apply a relation of "pitch identity", *defined* as the relation which holds for a pair of *matching* pitches (see p. 114, below) where *both* members of that pair *invariably* match *any* third pitch which matches *either* of them. By means of this definition we derive from a new "pass" over the data of our "piece" a "higher-level" structural interpretation of our *original*, first-level-derived vocabulary. This interpretation is *added* to that derived from our first "pass", rather than "replacing" it—this is the essential basis of that *functional multiplicity* exhibitable by musical entities, in which each distinct function is unambiguously determinate and uniquely assignable at its layer.

What our definition of "pitch identity" does is to constrain a *class*; and what our "pass" in terms of it does is to assign all the pitches of our "piece" to as few pitch-identity classes as possible. If there is at least one pair of pitch-identical pitches in the piece, there will be *fewer* pitch-identity classes than there are pitches, and therefore there will be at least one such class which is represented by two distinct entities regarded as "instances" of it. Thus the assertion of a class-definition effects a *reduction* in the vocabulary of distinct "observable" elements, and by the same token *in-*

creases the *functional* range of each vocabulary element by regarding specifically distinct things as variable *interpretations* of a single such vocabulary element, or "function". Thus are "intervals" reduced by "interval-identity classes", and then further reduced by "octave-equivalence classes", which enable the interpretation of members of different interval-identity classes as variable "values" of a single "interval class"—and this vocabulary is further reduced at the level of "complement-class" assertion (in which "inversional equivalence" correlates distinct interval classes).

Practically speaking, the reduction of our "piece" by "pitch-identity classes" means that we "still" register the *respect* in which each "pitch" is "distinct" (as "the one assigned to a given distinct pitch-instance slot"), while *superimposing* the respect in which it is a co-member of a pitch-identity class with other pitches. Hence we might find it less advantageous to speak of the two members of a pitch-identity pair as "the same pitch" than to designate them as "equivalent pitches". Here the use of a plural noun underscores the fact that it is only by virtue of having made a *comparison* among things designable as "several things", such comparison being regulated by a *concept* (i.e., of the relational and perceptual characteristics identifiable with "pitch identity"), that we allowed ourselves to arrive at the *empirical determination* through which we *assign* those two pitches to membership in the same pitch-identity class. The resultant pattern of identities, again, as conceptually interpreted, now enables us to ascribe a new cognitive coherence to the "piece" in question.

Here is a "model" of the procedure. Say we are in the presence of something we designate "a piece", whose content would not be misrepresented by the following notation, as conventionally interpreted:

C C D E C E D

At the "premusical" level, this is simply a "slice of auditory experience" without determinate *musical* content; its assignable "structure" is, at most, "a succession of seven sounds", or some such designation. After the introduction of the primitive notion of "pitch", this "piece" is interpretable as "a succession of seven slices of pitch experience". When "a pitch", also primitive, is further invoked, this tune is hearable as "seven pitches". At this level of determinacy, the tune is "the same tune as" *any* "seven pitches".

Thus its perceived pitch structure *is completely* characterized by the model:

{t, u, v, w, x, y, z}

for *any* t, u, v, w, x, y, z, in *any* order, where they are *pitches*.

Now under the "pitch-identity" concept, the entities in this model are *reinterpreted* as follows:[14]

tune-entity/model-entity correlation: $\begin{array}{ccccccc} C & C & D & E & C & E & D \\ t & u & v & w & x & y & z \end{array}$

pitch-identity-class structure: {(t, u, x), (v, z), (w, y)}
pitch-identity-class vocabulary: (t, u, x) = J
(v, z) = K
(w, y) = L

the "pitch-identity"-level "model" of the tune is:

{J, J, K, L, J, L, K}

Thus, auditorially, *any* tune consisting of the pitch-identity-class content represented by the above model would be an equivalent "instance" of our tune (e.g., F B F D♭ D♭ B F).

When we add the notion of "interval", then, we obviously reduce the number of possible "equivalent" interpretations. This type of reduction is what constitutes the "greater degree of determinacy" conferred by a higher-level model on its interpretations. At the other extreme, then, our "choice" of whether or not to call two things instances of the "same tune" when they both contain the same pitches in the same order, but when in one case those pitches are with "oboe" timbre and in the other they are with "violin" timbre, is clearly dictated by our contextual judgment of music-conceptual relevance, since there remains, after all, an *observable* and *specifiable* differentiation between the two events, even apart from their temporal nonsimultaneity.

So it appears that each definiential stage reduces the number of distinct vocabulary elements with respect to prior stages, increases the functional range of each such element, and also reduces the number of possible equivalent interpreting models (thus,

---

[14]This "reinterpretation" is actually premature, since it skips the essential stage of assigning sets of pitch qualia to syntactical pitch function classes (see explanation, Section 11, below). But this short-cut serves our present purpose more conveniently.

the number of equivalent interpretations of "seven pitches" would be greater than that of "seven pitches interpreting three pitch-identity classes", and still greater than that of "seven pitches interpreting three pitch-identity classes which interpret two interval-identity classes"—of all of which our "tune" *is* an interpretation—and so forth).

The ultimate "reduction" of "equivalent interpretations" is, of course, that under which a *whole piece is* determined as a "class", determined, that is, by a particular ordering of all relevant component functional sub-entities, and designated by some such label as "Beethoven's Sixth Symphony", understood as "nothing-but-a-particular structural "reading" of Beethoven's Sixth Symphony", which is a "class" with a unique member (assuming a given "performance" is also involved). This is "full circle" from the initial identification of "a piece", at the other extreme of musical determinacy, where the number of "equivalent interpretations" is limited only as "anything identified as "music", indifferently (but not necessarily) including any structural "reading" (or none) of "Beethoven's Sixth Symphony".

I recommend that readers actually perform such ear-training exercises on familiar musical entities in advance of a perusal of the sequel, to assure that the *musical* points being made (and I am aware of making no other sort) are not obscured in the seeming abstraction of formal definitions and their unfortunately, but unavoidably, complex notational representations.

9. SOME CONCEPTUAL CONSEQUENCES OF A MUSIC-CONSTRUCTIONAL SYSTEM

Before proceeding to the initial characterization of our system, I offer the following "conceptualization" to indicate the musical-epistemic import of the radical relativism implied by the successful construction of such a system:

> Suppose a "constructional-definition tree" that numbers among its "syntactical branches" (see schema, below) a "tonal" and a "twelve-tone"-systematic model. Consider a "compositional" (or "analytic") reconstruction proceeding along one branch and resulting in a particular "musical structure", and another proceeding along the other and resulting in another particular "musical structure". Suppose the symbolic-acoustic

concreta associated with the two compositions are indistinguishable. Then,

1. Are "they" the "*same piece*"?
2. Is there something wrong with a system in which such a result is obtainable?
3. If these are "two compositions", do they thus "exist" as simultaneously cotenable "*Gedankenerlebnisse*"?

The answer to each of the three questions is "No".[15]

Here follows a schematic representation of the "music-epistemological ordering" referred to, and which is also a basic "extrasystematic referent" in the constructions to follow; its "boundaries" are to be regarded as "relative to a context" rather than as "absolute" thresholds:

I. The domain of "General Epistemology":
   A. Notion of "structure" and of "coherence/complexity".
   B. "Structure" in the physical world.
   C. Linguistic-type structure (perceptual-rational interpretations of physical structures that generate relational structures in terms of syntactic-semantic interpretations of the "coherence/complexity" notion).
II. The domain of "Special Science": "Music Theory":
   A. Construction-definiential basis for *measuring* (realizing) musical interpretations of linguistic notions of "coherence/complexity".
   B. "Syntactical types".
   C. "Syntactical models" (musical "systems").
III. The Experimental Domain: "Analysis and Composition":
   A. Individual musical structures.
IV. The Explanatory Domain:
   A. Metalanguages for "intersystematic" and "interstructural" communication.

---

[15]In the first two cases, the reasons why the answer is "no" should be obvious from the preceding. The third case may be slightly more obscure; the reasoning here is that 1) the same "listener" may "hear" both, but not both at the same time; and 2) both may be heard at the same time, but not by the same listener.

10. THE BEGINNING OF THE SYSTEM

Beginning from our presystematic notion of a "pitch domain" we explicate our primitive predicate "is a pitch" as designating a *specified individual* contained in the domain; or, since the domain is representable as a continuum containing an infinite number of potentially "specifiable individuals", our predicate may be taken to designate a "perceptually specified *location* on the pitch continuum."[16] Thus, what qualifies as the interpretation of "a pitch" depends on the "experiential" thickness of such a "location"—whether the interpretation is in terms of "noises", "pitch-bands", or "pitches" as we know them, the systematic operations will hold regardless; it is only the *evidence* for what qualifies as the interpretation of "a pitch" that will differ. And the fact that what qualifies as the *minimum possible discernible difference* in the interpretation of "discrete *adjacent* positions on the pitch continuum" is dependent on "psychophysiological discriminative thresholds" is trivial, since we do not recognize as non-equivalent "locations" (henceforth called "pitches") any two "conceivable" and "realizable" ones that are not perceptually discriminable as "different". Here we assume intersubjectivity only with respect to the general criterion, not necessarily for any specific instance where variation among receptors may occur with respect to what is "discriminably different". For it is only in a general way that the criterion operates, the relevant specific interpretations being explicitly mediated by just such empirical preconsiderations, namely that the communicative range of existing interpretations of "pitch-vocabulary elements" seems to be maximized by restricting pitch-*function* (see below) thresholds to rather generous quantizations, readily discriminable (at least under appropriate conditions) by a virtually maximal range of non-pitch-deaf human receptors. Thus we distinguish the predicate P(x) ("x is a pitch") from the *derived* predicate Pf(A) ("A is a pitch function") where the "locational" relation of minimally discrete pitches, however various from sound-instance individual to sound-instance individual, is differentiated from the "minimal *syntactic* pitch difference"—which is thus also the basis for the assumption of "pitch-function-relational" (interval) identity. That is, given a succession of discriminably dif-

---

[16]Where *location* is regarded as *uninterpreted*.

ferent pitches, say, an alternation of two (abababababab, etc.) it is the pitch-functional interpretation that will operate to determine whether it is a "vibrato" (or if simultaneously presented, "choir-tone" or "out-of-tune playing"), or a "trill" (or a "two-pitch simultaneity").

Now the basic pitch-associative primitive relation we call, following Goodman, "x matches y". x and y need not be *identical* to match, so that it is possible to assert truly that "x matches y and y matches z, but not (x matches z)". This is where the pitch-functional interpretation is most significant: for we do not assume that, for example, we can specify the relative positions of all pitch qualia in a composition that are interpreted as belonging to a certain pitch function; indeed, we could easily accept, and often do accept, a pitch quale x that is "higher" than another pitch quale, y, such that, nevertheless, x is a member of a pitch function X "lower" than a pitch function Y of which y is interpreted as being a member, and the same "border" pitch quale may be taken as a member of different pitch functions in different presentations—and, of course, "syntactical" considerations may even convert the same pitch function into "different syntactical functions", and hence, into different "pitches", as A♭ in an A♭ major piece and G♯ in an "A major section" of that A♭ major piece. Thus, pitch functions not only define "intervals" as "pitches" alone cannot, but also define basic identifications of syntactical pitch-units which, under our "matching" test alone, would prove ambiguous.

For clarification, I quote Goodman: "Although distinct qualia must indeed be phenomenally distinct this is to say not that they fail to match but that there is some quale that is matched by one and not by the other. Thus the matching of non-identical qualia does not force us into a contradiction . . . the statement

$$x \text{ matches } y \supset x = y$$

does not hold, while the following statement

$$Qu(x) \supset \forall z ((z \text{ matches } x \sim z \text{ matches } y) \sim x = y)$$

does hold" (p. 161; see also the following discussion to p. 163).

This "functional" quantization, too, generates our "pitch vocabulary" inferred beyond simple identity-relations of actually presented pitches, in terms of a pitch-function-relational-equivalent degree-ordering of the entire pitch domain.

11. OUTLINE OF THE CONSTRUCTION

A. Musical objectives

Our purpose is to construct "music" in the broadest sense in which it is desirable to apply that designation to observable entities. This purpose entails that we account in a consistent and mutually commensurable way for everything presently regarded as "music" within some desirable limit, and that we allow as far as possible for the conception and inclusion as "music" of as yet nonexistent entities, as maximally extended from our present domain as can be projected. The result of our construction is, first, the trivial one that we are enabled to regard any slice of auditory experience as music; the limiting conditions, aside from the restriction to the auditory, are on *how* we regard that slice in order for it to be appropriately assertible that we are making music of it. Thus the non-trivial aspect of defining "what music is" resides in the explication of *what it means to make music of* any slice of auditory experience, which consists of the demonstration of *how to make music of* any such slice. Moreover, at even the first stage of construction beyond the most primitive, we are making it possible for any given slice of auditory experience to be music (i.e., to be made music of) in a, wishfully maximal, diversity of ways. Some of the "ways" that emerge at "higher" levels of the construction are, for example, designable as "twelve-tone", "tonal", etc.

Now the "openness" of our definitions is limited only by the fact that the concept of "making music" that they aggregately reflect is constrained by what is regarded herein as our intuitive notion of music, analyzed to its furthest possible limits to enable its maximum generalization. Thus it is not the intention of these definitions to demonstrate *that* "anything goes" as music, but rather to constrain the ways of regarding things which count as observing them to go "as *music*", to demonstrate, namely, *how* things *do* go as music, and how they *might* otherwise go as music in assertibly traditional, but perhaps unintuitive, senses.

We arrive at such an "open" but not "unbounded" condition by creating a chain of musical entities the order of whose links is guided by the objective of arriving by intuitively hierarchized steps at the foundational conditions which may be regarded as potentially generative for the whole of existing musical literature (although the non-necessity at any point in this initial chain of a

"12 pitch-class" interpretation of the "pitch-class octave", or even of a "semitone unit" interpretation of the "pitch domain", leaves these definitions open to account for considerably more than the existing "western musical literature", both in the direction of "non-western" literatures and in that of future "western" ones in which traditional western pitch-structural principles are applied to non-12-pitch-class domains). Subsequently (in Part III), we "branch" into two directions which account for the two principal syntactical-systematic types observable in western music, the types which may be loosely distinguished as "preeminently harmonic" and "preeminently motivic", or "serial". (The more explicit term-names used in the construction for the two types are "content-determinate" and "order-determinate".)

Such musical entities as our definitions create constitute a vocabulary of things by means of which musical structures are determined. The *primitives* of the system, e.g., "a pitch", are such entities. Every such entity subsequently created and added to the vocabulary is, explicitly, a *relation of primitives*. These latter entities are *musical functions*; and when we reach the completion of our (initial) construction, we have:

1. a "definition", by *extensional* constraint, of "music"—i.e., a set of guidelines to determine, for any conjunction of musical data with an interpretation thereof, whether and how that conjunction constitutes a "musical structure" (to say a "coherent musical structure" is unnecessary, for something is a structure only insofar as it is coherent);

2. a consistently defined *observational* (terminological) vocabulary in which to communicate *about* music with a minimum of ambiguity and a maximum of latitude for the extension of a common intelligibility to all kinds of musical phenomena (to everything we care about observing as music, and to every way we care about having things be observed as music);

3. an *ordering* of the musical concepts (the concepts whose aggregate constitutes the "notion of music"—or, better, the "music-conceptual scheme", which is thus subject to *revision* at any level when that appears advantageous to account for something we care about observing as "music", but which is so subject *relative* to the "deepness" of that level in this scheme). Such an ordering has the function of illuminating and designating the nature of the interdependence and hierarchical position of its component concepts.

If, for example, we succeed in defining every known variety of pitch relation without adding any assumptions or undefined terms to our original primitives, then we are able to regard each such relation as a *determinate compositional resource,* a potentially cognitive aspect of the individual identity of a given musical structure in conjunction with any of the other so-defined relations, rather than merely a "universal" of experience not subject to observable and controllable variability and volition. Thus "pitch domain", because it *is* taken as primitive, hence undefined, is *not* subject to variable interpretation; it is irreducible because undefined, although its experiential interpretation is not systematically but experientially determined.

An informal outline of the steps of the construction follows, after which the same steps are retraced in formal-definiential articulation.

B. Pitches, pitch functions, and pitch relations

First (1.0) "a pitch" is stipulated to be "atomic"—that is, indivisible into components not equivalent to the whole of itself. This designates the "basic" vocabulary of entities for music, i.e., "pitches".

Next (Df. 1.0) two pitches are designated as *distinct* if there is any third pitch such that one of the two, but not the other, matches it, or if the two do not match each other.

If there is no such third pitch, and the two pitches do match each other, they are equivalent pitches, and are assigned to membership in the same pitch-identity class (1.1 and Df. 1.1; note again that "pitch identity" is, properly speaking, a *relation,* not a "property"—the latter, insofar as it is applicable here, as a notion, is only so in the "property" of "being a pitch").

The vocabulary of "pitches" thus designated is not yet the functional pitch vocabulary of musical structures, but is interpretable by what an individual may regard as "minimally discriminable" distinct pitches. The music-structural pitch function is understood as served by whatever entities stand in pair-relation to each other as *intervals.* Such entities, then, are named "pitch functions", and are defined as *classes* of pitches, such that all of the members of any one such class are assigned the same value relative to the members of any other such class in interval construction. In music as we know it, the property of "perceptible pitch difference" is quite distinct from the determinant of "interval", some "perceptible pitch differences" being assigned the status of "inflections" (e.g., "vibrato", "out-of-tuneness", "sharpness", etc.). Such "inflections" are understandable as variations taking place within pitch-functional thresholds, and we are not accustomed to measure such "intervals of inflection" comparatively with the degree of specificity we assign to pitch-functional intervals. In fact, within pitch-functional thresholds, intervals are comparatively measured in "analog" fashion, for it is the pitch-function thresholds themselves which "digitize" our pitch-perceptual observations.

A pitch function, then, is defined as either a pitch-identity class or as a class of non-pitch-identical pitches lying between some boundary pitches. This definition, however, permits but does not necessitate the assignment of every pitch between those boundaries to be assigned to the same class, nor does it require the assignment to a class every pitch that is identical to a previously assigned member thereof. Such interpretive latitude is required if we are to account for the frequent assignment, within a single musical structure, of two equivalent pitches to different pitch functions (e.g., a "sharp E" and a "flat F"), and even of a "higher" of two pitches to a "lower" of two pitch functions (as, e.g., the case where the pitch regarded as a "sharp E" is actually higher than the one considered to be a "flat F") (Df. 1.2).

Pitch-functional *identity* is just the relation between two pitch functions that no pitch is assignable to one without thereby being assigned to the other (1.2); this still does not necessitate the assignment of any pitch to any pitch function because of such an assignment to an equivalent pitch (1.3, 1.4).

Intervals are defined as two-place relations among *functionally* qualified pitches (Df. 1.3a). Since the relation between two pitches that are members of a single pitch function and that between two pitches that are members of equivalent pitch functions are coextensive, the latter constitutes the intervallic interpretation of the former, and determines a class of intervals, designated the "unison" (1.5c).

Interval-identity classes in general are determined by invariance of assignment; their members are those intervals for which, if a pitch-pair is assigned to any one of them, it is thereby assignable to every other one of them (Df. 1.4a). Thus, for any two intervals to which the same pitch-pair is assigned, membership by one of them in an interval-identity class entails membership in that same class by the other, and membership by any two intervals in such a class entails that they are equivalent intervals (1.5a, 1.5b).

At this stage we have acquired a finite vocabulary of discrete pitches organized into a finite vocabulary of discrete pitch functions, the relations among which constitute a vocabulary of intervals, the latter being intersected by identity-classes the members of any one of which may be *distinct* pitch-pairs, and one of which is the class of all pitch-pairs both of whose pitch-element components belong to the same pitch functions, such class being designated the *unison*.

We now go on to a series of constructions that leads us to the interpretation of our vocabulary of distinct intervals as a set of *metrically ordered* entities; this construction enables us to specify *determinate relations among intervals,* beyond qualitative identity, as determinants of musical structures.

Our ability to do so depends on the *quantitative* determinacy of intervals, beyond the purely qualitative one we have used to generate pitch-function and interval-identity vocabularies. The basis for this quantization is our intuitive notion of "pitch height", or "relative directional relation in pitch space", which are here to be *defined* from our previously asserted primitives and previously defined relations, especially those of *pitch-function identity* and *interval identity*, as follows:

1. a pitch is *midway between* two others if it determines the same interval (*interval identity*) with each of those two others, but those two others are not (pitch-functionally) identical (*pitch-function identity*) (Dfs. 1.5, 1.6a);

2. a pitch x is *between* two others y and z if it is midway between y and z, or if there is some interval such that a "chain of midway betweenness" in terms of that interval may be constructed such that it begins with y and terminates with z and includes x as one of its (intervening) members. Such a chain will always run in what we would intuitively designate as "a single direction" because of the condition that the "outer" pitches of every "midway-between" trio are non-equivalent. This condition guarantees that the chain could never "fold back" on itself, since each successive link is constructed by generating a new "midway-between" trio one of whose "outer" elements is the "center" element of the "midway

between" trio from which the immediately antecedent link was constructed. Thus,

if x is midway between y and z
and y is midway between w and z,

then, e.g., w cannot be midway between y and z, and (w y x z) must determine a "chain of midway betweenness", and y must be *between* w and z (1.8a, 1.8b, 1.8c; Df. 1.6b).

Thus we have, by extrapolation of this relation, ordered every pitch in our vocabulary as a member (call it x) of a chain of "betweenness with respect to all pairs of functionally non-equivalent pitches neither of whose components is equivalent to x".

This ordering is further refined and functionally simplified into a set of two-place pitch relations by the next set of definitions and postulates. By reducing the three-place "betweenness" ordering in terms of a two-place relation we can bring it into correlation with the *interval* vocabulary previously generated, since that vocabulary consists just of all possible two-place pitch-functional relations. This correlation gives us a way to map our "distinct interval quality" vocabulary into a "relative degree-of-pitch-distance" vocabulary, through identity of membership, and hence it also makes available a vocabulary of determinate *relations among intervals* as potentially determinate components of musical structures.

3. This two-place conversion of a three-place relation is done by means of a relation called "higher than", which corresponds *either* to our intuitive notion of "higher than", *or* to our intuitive notion of "lower than"—the significant point is that in any single context it cannot correspond to both, once an initial assignment has been made. That is, the conditions stipulated in the definition of "higher than" are designed to guarantee intuitive *consistency* of assignment to relations with respect to the "direction relation".

We derive "higher-thanness" from "betweenness" *negatively*, by denying that something is between two other things, as follows: first we designate a pair of pitches x and y, of which we wish to say that "x is higher than y". We then define this condition by designating two pitches z and t, as any pitches such that *neither* is between x and y. Then, x is higher than y if, whenever one pitch (z) that is not between x and y is between x (or y) and another pitch (t), it will always be the case that that pitch (z) is also between *y* (or *x*) and the same other pitch (*t*). Thus are all pitches locked into an ordered set of two-place "higher-than" pairs. Since this ordering is conjunct (every pitch except the highest and lowest is both a "higher" member of at least one "higher-than" pair, and a "lower" member of at least one other such pair), it creates a *linear* ordering of the entire functional pitch vocabulary (Df. 1.7).

The relation also fits into our "identity" relations as follows: every pitch is either *higher than, lower than,* or *functionally equivalent to* every other (1.9a–d). Now the latter (equivalent) condition determines the unison ("zero-distance") class of intervals. All other intervals may be correlated with "higher-than"-"lower-than" classes by means of the answers that may be truly given to the question "how much higher than?". For then, "interval quality"-identity may be uniquely correlated with interval-size equality, which follows from the fact that we derived the "size" metric from observations based on the "quality" characteristic.

4. Then, the relation between two non-unison-related p.f.'s between which there exists no third designable p.f. is the minimal functional distance between distinct pitches. And two pitches having this relation are, obviously, *adjacent* elements in the "higher-than" ordering of the pitch vocabulary; the *interval* such pitches determine is thereby designated the "unit interval", since it represents the minimal non-zero distance and thus permits correlation of the elements of the ordered pitch vocabulary with integers, such that the "pitch distance" determined by non-zero-related pitch pairs can be correlated with integers representing the number of pitches lying between the two component pitches of any pitch-pair in question, such that where n is the number of intervening pitches, (n + 1) is the integer correlate of the "pitch distance" in question.

An important concept here is that the unit interval of a musical work, as we define it, may be *inferred* even if not actually *presented*. And this conjoins with another concept, namely that the unit interval determines uniquely "the background pitch vocabulary" inferred as universal for a given musical structure (by creating an inferable "midway-betweenness chain" in terms of itself over the entire auditory domain from any initial position therein). The larger the unit interval in any given case, the smaller the resultant inferred background pitch vocabulary.

Thus, where what is presented leads to the inference of a "semitone" as the largest possible unit interval, the necessary inference from this is of a minimal background pitch vocabulary consisting of all the pitches that would result from the assertion of a "chromatic scale" between the extremes of the auditory domain. Such an inference is, in fact, necessitated not only by music in which the "semitone" actually appears, such as that containing a single "diatonic collection", but even by that determined by such non-semitonal collections as the "pentatonic" (C, D, F, G, A), or even just the "triadic" (C, D, F) or (C, E, G). In fact, the only more-than-two-element pitch sets designable in our notation (i.e., so far occurrent in western music) that do not entail such a "chromatic" background pitch vocabulary are those which we know as "symmetrically octave-divisive", such as (C, E♭, F♯), etc. (C, E♭, F♯, A), etc. (C, E, G♯), etc., and (C, D, E, F♯, G♯, A♯), etc. (Dfs. 1.8, 1.9, 1.10, 1.11, 1.12, 1.13; 1.10, 1.11, 1.12a–c, 1.13).

Having correlated all distinct intervals with relative-size designations, we can now reduce the interval vocabulary still further, in correspondence with much western music, by regarding it as intersected by equivalence classes of intervals. The basis of such a reduction is normally the designation of a *modular* interval, such that modular equivalence in terms of that interval is the basis for assignment of distinct intervals into single interval-equivalence classes. These classes are defined by their *smallest* members, which are always intervals of *less than* the modular size, one such class, in fact, for *each* interval from zero to one unit smaller than the modular one. Thus the size of the modular interval determines the number of distinct interval-equivalence classes, and hence the number of interval-class *entities* there will be in a given musical structure. For there is just the number of interval-class entities that there are intervals smaller than the modular one.

The correlating relation that determines class membership is just the modular-interval relation itself. Every interval of modular size or larger is correlated with just that interval of smaller than modular size which is an integral number of modular-size intervals smaller than that larger interval. Thus the modular interval itself is correlated with the *unison* (since it is "one" modular-size interval larger than "zero"). The interval one unit-interval larger than the modular-size interval is correlated with the unit interval; and so forth. Obviously, the interval that is one modular-size interval larger than the modular interval is also correlated with the unison; which is to say that all three are assigned membership in a common interval-equivalence class; or, to put it yet another way, that all three of these *distinct* intervals are regarded as *interpretations* (or *instances*) of a single "interval class" or "interval type" or "interval function".

Such a function is obviously independent of the particular sound chosen in a particular case to interpret it (i.e., of *which* particular interval happens to be taken as "modular"). Equally obviously, however, the choice that is made will have a strongly determining influence on the range of possible interval-relation structures within any such case. And whether or not the interpretation as a modular interval of some other sound than our empirically validated "octave" is in fact empirically *feasible*, is determinable only by experiential test, not by theoretical postulation (Dfs. 2.0, 2.1, 2.2, 2.3; 2.0, 2.1).

From a vocabulary of mod-n interval-class entities we derive a further functional reduction of the pitch vocabulary, in which pitch-functionally distinct pitches are regarded as distinct instances of mod-n *pitch-equivalence classes,* or *pitch classes*. Pitch classes are, in fact, determined by the components of members of subclasses of the "unison" mod-n interval-equivalence class: a pitch class contains pitches, every possible pair of which determines a member of the unison interval-equivalence class (Df. 2.4).

Pitch-class intervals are then constructed; these interpret the relation between any two pitches as a relation "within" the modular domain ("pitch-class octave") of *one* of them, so that that one is regarded as determining the "zero-point" of the "pitch-class octave" within which the other pitch class is "quantized" as a certain "unit pitch-class interval higher than" the first (Dfs. 2.5, 2.6). Thus the relation "of" one pitch class "to" another is non-symmetric (2.2).

Pitch classes and their (pitch-class) intervallic relations are regarded as the highest-level "basic pitch-structural entities" that are assertible for *all* music. Syntactical relations are regarded as being constructed out of them. The syntactical operations that construct such relations are regarded as methods of reducing sets of greater than dyadic dimension by asserting super-dyadic bases of pitch-set isomorphism, such that distinct sets may be regarded as particular *transformations* of one another. Such operations also generate functional vocabularies of relations among such more-than-dyadic sets which generate larger sets, such that these larger sets are sets of transformationally equivalent smaller sets of one or more dimensions. Expansions into progressively larger sets of transformationally isomorphic sets ultimately define entire musical structures as macrosets with particular interval structures of variably isomorphic subsets of every possible degree from unit sets to the set whose dimension is equivalent to that of the set of all unit sets.

The total number of such pitch-set operations that suffices to generate all known western music is just three; and even these three operations are demonstrably interdependent, and ultimately reducible to just one of them, as we shall note. The three are, in order of definition, transposition, complementation, and partition.

Transposition of sets is easily extrapolated from an invariance of the "interval between members of distinct intervals" (2.3, 2.4, 2.5, 2.6, 2.7; Df. 2.7). Thus, the transposition of a *set x* of pitches is simply a *set y* of pitches which contains just one pitch, for each pitch of x, that determines a given (fixed) interval with respect to that pitch of x. Transposition is, thus, simply an explicit extension and redefinition of the notion of interval-size identity.

Complementation, on the other hand, effects a new reduction in interval vocabulary; methodologically, it could have been included among the basic pitch-structure class reductions, but it seems less universally applicable to western music unless we include only that composed since the beginning of the "tonal era". In any case, the reduction associated with complementation is produced by the correlation into complementary-interval-equivalence classes of pairs of interval classes which complement each other *within* the modular (or other specified) pitch-class interval. Thus we derive "complement classes" (the familiar "interval inverses" 0/0, 1/11, 2/10, 3/9, 4/8, 5/7, 6/6, as well as any resulting from complementation within other than the modular interval), as a "reductive reading" of the "transposition classes" (i.e., 0, 1, 2, 3, 4, 5, 6, 7, 8, 9, 10, 11)—trivial in the case of dyadic "one-interval sets", but significative in larger-set elaborations. The set-isomorphism determined by complementation may be described as "a relation between sets x and y such that for every pitch i of x, its mod-n complement $(n-i)$ is an element in y, for some specified interval n" (Dfs. 2.8a–c).

Partitioning is related to complementation and transposition; it may most informally be characterized as a slicing of a set of entities into subsets whose content is determined by a relation between successively specified entities. Thus a single interval implies a partitioning of the pitch domain into equal conjunct segments each of which determines that interval: this is also an avenue to the definition of "transposition". Moreover, an interval also implies the partitioning of any pitch-class or pitch octave into two complementary intervals: this is an avenue to the definition of "complementation". So partitioning is the most general operational notion in music, although its distinction from transposition and complementation in our definitions corresponds to musical usage and intuition. In particular, relations of more-than-dyadic pitch sets not accounted for by transposition and/or complementation may be generated from the same general principles of partitioning as those on which they rest; the way a set may be said to partition "pitch-class space" may be regarded as the principal basis for its isomorphism with other sets, and hence for its inclusion in the expanding isomorphic-set chain that ultimately asserts the total structure of a work as a set of overlapped partitionings of the pitch-class domain, from a "one pitch at a time" simple partitioning to a "whole piece at a time" total partitioning, with as many sub-partitioning levels in between as are cognitively designable and music-structurally productive (Dfs. 2.9, 2.10, 2.11a and b, 2.12, 2.13).

C. Time-order primitives, order classes, and order relations

Succession is an aspect of all musical structures; to date, it has almost invariably been correlated with time-order, although this is nonimperative—for example, the components of a "single attack" might be regarded as an *ordered succession* in some other dimension than time, and hence as a "musical structure". Such order relations might be determined by registral, dynamic, or timbral characteristics. Nevertheless, ordering, or succession, however determined, is simply equivalent to a *serial* interpretation of entities within a slice of musical experience, which is thus seen to be an essential aspect of *all* pitch-structural music. It is only the *way* in which serial aspects are involved in the determination of the identity of a musical structure that creates the categorical distinction of "serial" music from music with which it is contrasted. Time, however, serves additional relational functions in music; namely, as the basis of temporal-size relationships, in which a given time-slice is variably partitioned by some internal pitch- or other-dimensional differentia (as, syntactically functional pitch groups) into sub-slices of different sizes, themselves sub-sliced down to the single-attack-to-single-attack spans themselves. Thus rhythm, understood not only as the relative time-size structure of sub-slices of a musical whole, but also as the function-difference-extent-and-nature structure of the contents of those slices, seems to constitute the most embracing structural notion for music, although the term-name is frequently associated with some of the least embracing such notions.

Thus the time-relational entities to be constructed are, first, *time-span intervals* (relative durations between specified *moments*), and, second, *order* relations independent of temporal interpretation.

A time-span, first, is constructed as a set of moments, including an earliest and a latest moment and all moments lying between. A "time point" is not analogous to "a pitch", because it has no "thickness"; therefore a "moment" is chosen to designate the minimum significative time-span within a musical structure (Df. 3.0).

A time-span interval is the value assigned to a given time-span on the basis of the times of its earliest and latest moments (Df. 3.1).

A unit time-span is the largest time-span in terms of whose integral increments all component time-spans in a musical structure can be generated (Df. 3.2). Thus the proportional-size metric is the exclusive determinant of time-span interval identity, with nothing to correspond to pitch-interval "quality"; this difference undoubtedly underlies the difference in role between the two categories in the articulation of musical structures.

Our next task is to define order relations, by correlating pitch elements with order positions within ordered sets. Ordered pitch sets are defined as resulting from the assignment of integer co-labels to pitch elements within a set such that there is an invariant correlation between *lower co-label number* and *earlier time of occurrence* (or *position* of occurrence, if time is not the interpretant of ordering) (Df. 3.3).

Order-position reference independent of actual time-span is then defined for sets of the same dimension (an essential constraint), thus reducing the order-position numerical co-label assignment vocabulary (unconstrained except relatively by Df. 3.3) by the relation of order-position identity. Thus order identity among pitch elements of distinct sets is determined by counting the number of pitches "earlier than" each and those than which each is "earlier"; if the totals in each category are equal, the two elements are "order identical" relative to their respective sets (Df. 3.4).

By means of the order-identity relation we can create a vocabulary of order classes, whose members are order-identical pitch-set elements (Df. 3.5); we designate the class of *unprecedented* members as the "zero order class", which enables uniform label-assignment to all order-class members such that their numerical co-labels correspond to the number of successors of the zero-order-class elements there are up to and including themselves (Df. 3.6).

Two sets are ordered transpositions of one another if the pitch-class element associated with every order position of one set has a fixed pitch-class interval relation to the pitch-class element at the corresponding order number of the other (Df. 3.7). The interval that maps either into the other will be complementary to the interval that maps the second into the first (3.0). Sets are ordered complements of each other if the fixed relation between pitch elements at corresponding order positions is that of complementation rather than transposition (Df. 3.8).

Sets having the same pitch content may be compared in terms of uniform order transformation. Such relations, preeminently associated in the literature with "serial" music, are just as fully and essentially significant, if not as syntactically fundamental, in "content-determinate" music. Wherever succession is significative, whether it is melodic (single-pitch) succession, harmonic (pitch-subset) succession, or sectional (macroset) succession, the "operations" of order relation are also essentially involved in the assignment of structural identity. The operations that suffice to describe all relevant syntactical order relations in music are order transposition (rotation) and order complementation (retrogression). The observation of large-scale transformation relations is dependent on that of "order interval", which not only measures order-position distance between elements within a set, but uses order-class equivalence to compare order positions of pitch-equivalent elements in different sets (Df. 4.0; 4.0). By making independent observations of the pitch-equivalence relations of individual elements of two sets, it can be observed that, as a whole, the sets are pitch-content equivalent, and that their equivalent pitch elements are related by a single order interval. In such a case, the two sets are order transpositions of one another (Df. 4.1; 4.1).

Two pitch-content-equivalent sets are each other's retrogrades if equivalent pitch elements appear at complementary order-class positions (Df. 4.2; 4.2). Retrogression functions, of course, in any music in which it is regarded as significant that even a single dyadic succession xy is immediately or subsequently reversed to yx, whether x and y are pitches, chords, or complex successions of either.

Further relations fall within the province of special-syntactical construction, the matter of Part III. The vocabulary of functional characteristics that hold for the pitch-time structures of all music is considered to have been specified in the foregoing.

The remaining sections are devoted to one possible formal and metalinguistic realization of the links in the constructional chain outlined in the present section.

12. PRIMITIVE SYMBOLS AND OPERATORS

Here are listed the primitives of the system, with approximate metalinguistic "translations", in the usual sense. The logistic symbols used are those of Kleene [58].

APPENDIX (SEC. 12)

12.* Primitive symbols and operators
  1. Variables:
      a. Lower-case roman letters
      b. Upper-case roman letters
      c. Lower-case greek letters
      d. Upper-case greek letters
  2. Logical symbols:
      ¬   ("not")
      ∧   ("and")
      ∨   ("or")
      ~   ("is equivalent to"; "if and only if"; "mutually implies")

⊃	("implies"; "if...then"; "only if")		
∈	("is a member of")		
∀x	("for all x")		
∃x	("there exists an x such that")		
Q(x)	("x is (a) Q")		

3. Extralogical symbols:

>   ("is greater than");   < ("is less than)
=   ("is equal to")
⊆   ("is included in");   ⊂ ("is included as a proper part in")

X ∩ Y   ("the intersection of X and Y")
X ∪ Y   ("the union of X and Y")
X − Y   ("the difference of X from Y")
X + Y   ("the Boolean sum of X and Y")
$\wp(x)$ ("the power set of X")
+, −, /, ·   (arithmetical addition, subtraction, fractionalization, and multiplication)
(℩ x)   ("the x such that")

4. Primitive predicates:

P(x)   ("x is a pitch quale")
T(x)   ("the time of x")
Tm(x)   ("x is a moment")
Pm(x, y)   ("x pitch-matches y")

13. PITCHES, PITCH FUNCTIONS, AND PITCH RELATIONS

The definitions that follow hierarchize the normally assumed properties of pitch recognition in music. In defining them explicitly, it occasionally happens that unintuitive consequences appear, and these are noted in the commentary. I articulate the definitions with metalinguistic "translations", "narrative commentary", and demarcation of "stages" in the "ascension".

A. Pitches

I start, following Goodman, with the postulate that being a pitch quale entails "having no other quale as a proper part":

1.0:

(Strategy: The notion here is that "a pitch" is *atomic,* hence has no proper parts, i.e., no parts not identical to itself.)

Df. 1.0: "x and y are distinct pitches" ("Pd(x, y)")

(Strategy: Here the possibility that two pitches that match are nevertheless perceptually distinct is accounted for by invoking a third pitch matched by one but not the other of the two. (1.1): So, if there is no such third pitch, then the two must be equivalent.)

1.1: identity condition for pitch qualia

APPENDIX (Sec. 13A)

13A*   Pitches

1.0: $P(x) \supset \neg(\exists y \, (y \subset x))$.

("x is a pitch if there does not exist a y such that y is included as a proper part in x.")

Df. 1.0: $Pd(x, y) \equiv_{df} P(x) \land P(y) \land (\neg(Pm(x, y)) \lor \exists z \, (Pm(x, z) \land \neg(Pm(y, z))))$.

("x and y are distinct pitches if x is a pitch and y is a pitch and (either) x and y do not match or there exists a z such that z is a pitch and x matches z and y does not match z.")

1.1: $P(x) \supset (\forall z \, ((Pm(z, x) \supset Pm(z, y)) \sim (x \sim y)))$.

This defines identity for pitch qualia: ("If x is a pitch quale then for all z, z matches x implies that z matches y, iff x is equivalent to y.")

B. Relation-type I: *the pitch-identity relation*

    The extension of the pitch-identity (or equivalence) relation orders a given S (= "musical pitch-structure") into sets of equivalent pitch qualia each distinct from any pitch qualia that are members of any other non-equivalent pitch-identity set. This implies no further involvement of matching, or of grouping in terms of pitch functions, both of which are invoked at a later stage.

Df. 1.1: "A is a pitch-identity class" ("Pi(A)")

    The identification of pitch identity as a relational characteristic makes possible the identification of discrete pitches, without inferring discrete "pitch elements". I want to emphasize again the distinction between *perceptual distinctness* and *functional distinctness* ("what can be heard" from "what is relevant to be heard") because the property of interval identity attaches only to the latter, to *pitch functions,* not to *pitches* as designated herein, unless they are also the exclusive pitch-function discriminants in some S. Thus we do not construct intervals here, for it is not correct to postulate, for any pitch qualia x and y, that there is an interval X such that (x, y) is a member of X, and that for some discrete pitch qualia v and w, it is determinable whether, for some Y such that Y is an interval and (v, w) is a member of Y, Y is or is not equivalent to X, even if x matches v and y matches w, and even if x is equivalent to v and y is equivalent to w, since, as noted earlier, two pitch qualia may match or even be equivalent but still be "members"— by interpretation—of distinct pitch functions.

APPENDIX (Sec. 13B)

13B* Relation-type I: *the pitch-identity relation*

Df 1.1: $Pi(A) =_{df} P(x) \supset [(x \sim y) \sim (x \in A \sim y \in A)]$.

("A is a pitch-identity class if, if x is a pitch quale, then x is equivalent to y, iff x is a member of A iff y is a member of A.")

C. Pitch functions

Df. 1.2: "A is a pitch function" ("Pf(A)")

(Strategy: The final condition assures only ultimate contiguity among all the possibly scattered parts of a pitch function; the "breadth" of (i.e., the number of contiguous distinct pitches encompassed by) individual pitch functions (even within the same piece) is left open. And in fact the absence in a presented pitch structure of any of the members of the "chain" of contiguous pitches does not exclude the potential inclusion of such a "missing" pitch in the "inferred" contents of the pitch function; and hence the "existence" of that pitch in the pitch function is inferable from the actually present pitches within that pitch function (even if there are only two such "others", and these two are "widely separated"; in this case, the definition allows the inference of their connection by an inferred chain of intervening "minimally distinct" pitches. Two, of course, is the minimum number of *distinct* pitches contained in any pitch function that is not a pitch-identity class, which latter case is accounted for by the first condition of the definition.)

Note that if there are other members of the distinct pitch-identity classes B and C some of whose members belong to a pitch function A, these other members need not also be members of A, which conforms to our previous observations. Identity-classes of pitch functions are formed according to 1.2; note that we do not speak of pitch functions matching, for they match if and only if they are identical pitch functions.

APPENDIX (Sec. 13C)

13C*   Pitch functions

Df. 1.2: $Pf(A) \equiv_{df} Pi(A) \lor \exists x \exists y \ (x \in B \land y \in C \land Pi(B) \land Pi(C) \land \neg(B \sim C) \land (x \in A \land y \in A) \land \forall z \ (z \in A) \ \exists w \ (w \in A \land Pm(z,w)))$.

("A is a pitch function if A is a pitch-identity class or there exists an x and there exists a y such that x is a member of a pitch-identity class B and y is a member of a pitch-identity class C and B is not equivalent to C and x and y are both members of A and for all z such that z is a member of A there exists a w such that w is a member of A and z matches w.")

D. Relation-type II: *the pitch-function-identity relation*

1.2: pitch-function identity

1.3.⎫ non-entailment by pitch equivalence of either pitch-function
1.4.⎭ assignment or pitch-function equivalence

APPENDIX (Sec. 13D)

13D*   Relation-type II: *the pitch-function-identity relation*

1.2: $Pf(A) \supset \forall B \ [(Pf(B) \land \forall x \ (x \in A \sim x \in B)) \sim (A \sim B)]$.

("If a is a pitch function, then for all B, B is a pitch function and for all x, x is a member of A iff x is a member of B, iff A is equivalent to B.")

Note that, again, this does not rule out the possibility that for some other pitch y and some other identical pitch functions C and D, y may be a member of C but not of D. Thus

1.3: $\neg[\neg(A \sim B) \supset \forall x \ (x \in A \land (x \sim y) \supset \neg(x \in B))]$

where $Pf(A)$ and $Pf(B)$ and, of course,

1.4: $\neg(x \in A \wedge y \in B \wedge (x \sim y) \supset A \sim B)$.

E. Descriptive resources of relation-types I and II

On the basis of the above definitions alone, we can list all the discrete syntactical units of any S by grouping its pitch qualia into pitch-function-identity classes, such that for all members of any such class (remember the members are *pitch functions, not their member qualia*) no member of any other class is equivalent to it. If we add time-order relations (just in terms of "comes before" and "comes after"), we can offer a rudimentary "analysis" of S, such as, e.g.,

if $S = \{(t, x), (t + 1, y), (t + 2, z), (t + 3, x), (t + 4, y), (t + 5, z)\}$ where for each member (t, x) of S, (t, x) is a quale-complex in which t is a time-order position and x is a pitch quale, and there exist pitch functions A, B, and C such that x is a member of A, y is a member of B, and z is a member of C (no commitment is made to their identity or non-identity), then we can define a subset-predicate R such that, for all S, where S_1 and S_2 are proper subsets of S,

$R(S_1, S_2) \equiv_{df} \exists S_0 (S_0 = \{S_1, S_2\}) \wedge \forall(x, y) [(x, y) \in S_1 \wedge \exists(t - 1, z) (t - 1, z) \in S_1 \wedge \neg\exists(u, v) ((u > t - 1) \wedge ((u, v) \in S_1)) \supset (x + t, y) \in S_2]$

or, in other words, that S consists of the two subsets S_1 and S_2 such that S_2 is an *immediate recurrence* ("repetition") of S_1 (see discussion of "structural levels" in Part III). "Recurrence" (here "immediate" but definable as "non-immediate" as well) is thus a "syntax-independent" analytic category, also independent of higher "foundational" predicates such as interval identity or metric ordering of the pitch domain beyond a simple vocabulary "element-list". Of course, other predicates could also be defined; even a "polyphonic structure" could be inferred (see Part III) though not a *rationale* (or at least not a standard musical rationale) for one, except for "voices" defined entirely by pitch-function-identity characteristics, as,

from the ordered pitch array $\{(0, a), (1, b), (2, c), (3, a), (4, b), (5, c), (6, a), (7, b), (8, c)\}$ to infer the partitioning $\{\{(0, a), (4, b), (8, c)\}, \{(1, b), (5, c), (6, a)\}, \{(2, c), (3, a), (7, b)\}\}$,

where a, b, and c are pitch qualia and there exist pitch functions A, B, and C such that a is a member of A, b is a member of B, and c is a member of C, and A is not equivalent to B, and B is not equivalent to C.

F. Relation-type III: *pitch-function-relation (interval)*

Df. 1.3a: "X is an interval" ("I(X)")

(Strategy: This definition just asserts that intervals are two-place relations among pitches (x and y) that are identified as members of pitch functions (B and C).)

Obviously x may be equivalent to y and B may be equivalent to C; hence every pair of members of the same pitch function determines an interval, and that interval is equivalent to the interval determined by two pitches which are members of two *equivalent* pitch functions. Thus we can determine, to start with, the "unison" class of identical intervals. We return to interval-identity classes after introducing the following notation:

Df. 1.3b: "$X_{(A, B)}$"

(Strategy: The subscript identifies the pitch-function pair such that any pitch-pair consisting of one member of each pitch function named in the subscript determines an interval equivalent to that determined by any other such pitch-pair.)

APPENDIX (Sec. 13F)

13F* Relation-type III: *pitch-function-relation (interval)*

Df. 1.3a: $I(X) \equiv_{df} \forall x \forall y ((x, y) \in X \supset \exists B \exists C (Pf(B) \land Pf(C) \land x \in B \land y \in C))$.

("X is an interval if, for all x and for all y, (x, y) is a member of X only if there exists a B and there exists a C such that B and C are pitch functions and x is a member of B and y is a member of C.")

Df 1.3b: $X_{(A, B)} \equiv_{df} (\imath Z) [I(Z) \land Pf(A) \land Pf(B) \land \forall x \forall y$
$((x \in A \land y \in B) \lor (y \in A \land x \in B) \supset (x, y) \in Z)]$.

("$X_{(A, B)}$ is the Z such that Z is an interval, and A and B are pitch functions and, for all x and all y, if either x is a member of A and y is a member of B or x is a member of B and y is a member of A, then (x, y) is a member of Z.")

G. Relation-type IV: *interval identity*

G_0:

Df. 1.4a: "Γ is an interval-identity class" ("Ii(Γ)")

1.5a:

1.5b:

(Strategy: Df. 1.4a has the force for intervals that Df. 1.3b has for pitch functions; namely that all intervals containing the same pitch-functionally identified pitch-pairs as members are members of a class which confers equivalence on them, as 1.5a and 1.5b assert.)

G_1: the "unison" class:

1.5c:

(Strategy: The unison class is identified just as the Ii class consisting of intervals whose member pitch-pairs are identified with *single* pitch functions.)

The extension of this two-member class into an exhaustive identity-class can be demonstrated through the following sequence:

Df. 1.4b: "$\Gamma_{X,Y}$"

1.6: invariance of common interval-identity-class membership

1.7: equivalence of interval-identity classes with any common members

APPENDIX (Sec. 13G_0 and G_1)

13G* Relation-type IV: *interval identity*

G_0:

Df. 1.4a: $\text{Ii}(\Gamma) \equiv_{df} \forall X \forall Y [I(X) \wedge I(Y) \supset (X \in \Gamma \wedge Y \in \Gamma \supset \forall x \forall y ((x, y) \in X \sim (x, y) \in Y))]$.

("Γ is an interval-identity class if for all X and all Y, if X and Y are intervals then X and Y are members of Γ only if for all x and all y, (x, y) is a member of X iff (x, y) is a member of Y.")

1.5a: $\forall X \forall Y (((x, y) \in X \sim (x, y) \in Y) \sim \forall \Gamma (\text{Ii}(\Gamma) \supset (X \in \Gamma \sim Y \in \Gamma))$.

1.5b: $(X \in \Gamma \wedge Y \in \Gamma \wedge \text{Ii}(\Gamma)) \sim (X \sim Y)$.

G_1: The "unison" class

1.5c: $\forall x \forall y \forall z \forall w \, [x \in A \land y \in A \land Pf(A) \land (x, y) \in X \land I(X) \land z \in B \land w \in B \land Pf(B) \land (z, w) \in Y \land I(Y) \supset (X \sim Y) \land \forall \Gamma \, (\Gamma = \{X, Y\} \supset Ii(\Gamma))].$

("For all x, y, z, and w, if x and y are members of a pitch-function A and (x, y) is a member of an interval X and z and w are members of a pitch function B and (z, w) is a member of an interval Y, then X is equivalent to Y and for all Γ, if Γ is (X, Y), then Γ is an interval-identity class.")

Df. 1.4b: $\Gamma_{X,Y} \equiv_{df} (\imath \Delta) (Ii(\Delta) \supset \exists X \exists Y \, (I(X) \land (X \sim Y) \land X \in \Delta \land Y \in \Delta)).$

("($\Gamma_{X, Y}$) is the Δ such that if Δ is an interval identity class then there exists an X and there exists a Y such that X is an interval and Y is an interval and X is equivalent to Y and X and Y are both members of Δ.")

1.6: $\forall \Gamma \, \forall \Delta \, (Ii(\Gamma) \supset (X \in \Gamma \land Y \in \Gamma \supset (Ii(\Delta) \supset (X \in \Delta \sim Y \in \Delta)))).$

1.7: $Ii(\Gamma_{X, Y}) \land Ii(\Delta_{Y, Z}) \sim Ii(\Gamma_{X, Y, Z}) \land Ii(\Delta_{X, Y, Z}) \sim$
$(Ii(\Gamma_{X, Y, Z,...,W}) \sim Ii(\Delta_{X, Y, Z,..., W})).$

("$\Gamma_{X,Y}$ and $\Delta_{X, Y}$ are interval-identity classes iff $\Gamma_{X, Y, Z}$ and $\Delta_{X, Y, Z}$ are interval-identity classes, and iff $\Gamma_{X, Y, Z,...,W}$ is an interval-identity class iff $\Delta_{X, Y, Z,..., W}$ is an interval-identity class.")

1.7 follows trivially from Df. 1.4b, 1.5b, the transitivity of equivalence, and 1.6.

H. Relation-type V: *the relational predicate "higher than"*

From the above, we can derive the "direction relation" for pitches without taking it as primitive, as follows: if two intervals have a pitch in common then, if they are equivalent intervals, either they also have the other pitch in common as well, or one of the non-common pitches is higher than the other non-common pitch. The rest of the ordering of the pitch domain in terms of "higher than" follows. How "higher" *is interpreted,* however (as "our" *higher or* as our *lower)* has no effect on the operationality of this or any subsequent definition (thus, it may be *called* "lower than" in the metalanguage just as well; all we define is a relational symbol ↘).

Three preliminary definitions are needed; the first is that of "functional equivalence":

Df. 1.5: "x is functionally equivalent to y" ("x ≅ y")

Then we define a second special predicate, "midway between"; this is a three-place-predicate of the form w=/=x=/=y, designating "x is midway between w and y".

Df. 1.6a: "x is midway between w and y" ("w=/=x=/=y")

(Strategy: If two intervals are equivalent, and they have one pitch member in common, then either they have the other pitch member in common as well or the one they have in common is *midway between* the two they do not have in common.)

From the connectedness of midway betweenness, we can infer general betweenness, since there is always at least one interval such that if y is between x and z, there will be a "chain of midway betweennesses" in terms of that interval from x to y to z.

First, we introduce some useful notation (1.8a and 1.8b); then, we define "between" (Df. 1.6b):

1.8a.⎫
1.8b.⎭ notations for "chains of midway betweenness"

Df. 1.6b: "y is between x and z" ("x/y/z")

1.8c: invariance of betweenness relations for non-identical pitches

(Strategy: A pitch is between two others, if there is at least one interval such that there is a chain of conjunct pitch pairs determining that interval, such chain beginning from either of the "outside" pitches and proceeding to the *other* of the "outside" pitches *through* the "inner" pitch (i.e., including the inner pitch as an explicit member of the conjunct-chain); thus, for three pitches determining *any* intervals, it is possible to construct a "midway-betweenness" chain that intersects all three and determines, by their relative position in the chain, their "betweenness" relation to one another. Examples: take three pitches related as some particular C, F♯, and B♭; then the Ii-class of which (C, D) is a member will determine the chain:

<u>C</u> D E
    D E F♯
        E F♯ G♯
            F♯ G♯ <u>B♭</u>

which establishes that that F♯ is *between* that C and that B♭.

Consider a C, an E♭, and an A; here, the interval determined by C and E♭ will be part of an appropriate interval-chain:

<u>C</u> E♭ F♯
    E♭ F♯ <u>A</u>

and, for C, an E♭, and an F:

<u>C</u> C♯ D
    C♯ D <u>E♭</u>
        D E♭ E
            E♭ E <u>F</u>

and so forth. But note that this interpretation is to be understood as dealing with intervals not as *quantized* but only as *qualified*.)

From here, we can define ↘ directly in terms of x/y/z; we call ↘ "higher than" in the metalanguage, but it could equally be called "lower than" within any given system, but never either one indifferently (an essential feature of the definition as of the intuitive notion).

Df. 1.7: "x is higher than y" ("x ↘ y")

(Strategy: All pitches in a given pitch structure are "locked in" to relative "directional" positions by the specification of conditions for "betweenness"; thus if a pitch z is not between two others x and y, and another pitch t is not between x and y, then z is between x and t if and only if z is also between y and t, a condition which is significant only if x and y are not the same pitch. For to be between x and anything else not within the interval (x, y) is always either to be between y and that thing or never to be between y and it. The "interlock" feature that this definition incorporates guarantees that *opposite* "directions" cannot *both* qualify within the same system as "higher than" (because always distinguished by the distinction between being between x and something as well as y and something or x and something but not y and something or y and something but not x and something).)

1.9a: entailments of "higher-thanness" in a "between" trio with one predeterminate "higher-than" pair
1.9b.} entailment of non-equality of "higher-than"-related pitches, and
1.9c.} of "higher-than" relatedness of non-equivalent pitches

1.9d: transitivity of "higher than"

1.9e: entailed "higher-than" relations among pitches of a "between" trio

Df. 1.7 interprets "betweenness" to order the entire pitch-functional content of an S as a linear array. The "x is higher than y" predicate is, then, a two-place predicate deriving from a special relation of two elements in terms of their relations in the three-place predicate "between".

I choose to define "higher than" this way, rather than take it as primitive to derive interval identity from it, because I regard the interval-identity characteristic to be a "quality" at an epistemic level more basic than that at which it may be regarded, in terms of a "metric", as a "quantity"; that is, the point is not just to save a primitive, however formally attractive (and, indeed, musically relevant) that also is. But this path makes it evident why "composing with intervals" is nearly as fundamental to western music as is "composing with pitches", and the two seem virtually indistinguishable at levels above this one.

APPENDIX (Sec. 13H)

13H* Relation-type V: *the relational predicate "higher than"*

Df. 1.5: $x \cong y \equiv_{df} \forall A\, (Pf(A) \supset (x \in A \sim y \in A))$.

("x is functionally equivalent to y if, for all A, if A is a pitch function, then x is a member of A iff y is a member of A.")

Df. 1.6a: $w=/=x=/=y \equiv_{df} \forall A \forall B\, (Pf(A) \wedge Pf(B) \wedge x \in A \wedge y \in B)$
$\exists X\, [I(X) \wedge \forall z \forall t\, (z \in A \wedge t \in B \supset (z, t) \in X)$
$\wedge\, \exists v \exists u\, (v \in C \wedge u \in D \wedge Pf(C) \wedge Pf(D) \wedge \exists Y\, (I(Y)$
$\wedge\, \forall r \forall s\, (r \in C \wedge s \in D \supset (r, s) \in Y) \wedge (X \sim Y) \wedge$
$(x \cong v) \wedge (w \cong u) \wedge \neg (B \sim A) \wedge \neg(C \sim D) \wedge \neg(D \sim B)))]$.

("x is midway between w and y if, for all A and B such that A and B are pitch functions and x is a member of A and y is a member of B, there exists an interval X such that for all z and all t such that z is a member of A and t is a member of B, (z, t) is a member of X, and there also exist v and u such that v is a member of a pitch function C and u is a member of a pitch function D and there is an interval Y such that for all r and all s such that r is a member of C and s is a member of D, (r, s) is a member of Y and X and Y are equivalent; and x is functionally equivalent to v and w is functionally equivalent to u and B is not equivalent to A and C is not equivalent to D and D is not equivalent to B.")

1.8a: $(x=/=y=/=z=/=t) \sim (x=/=y=/=z) \wedge (y=/=z=/=t)$.

1.8b: $(x=/=y=/=...=/=z)$ designates "there are t, u, ..., v, w such that $(x=/=y=/=t)$ and $(y=/=t=/=u)$, and ..., and $(v=/=w=/=z)$"; for short, this schema will be called that of a "chain of midway betweenness from x to y to z."

So where x/y/z designates "y is between x and z" (after Goodman),

Df 1.6b: $x/y/z \equiv_{df} \exists X \ (I(X) \wedge \exists r_n \exists r_m \ [P(r_n) \wedge P(r_m) \ \forall r_i \ ((x, r_i) \in X \supset ((x=/=r_i=/=...=/=r_m=/=y) \sim (r_m=/=y=/=...=/=r_n=/=z)))])$.

("y is between x and z is there exists an X such that X is an interval, and such that there exist pitches r_n and r_m such that for all r_i such that (x, r_i) is a member of X, there is a chain of midway betweennesses from x to r_i to r_m to y iff there is a chain of midway betweenness from r_m to y to r_n to z.")

1.8c: $\forall x \forall y \forall z \ (x \neq y \neq z \sim (x/y/z) \vee (y/x/z) \vee (z/x/y))$.

Df. 1.7: $x \searrow y \equiv_{df} \forall z \forall t \ [\ \neg(x/z/y) \wedge \neg(x/t/y) \supset ((x/z/t \sim y/z/t) \wedge \exists u \ (x/y/u))]$.

("x is higher than y if for all z and for all t, if neither z nor t is between x and y, then z is between x and t iff z is between y and t, and there is a u such that y is between x and u.") (The last condition just assures "not (x = y)", and could so have been stated (see 1.9a and 1.9b, below).)

1.9a: $x \searrow y \sim (x/y/w \sim y \searrow w)$.

("x is higher than y, iff y is between x and w iff y is higher than w.")

1.9b: $x \searrow y \supset \neg(x \cong y)$.

1.9c: $\neg(x \equiv y) \sim (x \searrow y \vee y \searrow x)$.

1.9d: $x \searrow y \wedge y \searrow z \supset x \searrow z$.

(1.9b: "x is higher than y implies that x is not functionally equivalent to y." 1.9c: "x is not functionally equivalent to y iff either x is higher than y or y is higher than x." 1.9d: "If x is higher than y and y is higher than z then x is higher than z.")

1.9e: $\forall w \forall x \forall y \, (w/x/y \supset (x \searrow w \wedge y \searrow x \wedge y \searrow w) \vee (w \searrow x \wedge x \searrow y \wedge w \searrow y))$.

("For all w, x, and y, if x is between w and y, then either x is higher than w and y is higher than x and y is higher than w, or w is higher than x and x is higher than y and w is higher than y.")

I. Relation-type VI: *the "unit interval" "Γ_0"*

To infer from a presented pitch-functionally interpreted succession of pitches a total "background" vocabulary of pitch functions requires the inference of a basic unit-interval class in terms of which to partition the pitch domain such that every member of every such interval class is an ordered couple of minimally adjacent pitches (i.e., minimally functionally adjacent pitches). The definitions in this section also make possible the eventual ordering of all intervals into a vocabulary based on the metric of the "unit" interval as well.

First we define the quantization of the "unison" as Γ_0:

Df. 1.8: "Γ_0"

(Strategy: The unison class previously identified as an Ii-class is now assigned the subscript 0.)

Df. 1.9: "Γ_0"

(Strategy: A unit-degree-ordering of the entire pitch field can be inferred from the set of all pitches of an S as the "background pitch vocabulary macroset" of S by inference of a *unit* (hence, *minimal nonzero*) *interval*. Either the unit interval is the smallest presented interval (i.e., the interval such that for no pitch couple determining it is there another pitch "between" its members) or, in cases where that "least" interval is not a "common denominator" (as, for example, in a pitch set consisting of (C, E♭, F) where

(E♭, F) is the *least* interval, but not the *unit* interval because a degree-ordering in terms of (E♭, F) does not encompass C as well) it is possible to infer a unit interval having the property that for every distinct-pitch-pair (x, y) in a pitch set, there is an interval X such that if *one* member of a pitch-pair (z, t) that determines X is either *conjunct with* or *between* the members (x, y) of the pitch-set member interval, then if the *direction relation* between x and y is the same as that between z and t, then t will *always* be either "within" x and y, or t will be equivalent to y. Thus, (1) if x is *equivalent* to z, and y is *not equivalent* to t, then t is *between* x and *y;* and (2) if x is not equivalent to z, and y is not equivalent to t, then both z and t are between x and y; and (3) if x is not equivalent to y and z is equivalent to t, then z is between x and y; and (4) if x is equivalent to z and y is equivalent to t, then, of course, they determine equivalent intervals; and (5) x cannot be equivalent to t and y cannot be equivalent to z. Here is a "map" of the relevant situation:

1. x = z   3. x ≠
       t   z
   y ≠   y = t

2. x ≠   4. x = z
       z   y = t
       t
   y ≠

That is,
1. x = z and y ≠ t implies x/t/y and z/t/y and not x/z/y and not x/z/t.
2. x ≠ z and y ≠ t implies x/z/t/y.
3. x ≠ z and y = t implies x/z/t and x/z/y and not x/y/t and not z/y/t.
4. x = z and y = t implies not x/z/t and not x/z/y and not z/y/t and not x/t/y and not z/t/y.

It will be seen that any interval not qualifying as a *unit* interval will always "overlap" some other interval (rather than "intersecting" with both its members), as:

(C, E♭, B♭)

where the interval determined by (C, D) produces, within (C, E♭), the situation that (D, E) is a member of the (D, E)-equivalent (conjunct) interval chain, but while D is between C and E♭, E♭ is between D and E, which is disallowed for the unit interval by our definition. Only the interval of which (C, D♭) is a member will satisfy the conditions; since the last condition specifies that the unit interval is also the largest possible interval having the stipulated properties, i.e., that there is no interval not equivalent to it that has the unit function *to it,* no interval "within" (C, D♭) will satisfy the definition for (C, E♭, B♭). (This would obviate, e.g., the inference of the "semitone" for a system that was entirely determinable by a single "whole-tone scale", as well as irrelevant microtonal intervals, which otherwise could be inferred multitudinously.))

The extension of this "unit interval" orders the entire pitch-functional content of any S, since every interval can be $\Gamma_{0'}$-generated (see sec. J), and every interval implies a mapping in terms of itself onto the entire pitch domain as an implicit "metric".

1.10: assertion of the existence of at least one conjunct equivalent for every pitch couple (interval).

From 1.10, it follows that, by transitivity of implication, disjunct equivalent pitch couples always exist, too, for every interval, but this property needs to be separately asserted, since the above statement does not account for cases like the following:

02/13 or 02/35/68, etc.

1.11 is the most general form of 1.10, then: its demonstration is best done by assuming its denial and showing that under Df. 1.9 this leads to a contradiction .

1.11: assertion that every pitch is a member of at least two (not necessarily nonequivalent) (interval) members of every interval-identity class; i.e., that for every pitch x in an S, there are at least two pitches y and z for each interval-identity class such that the interval formed by x and y and that formed by y and z belong to that interval-identity class.

APPENDIX (Sec. 13I)

13I*   Relation-type VI: *the "unit interval" "Γ_0"*

Df. 1.8: $\Gamma_0 \equiv_{df} (\imath \Delta) (Ii(\Delta) \wedge \forall X (I(X) \wedge \forall A \forall B (Pf(A) \wedge Pf(B) \wedge (x \in A \wedge y \in B \supset ((x, y) \in X \supset (A \sim B)))) \sim X \in \Delta))$.

("Γ_0 is the Δ such that Δ is an interval-identity class and such that for all X such that X is an interval and for all A and B such that A and B are pitch functions and such that if x is a member of A and y is a member of B then (x, y) is a member of X only if A is equivalent to B, iff X is a member of Δ.")

Df. 1.9: $\Gamma_{0'} \equiv_{df} (\imath \Delta)$ {∀X∀S (I(X) ∧ ∀A (a ∈ S ⊃ P(a)) ∧ ∀(b, c)
((b, c) ∈ X ⊃ b ∈ S ∧ c ∈ S)) ∃A∃B (Pf(A) ∧ Pf(B) ∧ x ∈ A
∧ y ∈ B ∧ ¬(A ~ B) ∧ (x, y) ∈ S ⊃ [y ↘ x ∧ ∀z (z ∈ S)
¬∃C (Pf(C) ∧ z ∈ C ∧ y/z/x) ⊃ X ∈ Δ ∨ ∀Y (I(Y) ∧ (t, u) ∈ Y
∧ ¬(Y ∈ Γ_0) ∧ (t, u) ∈ S) ∃Z (I(Z) ∧ ¬(Z ∈ Γ_0) ∧ ∀(v, w)
((v, w) ∈ Z ∧ ((w ~ u) ∨ u/w/t) ⊃ (w ↘ v ⊃ (u ↘ t ⊃
(v ↘ t ∨ (v ~ t)))) ∧ ¬∃T (I(T) ∧ ¬(T ∈ Γ_0) ∧ ∀(r, s) ((r,s) ∈ T
∧ ((s ~ w) ∨ w/s/v) ⊃ (s ↘ r ⊃ (w ↘ v ⊃ (s ↘ v ∨
(s ~ v)))))) ∧ Z ∈ Δ)]) }.

("$\Gamma_{0'}$ is the Δ such that for all X and all S such that X is an interval and for all A such that, if a is a member of S then a is a pitch, and such that for all (b, c), if (b, c) is a member of X then b is a member of S and c is a member of S, there exists an A and there exists a B such that if A is a pitch function and B is a pitch function and x is a member of A and y is a member of B and A is not equivalent to B and (x, y) is a member of S then if y is higher than x and for all z such that z is a member of S there does not exist a C such that C is a pitch function and z is a member of C and z is between x and y then x is a member of Δ or for all Y such that Y is an interval and (t, u) is a member of Y and Y is not a member of Γ_0 and (t, u) is a member of S there exists a Z such that Z is an interval and Z is not a member of Γ_0 and, for all (v, w), if (v, w) is a member of Z and either w is equivalent to u or w is between u and t then, if w is higher than v then if u is higher than t then v is higher than t or v is equivalent to t, and there does not exist a T such that T is an interval and T is not a member of Γ_0 and for all (r, s), if (r, s) is a member of T and either s is equivalent to w or s is between w and v then if s is higher than r then, if w is higher than v, then s is higher than v or s is equivalent to v; and Z is a member of Δ.")

1.10: ∀X [(x, y) ∈ X ∧ I(X) ⊃ ∃z∃t ((z, x) ∈ Y ∧ (y, t) ∈ Z ⊃
Ii($\Gamma_{X, Y, Z}$))].

1.11: ∀Γ (Ii(Γ) ~ ∀x (P(x)) ∃y∃z ((x, y) ∈ Γ ∧ (x, z) ∈ Γ)).

("For all Γ, Γ is an Ii-class iff, for all pitches x there exists a y and there exists a z such that (x, y) is a member of Γ and (x, z) is a member of Γ.")

J. Intervals of all sizes

Next we seek ways to generate all intervals, and to generate, for any interval, a co-member of an Ii-class with respect to any pitch (as we know is possible from 1.11).

First we deal with the question of different-sized intervals. The definition here is based on the Γ_0, "successor" relation:

Df. 1.10: "Γ_1"

Df. 1.11: "Γ_n"

(Strategy: All intervals *not* the unison or the unit, can be measured and assigned relative numerical subscripts by means of a count of the number of (unit-interval-related) pitches that lie *between* the two members of the interval being measured; this is the class φ, which is the class of pitch functions whose members lie *within* intervals that are members of Γ_n (*between* pitches that are members of single members of Γ_n).)

1.12a:
1.12b:
1.12c:

These rules, first, introduce an interval-dependent subscript notation for pitches which, on the model of the contents of φ in Df. 1.11, are the "number of 1's apart" equal to one greater than the number of *intervening* pitches. 1.12b notes that the subscript difference identifies the interval-identity-class subscript as well, which links the two "systems", pitch function and interval. 1.12c states the same case another way, pointing out that the subscript-difference between any two pitch-functionally distinct members of any interval is the same as the subscript-difference of every other such member-pair of that interval (and of every member-pair of every interval equivalent to that interval) and, of course, that that difference is the same as the subscript of the Ii-class symbol.

We now have generated all pitch functions as unit-divisions of the pitch domain, and all intervals as determined by unit-distance increments in the pitch domain; and we have identified all pitch successions and relations as successions and relations of quantized-interval-related pitches.

Just one predicate remains to complete the "universal" pitch basis for music. This is the relation of "interval difference", which can be defined as a simple two-place relation, and enables the introduction in turn of some useful notation:

Df. 1.12: "The difference between (interval) X and (interval) Y" ("X − Y")

1.13:

1.13 relates the interval difference of two intervals to the interval classes to which they belong and the pitch-array relations of their determining pitches. Thus the difference between two intervals determines the differences between any other intervals formed among their component members, namely that such differences will be equivalent to one or another (or the sum) of those interval-class subscripts. A further property of x, y, z, and w not in the above rule is that if (x, y) is a member of Γ_i and (z, w) is a member of Γ_j, then if we can represent their possible relative dispositions in terms of betweenness, then,

if x/y/z/w, then $((x, w) - (y, z)) = (i + j)$
            and $((x, z) - (y, w)) = (i - j)$
if x/z/y/w, then $((x, z) - (y, w)) = (i - j)$
            and $((x, w) + (y, z)) = (i + j)$
if z/x/y/w, then $((x, z) + (y, w)) = (i - j)$
            and $((z, y) + (x, w)) = (i + j)$

So there is always a unique relation between the members of different intervals and the relative sizes of the intervals, a relation which depends on the relative positions of the pitches concerned, though in some cases it is the interval *sums* (the sum of the r-subscripts), while in others it is the interval *differences,* that are invariant.

A final notation in this section designates relative interval size:

Df. 1.13: "X is larger than Y" ("X > Y")

APPENDIX (Sec. 13J)

13J*   Intervals of all sizes

Df. 1.10: $\Gamma_1 \equiv_{df} \Gamma_{0'}$.

Df. 1.11: $\Gamma_n \equiv_{df} (\imath \Delta)$ (Ii (Δ) $\wedge$ $\forall X$ (I(X) $\wedge$ $\neg(X \in \Gamma_0$ $\wedge$ $\neg(X \in \Gamma_1)$ $\wedge$ $X \in \Delta$ $\wedge$ $(x, y) \in X)$ $\exists \varphi$ ($\forall z$ (P(z) $\wedge$ $z \in A$ $\wedge$ Pf(A) $\wedge$ $A \in \varphi \supset$ $x/z/y$ $\wedge$ $(z = z_1 \supset (x, z) \in \Gamma_1)$ $\wedge$ $(z = z_{n-1} \supset (z, y) \in \Gamma_1)$ $\wedge$ $(z = z_1 \vee z = z_2 \vee \ldots \vee z = z_{n-1})$ $\wedge$ $\forall i$ $((z_i, z_{i+1}) \in \Gamma_1$ $\wedge$ $x/z_i/z_{i+1})))).$

("Γ_n is the Δ such that Δ is an Ii-class and, for all X where X is an interval and X is not a member of Γ_0 or Γ_1, and X is a member of Δ, and (x, y) is a member of X, there exists a φ such that for all z, if z is a pitch and z is a member of A and A is a pitch function and A is a member of φ, then z is between x and y and $z = z_1$ implies that (x, z) is a member of Γ_1, and $z = z_{n-1}$ implies that (z, y) is a member of Γ_1, and z is z_1 or z_2 or … z_{n-1} and, for all i, (z_i, z_{i+1}) is a member of Γ_1 and z_i is between x and z_{i+1}.") (φ would be the null class if X were a member of (the Ii-classes) Γ_0 or Γ_1, contrary to the stipulated conditions.)

1.12a: $\forall x \forall y$ $((x, y) \in \Gamma_n \sim ((x = z_i) \supset (y = z_{i \pm n})))$.

1.12b: $\forall x \forall y$ $(((x = z_i) \sim (y = z_{i \pm n})) \sim ((x, y) \in X \supset X \in \Gamma_n))$.

1.12c: $\forall X$ {$X \in \Gamma_n \sim \forall x \forall y$ [$(x, y) \in X \wedge (x = t_i) \wedge (y = t_{i \pm n}) \supset$ $\forall z \forall w$ $((z, w) \in X \sim ((z = t_j) \sim (w = t_{j \pm n})))$] }.

Df 1.12: $X - Y \equiv_{df} (\imath \underline{n})$ $(X \in \Gamma_i \wedge Y \in \Gamma_j \supset i - j = \underline{n})$.

("The difference between X and Y is the $\underline{n}$ such that, if X is a member of Γ_i and Y is a member of Γ_j, then $i - j$ is $\underline{n}$.")

1.13: $\forall X \forall Y$ {$X \in \Gamma_i \wedge Y \in \Gamma_j \sim \forall x \forall y \forall z \forall w$ [$(x, y) \in X \wedge (z, w) \in Y \supset$ $\forall Z \forall W$ $(((y, z) \in Z \wedge (y, w) \in W \sim Z \in \Gamma_k \wedge W \in \Gamma_l) \supset k - l = j$ $\wedge$ $\forall T \forall V$ $(((y, z) \in T \wedge (x, z) \in V \sim T \in \Gamma_m \wedge V \in \Gamma_n) \supset$ $m - n = i$))] }.

("For all X and all Y, X is a member of Γ_i and Y is a member of Γ_j iff for all x, y, z, and w if (x, y) is a member of X and (z, w) is a member of Y then for all Z and all W if (y, z) is a member of Z and (y, w) is a member of W iff Z is a member of Γ_k and W is a member of Γ_l then $k - l$ is j and for all T and V if (y, z) is a member of T and (x, z) is a member of V iff T is a member of Γ_m and V is a member of Γ_n then $m - n$ is i.")

Df. 1.13: $X > Y \underset{df}{\equiv} (I(X) \wedge I(Y)) \supset (X \in \Gamma_i \wedge Y \in \Gamma_j \supset (i > j))$.

K. Interval-class equivalence

Most pitch-syntactical systems in music impose a further ordering on the pitch domain, beyond pitch-functional identity, interval identity, and their metric ordering in a linear array. This further ordering results from a "cyclic" interpretation of the pitch-interval domain, which further reduces the numbers of "syntactic elements" (as well as increases the number of *kinds* of things—levels—that are musically interpretable, just as "pitch functions" reduce the number of syntactical ways to interpret discriminably different pitches, at the same time creating a new category of "syntactic difference" (to be *added* to "discriminable difference") by creating a set of equivalence classes that join certain Ii-classes whose extensions are distinct. In general, the interpretation given classes of Ii-classes is that those remaining distinct under maximal extension represent the basic "syntactic interval" units, and that classes of particular members of Ii-classes of a particular type constitute the basic "syntactic pitch" units. The remaining differentia within these classes then create a multiple representability of the same syntactic functions in a non-syntactic "articulative" realm normally interpreted as the *registral* domain (just as discriminably different members of the same pitch functions are assigned to the still more "articulative" domains of "vibrato", "choir tone", "leading-tone sharpness", etc.). Essentially this amounts to partitioning the pitch domain in terms of a single Ii-class interpreted as modular, such that this modular class and all Ii-classes whose subscripts are multiples of the subscript of the modular class are uniquely correlated with the "unison class", their successors with the "unit class", and each of their further successors (up to the next modular multiple) with the Ii-class whose subscript is the residue of the subscript of the class in question after subtraction of all possible multiples of the modular subscript. We generate such interval-class equivalence classes (subscript residue classes) by first defining subclasses the unions of whose maximal extensions are the full extensions of the residue classes in question. We do this to distinguish the members of these subclasses as classes of residue-class equivalents whose member pairs all have a given element in common. In the case of the modular interval itself, these extensions give the complete set of modular equivalents with respect to each "within-the-modulus" pitch function, and the totality of such extensions defines the syntactical pitch-function relations as relations among members of *distinct* modular-equivalence unison-class sets. These are, of course, our "octave equivalent pitch classes" under the customary interpretation, but this interpretation is unspecified in the definition, as is the dimension of the modular interval (the numeral of the Ii-class subscript of the modular Ii-class), for the theoretical concept involved is quite definable and modellable without respect to those factors.

The first definitions required here are of predicates specifying the interval referents ($\Gamma_0, \Gamma_1, \ldots, \Gamma_{n-1}$) that are the bases for the eventual construction of interval-equivalence residue classes; we start by defining first a "mod-n minimal interval" (where, i.e., Γ_n is the modular interval), and then, the set of all mod-n minimal intervals in an S:

Df. 2.0: "R is a mod-n minimal-interval class" ("$Ms_n(R)$")

(Strategy: If n determines (is the subscript of) a modular ("octave-determining") interval, then a mod-n *minimal* interval is one *smaller* than Γ_n (i.e., one whose subscript is *less* than n).)

2.0: "induction" rule that asserts that a member of a mod-n minimal-interval class is a member of one of the *n* interval-identity classes whose subscripts range between 0 and (n – 1).

The next definition identifies intervals in terms of mod-n equivalence by virtue of modular reducibility to a member of a minimal set:

Df. 2.1: "X and Y are mod-n equivalent intervals" ("$X \equiv_n Y$")

The next definition isolates, for every interval, its minimal-set referent in terms of the subscript value of any mod-n equivalent of it that is a member of a mod-n minimal-interval set:

Df. 2.2: "X is the minimal mod-n referent of Y" ("$Mi_n(X, Y)$")

2.1: symmetricality of "$Mi_n(X, Y)$" for a given X and Y implies *equivalence* of X and Y.

Finally, we can define an interval class mod n as the class of all intervals that have a minimal mod-n referent belonging to the same Ii-class:

Df. 2.3: "A mod-n interval-i class" ("Σ_n^i")

APPENDIX (Sec. 13K)

13K*   Interval-class equivalence

Df. 2.0: $Ms_n(R) \equiv_{df} \forall X (X \in R \sim \forall \Gamma_i (X \in \Gamma_i \supset n > i))$.

("R is a mod-n minimal-interval class if, for all X, X is a member of R iff for all Γ_i, if X is a member of Γ_i then n is greater than i.")

2.0: $\forall X (X \in R \land Ms_n(R) \sim (X \in \Gamma_0 \lor X \in \Gamma_1 \lor ... \lor X \in \Gamma_{(n-1)}))$.

Df 2.1: $X \equiv_{\bar{n}} Y \equiv_{df} I(X) \land I(Y) \land \forall \Gamma_i \forall \Gamma_j [X \in \Gamma_i \supset$
           $(Y \in \Gamma_j \sim (i - j = k \supset (k = 0 \lor k = n \lor k = (n + n) \lor$
           $k = (n + n + n) \lor ...)))]$.

("X and Y are mod-n equivalent intervals if X and Y are intervals and for all Γ_i and Γ_j, if X is a member of Γ_i then Y is a member of Γ_j iff $i - j = k$ implies that $k = 0$ or $k = n$ or $k = (n + n)$ or $k = (n + n + n)$ or...")

Df. 2.2: $Mi_n(X, Y) \equiv_{df} X \equiv_{\bar{n}} Y \land \exists R (Ms_n(R) \land X \in R)$.

("X is the minimal mod-n referent of Y if X and Y are mod-n equivalent intervals and there exists an R such that R is a mod-n minimal interval set and X is a member of R.")

2.1: $Mi_n(X, Y) \land Mi_n(Y, X) \supset (X \sim Y)$.

("If X is the minimal interval of Y and Y is the minimal interval of X, then X is equivalent to Y.")

Df. 2.3: $\Sigma_n^i \equiv_{df} (\imath \Omega)(\forall X (X \in \Omega \sim \exists Y (X \equiv_{\bar{n}} Y) \land Mi_n(Y, X) \land Y \in \Gamma_i))$.

("A mod-n interval-i-class (Σ_n^i) is the Ω such that for all X, X is a member of Ω iff there exists a Y such that X and Y are mod-n equivalent intervals and Y is the minimal mod-n referent of X and Y is a member of Γ_i.")

L. Pitch classes and pitch-class intervals

    Note that, while we have defined equivalence classes mod n for intervals, we have not identified as interval equivalents relations such as, e.g.,

(a) C4, C♯5 and
(b) C♯3, C4.

(a) would be in the class Σ_{12}^{1} and (b) would be in the class Σ_{12}^{11}, a distinction we would wish, surely, to be able to preserve as a relation of "complementation". But for other, syntactically essential, purposes, we need a way to regard both C♯s as representing the same interval with respect to C. For if intervals alone are not the basic syntactic units of a structure, then the interval equivalence classes alone will not suffice as generating and identifying sufficiently "background" units of relation; for this we need to generate pitch classes as members of individual n-classes, and thus generate the *pitch-class intervals* which are the basic syntactic relations of, at least, tonal and post-tonal western music.

Df. 2.4: "a is a pitch class mod n" ("$Pc_n(a)$")

(Strategy: A pitch class is made up of pitches every possible pair of which has the unison class as its minimal mod-n referent.)

Df. 2.5: "the mod-n pitch-class interval of a to b"[17] ("$PcI_n(a \to b)$")

(Strategy (for Df. 2.5): Pitch-class intervals are defined as directional, "upwards" from the left-inscribed pitch-class member to the next closest member of the right-inscribed pitch class.)

Df. 2.6: "aRb" (an alternate notation for "$PcI_n(a \to b)$")

2.2: non-symmetricality of "pitch-class interval" relations

APPENDIX (Sec. 13L)

13L* Pitch classes and pitch-class intervals

Df. 2.4: $Pc_n(a) \equiv_{df} \forall x \, (x \in a \sim (P(x) \land \forall y \, (y \in a \supset (x, y) \in \Sigma_n^0)))$.

("a is a pitch class mod n if, for all x iff x is a member of a iff x is a pitch and for all y, if y is a member of a then (x, y) is a member of the mod-n interval-zero class.")

Df. 2.5: $PcI_n(a \to b) \equiv_{df} (\imath Q)\,[I(Q) \land \forall x \forall y \, (x \in a \land y \in b \land Pc_n(a) \land Pc_n(b)) \supset \exists z \, ((x, z) \in Q \land z \searrow x \land z \in b \land \exists R \, (Ms_n(R) \land Q \in R))]$.

---

[17]Note the distinction between *pitch-interval classes* and *pitch-class intervals*; the former is determined by a symmetric, the latter by a non-symmetric, relation.

("The mod-n pitch class interval of a to b is the Q such that Q is an interval and for all x and all y, such that x is a member of a and y is a member of b and a and b are mod-n pitch classes, there exists a z such that (x, z) is a member of Q and z is higher than x and z is a member of b and there exists a mod-n minimal interval set R such that Q is a member of R.")

Df. 2.6: $aRb \underset{df}{\equiv} PcI_n(a \rightarrow b)$.

("aRb" is a more convenient notation for "the mod-n pitch class interval of a to b", where the arrow is used to indicate the non-symmetrical nature of the relationship (since it is a measurement with respect to a *fixed* pitch class).)

This property is stated as a rule in 2.2:

2.2: $\neg(((aRb) = X) \supset ((bRa) = X))$.

M. Syntactical operations on pitch-class intervals

The operations considered in this section are regarded as exhaustive for existing pitch-syntactical systems, in the sense that they are considered adequate to describe any and all relations among pitch-class intervals and, by extension, among pitch-class sets of any dimension. This makes possible the coherent relation of sets of the same dimension, as "transformations" of one another, thus making possible also particular transformation-arrays (with respect to some fixed set of defined relations) of sets that are taken as syntactically referential (see Part III), as well as of all other possible macrosets and subsets, down to the dyadic interval and the monadic pitch, that are found in existing music. Additional relations have been proposed, particularly to explain problematic aspects of existing music,[18] and to serve as an added relational resource in the composition of new music.[19] But the desirability of adding these operations to a general system is not yet evident, and will depend on whether the explanatory and empirical power of these operations is comparable to those already in the system, whether the latter are either inadequate to portray the significantly

---

[18]See especially Forte [15] and Howe [16].

[19]See Howe [16], and Winham (on Weinberg) [41], and Randall (on Winham) [30].

perceived relations resulting from the new operations, or are capable of doing so only in an unacceptably cumbersome way, and whether the new operations appear useful in some as yet unforeseen way.

In any case, the operations here regarded as exhaustive are those extrasystematically named "transposition", "complementation", (or "inversion"), and "partition". Their definitions are in that order. The "arithmetic" aspects of the definitions are, of course, considered to represent perceptually confirmable characteristics, and the underlying assumptions of the perceptual validity of these operations as creating classes of unambiguously definable correlates have already been made in the definitions of interval identity (for transposition) and pitch-class interval equivalence (for complementation).

First we introduce ordering subscripts for pitch classes:

2.3:

This leads to the invariance rule for pitch-class interval transposition:

2.4:

Df. 2.7: "the t-transposition of the pitch-class interval $a_i R a_j$" ("$Tt(a_i R a_j)$")

Df. 2.7 specifies the transposition *function* that maps a pitch-class interval $a_i R a_j$ into its t-transposed equivalent $(a_{i+t} R a_{j+t})$ (mod n).

Transposition, then, corresponds to the function "adding a constant": "$Tt(a) = (a + t)$", which maps an interval "$T_t(a, b) = ((a + t), (b + t))$", and, generally, a set:

$$T_t(S) \equiv_{df} (\imath T) (\forall a \, (a \in S) \supset (a + t) \in T).$$

Complementation, on the other hand, constitutes "subtracting from a constant". Note that unlike transposition, complementation is dependent for its "meaning" on the modular interpretation of the pitch domain (not just for the interpretation of its results, but for its significativeness as a possible operation), if it is not to be interpreted merely as "contour inversion". For the sense in which, say (0, 3) is the inverse of (0, 9) is derived from the partitioning of the modulus 12 by 3: ((0, 3), (3, 12)). Thus:

2.5: complementary relation of pitch-class pairs with respect to the p.-c. interval-classes of which they are members

2.6: complements of the p.-c. members of a p.-c. interval form the complementary p.-c. interval

2.7: the p.-c. interval from a to b is the complement of the p.-c. interval from b to a

There is no dichotomy here between complementation in a twelve-tone sense and "interval inversion" in the tonal sense, since both involve mod-n complementation where n=12; for even though normally a succession (0, 3) will map, under inversion, into (0, 9) in twelve-tone-explanatory writings (which corresponds to our definition of complementation), it is also the case that the tonal (0, 3), (3, 0) "octave partitioning" is at the heart of the relationship.

This is the force of 2.5 and 2.7. The definitions Df. 2.8a–c, then,

Df. 2.8a:
Df. 2.8b:
Df. 2.8c:

read as follows: "The mod-n pitch-class complement of a_i is a_{n-i}, the mod-n pitch-class-interval complement of $a_i Ra_j$ is $(a_{n-i} Ra_{n-j})$; the mod-n inverse of Γ_i is Γ_{n-i}."

Of the operations described in this section, partitioning is the most fundamental in music-syntactical systems. Conceptually, in fact, it may be considered as *prior* to the transposition and complementation functions. If a question then arises as to the appropriateness of formulating its definition in terms of transposition, as is done below, the answer is that, in fact, we have already essentially involved the concept in our previous definitions. That is, any interval implies a degree-ordering of the pitch domain in terms of itself, and this is a *partitioning* of the pitch domain. Any ordered set of interlocked intervals partitions the pitch domain whether it explicitly exhausts it or not. The Γ_n "modular cycle" is a partitioning of the pitch domain in terms of Γ_n into "n-cycles". What we are concerned with here is the generation of syntactic *reference collections*; for whether regarded as ordered or unordered, a reference set partitions the *pitch-class* domain (a twelve-tone set is thus representable as an interval sequence, a "chord", which *might* be represented as a *registral* rather than a temporal ordering while still preserving some of the essential identificatory aspects of the system: a "pyramid chord" is such an instance), a construct partitions a set, an interval partitions a construct as well as any other interval, etc. So it is out of partitioning operations that all the basic syntactic constructs may be derived; for "generation" by, e.g., transposition, complementation, complementary transposition, and transposed complementation are only converses of partitioning (a transformational operation on a construct generates a set of constructs that constitutes a collection; a partitioning operation on a collection subdivides the collection into constructs; if they are isomorphic, the result may be said to be a partitioning of that collection by a single construct). And anything that is *generated* by something is thereby *partitionable* in terms of it. A "cyclic partitioning" is just such a case; obviously any set of elements may partition any domain of which the elements are elements; the "rationale" for a partitioning is to be found in the notion of a "cycle", whose dimension is from zero to the dimension of the entire domain. Thus (051423) may be a "one-cycle" partitioning of (012345), but the latter set also has (among others) the 2-cycle partitionings 021/354 and 012/345, the 3-cycle 01/23/45 and the 6-cycle 0/1/2/3/4/5. Any interval-class partitions any other; an interval partitions itself in a special, one-cycle way; thus the n-partitioning of Γ_n would just be a repetition of the interval itself. (0, 3) partitioned by 3 mod 12 is ((0, 3), (3, 3)) or ((3), (0)), intervallically; (0, 3) partitioned by 12 mod 12 is ((0, 0), (0, 3)), or ((0), (3)), intervallically. The "partitioning" of a "unison-class" relation, by itself, is a "zero-cycle" partitioning: (0, 0) → ((0, 0), (0, 0)). An "exhaustive" partitioning cycle is one whose single-valued operation orders the entire pitch domain; thus for any n, a j-cycle is exhaustive if j is prime to n; and, for any n, a (j + k) cycle is exhaustive if (j + k = l) if and only if l is prime to n; etc.

The first definition here is of simple partitioning, invoking the mod-n interpolation of a pitch-class interval (Γ_k) within another (Γ_j) to produce a two-interval set, whose members are thus mod-n j-complements:

Df. 2.9: "the mod-n k-partitioning of the pitch-class interval $(a_i Ra_{i+j})$" ("$\alpha_{n,k}(a_i Ra_{i+j})$")

Df. 2.10: "the set of mod-n i-complements" ("$¢_{n,k}$")

Df. 2.11a: "the mod-n k-cyclic partitioning of the pitch-class interval $a_i Ra_{i+j}$" ("$\alpha^c_{n,k}(a_i Ra_{i+j})$")

Df. 2.11b: "the mod-n (k + 1)-cyclic partitioning of the pitch-class interval a_iRa_{i+j}" ("$\alpha^c_{n, k+1}(a_iRa_{i+j})$")

$\alpha^c_{n, k+1}(a_iRa_{i+j})$, of course, generalizes to any number-of-element cycles. Such a cycle could also be expressed as a r-element partitioning of j mod n, as:

$$\alpha^c_{n, k+\ldots+1+m}(a_iRa_{i+j}) = \{\{(a_iRa_{i+k}), (a_{i+k}Ra_{i+j})\}\ldots,$$
$$\{(a_{i+k+\ldots+1}Ra_{i+k+\ldots+1+m}),(a_{i+k+\ldots+1+m}Ra_{i+k+\ldots+1+j})\}\},$$
where r > 2 and {k, ..., l, m} = r.

From the above, we can define a mod-n k-cycle of pitch classes that partitions j:

Df. 2.12: "the mod-n k-cycle of pitch classes partitioning j"
  ($C_{n, k}(a_iRa_{i+j})$")

Obviously a k + 1 cycle would consist of the first element of the first interval of every discrete set of a "$\alpha^c_{n, k+1}(a_iRa_{i+j})$" partitioning.

Every partitioning has a complementary partitioning with respect to some interval taken as modular for the complementation, whether or not it is equivalent to the interval taken as modular for the original partitioning. The m-complement of $\alpha_{n, k}(a_iRa_{i+j})$ is defined in Df. 2.13.

Df. 2.13: "the m-complementary mod-n k-partitioning of j"
  ("$\dfrac{m}{\alpha_{n, k}}(a_iRa_{i+j})$")

Now it might seem to be the case that some relationships produced by this partitioning (or some of the others) where n ≠ j are musically vacuous—as, e.g., the mod-m (m=12)-complementary k (k = 1) mod-n (n = 12) partitioning of the pitch-class interval j (j = 3) produces the relationship $\alpha = \{(0, 1), (1, 3)\}$ and $\dfrac{m}{\alpha} = \{(0, 11), (11, 3)\}$; but see Part IV for a conjecture about a vital role this partitioning type may be regarded as playing in an otherwise recalcitrant literature. Where n = j, the relationship is that of interval complements: $\alpha = \{(0, 1), (1, 0)\}$ and $\dfrac{m}{\alpha} = \{(0, 11), (11, 0)\}$.) But note that this $\alpha : \dfrac{m}{\alpha}$ - relation where n ≠ j is precisely the one that interrelates the major-triad-minor-triad partitioning of the diatonic "fifth"; thus, where (k = 4; n = 12; m = j = 7; α = {(0, 4), (4, 7)} and $\frac{m}{\alpha}$ = {(0, 3), (3, 7)}.) So both the complementary partitioning with respect to the octave, and with respect to syntactically partitioned intervals, are significant in the construction of musical structures.

This concludes the sketch of basic pitch-syntactical operations for all music; further stages require the introduction of time-order primitives to complete the pitch-time-elementary basis of existing musical systems, and, then, to initiate the construction of distinct classes of syntaxes themselves.

APPENDIX (Sec. 13M)

13M*   Syntactical operations on pitch-class intervals

2.3: $aRb \in \Gamma_i \supset (a = a_j \supset b = a_{j \overset{n}{+} i})$, where $j \overset{n}{+} i$ = "j + i mod n".

2.4: $a_i R a_j \in \Gamma_k \sim \forall t\, (a_{i \overset{n}{+} t}\, R a_{j \overset{n}{+} t} \in \Gamma_k)$.

Df. 2.7: $Tt(a_i R a_j) = (a_{i \overset{n}{+} t}\, R a_{j \overset{n}{+} t})$.

2.5: $aRb \in \Gamma_i \sim (b = b_j \supset a = b_{j \overset{n}{+} (n - i)})$.

2.6: $a_i R a_j \in \Gamma_k \sim (a_{n-i} R a_{n-j} \in \Gamma_{n-k})$.

2.7: $aRb \in \Gamma_i \sim bRa \in \Gamma_{n-i}$.

Df. 2.8a: $C_n(a_i) \overset{\equiv}{df} (a_{n-i})$.

Df. 2.8b: $IC_n(a_i R a_j) \overset{\equiv}{df} (a_{n-i} R a_{n-j})$.

Df. 2.8c: $IV_n(\Gamma_i) \overset{\equiv}{df} \Gamma_{n-i}$.

Df. 2.9: $\alpha_{n,k}(a_i R a_{i+j}) \overset{\equiv}{df} (\text{?}\, \beta)\, (\beta = \{(a_i\, R a_{i+k}), (a_{i+k}\, R a_{i+j})\})$.

Df. 2.10: $\mathcal{C}_{n,\,i} \underset{df}{\equiv} (\imath\, S)\, [\forall a \forall b \forall c \forall d\, (((aRb), (cRd)) \in S \sim ((a = a_j \land b = a_k \land c = a_l \land d = a_m) \supset k = l \land (m - j) = i \land (j + k) = m)))$.

(2.9): ("The mod-n k-partitioning of the pitch-class interval $(a_i Ra_{i+j})$ is the β such that β is the pitch-class interval set whose members are $(a_i Ra_{i+k})$ and $(a_{i+k} Ra_{i+j})$.")

(2.10): ("the set of mod-n i-complements is the S such that for all a, b, c, and d (aRb, cRd) is a member of S iff, if a is a_j and b is a_k and c is a_l and d is a_m, then k is equal to l and (m − j) is equal to i and the sum of j and k is m.")

Df. 2.11a: $\alpha_{n,\,k}^{c}(a_i Ra_{i+j}) \underset{df}{\equiv} (\imath\, \beta)\, \{[(\alpha_{n,\,k}^{0}(a_i Ra_{i+j}) = \{(a_i Ra_{i+k}), (a_{i+k} Ra_{i+j})\}) \land (\alpha_{n,\,k}^{1}(a_i Ra_{i+j}) = \{(a_{i+k} Ra_{i+k+k}), (a_{i+k+k} Ra_{i+k+j})\})] \supset [(\alpha_{n,\,k}^{p}(a_i Ra_{i+j})) \sim (\alpha_{n,\,k}^{0}(a_i Ra_{i+j})) \supset \beta = \{\alpha_{n,\,k}^{0}(a_i Ra_{i+j}),\, \ldots,\, \alpha_{n,\,k}^{p-1}(a_i Ra_{i+j})\}]\}$.

("The mod-n k-cyclic partitioning of the pitch class interval $(a_i Ra_{i+j})$ is the β such that if the zeroth mod-n k-partitioning of $(a_i Ra_{i+j})$ is the set whose members are $(a_i Ra_{i+k})$ and $(a_{i+k} Ra_{i+j})$, and the 1-th partitioning of the same interval is the set whose members are $(a_{i+k} Ra_{i+k+k})$ and $(a_{i+k+k} Ra_{i+k+j})$, then, if the pth partitioning is equivalent to the zeroth partitioning, β is the set whose members are the zeroth to the (p − 1)th mod-n k-partitioning of $(a_i Ra_{i+j})$.")

Df. 2.11b: $\alpha_{n,\,k+1}^{c}(a_i Ra_{i+j}) \underset{df}{\equiv} (\imath\, \beta)\, [\alpha_{n,\,k+1}^{0}(a_i Ra_{i+j}) = \{\{(a_i Ra_{i+k}), (a_{i+k} Ra_{i+j})\}, \{(a_{i+k} Ra_{i+k+1}), (a_{i+k+1} Ra_{i+k+j})\}\} \land \alpha_{n,\,k+1}^{1}(a_i Ra_{i+j}) = \{\{(a_{i+k+1} Ra_{i+k+1+k}), (a_{i+k+1+k} Ra_{i+k+1+k+j})\}, \{(a_{i+k+1+k} Ra_{i+k+1+k+1}), (a_{i+k+1+k+1} Ra_{i+k+1+k+j})\}\} \supset (\alpha_{n,\,k}^{p}(a_i Ra_{i+j}) \sim \alpha_{n,\,k}^{0}(a_i Ra_{i+j})) \supset \beta = \{\alpha_{n,\,k}^{0}(a_i Ra_{i+j}),\, \ldots,\, \alpha_{n,\,k}^{p-1}(a_i Ra_{i+j})\}]$.

("The mod-n (k + 1)-cyclic partitioning of the pitch class interval $(a_i Ra_{i+j})$ is the β such that if the zeroth mod-n k-partitioning of $(a_i Ra_{i+j})$ is the set whose members are the sets

$\{(a_i R a_{i+k}), (a_{i+k} R a_{i+j})\}$ and $\{(a_{i+k} R a_{i+k+1}), (a_{i+k+1} R a_{i\pm k+j})\}$ and the 1-th partitioning is the set whose members are the sets

$\{(a_{i+k+1} R a_{i+k+1+k}), (a_{i+k+1+k} R a_{i+k+1+k+j})\}$ and
$\{(a_{i+k+1+k} R a_{i+k+1+k+1}), (a_{i+k+1+k+1} R a_{i+k+1+k+j})\}$,

then, if the pth such partitioning is equivalent to the zeroth, β is the set consisting of the zeroth through the (p − 1)th such partitioning.")

Df. 2.12: $C_{n,k}(a_i R a_{i+j}) \equiv_{df} (\iota\, D) \{\alpha^c_{n,k}(a_i R a_{i+j}) = \{(X_0), (Y_0)\}, \ldots ,$
$\{(X_{p-1}), (Y_{p-1})\}\} \supset [\forall X_q \forall Y_q (X_q = \{a_q, b_q\} \wedge Y_q = \{c_q, d_q\} \supset$
$D = \{(a_0), (a_1), \ldots , (a_{p-1})\})]\}$.

("The mod n k-cycle of pitch classes partitioning j is the D such that if $\alpha^c_{n,k}(a_i R a_{i+j})$ is the set $\{\{X_0, Y_0\}, \ldots , \{X_{p-1}, Y_{p-1}\}\}$ then, for all X_q and Y_q, if X_q is (a_q, b_q) and Y_q is (c_q, d_q), then D is the set of pitch classes $\{(a_0), (a_1), \ldots , (a_{p-1})\}$.")

Df. 2.13: $\dfrac{m}{\alpha_{n,k}}(a_i R a_{i+j}) \equiv_{df} (\iota\, \beta)(\beta = \{(a_i R a_{i+(m-k)}), (a_{i+(m-k)} R a_{i+j})\})$.

("The m-complementary mod-n k-partitioning of j is the β such that β is the set whose members are the pitch-class intervals $(a_i R a_{i+(m-k)})$ and $(a_{i+(m-k)} R a_{i+j})$.")

14. TIME-ORDER PRIMITIVES, ORDER CLASSES, AND ORDER RELATIONS

A. Time and time-span

The principal roles of time in music may be characterized in terms of what Goodman ([53], pp. 355–359), calls "phenomenal time order", "temporal size", and "temporal shape". For our purposes, a *syntactical ordering* specifies the earlier than/later than relationships inferred as referential for a presented pitch collection, while the "temporal shape" aspect is understood as the *particular* time-point (attack-point) proportional partitioning of a total or partial "temporal size" that represents the particular interpretation of the ordering in a given musical structure, and "duration" is the most purely articulative aspect of time in musical structure, having to do just with the local interpretation of a time-span between partitioning elements of a minimal "temporal size-unit", i.e., whether the articulation of that span is realized by a pitch sustained throughout, sustained through some given portion, or occupying the minimum perceivable time-span. Again, as with pitches, we do not normally *assume* for structural purposes as precise discrimination of relations among *durations;* the minimal such unit is normally the "unit attack-successional duration",[20] comprising a relation between at least two pitch-times. Thus "staccato" and "tenuto", etc., are temporal analogs of the pitch category "vibrato" and under most circumstances "tremolo" is analogous to "glissando". The distinction is made by Goodman in terms of "persistence" and "endurance" ([53], p. 357):

> ...occurrence through a period is thus a quite different matter from the duration of a thing or event, and we had better observe the distinction by saying that the patch *persists* through the period.
>
> ...The endurance or persistence is continuous or discontinuous according as the period is...The result of adding to a persisting individual the times it occurs at is an enduring individual. The result of extracting from an enduring individual the times it persists at is a persisting individual.

It may be distorting Goodman's concept somewhat to correlate the "persistence" of a presented pitch with its actual sounding time, and its "endurance" with the "structural duration", for a pitch *quale* is, of course, timeless; but the relation seems justifiable, since the "pitch-time" individual associated with a "presented pitch-instance succession" "endures" throughout its "structural duration", but the "presented duration" is not necessarily equivalent to the "structural duration", as we have noted. Hence the "presented duration" may be called the "persistence time" with respect to a given "endurance time" of a "structural duration", especially since we have no need of the notion that a particular pitch-individual "endures" through a piece in a sense different from its "eternal endurance". For just as the composition is the entire "language"—or

---

[20]Thus, as Goodman points out, [53], p. 357, "the temporal size—or duration—of a thing or event depends on how many moments it contains". In musical structures, the "moments" are just the smallest *structural* temporal divisions, which is why the "same musical structure" may be perceived in performances at different tempos, and hence lasting different "clock times".

"universe"—under scrutiny, so *its* total time-span is its own "eternity".

The definiential path chosen here diverges from that chosen for pitch, because we have no sense of "time functions" or even "times" as entities except as relative positions in a succession. This is not to deny their logical status as *qualia* (although I avoid referring to them as such in the sequel), but only to consider the *musical* identities that appear significant; and there seems no comparable function for the "time-position" as for the "position on the pitch continuum" except as a basis for defining an ordering *of pitches*. In fact, I regard all non-pitch dimensions of auditory perceivables as, in music, defining *paths through the pitch domain* or, in other words, *partitionings* such as we have previously considered. Thus the purely pitch-generated "registral" domain is only one way to express such a partitioning; and only if a musical structure consists of a single "chord" would that be a sufficient means of describing a partitioning, for *registral succession* and *registral rhythm* obviously preinvolve pitch and time-conjunction identification, and the registral pitch-class time-ordering in discrete registers determines "sonority-succession", in the sense of successions of the pitch-complexes that are resultants of registral presentation at particular times.

But a similar point needs to be made about the other dimensions that we do not treat in this incomplete sketch; for loudness and "timbre" (the latter now on the brink of compositional reformulation as a syntactical function in terms of a "second-level" pitch-structural domain) are also invariant "components" of the auditory concretum, and also exhibit potentially functional variability in musical structures. But once again, I view these as ways of projecting time-successional paths through the pitch domain. In traditional music, the dynamically, timbrally, and temporally determined pitch paths tend to function mainly as congruent conjuncts of a more basic set of *registral* paths; in later music, multiple simultaneous counterpoints of pitch voices are projected through each dimension independently.

Our procedure, then, is not to introduce "time qualia" as primitive, but to use the primitive predicate "$T(x)$" for "the time of x", which may or may not be accompanied by a specification of another predicate for x, as "$P(x)$", which is normally the case. We also take as primitive the "earlier than/later than" relation; as

Goodman suggests, it too can be defined, on the basis of "matching", and clearly we can define "between" for time in those terms, and invoke the transitivity of "betweenness" to order the entire time-position domain for a piece. But this would be a purely formal exercise for us, since time-positions have no structural functions *in se,* so it represents no methodological or epistemic disadvantage to take the time-order relation as primitive.

For these "relative time" descriptions we infer "timeless" "order classes", whose *interpretations* are multivariable in total temporal size and in every aspect of temporal shape, as compositionally particular articulations at various levels of structure, from the duration of a "movement" to that of a "repeated section" (or a non-repeated one) to the relative durations of phraseological units of all kinds, as defined by the pitch content or content-classes into which the presented succession is multiply sliced by inference. The totality of these "temporal shape" descriptions *in conjunction with the descriptions of what they are the temporal shape of* is what is (or ought to be) called "rhythmic structure" (see Part IV).

I begin by listing the possible "persistence" relations among the boundaries of two pitch-times; the notation is informally introduced.

> Let $T((x)$ be "the time of initiation of x"
> Let $T(x))$ be "the time of termination of x"

(At this stage we could not consider these variably "persistence" *or* "endurance" relations for, without persistence, endurance is *syntactically* defined—e.g., by whether "registral succession" or "timbral succession", or some other dimension, is the, or a, structurally significant determinant of "displacement". Moreover, we could also not guarantee "endurance" on the basis of "persistence"; else how could a "tied note" *change pitch function* in a tonal piece, or *change order-position reference* in a twelve-tone one?)

> Then, if
> $T((x) = T((y) \equiv_{df}$ "the initiation of x is simultaneous with the initiation of y"
> and
> $T((x) < T((y) \equiv_{df}$ "the initiation of x is earlier than the initiation of y"
> then the list of possible order relations is:

1. /T((x) < T((y)/and/T(x)) < T((y)/
2. /T((x) < T((y)/and/T(x)) = T((y)/
3. /T((x) < T((y)/and/T((y) < T(x))/and/T(x)) < T(y))/
4. /T((x) < T((y)/and/T(x)) = T(y))/
5. /T((x) < T((y)/and/T(y)) < T(x))/

6, 7, 8, 9, 10, are derived from nos. 1–5 by substituting x for y and y for x.

11. /T((x) = T((y)/and/T(x)) < T(y))/
12. /T((x) = T((y)/and/T(x)) = T(y))/
13. /T((x) = T((y)/and/T(y)) < T(x))/

(This list is due primarily to Babbitt [3]; nos. 2 and 7, omitted there, are included here for completeness.)

In no. 11, x and y are *co-incidental*.
In nos. 1, 2, 6, and 7, x and y are *temporally disjunct*.
In nos. 3, 4, 5, 8, 9, 10, 12, and 13, x and y are *partially co-incidental*.

In general, music-syntactical systems create references for only *order of initiation* and *sonority content* at any given time. The aggregate of distinct pitch-function "tokens" coincidental in a given pitch structure S at a given moment t is the *sonority content of S at t*; while the totality of distinct pitch functions represented between times t_i and t_j in a pitch structure S is the *sonority content of the time-span* Ts(i, j). Since, in fact, a time point has no duration (i.e., there are an infinite number of possible time points t in any time-span interval and a time point has no "temporal thickness", or "size"), a "moment"—actually, a minimal discriminable time-span (on the model of "a pitch")—is the actual interpretation of "t" as a minimum time-span interval. Note the nonanalogous nature of this situation to that of pitch functions, for any of the infinite number of "specifiable" pitches, though not necessarily *distinguishable* from any other pitch at a remove less than that determining a "minimally discrete" adjacency, is still palpable, but *no* time point is, since it is "without thickness", whereas the perceptual correlate of a 'sine wave' is the "thinnest" pitch slice we need to consider. And we cannot, obviously, assert the "sonority content" of a "timespan without duration". So the *only* perceptual factors in time order are "time-spans". But there is, with respect to every S, also a maximal syntactical unit time-span $\perp'$ (on the "pitch-function" model), where "Ts(i, j) $\in \perp'$ " if if T(x) = i and T(y) = j then

$t = (j - i)$, or the *durational index* of Ts(i, j) is equivalent to t and t is a *time-span interval*. Let us, then, take as primitive "x is a moment" (as the designatum of Tm(x)), as well as T(x):

Df. 3.0: "the time-span (i, j)" ("Ts(i, j)")

(Strategy: A time-span is defined as a set of *moments*, including an *earliest* and a *latest* moment and all those in between.)

Df. 3.1: "the time-span interval t" ("$\bot(t)$")

(Strategy: A time-span is quantized as the *difference between* the integer assigned to its earliest and that assigned to its latest component moment.)

Df. 3.2: "t is the unit time-span (of an S)" ("$\bot'(t)$")

(Strategy: Time-span relations are proportional divisions of a finite total time-span, hence they are always representable as integer ratios, hence there must be a largest integer of which all time-spans within a given total time-span are multiples, and this integer is identified as the value of the *unit* time-span.)

Note the analogy here between $\bot'(t)$ and Γ_0', as well as the essential difference between them in both notation and definition, a difference which corresponds to the fact that since there is no "element identity" for *a time,* there is no "zero-class" time interval, and no "interval quality" for a time interval distinct from a proportional metric. Thus all time relations are expressible in terms of relations to the unit metric or its compounds, as (1:2), (2:3), etc. Such a unit time-span, however, may of course be the interpretation in an empirical presentation of the "time-point function" in a constructional system, just in that such a unit constitutes the minimum functional duration, hence the minimum duration between discrete timepoints, and perceivable smaller durational differences are not assumed to be proportionally measurable with precision or equivalent significance, but are regarded as articulative inflections of an associated unit time-span (as noted above).

APPENDIX (Sec. 14)

14*   Time-order primitives, order classes, and order relations

A.

Df. 3.0: $Ts(i, j) \equiv_{df} (\imath S)(\forall x (Tm(x) \wedge ((T(i) \leq T(x)) \vee (T(x) \leq T(j))) \supset x \in S))$.

("The timespan (i, j) is the S such that for all x, if x is a moment and the time of i coincides with or is earlier than the time of x, or the time of x coincides with or is earlier than the time of j, then x is within S.")

Df. 3.1: $\bot(t) \equiv_{df} (\imath Q)(\exists i \exists j ((i, j) \in Q \supset Ts(i, j) \wedge t = j - i))$.

("The timespan interval t is the Q such that there exists an i and there exists a j such that if (i, j) is a member of Q then (i, j) is a timespan and t is (j − i).")

Df. 3.2: $\bot^1(t) \equiv_{df} \bot(t) \wedge \forall s (\bot(s) \exists r (r = 1 \vee r = 2 \vee \ldots) \wedge t \cdot r = s) \wedge$
$\neg \exists q (\bot(q) \wedge (q = 1 \vee q = 2 \vee \ldots) \wedge q > t \wedge$
$\forall m (\bot(m) \exists p ((p = 1 \vee p = 2 \vee \ldots) \wedge q \cdot p = m)))$.

("t is the *unit timespan* (of an S) if t is a timespan interval and for all s such that s is a timespan interval there exists an r such that r is an integer and the product of t and r is s, and there does not exist a q such that q is a timespan interval and q is an integer larger than t and for all m such that m is a timespan there exists an integer p such that the product of q and p is m.")

B. Ordered sets and order classes

Df. 3.3: "S is an ordered pitch set" ("Π(S)")

Df. 3.4: "(x, y) and (z, t) are order-equivalent" ("Oi((x, y), (z, t))")

(Strategy (for Df. 3.3): This simply identifies a set whose members are order-number/pitch-number couples as an *ordered pitch set*. (For Df. 3.4): Where *n* is the number of members of an ordered pitch set S whose order numbers are less than the order number *x* of a given member of S (x, y), and if *m* is the number of the members of S whose order numbers are greater than *x*, then, if *a* is the number of order numbers of members of an ordered pitch set T that are less than the order number *z* of a member of T (z, t), and *b* is the number of order numbers of members of T greater than *z*, then, if a = n and b = m, then (x, y) and (z, t) occupy *order-identical* positions in S and T, respectively (and of course this entails that S and T have the same total number of members).)

Df. 3.5: "Δ is an order class" ("Oc(Δ)")

Df. 3.6: "Δ_0"

All earliest-time pitch members of ordered sets are members of the "Δ_0" order-equivalence class; accordingly, we assign order-number members of this class the value zero. The relevance of this order-identification of elements of different sets may be seen to go beyond its obvious application in "serial" music if we ever regard it as both recognizable and significant that in some piece some pitch succession S is not "identical to" some *later* pitch succession T, and that it is perceivable and significant that this non-identity occurs, let us say, even in a rather extensive and elaborate articulative complex, by virtue of the fact that in just one order-position of T there is a pitch that is different (to within total set transposition) from the pitch in the order-identical position in S. Thus, too, it may be a matter of considerable structural importance to notice what the pitch-intervals are between each order-position pair in some T and its corresponding order-position pair in S, especially since it is only thus that the fact that they are total transpositions of one another (should that be the case) is ascertainable. Thus, if for all ordered pitch-order couples in S, a uniform transposition is applied to the pitch elements with the order elements unchanged, to produce a pitch-order couple of T, then T and S are *ordered pitch transpositions* of one another (Df. 3.7):

Df. 3.7: "T is a mod-n ordered t-transposition of S" ("$T_{n,t}(S, T)$")

(Strategy: Where every pitch at a given order position in an ordered pitch set T is in the same pitch-class interval relation t (mod n) to the pitch at that order number in an ordered pitch set S, then T is an ordered transposition by t (mod n) of S.)

Obviously, if S is derived from another set Q by complementation, the ordering question is different; for where there does not exist a t such that S is an ordered t-transposition of Q, then there may still be a q such that S and Q are ordered q-complements of each other. First, however, let us note the trivial condition that if T is an ordered t-transposition of S, then S is an ordered (n − t)-transposition of T:

3.0:
Next, the definition of "ordered t-complements":

Df. 3.8: "T is the mod-n t-complement of S" ("$Cp_{n,t}(S, T)$")

APPENDIX (Sec. 14B)

14B*   Ordered sets and order classes

Df. 3.3: $\Pi(S) \equiv_{df} \forall x \forall y \forall z \forall t ((x, y) \in S \wedge (z, t) \in S \supset P(y) \wedge P(t) \wedge (x < z \sim T(y) < T(t)))$.

("S is an ordered pitch set if, for all x, y, z, and t, if (x, y) is a member of S and (z, t) is a member of S then y is a pitch and t is a pitch, and x is less than z iff the time of y is earlier than the time of t.")

Df. 3.4: $Oi((x, y), (z, t)) \equiv_{df} \forall S \forall T (\Pi(S) \wedge \Pi(T) \wedge (x, y) \in S \wedge (z, t) \in T \supset \forall(p, q) (((p < x) \wedge (p, q) \in S \supset \exists(r, s) ((r < z) \wedge (r, s) \in T)) \wedge ((p > x) \wedge (p, q) \in S \supset \exists(u, v) (u > z \wedge (u, v) \in T))))$.

("(x, y) and (z, t) are order-identical if, for all S and all T, if S and T are ordered pitch sets and (x, y) is a member of S and (z, t) is a member of T then for all (p, q), if p is less than x and (p, q) is a member of S then there exists an (r, s) such that r is less than z and (r, s) is a member of T and if p is greater than x and (p, q) is a member of x then there exists a (u, v) such that u is greater than z and (u, v) is a member of T.")

Df. 3.5: $Oc(\Delta) \equiv_{df} \forall x \forall y \forall z \forall t ((x, y) \in \Delta \wedge (z, t) \in \Delta \supset \exists S \exists T (\Pi(S) \wedge (x, y) \in S \wedge \Pi(T) \wedge (z, t) \in T \wedge Oi((x, y), (z, t))))$.

("Δ is an order class if for all x, y, z, t, if (x, y) is a member of Δ and (z, t) is a member of Δ then there exists an S and there exists a T such that S and T are ordered pitch sets and (x, y) is a member of S and (z, t) is a member of T and (x, y) and (z, t) are order identical.")

Df. 3.6: $\Delta_0 \equiv_{df} (\imath \varphi)(\forall(x, y) ((x, y) \in \varphi \sim \forall S (\Pi(S) \wedge (x, y) \in S) \neg\exists(z, t) ((z, t) \in S \wedge z < x)))$.

("Δ_0 is the φ such that for all (x, y), (x, y) is a member of φ iff for all S such that S is an ordered pitch set and (x, y) is a member of S there does not exist a (z, t) such that (z, t) is a member of S and z is less than x.")

Df. 3.7: $\text{Tr}_{n,t}(S, T) \equiv_{df} \forall x \forall y \, ((x, y) \in S \sim \exists z \exists w \, ((z, w) \in T \wedge (y \in a_i \supset w \in a_{i+t}) \wedge \forall \Delta_n \, ((x, y) \in \Delta_n \sim (z, w) \in \Delta_n)))$.

("T is a mod-n ordered t-transposition of S, if, for all x and all y, (x, y) is a member of S iff there exists a z and a w such that (z, w) is a member of T, and (iff) y is a member of the pitch class a_i iff w is a member of the pitch class a_{i+t}, and (x, y) and (z, w) are members of the same order class, where S and T are ordered pitch sets.")

3.0: $\text{Tr}_{n,t}(S, T) \sim \text{Tr}_{n,(n-t)}(T, S)$.

Df. 3.8: $\text{Cp}_{n,t}(S, T) \equiv_{df} \forall x \forall y \, ((x, y) \in S \sim \exists z \exists w \, ((z, w) \in T \wedge (y \in (a_i) \wedge \text{Pc}(a_i) \supset w \in a_{(t-i)}) \wedge \forall \Delta_n \, ((x, y) \in \Delta_n \sim (z, w) \in \Delta_n))) \wedge \Pi(S) \wedge \Pi(T)$.

3.1: $\text{Cp}_{n,t}(S, T) \sim \text{Cp}_{n,t}(T, S)$.

("T is the mod-n t-complement of S if, for all x and y, (x, y) is a member of S iff there exists a z and a w such that (z, w) is a member of T, and if y is a member of the pitch class a_i then w is a member of the pitch class $a_{(t-i)}$, and (x, y) and (z, w) are members of the same order-class, and S and T are ordered pitch sets.")

C. Order intervals, order transposition, and order complementation

Order transposition, called "rotation" in the literature relating to music whose principal syntactical bases are order-referential pitch sets, is actually more frequently a factor on the "articulative" levels of tonal, or other content-referential music, than in the structural background of, say, twelve-tone music, although some of the recent literature (see Babbitt [3], and Krenek, "Extent and Limits of Serial Technique", *The Musical Quarterly* [April 1960], and Rogers, "Some Properties of Non-duplicating Rotational Arrays", *Perspectives of New Music*, Vol. 7, No. 1 [1968]), indicates a considerable interest in its exploration on those levels as well. But in fact, the inference that a tonal tune and its texturally coincidental pitch successions and another, distinct such tune, and associated texture elsewhere in the same structure, are "content-equivalent", and that both are "permutations" of a given "background" content-set depends on the capacity to regard a given presented *or-*

dering of that content as an order-permutation of every other; for whether an analysis proceeds *from* the surface by inference or *to* the surface by construction, it is necessary at some point, on some levels, to account for the ordering of the "presented pitch surface" as well as more background successions. And thus a general permutational notation is essential, since (unlike "syntactical" operations) the relevant operations involved are the very things *most* particular to the individual composition (that is, when the ordering is of the "presented pitch successions"). By now, then, the point should be clear that in any *pitch*-syntactical systematic description of a musical structure, a time-ordering dimension is essential at every level beyond the elementary partitioning of the pitch domain by referential collections, constructs, intervals, etc.; as soon as *succession* is involved, as defined by a derived "model for succession" (as the 0-7 "harmonic model" of tonal music) or otherwise, *time* dependency is involved. And of course the elementary basis of order-referential music is usually given its interpreted identity through time-dependence. Thus we first give a definition for the general notion of an "order interval", then definitions of the "order-syntactical" operations of order transposition and order complementation, and finally a general definition of "T is a permutation of the ordered pitch collection S". This latter implies an unordered pitch collection X such that for all x such that if x is a pitch, and if, for all (z, t) such that (z, t) is a member of S implies that x is a member of the pitch class a_i only if t is a member of the same pitch class, there exists a (v, w) such that (v, w) is a member of T and for all a_j, t is a member of a_j implies that w is a member of a_j, then x is a member of X. Note that such observations are made only about sets of equivalent dimension. This seems a significant principle with respect to the notion of "structural levels", namely that sets on the same structural level must be of equivalent dimension (see Part III).

The first definition in this section is of "order interval", a relation which enables the representation of such "normal" observations as, "The first four notes of the tune in the oboe at measure 7 are the same [*sic*] as in the fifth through the eighth notes of the tune in the first violins at measure 10", a not infrequent sort of "foreground" observation that has analogs at many structural levels in tonal music, and plays a significant role in the more basic "compositional" operations of twelve-tone music (see Babbitt [3]).

Df. 4.0: "The order interval of (x, y) to (z, t)" ("(x, y) ○→ (z, t)")

If (x, y) is a member of S, and (z, t) is a member of T, and if S and T are equivalent sets, the order interval between (x, y) and (z, t) will also be a relation *within S;* e.g., if the dimension of S is 8, the order interval of the element with order number 6 to that with order number 3 is 5 (3 − 6 mod 8).

4.0: complementary nature of "(x, y) ○→ (z, t)" and "(z, t) ○→ (x, y)"

Next we define order transposition:

Df. 4.1: "T is a mod-q order-r-transposition of S" ("$Ot_r^q (S \to T)$")

(Strategy: If all and only the pitch elements of T are also pitch elements in S, and if the order number of each pitch element of T is r (mod q) greater than the order number of the same pitch element in S (where q is the highest order number in S plus 1) then T is an order transposition of S by r (mod q).)

4.1: complementary nature of "$Ot_r^q(S \to T)$" and "$Ot_r^q(T \to S)$"

Df. 4.2: "T is the retrograde (order complement) of S" ("$R(S \to T)$")

4.2: symmetricality of retrogression

Df. 4.3: "T is a permutation of S" ("$Op(S, T)$")

Aside from its manifestly important role in "serial" music, retrogression, like all the other order operations considered herein, has nontrivial applications in "tonal" music as well. For "pitch retrogrades" are necessarily inferable to explain some of the things we understand and regard as significant in traditional respects in connection with "tonal" musical structures. I am not speaking merely of "retrograde canons", but of any, however restricted—even just dyadic—order-compared sets, where it is considered both "perceivable" and significant that a particular relationship exists between, say, a presented set $\{(x_0, y), (x_1, z)\}$ and another presented succession $\{(x_n, z), (x_{n+1}, y)\}$. Here the "complementation" seems trivial, but its logic is consistently assertible as analogous to the assumption that obtains in "serial" music regarding "equivalence class" relatedness of elements in "complementary order positions". Thus, whether or not these order-operational rules actually function for sets of large dimension in any tonal-musical structure, the fact is that their construction requires no further definitional postulates than those necessary to account for order-recognitional characteristics normally regarded as significantly functional in tonal music at many structural levels. Thus, in "serial" music, their invocation may be regarded as the extension to a maximal functional range of relations operating in all music on lesser functional ranges. This idea is further elucidated in the sections to follow, but it does seem worthwhile to note here this indication of a broader shared assumptive basis for tonal and twelve-tone music than has perhaps been generally supposed.

APPENDIX (Sec. 14C)

14C*   Order intervals, order transposition, and order complementation

Df. 4.0: $(x, y) \circ \!\!\!\to (z, t) \equiv_{df} (\imath\, n)\, \{\forall S \forall T\, (\Pi(S) \wedge \Pi(T) \wedge (x, y) \in S \wedge (z, t) \in T \supset ((\forall a \forall b \forall c \forall d\, ((a, b) \in S \wedge (c, d) \in T \wedge \exists q\, (\forall \Delta_r\, (r \geq q \supset \neg((a, b) \in \Delta_r \vee (c, d) \in \Delta_r)))) \wedge ((x, y) \in \Delta_i \wedge (z, t) \in \Delta_j) \supset n = (i - j(\text{mod}\, q))))\}$.

("The order interval of (x, y) to (z, t) is the n such that for all S and all T, if S is an ordered pitch set and T is an ordered pitch set and (x, y) is a member of S and (z, t) is a member of T then if, for all a, b, c, d such that (a, b) is a member of S and (c, d) is a member of T there exists a q for all Δ_r such that if r is greater than or equal to q then neither (a, b) nor (c, d) is a member of Δ_r, and if (x, y) is a member of Δ_i and (z, t) is a member of Δ_j, then n is the difference mod q of j from i.")

4.0: $((x, y) \circ \!\!\!\to (z, t) = n) \sim ((z, t) \circ \!\!\!\to (x, y) = (q - n))$.

Df. 4.1: $Ot_r^q(S \circ \!\!\!\to T) \equiv_{df} \Pi(S) \wedge \Pi(T) \wedge \forall (x, y)\, ((x, y) \in S \supset \exists (z, t)\, [(z, t) \in T \wedge \forall a_i\, (Pc(a_i) \wedge (y \in a_i \sim t \in a_j)) \wedge \forall \Delta_j\, ((x, y) \in \Delta_j \sim ((z, t) \in \Delta_{j + r(\text{mod}\, q)}))\,]\wedge \forall (a, b)\, (((a, b) \in S \wedge (a, b) \in \Delta_{j-1}) \supset \forall k(k \geq j)\, \neg \exists (c, d)\, ((c, d) \in S \wedge (c, d) \in \Delta_k))\,] \supset q = j$.

("T is a mod q order-r-transposition of S if S and T are ordered pitch sets and for all (x, y) such that (x, y) is a member of S there exists a (z, t) such that (z, t) is a member of T and, for all a_i, a_i is a pitch class and y is a member of a_i iff t is a member of a_j, and for all Δ_j (x, y) is a member of (order class) Δ_j iff (z, t) is a member of (the order class) $\Delta_{j + r}(\text{mod}\, q)$; and, if for all (a, b), if (a, b) is a member of S and (a, b)

is a member of order class Δ_{j-1} then for all k such that k is equal to or greater than j there does not exist a (c, d) such that (c, d) is a member of S and (c, d) is a member of the order class Δ_k, then q is j.") (In other words, if the ith member of S is the last member of S, then q is i + 1.)

4.1: $\text{Ot}_r^q(S \circ\!\!\to T) \sim \text{Ot}_{q-r}^q(T \circ\!\!\to S)$.

Df. 4.2 (order complementation):

$R(S \to T) \equiv_{df} \Pi(S) \wedge \Pi(T) \wedge [\forall(x, y) ((x, y) \in S)$
$\exists(z, t) ((z, t) \in T \wedge \forall \Delta_i \,`((x, y) \in \Delta_i \sim (z, t) \in \Delta_{(r-i)}))\,] \wedge$
$\{[\forall(a, b) ((a, b) \in S \wedge (a, b) \in \Delta_j \supset \forall k \,(k > j)$
$\neg\exists(c, d) ((c, d) \in S \wedge (c, d) \in \Delta_k))\,] \supset r = j\}$.

("T is the *retrograde* of S if S is an ordered pitch set and T is an ordered pitch set and, for all (x, y) such that (x, y) is a member of S, there exists a (z, t) such that (z, t) is a member of T and for all order classes Δ_i, (x, y) is a member of Δ_i iff (z, t) is a member of $\Delta_{(r-i)}$ and if for all (a, b), if (a, b) is a member of S and (a, b) is a member of Δ_j then for all k where k is greater than j, there does not exist a (c, d) such that (c, d) is a member of S and (c, d) is a member of Δ_k, then r is j.")

4.2: $R(S \to T) \sim R(T \to S)$.

Df. 4.3: $\text{Op}(S, T) \equiv_{df} \exists X ((\forall y \,(y \in X \supset P(y))) \wedge \forall x \,(P(x) \wedge$
$\forall(z, t)\forall(a_i) ((z, t) \in S \wedge \text{Pf}(a_i) \supset (x \in a_i \supset t \in a_i))$
$\exists(v, w) ((v, w) \in T \wedge \forall a_j \,(t \in a_j \supset w \in a_j)) \supset x \in X))$.

15. CONCLUSION OF THE ALL-MUSICAL SYSTEM[*]

These definitions complete the sketch of the shared pitch-time basis for "all music", creating a "vocabulary" of relation-types from which, at this point, individual music-syntactical systems can be constructed. A key feature of these definitions that encourages the boldness of the claim of "all-musicality" advanced for them is that all the relations are described operationally, so that virtually all "actual" interpretations and quantizations are "open". This allows,

---

[*] (1995:) A second thought on the name "All-Musical System" was explicated in "The Logic of What?" (*Journal of Music Theory* Vol. 33, No. 1, Spring 1989); here is an excerpt from note 4: "[As to the construct called "The All-Musical System":] This title is, as I subsequently perceived, significantly misleading; I am sure it

for example, for the identification as "music" under our system of compositions having different pitch-interval quantizations, different "octaves"—or none at all (in which case they would have no "registral" dimension, since their modular interval would just be the largest possible one in the system, and every "pitch class" would have just one member). Neutrality is also maintained regarding the dimensioning of the pitch domain itself (what constitutes "a pitch", a "pitchband", etc.). And note that only operations on the "total pitch domain" of any composition are engaged here, the *referential,* or "syntactical" basis being left for the actual construction of syntactical systems, a restriction which is again advantageous in providing ample room for common reference for systems of widely disparate structure—e.g., the common "twelve-tone" basis of tonal and twelve-tone music is derivable at this level without systematic bias toward either.

---

had misled even good readers into confusions concerning its interpretation (see, for example, Jay Rahn's *A Theory For All Music*). The 'universality' of the definiential ascension-structure which is described in this section purports to lie explicitly in the *openness* of the space it creates for the invention of sound-materializations of the attributing predicates it defines. Significantly: this openness to creative interpretation is absolutely autonomous for *each* distinct act of musical entification; no such act is *systematically*—in principle—contingent upon any other (however so contingent it may be on account of the psychological conditioning and experiential history of any particular individual). What is specified for each defined predicate is precisely and exclusively a *sense* which may be attached (attributed) to an acoustical signal whereby it is heard as a particular sound, a sense which I considered to be a meaningful and intuitive sub-literal reading of its given name (as, for example, 'interval'); and there is also specified a *structure* of such senses such that each derives its (logical as well as epistemic) intelligibility from the sense in which it 'reinterprets' its (lower-order) predecessors within the global structure. But no *one* global *interpretation* of the structural universe (that is, no interpretation which might characterize some single musical instance) compromises the interpretive liberty of any other, from top to bottom; thus the system never actually refers to 'all' music in any univocal sense, but rather—crucially and explicitly—to '*any*' music. And thus it is only in the sense of holding for any music that the system offers itself as holding for "all" music, so it should, clearly, have been named accordingly: "The Any-Musical System"."

V.
Part III:
Systematic and Extrasystematic Preconditions for the Construction of Musical Syntax

1. THE NOTION OF REFERENCE

In the absence of lexical or conventional referents for the ordering of musical elements in a "semantically interpreted" structure, the construction of coherent musical entities depends on a contextually inferable referential basis. Such dependence requires that it be possible to *distinguish among* individual musical things, and to distinguish classes of such things, on no more elaborate a *prior* basis than that on which those things are just *identified as* musical things in the first place. If our subject were (verbal) language, the claim that the above requirement could be met would amount to a claim that given only notions of what "language" was, of the kind of data that was pertinent to the construction of "linguistic entities", and of the varieties of identity and function designable for linguistic entities, it would be possible to *infer* from the perceptual quality-patterns of successions of sounds and/or inscriptions associated with any "linguistic utterance" the particular vocabulary and syntax through which to interpret the "meaning" and "structure" of that utterance—i.e., to *distinguish* it as a *particular* linguistic individual. Thus "English", while it would be a cognitively designable stage in the definiential ascension from "language" to "this utterance", would no longer be an *essential* stage to account for by the introduction of new assumptions and conventions, since all the essential characteristics of "this utterance" would be determinable through construction on the original primitives without the mediate intervention of a conventional English dictionary and grammar.

This designability but non-essentiality of a crucial linguistic "stage" is, of course, unavailable in verbal language, at least presently, but the analogous stages of determination in music, i.e., of "tonal", "12-tone", etc. determination, do present such a methodological superfluity; they are *convenient* but not *essential* stages to distinguish explicitly in the construction of individual musical entities. And thus musical structures do seem rather special among "linguistic-type" entities (see Part I, p. 69ff.); for their entire "meaning" or, to be less fanciful, their significative relations, and the determinations of complexity and coherence that measure their "cognitive contents", can be derived solely from the conceptually guided processing of such "musically basic" information as the perceived patterns of difference among the qualia of individual auditory concreta in associated successions, and of *degrees* and *kinds* of difference among sub-complexes of such concreta inferred from ("sliced out of") the total succession. The degree to which a musical structure approaches *maximal* coherence (i.e., maximal individuality) is proportionate to the degree to which the metrically determinate data are multiply exhausted by such slicings, as members of sets of interrelated "relation-class" extensions. Such sets, in most "western" music, are understood as tracing "paths through the data" whose totality presumably constitutes "the musical structure".

The kinds of information processed in the pitch-time dimensions, and the fundamental relations in terms of which the processing takes place conceptually-perceptually, are the subjects of the second part of this essay. The present section begins at the point where the general ("universal musical") *resources* of relation are marshaled into interconnected sets of particular relational syntactical *functions*. Through such functions, ultimately, maximally coherent individual structures may be constructed (or reconstructed) as particular orderings—in particular sequences and multiplicities—of particular values of these functions in particular (quantized) empirical interpretations. There is, thus, compositional "latitude" up to this last, "notational" stage—and beyond that there is latitude in the "articulative" decisions of "interpretative performance" which have to do with determining what happens in perceptual dimensions whose most minute distinguishable aspects of identity, similitude-differentiation, or proportionality are not considered to be *syntactically* determinate or determining.

The room for "choice" at every level of the construction, both in concrete interpretation and in more formal determinations—even well below the first "syntactical" stages—seems to evidence that maximum determinacy in every dimension of structure is a prerequisite for maximum "creative freedom", if that is considered to be significative only when what is "created" is "something". For the "freedom" to create and perceive vacuously is hardly to be preferred to a completely conventionalized "determinacy", where the "rules" are not *chosen* but *given* (in both composition and audition); in both cases the "musical individual" is severely circumscribed in the degree to which it can be perceived as "individual" or is even "identifiable" at all, by precisely the degree to which its perceivables are determinably interpretable, in the first case, and contextually interpretable, in the second. For to the extent to which a "lexical-conventional" predetermination is brought to musical structures, they are merely "representative" ("in a language"), and, as such, non-particular. Hence, no "ideas" emerge except *above* the highest such lexical-conventional level. But without references for the consistent measurement of similitudes and differentia at all, no "characteristics" can emerge either, except in the most general dimensions (such as the dimensions that seem to be principally functional in some recent music, by, e.g., Penderecki and Xenakis) where the metricizations are restricted to aspects of sonic perception not conceptually unique to music, as (grossly) "louder-softer", "denser-thinner", etc., dimensions which in maximally determinate music are merely part of the articulative surface *through* which the structurally relevant paths through pitch complexes are extended.

Thus, since our music is largely pitch-structural music, the most favorable central referents for most of its instances are single, particular partitionings of the pitch domain. The "singleness" of such partitionings is, of course, fundamental to our notion of "total structure", a notion which is expressed implicitly any time we speak of a piece as "the piece" or anything that characterizes it as "*a* thing". Such partitionings, in existing musical systems, make possible a hierarchization of relations and their relations which, in the most fertile of such systems, also makes it possible to overlap the pitch domain manifoldly in terms of determinate relations at *hierarchically distinct levels* (generating the "distinct meanings" for the "same relations" referred to above). Thus a musical syntax is essentially a model for the determination of the interlocking structure of hierarchically connected relations through which the range of significations of a discriminable set of data can be interpreted. The more "efficient" the model, the larger the number of distinct and unambiguously determinate relational functions that can be inferred from a single datum-succession. This standard of unambiguousness, however, is often misunderstood; without dwelling on the point, I suggest consideration of the essential difference between *unambiguous multivalence* in which an event has multiple "meanings", simultaneously cotenable and perceivable but not "identical", and *ambiguity,* where it is not determinable whether any one particular relational "meaning", of a given nature, is significantly ("meaningfully", determinably) ascribable to the event in question .

And since there are two principal bases for the construction of a partitioning referential set, and it turns out that these are mutually incompatible, it is just here that our system experiences its first major "fork". The imperatives that underlie this divergence are the subject of the sequel.

2. CONTENT-CENTRICITY AND ORDER-DETERMINACY

Given that a presented pitch collection may be perceptually identified in terms of three factors, *dimension* ("number of token-slots"), *content* ("identity and relation of distinct element-types [i.e., things representable by distinct primitive symbols] represented by the totality of element-tokens"), and the *order* of the content-tokens, it is evidently possible to rest a pitch-syntactical system on the discriminative basis of either of the latter two (the first, dimension, alone could function as a primary referent only in a non-pitch-based musical syntax since it cannot be used to take into account pitch identities and relations, and therefore the identities of the partitioning sets within any sound-presentational array would have to be determined by other means than their pitch aspects). Consider, for example, the pitch succession (however interpreted) (A-A-B♭-A). If *token dimension* alone were determinate, we would have as the identity of this set just the quantity 4, as the "number of slots" in the set:

$$(x_0, x_1, x_2, x_3)$$

If, however, we define *content* to within just pitch identity/nonidentity, we obtain the result:

$$(x, x, y, x)$$

by which we can assert *distinct content dimension* (2, as (x, y)); *order* of content representation (x-y-x); *dimension* of primitive-symbol multiplicity (3x, 1y); and finally, order of distributed tokens (x-x-y-x).

If, further, the token-referents are intervallically *quantized*, it is further possible to assert relations among the elements, as:
1. content = (0, 1) (where x = 0, y = 1)
2. order of content = (0 1 0)
3. content-token order = (0 0 1 0)

As far as *interpretation* is concerned:

1. At the *dimension*-determinate level (A-A-B♭-A) is music-ontologically equivalent to any four-token pitch set.

2. At the *content-dimension*-determinate level, any sets of whatever dimension or order whose tokens are all tokens of one of exactly two distinct pitch elements, such that there is at least one token in each set of each pitch element, are equivalent. Thus (A-A-B♭-A) = (C-F-F-C-C-F-C). (2a.) With token-dimension determinacy added to content-dimension determinacy (A-A-B♭-A) = (C-C-C-F).

3. With *content-identity* determinacy, any two sets representing just two distinct pitch elements related by the interval 1, each of the elements of which may be mapped into an element of the other by the identity operation, are equivalent. Where the latter mapping is not by the identity operation but by the addition of or subtraction from a given integer, such two sets are transpositionally or inversionally equivalent, respectively. Thus, in the first case (A-A-B♭-A) = (B♭-B♭-A-B♭-B♭-A-A); and in the second (or the third) case (A-A-B♭-A) = (C-B-B-C-B). (3a.) Where token-dimension determinacy is added to content-identity determinacy (A-A-B♭-A) = (B♭-A-A-A).

4. At the *order-of-content*-determinate level, any two sets of any token-dimensions in which the first tokens are tokens of the same pitch element, and the next distinct pitch elements represented are the same in both sets, etc., are equivalent. Thus (A-A-B♭-A) = (A-B♭-B♭-A-A). (4a.) With token-dimension determinacy added to order-of-content determinacy (A-A-B♭-A) = (A-A-B♭-A). Transpositionally and inversionally related sets are processible as transformationally equivalent under this condition, also.

Thus we may speak of content-determinate pitch systems (or content-referential, or content-generative, systems), and order-determinate pitch systems, noting that where order is syntactically determinate this involves a more complicated referential basis than where content alone is, since "order" is not independent, but a referential ordering of the content of a pitch set.

But what do we mean by "syntactical system" or "syntactical function"? And how are "content" and "order" inferred as "bases" of musical structures? Briefly, this is what is meant: if a particular "slice" made of auditory experience consists of an ordered array of pitch events, a "musical structure" may be inferred as the global interpretation of this array by means of a series of more local partitions of the array into proper subsets of pitches (or even into just a single subset equivalent to the whole, but that is in one respect a trivial and in another respect a nonstandard instance). These partitionings are not necessarily limited by temporal adjacency; and all partitionings of the actual pitch data are conceived in terms of some inferred partitioning of the pitch or the pitch-class domain which functions as a unitary referent (in dimension and content, or dimension, content, and order) for every partitioning subset of the presented array. Reference to this referent is enabled through inference of a delimited set of mapping functions (e.g., "transposition") by means of which the "isomorphism" of the array-partitioning sets to the referential set and to one another can be asserted. The sequences in which such mapping functions are applied, and the rationale through which their successive applications are interrelated, maximally specifying the characteristics of the presented array in terms of the referential *aspect* (dimension, content, or order) of the referential *collection* (thus maximally determining the partitioning subsets, or, rather, producing a maximum hierarchically ordered set of subset-types in which adjacent types are minimally distinct, whose least member is as close to having a monadic content as possible, and in terms of each of which the entire presented succession can be ordered), can be considered the "structure" of the composition; and whatever is chosen as the "background" system of hierarchies, functions, and relations may be considered the syntax, and the hierarchies, functions and relations themselves may be considered *syntactical* ones.

Retrospectively, then, the definitions of Part II can be regarded as a hierarchized specification of basic relations and functions by means of which the references for any pitch-syntactical system can be constructed. We have, in turn, specified content operations and order operations and shown them to be conceptually and formally analogous (that is, we have seen that "transposition", "complementation", and "partition" are analogously operative on both content and order). But here we need to consider what general concepts can be explicated as the cognitive dimensions in terms of which observable content- and order-differentia function to produce references for syntactical functions.

When we talk of "partitioning subsets" and their interlocking interrelations as "defined" by referential (unordered or ordered) sets of primitive elements and "rules of relation", what we are talking about is comparison: comparison of such subsets to others of the same subset-type level, in terms of their constituent proper subsets (of, in turn, the same [subset-of-subset]-type levels), as well as in terms of their relative time-order positions.[1] Thus when we speak of "content-determinate" systems we mean systems such that the *primary* basis of subset comparison determined by them (that is, the basis for comparison of subsets whose content- [or token-] dimension is equivalent to that of the principal reference set, which thus begins with comparison at the most "background" structural level but is not limited to it) is the measurement of content intersection, both of its *degree* (amount), and its *nature* (relational content). These two factors are then interpreted as the determinants of the degree of "P"-similitude exhibited by compared subsets, for some "P" such that "P" is a relevant "syntactical function" within S. (There may be several independent, or interdependent, functional predicates substitutable for "P", as, e.g., "interval similitude", "pitch-element similitude", "token-dimension-per-pitch-element similitude", etc.)

Now to determine degree of simple pitch-element similitude only identity, number, and position of discrete element-types within subsets to be compared need be defined, as:

$$A = \{a_0, a_1, ..., a_i\}$$
$$B = \{b_0, b_1, ..., b_j\}$$

---

[1] What constitute boundary conditions for membership in a given subset-type cannot be stipulated independently of contextual determination, just as the referential aspect of the referential set is not uniquely determinable from an examination of the contents of the set itself, alone. Even the relevant dimension-limitation is not determinable independently of context. Thus, for example, at some levels of some composition in some syntactical system (C, D, C) and (C, D) may be members of the same subset-type, while at some other level of the same composition (not to mention some other composition in the same syntax or in a different syntax) they may not be members of the same subset type.

$$C = \{c_0, c_1, ..., c_k\}$$
$$D = \{d_0, d_1, ..., d_l\}$$

For any pitch-structure S, where A is the reference set for S, and B and C are proper subsets of S, if B and C are *primary subsets* of S (at their respective structural levels), then all the tokens of B as well as all those of C represent distinct element-types and $i = j = k$, or (in a relatively weaker system) there are in A, B, and C the same number of distinct elements. (If token-dimension alone were stipulated as the relevant "syntactical criterion", its capacity to function as such would depend just on the satisfaction of the condition that the primitive elements were all of the same general type, e.g., "all pitches", etc.) Now for a structure to be content-determinate, the subsets regarded as discrete within it must be comparable (and differentiable in varying degrees and ways) on the basis of their element-type content. Thus if we know only that

$$\begin{array}{ll} b_0 = w & c_0 = x \\ b_1 = x \quad \text{and} & c_1 = y \\ b_2 = y & c_2 = z \\ b_3 = z & c_3 = t \end{array}$$

and $j = 3$ and $k = 3$ (i.e., $B = \{w, x, y, z\}$ and $C = \{x, y, z, t\}$)[2] then, without knowing anything about the quantized interpretations of w, x, y, z, t (except for the condition $w \neq x \neq y \neq z \neq t$, or, w, x, y, z, t are *distinct*), we can content-compare the sets as follows:

$$\begin{array}{l} B \cup C = \{w, x, y, z, t\} \\ B \cap C = \{x, y, z\} \\ B - C = \{w\} \\ C - B = \{t\} \\ B + C = \{w, t\} \end{array}$$

and, of course, $\wp(B)$ and $\wp(C)$ will have the same dimension and:

$\wp(B) = \{ \{ \}, \{w\}, \{x\}, \{y\}, \{z\}, \{w, x\}, \{w, y\}, \{w, z\}, \{x, y\}, \{x, z\}, \{y, z\}, \{w, x, y\}, \{w, x, z\}, \{w, y, z\}, \{x, y, z\}, \{w, x, y, z\} \}$

---

[2] I.e., dimension of B = dimension of C; thus, while the "reference set" defines just the referential-aspect dimension of compared subsets of "primary degree", here that referential-aspect dimension (i.e., distinct element-type dimension) is, in fact, identical with the *token-dimensions* of the members of the particular array of "primary-degree" subsets.

℘(C) = { { }, {x}, {y}, {z}, {t}, {x, y}, {x, z}, {x, t}, {y, z}, {y, t}, {z, t}, {x, y, z}, {x, y, t}, {x, z, t}, {y, z, t}, {x, y, z, t} }
and:
  ℘(B) ∩ ℘(C) = { { }, {x}, {y}, {z}, {x, y}, {x, z}, {y, z}, {x, y, z} }
  ℘(B) − ℘(C) = { {w}, {w, x}, {w, y}, {w, z}, {w, x, y}, {w, x, z}, {w, y, z}, {w, x, y, z} }
  ℘(C) − ℘(B) = { {t}, {x, t}, {y, t}, {z, t}, {x, y, t}, {x, z, t}, {y, z, t}, {x, y, z, t} }
  ℘(B) + ℘(C) = { {t}, {w}, {w, x}, {w, y}, {w, z}, {x, t}, {y, t}, {z, t}, {w, x, y}, {w, x, z}, {w, y, z}, {x, y, t}, {x, z, t}, {y, z, t}, {w, x, y, z}, {x, y, z, t} }

Similar observations could be made regarding the number and content of all possible subsets of S of the given reference-aspect dimension (since the *reference* dimension is regarded as defining the reference-aspect dimension of a *maximum* relevant subset of S; all larger subsets are "described" as multiple representations of such a subset or "compositions" of several such subsets, as: {w, x, y, z, t} may be "understood" as B ∪ C, etc., but not as a potentially primary "syntactical" subset in itself), within the total set S (the total pitch array). S itself is thus always describable as one instance of a succession of instances of the reference set (i .e., of defined transformations of the reference set); each such description occupies a "structural level", and a consequentially ordered succession (or "nest") of such descriptions constitutes "the structure" of the S in question.

If the element types are quantizationally interpreted as, e.g., pitch classes, then the reference set may specify not only token- and content-dimension but also content-*relation*; and operations may be defined, for any two subsets of a given syntactically relevant subset-type, to determine their content-relational isomorphism.[3,4]

---

[3] These operations, like every theoretical term defined on a set of primitives in a system, serve to reduce the number of distinct vocabulary elements by asserting functional correlations for classes of such elements. Thus every sound-token in an array must be taken as a distinct pitch element before the assertion of the property of *pitch identity,* which reduces the number of distinct element types by its application. Similarly, before *interval identity is* asserted, every distinct pitch pair is a "different interval" (since interval is just "the relational entity determined by two pitches"). Again, reduction in vocabulary (distinct interval types) and increase in functionality (multiple possible [distinguishable] interpretations of

Thus, in our present example, we can describe not only the *degree* (amount) of pitch intersection, but the identity (pitch content) thereof, though not its relational nature (interval content):

$$
\begin{aligned}
\text{if } B - C &= \{w\} \\
\text{and } C - B &= \{t\} \\
\text{and } \qquad D &= \{v, w, x, y\} \\
\text{so that } B - D &= \{z\} \\
\text{and } D - B &= \{v\} \\
\text{and } C - D &= \{z, t\} \\
\text{and } D - C &= \{v, w\}
\end{aligned}
$$

then we can assert a hierarchy of "degrees of closeness" and one of "kinds of closeness" among B, C, and D. If A is the reference set, and A is $\{u, v, w, x\}$, then we can also assert "closeness to A", defined as the inverse of "difference from A". So if E is a *presented* subset in S, and E = $\{u, v, w, x\}$, then

$$
\begin{aligned}
A - E &= \{\ \} \\
\text{and } A &\sim E.
\end{aligned}
$$

---

each type, and functional independence, for each pitch pair, of its pitch-vocabulary "meaning" and its interval-vocabulary "meaning") result. Further, interval vocabulary is again reduced by interval-class correlation (mod-n—"octave"—equivalence) and then by complementary-interval-class ("inversional") correlation, and pitch vocabulary is reduced by pitch-class formation, generated out of interval-class correlation. Thus, the operations of transposition and complementation on complexes of pitches and intervals similarly reduce the "distinct set type" vocabulary and increase the functional range of each set type (i.e., enable us to regard *distinct sets* as *distinct instances of single set types);* and they do so by extending the same principles of interval and interval-class identity (for transposition) and interval-class-complement correlation (for inversion) through which the basic vocabulary of musical elements was reduced by the elaboration of the basic vocabulary of musical functions at the most general levels of their definition (see Part II, above).

[4] In the tonal system, *transposition is* the only *necessary* such operation, but *complementation is* also *significative* at every level, even though every complementation of the diatonic collection is describable as a transposition thereof (T7I of a "major" collection produces the "tonic minor" T3S, while the "dominant" and "subdominant" collections are produced by the "complementary transpositions" T7S and T5S, respectively. The T7I-T0S relation (particularly in view of the interval (7) of complementation involved) is especially significant in our later view of the "major"- and "minor"-oriented generations of the diatonic collection as inversionally symmetrical).

In this case, we can "map" E into A by an *identity* operation. But we have no way of mapping B, C, or D into A or into each other; for our specification tells us only of the *identity*-nature of the intersection, not its *relation*-nature; for {u, v, w, x, y, z, t} could be *any* pitches.
Thus,

if u = 0, v = 3, w = 4, x = 6, y = 8, z = 9, t = 1,
then A = {0, 3, 4, 6}
B = {4, 6, 8, 9}
C = {6, 8, 9, 1}
D = {3, 4, 6, 8}
E = {0, 3, 4, 6},

all the relations described above still hold, even though there is no transposition that will map any two nonidentical sets into one another. When complementation is added, B = T0I (D)[5], but no similar relation exists among any other pair, even though they can clearly be ranked in *"degree"* -*of-intersection hierarchy with respect to A*:

A = {0, 3, 4, 6}
1. E = {0, 3, 4, 6}   ("0 different")
2. D = {3, 4, 6, 8}   ("1 different")
3. B = {4, 6, 8, 9}   ("2 different")
4. C = {6, 8, 9, 1}   ("3 different")

And each could be a "reference set" for a similar arrangement of the others; also the "*identities* of the *differences*" could order an array even where more than one set had an equivalent *amount* of difference from the reference:

if F = {11, 0, 3, 4}   ("1 different")
G = {10, 11, 0, 3} ("2 different")
H = {7, 10, 11, 0} ("3 different")

then the "array with respect to A" would look as follows:

---

[5] T0I(D) = "The transposition-zero set of the mod-n complement set of D".

[6] Here the "identities of difference from A" are associated with relative amounts of intersection among the sets being compared to A; hence the "linearity" of the

for	F − D = {11, 0}	("2 elements different")
and	D − F = {6, 8}	
while	D − C = {3, 4}	("2 elements different")
and	C − D = {9, 1}	

so that "number of places away from N along the array" is equivalent to "number of elements different from N"; in particular, "number of places away from E in the array" is an index of "number of elements different from A (the reference set)". But *direction,* or *relative direction* away from E along the array yields no additional information about "content relation to A", but only about the content-intersection relations among the sets along each "directional vector".

But if Tt(x) = (x + t) (transposition) and Ir(x) = (r − x) (complementation) such that x is a pitch-class element number and t ranges over the domain defined by the totality of pitch-class element numbers, are admitted as syntactical ("f-") operations, then only D and B, and G and H have assertible f-relations to one another; but there exists no possible reference set such that *both pairs* have the relation to it. In other words, there is no t such that Tt or Ir + Tt will map D or B *into* G or H (where r = 12); for if there were any such t, there would be at least one possible reference set K such that D, B, G, and H could all be mapped into K by various Tt or Ir + Tt operations, and the relations of D, B, G, and H to one another could be characterized in terms of such a *relation to a common reference.*

In such comparability of all primary subsets of an S by means of such a "relation to a common reference" rests the *centricity* of the reference set that is inferred for a content-determinate system. The *degree of content determinacy* defined by such a system depends on the extent to which the reference set is (or can

---

array. If, for example, there were a set I whose contents were {2, 0, 3, 4}, it would create a new "path", which might or might not "join" one of the other paths at some point:

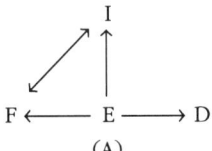

(A)

be) regarded as being *isomorphically partitioned* by, successively, subsets of decreasing dimension, where the subsets of the reference set determined by such partitionings are also regarded as "syntactical"—i.e., normative for every instance of the reference set at every level of the structure.[7] The reference set, thus, may be regarded as *generated by* the conjunction of sets at the immediately preceding subset-type level. This latter "ordering" is essential if *all* subsets so arrived at are to be regarded as "syntactically significant".

Thus the *minimum* degree of content determinacy is *collection centricity*, or determinacy of content of the reference collection taken as a whole. This is the necessary and sufficient condition for *primary content determinacy* of a syntax. Next are the various degrees of *construct centricity*, i.e., the inferences of complex subsets (constructs that are regarded as "normatively" [i.e., for all of a piece] generating or partitioning the reference collection isomorphically; e.g., the *triad* as a three-element generator of the diatonic collection, the "fifth" as a two-element partitioning thereof whose own (4 + 3) partitioning generates the triad, then the octave itself as partitioned by the fifth, and then the unit pitch domain as partitioned by the referential octave).[8] So we have, in order of weaker to stronger determinacy:

---

[7] Hence they would define *subset types* relevant to every structural level, though not accounting for all subset types appearing at all structural levels (except in the unlikely case where the "syntax" and the "structure" were totally indistinguishable, a situation which is logically possible [as a territory is a map of itself] but practically undesirable since it would represent as a "general relation" everything assertible about a particular piece, with nothing in that piece designated as constituting a particular interpretation chosen from a range of possibilities constrained by the general relation).

[8] Thus the "pitch centricity" of the "tonal system" seems to be an important aspect of it even presystematically (despite, e.g., Randall's attempt, now withdrawn, to generate it noncentrically), one that seems strongly inferable from the Schenkerian model, for example. Although the diatonic collection (even as triadically partitioned) does not itself "predetermine" or "presuppose" pitch or construct centricity, nor, obviously, need it be generated by an initially pitch-centric or construct-centric approach, nor, equally, *need* it function *only* in a pitch-centric context (it seems likely that there are instances in late 19th-century Russian music, perhaps in Debussy, and probably in Stravinsky [see example below] of pieces most favorably regarded as having combinational diatonic-collection, even triad, centric, but non-pitch-centric syntaxes), I think it essential to the maximization of congruities among the relations between the ultimately

collection centricity (determining the membership of an element or a relation in the reference collection; the range of memberships of an element or a relation in the member collections in the "syntactical array" determined by the reference set; and the range of "within-collections" and "between-collections" relationships determined by any pair or larger complex of elements);

construct centricity (ordering the elements of the reference collection in terms of "within a construct" and "between constructs" relations, and possibly [but not necessarily] hierarchizing the constructs with respect to a "central" construct regarded as generating "subsidiary" constructs through defined transformations, such that the union of central and subsidiary constructs generates the reference set. At this level, each construct [or "*the* construct"] is not regarded as "internally ordered" or hierarchized, but just as a *complex* of discriminably distinct components); (*sub-construct centricities* of dimension-degrees less than the dimensions of the principal collection-partitioning construct, equal to or greater than a dyad; these sub-constructs may be regarded as implying a hierarchization within the principal constructs such that the smaller the sub-construct dimension, the more primary its hierarchical position within the principal construct, on the one hand, and the less uniquely it determines [i.e., the less completely it specifies] the total content of the principal construct, on the other);

---

available properties of a collection (as actually engaged) and the generating basis inferred for it and (perhaps) extended beyond it in the "system" that the *functionally primary* elements and relations be as far as possible *systematically prior* as well. This would insure that the collection—as constructed, or reconstructed—has the relevant hierarchization "built in", as it were, to its "conceptual scheme", as represented by the sequence and nature of its construction. Thus we will want to construct secondary individuals as complexes (or subsets) of primary ones (or their subsets); and we will also want to redefine basic relations with respect to their syntactical functions within the system. Thus, for example, after our construction of the diatonic collection we can construct, by repeated application of the notion of adjacency, the "normal-form" representation, or scale, after which we can define, for essential syntactic reasons, the notion of "scale-degree interval", whence the "conventional" interval terminology arises as a *particular* syntactical interpretation of constructs which have more general (i.e., pitch-class-relational) names as well. It is this scale-degree-syntactical aspect that accounts for the fact that there are "particular" intervals of, theoretically, any general-interval size, and that the frequent use of the scale-degree interval terminology in descriptions of nontonal music (or at least non-diatonic-collectional) music is generally so awkward.

pitch (monadic) centricity (the strongest degree of content determinacy, comprising an ordering and hierarchization of the least-discriminable elements themselves, in terms of their defined relations to a single, referential, such element).

Thus one could perhaps explain much post-tonal "diatonic" music as collection, or even construct, centric, without also regarding it as pitch centric. Thus, e.g., a hexachordal segment of the diatonic collection is partitioned in Stravinsky's *Petrouchka* first in terms of the "dyadic construct" (0 2):

T0S: (0 2) (5 7) (9 11)/(5 7) (0 2) (8 10) : T7I (0 = "D")

but later in terms of the "triadic construct" (047/037):

(10 2 5) (8 0 3) : T3S

which suggests a local construct centricity but a global ("syntactical") centricity at the collectional level only.

Now, with respect to order-determinacy, the necessary and sufficient condition for its implementation is that sets be comparable in terms of the variable *orderings* they determine on a given set of elements (i.e., that all sets be transformable into all others by operations on *order* positions alone). This requires a dyadic interpretation of the elements of every presented set:

$A = \{a_{x, y}, a_{z, v}, ..., a_{m, n}\}$ where for all $a_{i, j}$, i is order position and j is a (relative) pitch-class number. Then, of course, the same observations hold for the amount of order-determinacy possible, given only identity-or-nonidentity-of-order-position information, which becomes more determinate under position-relational quantization ("order-class relations") and still more determinate under durational interpretation (perhaps like the relation of pitch class to registrally determinate pitch).

In every system (i.e., for every pitch-time structure) we can speak of the degree of order-determinacy relative to the degree of content-determinacy, and note that they are never co-operative at the same levels. The corollary of this is that, by extension, no system can be both content-determinate and order-determinate *primarily*. A demonstration of this assertion is offered in the Appendix to this section.

But first, it should be noted that the progression collection centric/construct centric/element centric has its analog in order-determinate systems as:

1. determinacy of collection-order (i.e., "12-content" aggregates as "partitions" of the pitch-class domain: chromatic completion)
2. determinacy of segment order, for segments of various dimensions, as:
  2 (internally unordered) hexachords
  3 (internally unordered) tetrachords
  4 (internally unordered) trichords
  6 (internally unordered) dyads
  12 monads,

the last constituting the maximum degree of order-determinacy. Note the analogy to our *Petrouchka*-vs-tonal music divergence in the fact that not all 12-tone music that is locally monadically determinate is globally so determinate (i.e., determinate in the same way for any segment larger than one reference set). Our ability to discover the minimum level of order-determinacy that does function globally should enable us to fix for each such piece the level of order-determinacy relative to the (internal) *level of content-determinacy*. Similarly, for tonal pieces, order of presented pitches is an essential operative factor, but, like content-determinacy in 12-tone pieces, it functions at a less globally determinate level than the deepest level at which content-determinacy operates.

2a. APPENDIX

The following demonstration illustrates the nature of the relation, for any array of sets, between content- and order-determinacy, and indicates why in music interpreted as unfolding within a twelve-pitch-class octave, the "12-tone system", to varying degree of contextual determination as to whether it is representable in given instances as "1", "2", "3", "4", "6", or "12"-determinate, is the only possible primary order-determinate syntax (to within interpretation of "order" as "registral order" or "temporal order", and where Tt and Ir remain the only relevant syntactical operations):[9]

Syntactical Operations (rules of transformation):

If A is a set, and (x, y) is a member of A, then

1. $[(((f0_q(x)), y) = (z, t)) \supset (z, t) \in PqA]$

---

[9]Although the relations also maintain to within various segmental determinations under the "M"-operations so called and described in Winham [41], and variously named in Howe [16], and Forte [15].

2. [(((f1$_q$(x)), y) = (z, t)) ⊃ (z, t) ∈ RqA]
3. [(((x, (f0$_q$(y))) = (z, t)) ⊃ (z, t) ∈ TqA]
4. [(((x, (f1$_q$(y))) = (z, t)) ⊃ (z, t) ∈ IqA]
where   f0$_i$(x) = (x + i) (mod (s + 1))
and   f1$_i$(x) = (i − x) (mod (s + 1))
and   f0$_i$(y) = (y + i) (mod (w + 1))
and   f1$_i$(y) = (i − y) (mod (w + 1))
and where s = (⁊ p) (∀q (p, q) ∈ A ⊃ ¬∃r∀v ((r, v) ∈ A ∧ r > p)).
and where w = (⁊ q) (∀p (p, q) ∈ A ⊃ ¬∃v∀r ((r, v) ∈ A ∧ v > q)).

Comment: Note that these rules incorporate the principle that we "compare", as referential sets" or "macrosets" or "subsets"—i.e., at any given "structural level"—only sets of *equal* dimension (as presented or "canonically" reduced). *Syntactic* operations are restricted to uniform operations on the *entire* contents of sets of the relevant dimensional degree.

Definitions:
      Let A be an *ordered pitch set* and (x, y) be an *order number pitch number couple*.
Then,

1. If B is an ordered pitch set, A and B are *order comparable* if, for all y such that (x, y) is a member of A, there is a z such that for some q (fn$_q$(x)) = z, where n = 0 or n = 1, and (z, t) is a member of B, and t is equivalent to y.

2. If B is an ordered pitch set, A and B are *order differentiable* if A and B are *order comparable* and there exists an (x, y) such that (x, y) is a member of A and there is no (z, t) such that (z, t) is a member of B and x = z and t is equivalent to y.

3. If B is an ordered pitch set, A and B are *content differentiable* if there exists a y such that for some x such that (x, y) is a member of A there does not exist a q such that for some p (p, q) is a member of B and y is equivalent to q.

Comment: All ordered pitch sets of equal token-dimension or of equal content-dimension are *content comparable*.[10]

---

[10]Content-comparability just requires that every element of one set be derivable from an element of the other by an operation on the *pitch number* alone (i.e., by pitch-class transposition or complementation).

4. C_A^q is the *q-level syntactic content array of A* if
   $C_A^q = \{(TqA), (IqA)\}$.
5. C_A^{q+1} is the *q + 1-level s.c.a. of A* if
   $C_A^{q+1} = \{(Tq + 1A), (Iq + 1A)\}$.
6. Δ_A is the *maximal syntactic content array of A* if
   $\Delta_A = \{\{C_A^q\}, \{C_A^{q+1}\}, ..., \{C_A^{q+n}\}\}$ where n = w (see above).
7. O_A^q is the *q-level syntactic order array of A* if
   $O_A^q = \{(PqA), (RqA)\}$.
8. O_A^{q+1} is the *(q + 1)-level syntactic order array of A* if
   $O_A^{q+1} = \{(Pq + 1A), (Rq + 1A)\}$.
9. Π_A is the *maximal syntactic order array of A* if
   $\Pi_A = \{\{O_A^q\}, \{O_A^{q+1}\}, ..., \{O_A^{q+n}\}\}$ where n = s (see above).
10. $X_A^{p,q}$ is the *p, q-level syntactic array of A* if
    $X_A^{p,q} = \{\{C_B^q\}, \{C_C^q\}\}$ where, for all D and all r, C_D^r is the r-level syntactic content array of D, and where B = (PpA) and C = (RpA).
11. Γ_A is the *maximal syntactic array of A* if
    $\Gamma_A = \{\{X_A^{p,q}\}, \{X_A^{p,q+1}\}, ..., \{X_A^{p,q+n}\}, \{X_A^{p+1,q}\}, ..., \{X_A^{p+m,q+n}\}\}$
    where m = s and n = w (see above).
12. If Γ_Q is a maximal syntactic array, then: Γ_Q is *primary content-generated* if for all ordered pitch sets A such that A is a member of the syntactic array X and X is a member of Γ_Q, there exists a B such that B is a member of S and S is a member of Γ_Q and A and B are content-differentiable.
13. Γ_Q is *primary order-generated* if for all ordered pitch sets A and all ordered pitch sets B, if A is a member of a syntactic array X and X is a member of Γ_Q, then, if B is a member of a syntactic array Y and Y is a member of Γ_Q, then A and B are order comparable and there exists an ordered pitch set C such that there exists a syntactic array Z such that Z is a member of Γ_Q and C is a member of Z, and A and C are order differentiable.
14. Γ_Q is *uniquely primary order-generated* if Γ_Q is primary order-generated and, for all ordered pitch sets A such that there exists a syntactic array X such that X is a member of Γ_Q and A is a member of X, if there exists an (order number) x and there exists a (pitch

class) y such that (x, y) is a member of A, then, for all (order numbers) z and all (pitch classes) t if t is equivalent to y then (z, t) is not a member of A, or there is a (are) syntactical rule(s) whose application results in a set B for which the stipulated conditions hold.

From the foregoing it follows that:

A. Γ_Q is primary content-generated iff for all ordered pitch sets S such that S is a member of a syntactic array X and X is a member of Γ_Q, and n is the number of distinct pitch-class elements contained in S, then if m is the total number of distinct pitch-class elements contained in the union of all ordered pitch sets that are members of syntactic arrays contained in Γ_Q, *m is equal to or greater than n + 1*.

Comment: In other words, in order for a syntax to be pitch-class content-determinate at the *primary* level, the referential pitch-class collection must be a proper subset of (fail to contain at least one element contained in) the referential pitch-class domain; and whenever the referential collection is such a proper subset, the syntax is necessarily content-referential at its primary level.

B. Γ_Q is uniquely primary order-generated iff for all ordered pitch sets S such that S is a member of a syntactic array X and X is a member of Γ_Q and n is the number of distinct pitch-class elements in S, then if m is the total number of distinct pitch-class elements contained in the union of all ordered pitch sets that are members of syntactic arrays contained in Γ_Q, then *m is equal to n*.

Comment: In other words, a syntax is primary order-referential if and only if the referential collection contains exactly one token of each primitive symbol in each place of its ordered couples; i.e., if the element-content of each set exhausts the referential pitch-class domain, and the token-dimension is equal to that of the referential pitch-class domain.

C. There does not exist an ordered pitch set A such that Γ_A is both primary content-generated and primary order-generated.

Comment: C follows immediately from assertions A and B. With respect to other than primary levels of reference, the following definitions provide principles for comparison:

Definitions:

15. If for all S such that S is an ordered pitch set in Γ_A, there exists an S' such that S' is an ordered pitch set such that for all y such that (x,

y) is a member of S' there exists a z such that z is equivalent to y and, for some w, (w, z) is a member of S; and, for all (u, v) such that (u, v) is a member of S' there is an (s, t) such that (s, t) is a member of S and, if v is equivalent to t, then if $x + i = u$ then $w + i = s$; and, for all (q, r) if $q = n$ then, if (q, r) is the *last* ordered couple contained in S' then there exists a p such that (p, k) is a member of S and p is greater than n, or, if (q, r) is the first ordered couple in S', there exists an l such that (l, m) $\in$ S and $l < r$; *then S' is a proper segment of S*.

16. If Σ_A^n is the array of all arrays of n-dimensional proper segments, of corresponding order position, of distinct ordered pitch sets in Γ_A, and every array within Σ_A^n is primary content-generated, then Γ_A is n-dimensionally *partially content-generated*.

17. If $\Theta_A^{S'}$ is the set whose members are S' and all other sets in Γ_A that contain a proper segment that is order comparable to S', then, if $\Theta_A^{S'}$ contains m sets, Γ_A is n^m-dimensionally *partially order-generated with respect to the S' array* (where S' contains just n distinct elements).

From the above, it follows that:

D. If Γ_A is primary order-generated it is n-dimensionally partially content-generated for all Σ_A^n where, if the dimension of A is m, n is equal to or less than $m - 1$.

E. If Γ_A is primary content-generated it is n-dimensionally partially content-generated for all Σ_A^n where n is equal to or less than m, where m is the dimension of A.

F. If Γ_A is primary content-generated, it is n^m-dimensionally partially order-generated with respect to all S'-arrays where if the dimension of A is n, then the dimension of S' is equal to or less than $n - 1$ and $m = (q \cdot r)$ where q is the number of members of Π_A contained as proper segments in the array {S + S} and r is the difference between $(s - 1) \cdot 2$ and the dimension of Π_A where s is the dimension of S'.

Comment: All syntactic arrays are either primary content- or primary order-generated, but none is both. An array may be partially content- or partially order-generated at given array-levels whether it is primary order- or primary content-generated, but never both partially content- and partially order-generated at the same levels (i.e., with respect to the same internal arrays). Here follow two models that satisfy the above conditions for a domain of four elements, one primary content-generated and one primary order-generated.

Domain: {0, 1, 2, 3}

Let A be an ordered pitch set whose members are (0, 0), (1, 2), (2, 1), represented below as (0 2 1). Then
Δ_A is:

<table>
<tr><td>(T0A = (0 2 1))</td><td>C_A^0</td><td>(I0A = (0 2 3))</td></tr>
<tr><td>(T1A = (1 3 2))</td><td>C_A^1</td><td>(I1A = (1 3 0))</td></tr>
<tr><td>(T2A = (2 0 3))</td><td>C_A^2</td><td>(I2A = (2 0 1))</td></tr>
<tr><td>(T3A = (3 1 0))</td><td>C_A^3</td><td>(I3A = (3 1 2))</td></tr>
</table>

and Π_A is:

<table>
<tr><td>(P0A = (0 2 1))</td><td>O_A^0</td><td>(R0A = (0 1 2))</td></tr>
<tr><td>(P1A = (1 0 2))</td><td>O_A^1</td><td>(R1A = (2 0 1))</td></tr>
<tr><td>(P2A = (2 1 0))</td><td>O_A^2</td><td>(R2A = (1 2 0))</td></tr>
</table>

and Γ_A is:

$(X_A^{0,0} = ((0\ 2\ 1), (0\ 2\ 3)), ((0\ 1\ 2), (0\ 3\ 2)))$
$(X_A^{0,1} = ((1\ 3\ 2), (1\ 3\ 0)), ((1\ 2\ 3), (1\ 0\ 3)))$
$(X_A^{0,2} = ((2\ 0\ 3), (2\ 0\ 1)), ((2\ 3\ 0), (2\ 1\ 0)))$
$(X_A^{0,3} = ((3\ 1\ 0), (3\ 1\ 2)), ((3\ 0\ 1), (3\ 2\ 1)))$
$(X_A^{1,0} = ((1\ 0\ 2), (3\ 0\ 2)), ((2\ 0\ 1), (2\ 0\ 3)))$
$(X_A^{1,1} = ((2\ 1\ 3), (0\ 1\ 3)), ((3\ 1\ 2), (3\ 1\ 0)))$
$(X_A^{1,2} = ((3\ 2\ 0), (1\ 2\ 0)), ((0\ 2\ 3), (0\ 2\ 1)))$
$(X_A^{1,3} = ((0\ 3\ 1), (2\ 3\ 1)), ((1\ 3\ 0), (1\ 3\ 2)))$
$(X_A^{2,0} = ((2\ 1\ 0), (0\ 3\ 2)), ((1\ 2\ 0), (3\ 2\ 0)))$
$(X_A^{2,1} = ((3\ 2\ 1), (1\ 0\ 3)), ((2\ 3\ 1), (0\ 3\ 1)))$
$(X_A^{2,2} = ((0\ 3\ 2), (2\ 1\ 0)), ((3\ 0\ 2), (1\ 0\ 2)))$
$(X_A^{2,3} = ((1\ 0\ 3), (3\ 2\ 1)), ((0\ 1\ 3), (2\ 1\ 3)))$

Let B be an ordered pitch set whose members are (0, 0), (1, 2), (2, 1), (3, 3), represented below as (0 2 1 3). Then
Δ_B is:

<table>
<tr><td>(T0B = (0 2 1 3))</td><td>C_B^0</td><td>(I0B = (0 2 3 1))</td></tr>
<tr><td>(T1B = (1 3 2 0))</td><td>C_B^1</td><td>(I1B = (1 3 0 2))</td></tr>
<tr><td>(T2B = (2 0 3 1))</td><td>C_B^2</td><td>(I2B = (2 0 1 3))</td></tr>
</table>

(T3B = (3 1 0 2)) C_B^3 (I3B = (3 1 2 0))

and Π_B is:

(P0B = (0 2 1 3)) O_B^0 (R0B = (0 3 1 2))
(P1B = (3 0 2 1)) O_B^1 (R1B = (2 0 3 1))
(P2B = (1 3 0 2)) O_B^2 (R2B = (1 2 0 3))
(P3B = (2 1 3 0)) O_B^3 (R3B = (3 1 2 0))

and Γ_B is:

$(X_B^{0,0}$ = ((0 2 1 3), (0 2 3 1)), ((0 3 1 2), (0 1 3 2)))
$(X_B^{0,1}$ = ((1 3 2 0), (1 3 0 2)), ((1 0 2 3), (1 2 0 3)))
$(X_B^{0,2}$ = ((2 0 3 1), (2 0 1 3)), ((2 1 3 0), (2 3 1 0)))
$(X_B^{0,3}$ = ((3 1 0 2), (3 1 2 0)), ((3 2 0 1), (3 0 2 1)))
$(X_B^{1,0}$ = ((3 0 2 1), (1 0 2 3)), ((2 0 3 1), (2 0 1 3)))
$(X_B^{1,1}$ = ((0 1 3 2), (2 1 3 0)), ((3 1 0 2), (3 1 2 0)))
$(X_B^{1,2}$ = ((1 2 0 3), (3 2 0 1)), ((0 2 1 3), (0 2 3 1)))
$(X_B^{1,3}$ = ((2 3 1 0), (0 3 1 2)), ((1 3 2 0), (1 3 0 2)))
$(X_B^{2,0}$ = ((1 3 0 2), (3 1 0 2)), ((1 2 0 3), (3 2 0 1)))
$(X_B^{2,1}$ = ((2 0 1 3), (0 2 1 3)), ((2 3 1 0), (0 3 1 2)))
$(X_B^{2,2}$ = ((3 1 2 0), (1 3 2 0)), ((3 0 2 1), (1 0 2 3)))
$(X_B^{2,3}$ = ((0 2 3 1), (2 0 3 1)), ((0 1 3 2), (2 1 3 0)))
$(X_B^{3,0}$ = ((2 1 3 0), (2 3 1 0)), ((3 1 2 0), (1 3 2 0)))
$(X_B^{3,1}$ = ((3 2 0 1), (3 0 2 1)), ((0 2 3 1), (2 0 3 1)))
$(X_B^{3,2}$ = ((0 3 1 2), (0 1 3 2)), ((1 3 0 2), (3 1 0 2)))
$(X_B^{3,3}$ = ((1 0 2 3), (1 2 0 3)), ((2 0 1 3), (0 2 1 3)))

Comment: Note that for all S of dimension n where n is greater than 3, the syntactic array is a proper subset of the array of all order permutations of the content elements of the referential domain taken j at a time for all j where j is equal to n. Where n is 3 or less, the two sets are equivalent. So our syntactic operations cannot uniquely determine a syntactic array for any S of dimension 3 or less.

From the above, the verification of assertions A through F is unproblematic.

3. MUSICAL SYSTEMS: SOME PRELIMINARY REMARKS

Here we enter the domain of "musical systems", the normal subject matter of what is traditionally thought of as "music theory", though it is still "metatheory" relative to the "foreground" layers of theoretical discourse. It is at this stage that a point of divergence from maximum generality is reached by our music-structural system; the necessity of such a divergence arises as a direct consequence of the implementation of certain of our systematic objectives which, as the preceding section reveals, are mutually incompatible within a single system at a single functional level—in particular, the systematic incorporation of both content-determinacy and order-determinacy presents a difficulty of this nature.

Further construction, moreover, awaits the explicit articulation of such syntax-building objectives as are essential for the conceptual guidance of our systematic formulations, if those formulations are to lead us to a system offering ranges and types of functions adequate to the construction of, say, "tonal" and "12-tone" *syntactical* models into which we could cleanly plug adequate *analytic* models of, respectively, the Schenker-tonal and Babbitt-"serial" types. Such syntax-building objectives are perhaps better represented as extrasystematic than as systematic notions,[11] since they may be favorably viewed as concepts whose observable implementations are practically *enabled by,* rather than formally *generated by,* or *generative of,* the constructions under consideration.

So, in connection with the elaboration of a notion of pitch centricity within a general modular pitch model into a particular reference collection (on the way to constructing a "tonal system"), it seems vital to have in hand, as a guiding "first principle", a well-analyzed concept of "polyphony"—one which, on investigation, appears to be itself explicable by way of a still deeper notion of "structural level".[12] Then, "polyphony" itself may be regarded as

---

[11]N. B., however, that the name of a notion introduced extrasystematically at some point may also serve as the name of a systematically defined predicate at some other, where such a definition is intended to correspond nontrivially to the intuitive sense of the notion.

[12]The contention implicit here is, of course, substantive: if such a hierarchical relation and degree of significance can be demonstrably attributed to the notions of "polyphony" and "structural level", the demonstration would offer a

an underlying basis for the explication of such other essential extrasystematic concepts as "simultaneity and succession", "rhythm", etc.

The principal contention of what follows is that the notion of "structural levels" is inferable from any instance of (Western) music that we care to (and can find some way to) regard as "articulate" (to choose the weakest word that comes to mind) in more than a single sound attack-to-single sound attack sense. As soon as we speak of "this segment" and suppose that we are speaking cognitively, we are necessarily invoking some "segment-isolating" characteristic that, for better or worse, entifies "segments" as complex individuals. The basis on which that identification is made for any given segment is also a basis on which it can be compared to other such individuals. And while we may easily construct an algorithmic instruction to generate such a passage or succession of passages as a whole, the purely formal content of the algorithm might not incorporate anything from which the notion involved could be inferred as the "reason" for the construction of a particular succession of more-than-one-element "events". So the awareness of the extrasystematic notion (which, as noted, may elsewhere be systematic) that motivates the particular slicing of the element-stream is indispensable to confer *structural* significance on the results of applying the algorithm (especially since there is an unlimited number of algorithms capable of generating the same successions, however extended, and, presumably, equally no limit on the number of *possible* motivating notions).

4. STRUCTURAL LEVELS

The construction of "structural levels" in music consists of making inferences of relations on a more than "one element-one element" scale, which thus *groups* sets of pitches (however minimally) so that "larger-scale" complex-unit ("thing") structures are assertible *as well as* a unit-to-unit structure. The interdependence of any two such structures generated for a given composition is, of course, not entailed or determined by this construction, but it is taken as a normative objective of explanation (and hence, presumably of composition) to maximize the degree of interrelation that

---

striking indication of the music-epistemic depth to which Schenker's strictly tonal-analytic notion of *Schichte* may be perceived to descend.

may be asserted to obtain among them. (The latter, in fact, seems to be one of the principal criteria for the adjudication among "ways of hearing" a given *local* relational structure when several ways may, on local evidence alone, appear to be equally supported experientially; moreover, it may also reasonably be regarded as a criterion for preferring, at any *single* "place" or local complex, an interpretation which would be, were that "place" the field of a "global structure", "far-fetched" or less desirable than some other, as, for example, choosing an interpretation more elaborate or remotely inferred than some other because of the preference for some "global" explanation of which the former is a consistent part.)

Example:

Let us consider only macrorelations that are assertible "premetrically", i.e., before the placing of elements in a linear (higher than-lower than) array, thus using only pitch identity and interval identity decidability as determinants of relatedness. Then, from an element-string

$$(a\ b\ c\ a\ b\ c) \qquad \text{where } a \neq b \neq c$$

which symbolizes a "unit structure", there may be inferred the "complex-unit structure" $((a\ b\ c)/(a\ b\ c))$, which corresponds, where $A = (a\ b\ c)$, to $(A\ A)$, and to the (possible) "syntactical unit" (A). The basis for such a slicing of the succession, and for the identification of the names of its two subsets, is an extrasystematic notion of "repetition", whose status as a quite fundamental structural-level-creating notion corresponds to its operationality at such a minimally specified level of pitch-functional interpretation (as compared, say, with "transposition"). But the conversion of this "intuitive" notion into a "systematic" definition, as a two-place predicate of the form "B is a repetition of A", might take several forms, depending on syntactical objectives or desired analytic range or the emphasis within the intuitive notion that is desired to be captured. Here is one possibility:

$$\text{Rep}(B, A) \equiv_{df} \forall a\ [(a \in A \lor a \in B \supset P(a)) \land (a \in A \supset \exists b\ (b \in B \land (a \sim b) \land T(a) < T(b) \land \forall c\ (c \in A)\ \exists d\ ((c \sim d) \land d \in B \land (T(a) < T(c) \sim T(b) < T(d)))))].$$

"B is a repetition of A if B and A are sets of pitch elements, and if, for every pitch element in A, there is an equivalent pitch element in B, and if all the elements of A precede all the elements of B in time-position, and if all elements that precede any elements in A also precede them in B". The latter condition preserves one-to-one identity mappings in terms of order position without invoking order-metric interpretations. The definition makes repetition irreflexive, asymmetric, and transitive, so that the time-dependency of repetition is incorporated, which seems to me to preserve the essential feature that distinguishes it from simple *identity*, or *equivalence*, so that nothing is a repetition of *itself* or of something that *follows* it.

Note, too, that this definition is not formulated as an "effective procedure" that could dig out of a string of tokens "the fact that" it contained subsets relatable as "repetitions". The reasons that such a procedure does not seem preferable are, first, a basic doubt about the explanatory value of procedures that "discover" relationships and articulations rather than providing a basis for defining, comparing, and ordering those articulations one chooses to adopt. And second, it would seem in any case that such effective procedures could operate only trivially without a multitude of conjoined boundary conditions involving syntactic definitions of a much higher order than any available at this stage of definition. Finally, the question of which "things" assertible as "repetitions" (of what dimension, within what other syntactical boundaries, etc.) might be significant at a deep level and which at a relatively shallow level would require other analytic decisions as well.[13]

---

[13] An alternative reading for "repetition" might be a definition that still further generalizes the "order" aspect from a specifically time-dependent one, to an "ordering" in some dimension" one:

$Rep_1(B, A) \equiv_{df} \forall a\ [(a \in A) \supset (P(a) \land \exists b\ ((b \in B) \land (a \sim b) \land T(a) < T(b) \land ((A = \{a_0, a_1, ..., a_n\}) \land (B = \{b_0, b_1, ..., b_m\}) \supset m = n \land (a = a_j \supset b = b_j)))].)$

Or, the definition might be generalized to specify only pitch-*content*, rather than also pitch-order, invariance:

$Rep_2(B, A) \equiv_{df} \forall a\ ((a \in A) \lor (a \in B) \supset P(a) \land (a \in A \supset \exists b\ (b \in B \land a \sim b) \land T(a) < T(b)))).$

This simply equates "repetition" with "transposition by 0", or the "identity" transposition operation on pitch sets, and perhaps the distinction between the two is worth preserving.

On the other hand, the definition might be strengthened to require duration-contour equivalence as well as pitch succession equivalence:

I have focused attention on a relatively simple example to show, first, how even at a very primitive systematic level basic "analytic" notions can be accounted for, by definitions restricted to terms defined in the primitive basis of the system, and also to show, within an area limited enough so that a relatively exhaustive investigation is practical, *how* extrasystematic notions such as we are concerned with here are continuously interconnected with the "systematic" definition chain, acting in many cases as criteria for priorities of definition and choices of primitives (see also the notes on content-centricity and order-determinacy, above). Also I have wished to indicate how fundamental to our "normal" music-conceptual scheme the notion of "structural level" is, and how misguided are attempts to equate it with Schenker-type analyses instead of recognizing in Schenkerian thought an effort to impose orderings in terms of such a general, "musical", notion up to the level of its particular applicability to particular, "tonal", contexts.

On the other hand, this characterization of "structural levels" as interrelated "slicings of the data" may seem counterintuitive to Schenker-oriented readers accustomed to thinking of more

---

$\text{Rep}_3(B, A) \equiv_{df} \forall a \, \{(a \in A \vee a \in B \supset P(a)) \wedge a \in A \supset \exists b \, (b \in B \wedge (a \sim b) \wedge T(a) < T(b) \wedge (a = \{a_0, a_1, ..., a_n\} \wedge B = \{b_0, b_1, ..., b_m\} \supset m = n \wedge (a = a_i \supset b = b_i) \wedge \forall c \, (c \in A \wedge (c = a_i \wedge i < j \supset \exists d \, (d \in B \wedge T(b) = r \wedge T(d) = s \wedge T(c) = t \wedge T(a) = u \supset (r - s) = (u - t)))))\}$.

But this probably overspecifies the conditions normally presupposed by the notion of "repetition" since it is often advantageous to regard some passage as an "ordered pitch set repetition" of some other, preserving pitch order but not necessarily durational contour (in fact, this seems one of the more nontrivial applications of the repetition notion). Thus it might seem best to leave the definition "open" to allow pitch successions and duration-contour successions to be compared independently, so that one could always specify a repetition in either occurring in conjunction with a nonrepetition in the other. Note, too, that given the two primitive relations of pitch and interval identity, a range of macrorelations is assertible beyond "complex" identity, e.g., interval-content identity: $(a, b) \in A \supset \exists c \exists d \, ((c, d) \in B \wedge ((a \, R \, b) \sim (c \, R \, d)))$; degree of pitch- (or interval-) content similitude:

Given (a b c), (a b d), if $A = (a \, b \, c)$ and $B = (a \, b \, d)$, then $A \cap B = (a \, b)$ (or if degree of pitch-intersectional similitude [where "X and Y have a degree of pitch-intersectional similitude equal to n" is reflexive, symmetrical, and transitive] = number of pitch elements intersecting/([dimension of set A_0 + dimension of A_1 + ... + dimension of A_k]/k), then "The degree of similitude of A and B is $\frac{2}{3}$"). But prequantizationally, no functions except identity can be asserted to map elements of A into B.

background levels as "containing" fewer entities than are contained in more foreground levels, such that the larger numbers of entities at more foreground levels are derived by compositional elaboration. In fact, the Schenkerian notion is not denied but explicated by my characterization; for the notion here is just that the "levels" constitute—each individual level as well as all the levels collectively—*a model of (all) the distinguishable data* of the composition, such that each level specifies a particular *degree of* (and *kind of*) *determinacy* for that data. Such determinacy does in fact proceed from the "most background" (least determinate) stage, where the entire data-array is regarded as "a single entity"—an entity which "contains" all the discernible data of the actual array in question but determines them only to the degree that a relatively large number of other arrays might equally constitute an instance of that entity. And at the "most foreground" (most determinate) stage, the entities individually specified and thus accounted for include "all possible things" discernible in the array (i.e., "things" each consisting of one atomic element [pitch], having no distinguishable proper parts): each discernible datum may, in fact, be accounted for *more than once* in this "structural foreground", which could thus possibly include more entities than there are distinguishable data. So the "Schenker graph" or any other structural-level-notational model is meaningful insofar as it is regarded at every stage as laid against the data, as a model of a particular (and presumably significative) *determinate thing-stage* with respect to that data. Such a graph, moreover, is *extrasystematically* regardable as symbolizing a *data-generative* stage (i.e., of composition) as well. Thus both "the background" and "the foreground" are just *relatively determinate* ways of hearing "the piece". And so there is no discernible sense to the dichotomy asserted by some theorists between "going from the background to the foreground" and the reverse procedure as a way of hearing, describing, or understanding a piece; the assertion of such a dichotomy must be predicated upon the notion that only "the foreground" accounts for all the data, and that "the background" somehow "reduces" the piece to some tiny subset of the data, a notion which seems to result from the confusion of a model with the entity it models.

In my reconstruction, "structural levels" are regarded as an ordered "nest" from the "most background" (0th) level to the "most foreground" (nth) level. All stages at which "the piece" is regarded as an assertion of "a single entity" are "syntactical" stages (symbolized as various "0-stages" distinguished by subscripts to 0; for a content-determinate piece, the 0_0th level is determined by the degree of content-determinacy assertible for the piece—for a tonal piece, it would be represented by a single pitch (class). Subsequent "syntactical" stages include those where "the piece" is regarded as instantiating "a construct" (e.g., "the tonic triad"). The *maximal* "syntactical stage" is that where the piece as a whole is regarded as instantiating (once) the referential collection. Thus the "1th" stage is just the first stage at which *succession* (of normatively partitioned reference collections or of constructs *within* a collection) is asserted (determined). This successional or ordering characteristic may be regarded as distinguishing the "1th" and all higher-numbered stages as "structural" rather than "syntactical" levels. The "nth" stage is *minimally* one at which *every distinguishable* datum (or every "atomic element" as defined by the complexity [dimension] of the entity represented at the 0_0th stage) is accounted for individually as *at least one entity*. This, then, constitutes a "foreground" concept which actually suggests the possibility of proceeding further "upward" from the *minimally assertible foreground*—which makes the notion that the "arrival at" or "departure from" the notational foreground represents some "ultimate" and thus universally dependable index to "what's there" seem particularly impoverished musically. For as we have noted, the "foreground" of "distinguishable data" may not only fail to account for all the entities in the eventual "structural" foreground, it may also contain (in a less than monadically determinate piece) *more* entities than the "structural foreground" does. In the latter case, maintaining the requirement of "arrival at" the distinguishable-data foreground as a criterion for the conferral of "analytic cognitivity" on a structural model would result in the exclusion from the literature of "music" of any piece falling within the class of less than monadically determinate pieces.[14]

---

[14]I believe, too, that the "model-entity" confusion is also the reason that Michael Kassler's representation of each Schenker-level graph as "a piece" has been misunderstood (e.g., by Eric Regener). Such a graph is indeed not "*the* piece" insofar as each single "entity" of each pre-foreground-level model is interpreted in "the piece" by a complex entity (whether or not the components of the complex are entified in "more foreground" structural levels). But to be comprehensible as a "stage of generation" of "the piece", each "structural level"

It should be clear from the foregoing that my notion of structural levels entails representation, for every level, in three interdependent notational models: 1) the distinguishable data as partitioned into "things"; 2) the symbolic notation of the "things" occasioning that partitioning (i.e., notation specifying just the determinate aspects of the "thingness" in question); and 3) a commentary explicating the relation-concept to be understood as generating each partitioning "out of" the preceding level. At the 0_0–0_n stages, the assertible relations among distinguishable components of "the thing" are as elements *within* the thing, in terms of such observables as relative order position and the identity or nonidentity of each component with the determinate (referential) entity that all the components are collectively being presumed to "represent". Non-referential elements at any given syntactical stage are *determinately non-referential* for the piece if they are *referential* at any *subsequent* syntactical stage (but they are in no case systematically determinate within any syntactical stage where they are *non-referential*). Thus, at the "0_0th" level of a tonal piece, every distinguishable pitch datum of "the piece" is simply either "the tonic pitch" or "not the tonic pitch"—the only other relation (omitting for brevity the pitch/pitch-class distinction) being relative attack position within the boundaries of "the piece" (as, "adjacent to", "three attack positions subsequent from", "simultaneous with", etc.). At the "0_1th" level, the identification might be in terms of "the tonic fifth" (so that *at this level,* "the tonic" would be indifferently "major" or "minor", since "the third" is at this stage not yet a determinate element). At the "0_2th" level, "the tonic triad" determines "the piece" (thus also determining the "major" or "minor" character of the piece by fixing the "referential third"). And at the "0_{2b}th" level, the "diatonic collection" is what "the piece" represents. Since all subsequent levels model the piece as *succession* they may be considered "structural" rather than "syn-

---

must itself *be* a possible one-to-one model of "*a* piece" (i.e., must itself be something potentially regardable as a notation of "a piece"), for a succession of "structural levels" explicates "the piece" just by invoking all the same determining referents for succession and simultaneity for every "level". Hence there is no way internal to the characteristics of the structural-level array to distinguish the "arrival at" the foreground from any other relation of adjacent levels; such an "arrival" can only be determined as such by reference to the "actual" foreground of a *particular piece.*

tactic" levels. (Thus, at the "1th" level, successions are of instances of the reference construct—the triad—within the reference collection. This is a pre-*Ursatz* level; the *Ursatz* itself is describable as representing "the basic succession" as well as "the basic structure" of "the basic composition", since "structure" in [most] music is successional structure. At more foreground levels, the successions represented are of instances of the reference collection as internally partitioned by the basic triad-successional model.) And the relations that each "structural" level uniquely adds to the "within-things" relations defined at the "syntactic" levels are new "between-things" relations. Thus all temporally "adjacent" elements at any 0-type level are related simply as "adjacencies within 'the piece'" (although they may be distinguished as determinate [referential, defined] or indeterminate [non-referential, undefined] pitch elements). But the assertion of *succession* creates a new situation (*superimposed* on, not *superseding*, the more background situation) in which *some* adjacencies are *within* and some are *between* the new sub-things created by the partitioning slices determined at that level.[15]

Here is an example of a simple tonal piece, illustrating how the "slicing" and the "generating" are mutually representable as ef-

---

[15]Thus structural levels, as determinate slices of particular stretches of a given acoustical foreground, determine the *rhythmic structure* of a composition in every relevant sense of the notion. For spans are of certain time extents, creating specific duration contours at every layer. And the "accentual" question in rhythmic structure is answered by the *relative backgroundness* attributed to a span since every span-boundary that appears at a given level is repeated in every more foreground level. "Backgroundness" is obviously a direct index of "degree of articulation" represented by a given span-boundary, understood as the "divider" between the last attack of a span and the first attack of the next succeeding span. Thus the "strength" of the "division" inferred between successive attacks (the degree to which they are heard as "attached to" or "separated from" one another) is indexed by the number of different-leveled span-boundary crossings which that succession represents. (Obviously, by intensive elaboration. a single attack may embody a span-boundary crossing, insofar as that single attack is understood as a concatenation of (at least) the last attack of one span with the first attack of its successor.) The functional contents attributed to the spans of a structure (e.g., the expression of a triad) are, then, the motivating *rationale* for distinguishing just those particular spans, and for distributing them in a particular way in hierarchically relative layers; such distinctions and distributions represent a crucial determination *through analytic attribution* of the rhythmic identity of the composition involved.

fectively constituting the same "structural level"-making activity: Let us begin with a "minimally elaborated" "tonal" composition:

$$\begin{matrix} E & F & E & D & C \\ C & C & C & B & G \\ G & A & G & G & E \\ C & F & C & G & C \end{matrix}$$

At the highest "0" level, this composition is representable as "the reference collection":

Level	Partition Array	Generation Array I. "Syntactical" Stages:	Commentary[16]
0_0:	$\begin{bmatrix} E & F & E & D & C \\ C & C & C & B & G \\ G & A & G & G & E \\ C & F & C & G & C \end{bmatrix}$	{C}	
0_1:	$\begin{bmatrix} E & F & E & D & C \\ C & C & C & B & G \\ G & A & G & G & E \\ C & F & C & G & C \end{bmatrix}$	{C, G}	
$(0_{1a}$:		{(F, C), (C, G), (G, D)}	)
0_2:	$\begin{bmatrix} E & F & E & D & C \\ C & C & C & B & G \\ G & A & G & G & E \\ C & F & C & G & C \end{bmatrix}$	{C, E, G}	
$(0_{2a}$:		{(F, A, C), (C, E, G), (G, B, D)}	)
$(0_{2b}$:		{C, D, E, F, G, A, B}	)

At the first "structural" level, the composition is represented as a succession of "2 things"; level 2 is recognizable as an *Ursatz* instantiating a "normative model for succession" for tonal-systematic pieces:

---

[16] The commentaries specify how to "get" from any level to the subsequent level. For the "commentary" on the succession from 0_0 to 0_{2b}, see Section 8, below. The sets designated at the 0_{1a} and 0_{2a} levels are the "maximized reference sets" for their levels (Section 8C, especially note 28), and hence are considered as generating complete "syntactic arrays" with respect to every level; some of the normative "limiting conditions" that generate for each level its "maximum reference set" are also given in n. 21 below.

Level	Partition Array	Generation Array	Commentary
		II. "Structural" Stages:	
1.	$\left\{\begin{array}{ccc\|cc} E & F & E & D & C \\ C & C & C & B & G \\ G & A & G & G & E \\ C & F & C & G & C \end{array}\right\}$	$\left\{\begin{array}{c\|c} E & C \\ C & G \\ G & E \\ C & C \end{array}\right\}$	from 0_2 by "arpeggiation" operation
2.	$\left\{\begin{array}{ccc\|cc} E & F & E & D & C \\ C & C & C & B & G \\ G & A & G & G & E \\ C & F & C & G & C \end{array}\right\}$	$\left\{\begin{array}{c\|cc} E & D & C \\ C & B & G \\ G & G & E \\ C & G & C \end{array}\right\}$	from 1 by "linear" and "registral" operations
3.	$\left\{\begin{array}{c\|c\|c\|cc} E & F & E & D & C \\ C & C & C & B & G \\ G & A & G & G & E \\ C & F & C & G & C \end{array}\right\}$	$\left\{\begin{array}{c\|c\|c\|cc} E & F & E & D & C \\ C & & C & B & G \\ G & (A) & (G) & G & E \\ C & & C & G & C \end{array}\right\}$	from 2 by "arpeggiation" and "linear" operations
4.	$\left\{\begin{array}{c\|c\|c\|c\|c} E & F & E & D & C \\ C & C & C & B & G \\ G & A & G & G & E \\ C & F & C & G & C \end{array}\right\}$	$\left\{\begin{array}{c\|c\|c\|c\|c} E & F & E & D & C \\ C & C & C & B & G \\ G & A & G & G & E \\ C & F & C & G & C \end{array}\right\}$	from 3 by "pitch-class-polyphonic" interpretation
5.	$\left\{\begin{array}{c\|c\|c\|c\|c} E & F & E & D & C \\ C & C & C & B & G \\ G & A & G & G & E \\ C & F & C & G & C \end{array}\right\}$	$\left\{\begin{array}{c\|c\|c\|c\|c} E & F & E & D & C \\ C & C & C & B & G \\ G & A & G & G & E \\ C & F & C & G & C \end{array}\right\}$	from 4 by registral (pitch-counterpoint) interpretation

Note that level "3" accounts for "everything" in the data foreground as an entity, but not as determinately as does level 4. At the

O_0-O_{2b} levels, there is one "thing", at the 1th level there are 2 things, at the 2th and 3th levels there are 3 and 5 things, respectively; the 4th level begins to individuate the construct-things into pitch-things, etc. (in the "model" it looks otherwise, namely that construct-things are generated out of previous pitch-things, but that is just because the determinacy of the construct associated with F at level 3 is specified only to the extent that it "expresses" F, whereas at levels 4 and 5 the total individual pitch content is determinate). And at levels O_0–O_{2b} the relation E-F is one of "adjacencies within the piece"; at the O_0 and O_1 stages it is also a relation of two "non-referential elements". At O_{1a} the relation is that of a "reference element" (E) and a "non-reference element" (F), and at O_{2a} and O_{2b} it is that of "two reference elements", at 2 it is "2 elements within a sub-thing", at 3 it is "an element (E) of a sub-thing" and "an element (F) of the adjacent subsequent sub-thing" (i.e., an element each of two adjacent members of the succession). At 4 they are adjacent pitch-class things (here there are 3 different entities accounted for with respect to each simultaneity). And at 5 they are adjacent pitch entities (accounting for their registral relation, and thus distinguishing 4 distinct entities per simultaneity).

Other extrasystematic (but potentially definable) properties inferable within the immediate range of "structural levels" are such generalities as "size" (relative dimension of articulated sets), "contour" (size- and direction-patterns, more or less precisely determined by interval measurement or merely by "higher than-lower than" comparisons), "span" (highest-lowest pitch-interval comparison, including highest-lowest pitch identity or "overlap"), etc.

While the notion of "structural level" does not *account for* that of "polyphony", the latter is very strongly determined in terms of the former, as a special interpretation of it, as shall be seen below. But first, it is perhaps worthwhile to note that the "structural level" idea and its range of associated notions is, if not surely sufficient, at least necessary for any analysis of music which is to be considered "pre"- or "non"-polyphonic; and this also indicates the strength of the assertible link between polyphonic music and its non-polyphonic predecessors, which might otherwise appear as one of those unbridged disjunctions too frequent in music-historical discourse. As we shall see, the idea of "reference set", fundamental to even a primitive attempt to attribute *coherence* to any music, is a vital conceptual link between the two "kinds" of music. Thus, many remarks of Treitler in [34] (pp. 81–85), invoking numbers of undefined "macrorelational" terms, could be subsumed under a group of simple "referential set" definitions that would eliminate the difficulties occasioned by synesthetic transference of notions like "antecedent-consequent" (which here seems to mean only "comes before/comes after"), "phrase", "open/closed", "dominant-tonic", "cadences", etc. And a basic methodological problem here, as in some recent writings of Leonard Meyer, is the belief that analysis answers the question *whether there is a syntax* as well as *what the syntax is*. That the first of these is an empty question (the answer to which is always trivially "yes", because every "thing" "has a form") should already be evident from *Meta-Variations,* Part I. As to the second, its answer is, also trivially, "anything", since, as the present chapter demonstrates, syntaxes are universal collections of functions able to account for any actual musical events whatever.

5. POLYPHONY

"A path (p) through the data (of S)" may be defined as follows: if p is an ordered subset (proper or improper) of an ordered set S such that for any elements x and y in p where x precedes y, there are elements z and t in S such that z is equivalent to x and t is equivalent to y and z precedes t, then p is a *path through the data of S* (and may be identical with S). In such a path, every element is regarded as being *displaced* by its immediate successor. Where the union of the members of a set P of paths ($p_0, p_1, ..., p_n$) through the data of a given S *exhausts* the elements of S, then P is a *structural-level partitioning of* S. And if no element x in any member p_i of P is displaced by an element y which does not also displace it in S, then P is a *monophonic structural-level partitioning of* S. If, however, there is at least one element z in any member p_j of P such that z is displaced by an element t in S, but such that t does not also displace z in p_j, and t is not a member of p_j and there is a member m of p_j such that m is a (immediate or nonimmediate) successor of t in S, then P is a *polyphonic structural-level partitioning* of S. In the latter case, too, z and t are defined as determining a *simultaneity in S* (regardless of their presented simultaneity or nonsimultaneity), so that t is a *temporal displacement* but not a [P-level] *structural displacement* of z. If Pa is an ordered subset of P such that for every member p_k of Pa that contains an element q such that q precedes in S an element r of any other member p_1 of Pa, and there is no element s contained in p_k such that s is preceded in S by r; and if Pb is another such subset of P then, if the members of Pa and Pb are (as they have been defined as being) paths through the data of S, then Pa and Pb are also paths through the data of S. And if at least one element of Pa precedes in S at least one element of Pb, *and* at least one element of Pb precedes at least one element of Pa, and no member of P is not a member of Pa or Pb (or of both), then Pa and Pb are *polyphonic voices* of S. If Q is the set containing Pa and Pb, then Q is a *two-voice polyphonic structural-level partitioning* of S.

Thus polyphony is most generally describable as the notion that multiple relational paths may be inferred from pitch successions by the isolation and association of pitch elements into inferred "successions" by criteria independent of presented temporal adjacency. Such "successions" are considered to associate such elements both within and between sets inferable on "structural-level"-type grounds alone so that the entire pitch-adjacency-successional "map" is accounted for (most often, multiply accounted for) by conjunctions of "lines" varying, by virtue of their temporal independence, *simultaneously* over the total temporal extent of the array, and (although the *rationale* involved is not a precondition for the *notion* to be applicable) *interdependently,* in terms of determined pitch-relational constructs. These constructs[17] may be construed as *partitionings* of the pitch domain into mutually determinate sets whose union totally determines the *primary* reference sets of the structure[18] involved (which might be the same as those which, on other grounds, had also been inferable as such at the "structural-level" stage).

Example:
From the succession

        A   B♭   C   D   E♭   C   F   B♭

may be inferred the 2-voice "polyphony"

        A   C   F
           B♭   D   E♭   C   B♭

---

[17] In tonal music, the triad.
[18] In tonal music, the diatonic collection.

which contains the "simultaneities"

(A, B♭), (B♭, C), (C, D), (C, E♭), (C, C), (F, C), (F, B♭).

From the same succession there may also be inferred the 2-voice "polyphony"

```
A       D    C F
  B♭ C     E♭      B♭
```

with the "simultaneities"

(A, B♭), (A, C), (C, D), (D, E♭), (E♭, C), (E♭, F), (F, B♭),

or the 3-voice "polyphony"

```
A            C    B♭
  B♭      E♭
     C D       F
```

with the "simultaneities"

(A, B♭, C), (A, B♭, D), (A, E♭, D), (C, E♭, D), (C, E♭, F), (B♭, E♭, F)

or the 4-voice "polyphony"

```
A                 C
  B♭                F
     C              B♭
        D E♭
```

with the "simultaneities"

(A, B♭, C, D), (A, B♭, C, E♭), (C, B♭, C, E♭), (C, F, C, E♭), (C, F, B♭, E♭)

or the 4-voice "polyphony"

```
A       C D    C F
  B♭ C              B♭
A       D E♭ C    B♭
  B♭      E♭    F B♭
```

with the "simultaneities"

(A, A, B♭, B♭), (C, C, A, B♭), (D, C, D, B♭), (D, C, E♭, E♭),
(C, C, C, E♭), (F, C, C, F), (F, C, B♭, B♭), (F, B♭, B♭, B♭),

etc., etc.—as the last example indicates, the "possible" distinct polyphonies are *infinite,* and any of them "can" be inferred *as* polyphonies "at will" without necessarily involving any "music-syntactical" or "structural" *rationales.*

The partitionings so determined define, for any two (adjacent or simultaneous) pitches, whether the relation they present represents a relation between two pitches *within* a partitioning construct, or one between two pitches *between* such constructs, or both. In a content-determinate system, where significant relations are defined as "content comparisons" of discrete pitch sets, and where, therefore, particular *orders* of pitch-to-pitch succession are not referential at the primary syntactical level, these partitioning constructs may be considered to define "pitch-voice regions" within the pitch domain, in which the elements of the "referential construct" itself are considered the interdependently principal referents for their "regions"—hence, their association as presented conjunctions (whether literally simultaneous in presentation or not is beside the point) is considered "normative" in defining a "simultaneous" conjunction within which each "voice" is represented by its principal referential pitch class (the relevant member of the referential construct). In this sense, such a partitioning may be considered to assert a "model for simultaneity" (where "simultaneity", again, is understood as "inferred temporal overlap of distinct pitch-voice elements", i.e., the totality at every "moment" of "non-displaced" [or not structurally suppressed] pitches in all voices)—or plurally, as "models for simultaneity", if the partitioning constructs taken as normative are non-isomorphic with one another. (This latter condition, however, if a criterion of maximally unique distinctness of "interpretation" on a given level is invoked, would seem to be decidedly disadvantageous.) Thus would be defined "intervals of simultaneity" (those occurring within constructs, hence always "between voices"), and "intervals of succession" (those occurring *only between* constructs, either within or between voices—for a stronger specification, see "Linearity and Adjacency", below).

Under this definition, the assertion as a presented simultaneity of two pitches in a defined relation of succession constitutes a situation in which the locally referential construct is inferred to be *either* one to which one of the two pitches belongs, *or* one to which the other does; this requires an amount of inference at any given level greater than that required at the same level where the presented simultaneity is among pitches all construable as belonging to the same local-referential construct.[19] This "resolution-re-

---

[19] This "greater amount of inference" arises from the condition that any such simultaneous presentation of succession-related pitches results from an

quiring" situation (the resolution required being *inferential,* not in any *necessary* sense an actual *presented* simultaneity or displacement) is the functional—and the only necessary syntactic—meaning of "dissonance", and the local indicators of which pitch of a non-referential simultaneity is to be taken as "referential" for the totality (or for the "others", if one prefers) is the essential meaning of "resolution" (and whether the "backward" or the "forward" resolution is at a higher structural level is a significant consideration for time ["rhythmic"] structure—see Komar [21]). "Consonance", of course, simply designates the simultaneous presentation of elements in a syntactically defined relation of simultaneity. Where no such simultaneity-succession distinction is operative, the "dissonance-consonance-resolution" complex of (interrelated) notions is equally inapplicable. And in any case, such syntactical determinants are completely detachable from any particular *sonic* interpretation, so that no "sound" is a priori dissonant—even in a system where dissonance is a relevant predicate—but this is not merely to say that such a sound might in fact be "consonant", but also that the very determination of whether the notions are applicable *precedes* the further determination of the consonant-dissonant status of any given "sound".[20]

"intensive" elaboration of a preceding, "extensive" elaboration in which *both* simultaneities "implied" by the presented event appear *as a succession.* Thus a "more background" level may have *more entities* than a "more foreground" level generated out of it by intensive elaboration. So, for example, one might expect to find pre-foreground levels of Brahms's Op. 116 No. 3 (g minor) containing a considerably greater number of distinguishable (attack-specified) "events" than are represented in the "notational" foreground.

[20] And it might be added that no sound is a priori consonant either, though it might be "prima facie consonant" by virtue of not being *excluded* as potentially expressive of a single reference simultaneity. Thus the chord (C E G) is not prima facie excluded from representing a single triad, and hence from being regarded as consonant, but, in a given context, it might in fact be regarded as representing a simultaneous conjunction of, say, the C, the E, and the G triads, in which case it would *be* dissonant. This explains the $^6_4$-chord question—and, in general, the question of the "perfect fourth" as sometimes a consonant, sometimes a dissonant, interval. For the case is that wherever the two elements of a perfect fourth are taken to represent the same triad, the sounded interval is consonant; but wherever they are taken to represent distinct triads, the sounded interval is dissonant. Thus, since the bass of the $^6_4$ is frequently taken to represent the triad of which it is root (say, V, in the case of a so-called "I$^6_4$" but the other two pitches are regarded as components of a distinct triad (the I) which has been generated linearly as a subsidiary elaboration of the locally referential triad (the V), the

Moreover, the "areas" defined by the "simultaneity model" *may* be further functionally hierarchized as well, though not necessarily, in a manner corresponding to the extrasystematic notion of pitch-(class) centricity (deriving a referential *construct* from a referential collection already confers "construct-centricity" on a syntax already collection-centricity determined by virtue of "structural-level" inference alone), which enables the hierarchical ordering of the individual pitches in the referential construct. This accounts in part for the relation of the *tonic triad* to the Schenker *Urlinien*, which are models for "resolving" the *secondary* pitch-voice areas defined by the tonic triad "into" the *primary* pitch-voice area. That these are in particular "linear" models requires further extrasystematic considerations, in particular that of "linearity" (q. v.).

In summary: note that in a content-determined system the "meaning" of a given succession is defined solely with respect to the total interval content of the referential construct; "succession" is defined in terms of the constructs as "relations holding between but not within constructs". Actual simultaneity is only an explicit realization of the concept of simultaneously varying "voices", which by containing pitches that are inferred to "hang over" (remain undisplaced by) intervening pitches in the "other voices" *imply* simultaneity as an aspect of the structure even where it is not literally present.

Now in an order-generated system, the partitioning constructs *exhaust* the pitch domain (as we have seen), which renders inoperative the notion of "voice areas" defined for content systems (see n. 24, p. 219, below). What, then, do these partitionings define? Of course, they constitute "content groups" in themselves, as proper subsets of the "universal pitch vocabulary", but they cannot be asserted as "pitch-voice-area"-defining "constructs of simultaneity", as just noted. What they determine, then, are *defined* relations of *precedence* and *subsequence,* distinguishable as such from any *presented* precedences or subsequences. Thus with respect to any presented simultaneity, it is determinable whether any

---

whole $^6_4$ is—in such a case—dissonant, since it is heard as representing the superposition of two distinct triads (V and I). But since the intervals it contains are all compatible with a single-triad interpretation, the "dissonance" of such a $^6_4$ is imposed entirely by contextual preference, and a "consonant" interpretation is in no way *systematically* counterentailed.

interval it contains represents an interval of *immediate* or of *nonimmediate* succession (as well as, if nonimmediate, what *order interval* it represents under any given possible interpretation). This determination might, for example, contribute in turn to a determination of whether a presented succession (either including or not including simultaneities) represents a "single-set" or "multiple (distinct)-set" unfolding. Here, if the inference is "multiple set unfolding", the inferred partitioning would be of the total pitch domain, multiply exhausted by as many unit-strings as there are inferred sets unfolding, *each* of which constitutes a "total" set, however related (relatable) to the others.

But the "immediate-nonimmediate" distinction may also enable an inference of "referential sub-construct partitionings" of the pitch domain as the *generators* of the total referential set. (The plural is used to allow for the possibility of different such partitionings being operative at different structural levels.) Here, any interval may be defined as obtaining between pitches in a *defined* adjacency-relation *within* a construct (or several), as a *non-adjacency, within-construct* relation, or as a "between-construct" relation, of adjacency (last-first), or non-adjacency (in local structure "adjacency-between-constructs" may not be determinable without invoking macrostructural considerations). Now the *dimensions* of such partitioning constructs determine the number of *structural voices* (always *at a particular level of structure*—the urgency of this stricture should be obvious to anyone familiar with complexly aggregate-forming 12-tone music). Thus, an array such as

$$(0, 1, 2, 3, 4, 5)$$
$$(6, 7, 8, 9, 10, 11)\,{}^{21}$$

is a 6 × 2 partitioning, so that *two* "structural voices" are implied, and the only "harmonic" criteria asserted are the distinctions of relations "*within* the 6s" and those "*between* the 6s". The "structural level" stricture applies to cases like the following:

---

[21]Independent of ordering; the convention employed here (to avoid the encumbrance of order-number/pitch-number couple specification in every case where left-to-rightness can substitute for the former) is that *unordered* sets are inscribed with intervening commas between element-inscriptions, and *ordered* sets are inscribed with blanks only intervening between element inscriptions.

$$\begin{array}{cccccc}(0 & 1 & 2 & 3 & 4 & 5) \\ (6 & 7 & 8 & 9 & 10 & 11) \\ (5 & 4 & 3 & 2 & 1 & 0) \\ (11 & 10 & 9 & 8 & 7 & 6)\end{array}$$

where at one level a 6 × 2 partitioning is still inferable where (0 1 2 3 4 5) and (5 4 3 2 1 0) belong to the same "structural voice"); but a 3 × 4 partitioning is also inferable, in which it is no longer "immaterial" whether (0 1 2) and (5 4 3) "appear" in the "same harmonic association", as it is in an inference at a purely hexachordal partitioning level.

Thus here, "structural voices" consist of determinate interval-contents within the partition-dimensional limit. (Obviously, the degree of "ordering" determines the dimension of the "smallest possible inferable partitioning unit" interlocked in any "textural counterpoint".) This suggests a link between descriptions of order-determinate and content-determinate structures in terms of patterns of "within-between" relations, with interpretations as order or content unspecified (see Part IV). But the "within-a-voice" criteria that are regarded as assertible for the two types of polyphony in the section following this seem to me to indicate that the usual equation of pitch-class adjacency with "voice"-connection, transferred from tonal to order-determinate music, represents a serious error of level-confusion. Thus I introduce the governing notions involved before returning to further consideration of polyphony in general.[22]

6. LINEARITY AND ADJACENCY

Linear adjacency and order adjacency are the "counterpart" notions in content- and order-determinate systems, respectively, that determine "within-a-voice" or "between-voices-but-also-between-constructs" inferences. Now, certain intervals are defined in content systems as "intervals of adjacency" and certain as "intervals of nonadjacency"—the latter being either intervals of simultaneity or intervals "between constructs and voices". In order systems,

---

[22]The "counterpoint" of order-determined music thus consists of particular partitionings through ordered successions of *normatively nonadjacent* segments (down to monads), while its *polyphony* is defined as the ordering of successions of segments of these dimensions as defined *adjacencies* in the referential set.

"adjacency" is defined not as "higher than-lower than" adjacency but as *order-positional* adjacency, which makes the *linear* adjacency criterion inoperative in order-determined music. So one possible (and frequent) "within-a-voice" notion associated with content systems, i.e., an empirically viable determinant of "pitch-voice areas", is *pitch-class adjacency*. Its determination is distinct from that of *pitch*, or *registral* adjacency, which is in the articulative rather than the functional direction[23] within a given structure. This characteristic may be called *linearity*. And the relevance of its application is entirely dependent on syntactic definition. It is plainly a prime criterion for determining structural voice succession in tonal and pretonal music, but in transferences to later music it seems most often to be equated with registral adjacency *alone*, an equation which would *not* be regarded as appropriate to content-music. In tonal music, for example, the explicit association of each tonic-triad pitch with a specific "neighbor-note" region is a syntactical factor in determining a "background line". The transference of such a particular normative criterion to nontonal music (even nontonal content-music) to support the derivation of an analogically background line seems highly problematic.

This attempt at transference is made even by quite rigorous theorists, most notably by Peter Westergaard in a series of articles on rhythmic and polyphonic structure in 12-tone music ([37], [38], [39], [40]). But, especially with respect to the subject matter of [37] and [38], I do not believe that linear adjacency has the same functional meaning, and surely not the same structural depth (in the sense noted above, that it seems a mostly articulative characteristic), in, for example, the Webern Op. 27, as an instance of order-generated music, as it does in content-generated music, and hence I regard the proffered transference of the *Urlinie* notion that depends on the affirmation of such a correspondence of functional

---

[23]I use "direction" here and elsewhere to relativize notions most frequently used absolutistically. Hence, I don't distinguish categorically between, "explanation" and "description", but rather consider them conceptual polarities between which relevant observations may be arrayed relative to a particular discourse. Thus some "analysis" may be "less explanatory" than another, which (if not counterintuitive or counterfactual) may be therefore considered "more purely descriptive". Note that this notion is already introduced in Part II with respect to "coherence", "opacity", complexity/simplicity", etc. In default of this relativization, people would spend a great deal of time (as some seem to do) wondering, in ascending, just when they had got "up".

meanings as unconvincing. The associations uncovered by Westergaard seem better understood as part of a "conceit", like "diatonic neoclassicism" in Stravinsky, or "Sonata Form"—or perhaps, better, "classical phrase contour"—in Schoenberg, but such an analogy would occupy a considerably different explanatory niche from the one seemingly claimed in Westergaard's articles. In particular, the tonal "neighbor-note" criterion is defined in terms of a non-indifference with respect to "upper" or "lower" neighbor, only the tonic having both kinds associated with it (and each of those is intervallically, hence functionally, distinguishable), whereas no such or analogous criterion is asserted for Webern. And here, too (in Webern), not only is the semitone defined in *particular* order-successional terms rather than as a "kind of interval" of "general adjacency", but it is also universally inferable in an extraregistral sense at the *pitch-class* level and hence seems "trivial" on that level (i.e., as a consequence of the "12-tone"-ness of the structure). But this "pitch-class" level would seem to "correspond" to just that level in tonal music where "interval of adjacency" is particularly "nontrivial". Thus the "structural line" in Westergaard's analysis is evidently not the result of a transference of the *Urlinie* notion, since the context of its generation does not conform to the situation in the Schenker model of tonality in which the "registral" and the "linear" are at least separably definable. What this "structural line" seems actually to be is, rather, a selection from a *registral* line based on a single interval, the interval of maximum presented adjacency (i.e., the semitone). This may be "equally" as explanatory as is the Schenker *Urlinie*, but surely it is *differently* explanatory from it. On the other hand, the actual determinant of structural-polyphonic "voices" in order systems is, as I have indicated, rather the *ordering within sets* (of elements or of whatever partitioning subsets are regarded as "subreferential", quasi-analytically speaking—as the "triad" is subreferential for the tonal collection), such "voices" being articulatively delineated (as "counterpoint") through *whatever* experientially "possible" dimension is also considered relevant (i.e., through registral, dynamic, timbral, etc., counterpoint, either independently or conjunctly). This difference in the defined basis of polyphony in the two types of systems follows from the difference between the derivation of *simultaneity*-interpretation in order-generated music from coincidences of, or of parts of, order-successional "lines", and the derivation of *lines* in content-generated music as inter-construct- and construct-definitionally partitioned successions.

Now to return to polyphony itself: the above considerations suggest that the inference of polyphonic voices on a functional basis enables inferences of "multiple function" for elements, as parts of various "local" and ultimately of (single or multiple) "global" structures. Inference of "constructs of simultaneity" in content systems widens this potential functional multiplicity by placing each atomic element into a new set of classes of relations with each other atomic element (the same, of course, is true for inferences of "constructs of succession" in order systems). The range of such an increased functional multiplicity (i.e., a *higher degree of determinacy*) is thus in direct proportion to the *dimensions* of the constructs themselves and the *uniqueness* of function of each contained element within the construct. Hierarchization extends still further the range associated with single elements (here the defined "voice areas" are in a hierarchical relation, that is, a stage beyond simple *conjunction*). And this is still further extended by a defined "model for succession" determining a normative relation among successive simultaneities. Thus, the more determined (or defined) on the more levels of function a syntax is, the *wider* the range of possible cognitive relational paths and multiple associations it may account for (or generate).

An analogous sequence of increasing determinacy can be traced for order-generated music as well, from the primary referential-order model to the "segment-associative" models; in this sense, the "interval element" in order-generated music directly correlates with the interval element in content-generated music, in producing functional multiplicity between and within sets, between and within segments, or, transformationally, in identifying such sets and segments as "adjacent" or "nonadjacent". And the *order* position of a pitch-class element in an order relation is like a hierarchical (voice) position of a pitch-class element in a content relation (i.e., being in "first", "second", or "third" position in a 12-tone set trichord is a determinate function, as determinate as, and "analogous" to, that of being "root", "fifth", or "third" of a tonal triad). Note, too, that although we have not ruled out the possibility of an *identity* of criteria of (i.e., normative intervallic models for) succession and simultaneity within a given system, it seems doubtful that such an identity would be usefully asserted at a single level of structure. (If both, "how both?" is the relevant explanation-seeking question, and the answer would presumably involve distinctions such as we have been drawing.) Consider the following *ordered* succession, for example, as an instance of a "serial" succession:

$$\begin{array}{ccc} C & E & G\sharp \\ G\sharp & C & E \\ E & G\sharp & C \end{array}$$

At the level of individual sonority ("chords"), this succession can be construed as exhibiting a simple "exchange of structural voices" among successive "presented-voice" attacks. Note that *at this level* none of the particular "melodic" intervals (be they registral, timbral, dynamic, or other kinds of melody) is "syntactically" determinate. This becomes especially evident if the succession is followed by another "harmony":

$$\begin{array}{llllll} C & E & G\sharp & G & B & D\sharp \\ G\sharp & C & E & D\sharp & G & B \\ E & G\sharp & C & B & D\sharp & G \end{array} \quad \begin{array}{l} (0 \ 4 \ 8 \ 7 \ 11 \ 3 : \ T0S \text{ or } T0RI) \\ (8 \ 0 \ 4 \ 3 \ 7 \ 11 : \ T8S \text{ or } T8RI) \\ (4 \ 8 \ 0 \ 11 \ 3 \ 7 : \ T4S \text{ or } T4RI) \end{array}$$

For here the "in-between" interval 1/11 is strongly explicable on successional (between partitioning constructs) rather than "partitional" (within partitioning constructs)[24] grounds—which in the

---

[24] I use "partition" here rather than "simultaneity" to emphasize the fact that simultaneity in the *presented* sense is a special case of the partitioning notion. Much of, e.g., early Stravinsky would seem to me polyphonically "incoherent" without this liberalization, since the "collection centricity" that I infer for works like *Petrouchka* (see Part IV) does not either entail *or* counter-entail the representation of particular segments, or even all of the referential collection as *actual* simultaneity, but rather determines just the partitioning of pitch-class space by the totality of the components of the reference collection. Variant sub-partitionings of the reference collection are thus regarded as a variable of local articulation (compare the opening partitioning of the collection into 2 + 2 + 2 by the interval 2 (D E) (G A) (B C♯/B♭ C), with the later "triads"). Insofar as these components are not *internally* hierarchized (even locally), the various unfoldings may be considered aspects of "structural levels" in the simpler sense, with "heterophonic" articulation but in a crucial sense "nonpolyphonic" structure—which is to suggest that the obverse of the coin of one-*line* polyphonic music is multilinear "monophonic" music (thus distinguishing "voice" as "deeper-structural" and "line" as "more foreground-articulative", as we have been doing all along). Although I suspect that *Petrouchka* might ultimately be convictable of polyphony (perhaps by tracing paths over intervening "cuts" in the manner suggested by Cone in [11], as well as on the macrolevel of this very variability of simultaneity-partitions), there are pieces of Debussy and perhaps

"global" (whole-array) sense "explains" the local (first or second-half), "purely content-exchanging" succession in terms of which each harmonic unit *alone* may be "completely" accounted for. (Of course contour, register, etc., are not intended to be specified, just "some" way of projecting *these* "voices" as "most favorably inferable" "paths", rather than, say, E E E/G♯ G♯ G♯/C C C/, etc. The point, however, is that the first, "content-only" explanation is *indifferent* with respect to this path-determining inference.)[25]

A last observation here: if the "harmonic" structure of a 12-tone piece is not evidently derivable from segmental partitioning relations, or from an "aggregate-formation" criterion (with or without "weighting"), we may at worst decide that the simultaneity dimension is relatively weakly determinate with respect to other compositional instances, or we may invoke "associative" criteria to elucidate the "interiors" of the smallest inferable "harmonic units" as locally rather than globally functional structures. But all of these retrenchments would presumably have some bearing on the coherence-complexity depth that we would assign to the composition in question.

7. STRUCTURAL COHERENCE IN "ORDER" AND "CONTENT" MUSIC

The notions discussed in the preceding, then, represent conceptualizations that discover and govern *functional resources* of musical systems; and any construction of particular systems will, then, legitimately be guided by a wish to make choices that maximize the range, complexity, and unity of such resources available under a consistent single interpretation. We will, in other words, never shrink from "justifying" a constructional step, choice, or

---

Moussorgsky where I suspect the notion might prove useful, not to mention the various instances of "parallel organum" in its own time as well as ours.

[25]This "presentation"-"definition" distinction hints at a problem in the "explanation" of certain compositions where such differentia as, e.g., the "characteristic interval" of an actual *instrumental part* are given as primary syntactical functions, with no accompanying criteria for the relations of "intervals between intervals" in those parts, for those between adjacent boundary pitches, or for those among pitches coincident in different parts (obviously *these* cannot be interpreted as the analog of those *within* a part, since that would seem to reduce the criterion to virtual absurdity). See, especially, discussions of Elliott Carter's Second String Quartet.

priority on "ideological" grounds—that it will "give us what we want"—because we don't mean to pretend that we don't *know* what we want, and where we want to arrive. Clearly, such a program of maximization derives its desirability from the insight that the more definitionally distinct respects there are in which function can be asserted, the more the unique variability that can be "read out of" or "composed into" a given composition. This suggests the notion that the more "bound" a composer's or an analyst's syntax with respect to (and in terms of) a given composition, the more "creative freedom" he can assert, an idea proposed earlier in this essay, and one which might be pondered with profit by those who seek to "liberate" music from syntactic constraints.

As far as the construction of particular systems beyond the general basis described in Part II is concerned, we will here terminate our consideration of order-generated systems with a few general remarks, and then proceed to sketch in outline some of the steps that might be taken in generating a content system. The reason for this reticence regarding order-generated systems is just that the amount of "precomposition" inferable from pieces regarded as instances thereof is sufficiently great that the generalizable "systematic" dimension is relatively trivial except for some theorems that can be proved about available properties of various structures under various constraints, and most of the existing literature is devoted to just such questions.[26] Note, especially, that by virtue of what has already been said, it can be seen that "precomposition" is the relative depth in the music-derivational chain at which thought particularly directed toward the generation of a particular piece may be said to have significantly begun; put another way, it is indexed by the relative number of levels that we find it *necessary* to descend down the systematic definition-ladder to explain the non-shared aspects of a given composition (as distinct from the number of levels that it is desirable to descend, or *possible* to, which latter, in principle, is always "all"). And put still another way, the notion represents the "degree of contextuality" exhibited by the individual instances of some set of compositions we find it convenient to regard as comprising a "literature". (The latter considera-

---

[26]See, for example, Babbitt [1], [2], [3], [4]; Lewin [24], [26]; Krenek [22]; Howe [16]; Winham [41]; even most of Forte [14] and [15], despite some evident claims to greater explanatory scope. All of this makes Westergaard [37], [38], [39] and [40] particularly significant as attempts to theorize analytically.

tion is relevant to *historical* matters, manifestly, in that it may be interesting to find ways that historically proximate compositions share characteristics which can be generalized into "the musical language of a time"; but it also may be relevant to extrahistorical investigations that group compositions for given explanatory purposes along quite otherwise-determined lines. An interesting "historical" experiment might be the examination of compositions for order- or content-generation to discover whether prevalent "historical-literature" beliefs actually prove descriptively relevant.) Thus, the analysis of the literature of tonal music does not *require* the reconsideration of the generation of referential sets in the reconstruction of each composition, whereas the analysis of the literature of 12-tone music does, symptomizing what we can consider the "greater contextuality" of the latter. I stress the point to distinguish the degree of contextuality that *can* be asserted for any music from that which, as it turns out, *must* be discovered for each composition in a "literature" where the "precompositional" chain for one or more pieces has been previously defined; simply, the number and level of *shared* characteristics of this nature differs from literature to literature. The extreme case is of that music which Babbitt calls "contextual", where each piece is—in the most extreme view—its own entire "literature". But this designation is itself slightly elliptical, since there are plenty of respects in which those ("free atonal") pieces can be seen to *resemble* each other; the problem is rather that for each *individual instance* no complete description of a comparable satisfactoriness to those we can give of members of earlier and later "literatures" can be derived. So in those cases, we are forced to make strategic retrenchments, from regarding the minimum "discernible element" in delimited relational complexes, as "referential", or functional, to regarding as minimally functional larger "basic units" whose interiors remain relationally undefined and which thus "function" in a sense grosser than we should like. For example, we may find a local structure in such a composition that exhibits a high degree of definable coherence, through which however we cannot account either for the interior structure of other localities, or for the relations between localities. Thus in order to produce a "global structure" we need to retreat to a *more complex* elementary unit, or "atom", admitting our "incoherence" at more individuated levels (such as, optimally, that of "minimum discriminable detail") with respect to that piece.

This retrenchment may, of course, proceed all the way to the boundaries of the compositional data, in which case we are, surely, *incoherent with respect to that composition* (see the earlier remarks on this subject, in Part I, and a reconsideration of the position in terms of analytic criteria in Part IV).

So, with respect to order-generated systems, I will simply indicate the "paradigm" procedure for their construction as consisting in the generation of a "referential set" which constitutes an ordering of the total pitch-class vocabulary. In other words, where n is the total number of pitch-class elements, then, for any ordered pitch array

$$(a_i \, a_j \ldots a_q)$$

the referential set will be an ordered partitioning of the set

$$(a_0, a_1, \ldots, a_{n-1})$$

with n-related pitches considered equivalent. The nature (interpreted "sound") of "n", and the *number* of partitioning elements (to within the symmetrical requirements that no "common denominator" not actually present is inferable) are left open to individual-systematic interpretation. The notion of partitioning involved here can be easily extrapolated from the definition of pitch-class partitioning given elsewhere. But the primary referential set resulting from such partition may itself be considered as having been generated by compositions of partitioning subclasses (not necessarily by isomorphic ones—e.g., compositional manifestation may make a segmental sub-partitioning relevant, as in the tetrachordal disposition of Schoenberg's Op. 25, even where the "derived-set" criterion is inoperative; and, conversely, the degree to which it is *useful* to notice an isomorphic segmentation, even where one or several *can* be asserted is contextually dependent—cf. various discussions of the set of Schoenberg's Third Quartet). The degree of determination of the *whole* by such subpartitions can also be variable (i.e., hexachord *content* may generate deeper structural levels, as a basis of isomorphism, than within-hexachord element *order,* and similar remarks apply to trichordal and/or dyadic partitionings that generate hexachords or tetrachordal [or trichordal, or dyadic] partitionings of whole sets). The crucial systematic point here is that we regard the syntactical-referential norm as in all cases the *maximal construct* along certain lines generated by defined relations among sub-constructs.[27]

8. OUTLINE OF A TONAL-SYNTACTICAL SYSTEM

Now we proceed to our final task in this Part, the sketch of a "syntactical model" for the tonal system, one that provides a basis into which the "Schenker model" of tonal structure can be plugged. What follows is merely an informal outline of such a construction, mentioning relevant considerations and interesting properties in the process.

Since what is being generated is a content system, whose referential set will therefore be a proper subset of the total pitch-class vocabulary, it may be useful to indicate in advance the necessity, in generating a system isomorphic with the tonal one, of dimensioning the pitch-class "octave" at 12, though the "actual" interpreted modular "size" (sonically speaking) is irrelevant; that is, what constitutes a "1", or a "1/12 octave" relation is open to indi-

---

[27]That such considerations of varying *degrees* of order-determinacy within "the 12-tone system" are not reflected within the scope of Kassler's models [in [20]; see Part I, pp. 76ff.) is, though understandable from his point of view, one of the principal contributors to the "epistemic shyness" I have noted therein. In particular, it would seem that some of the "analytic puzzles" described in his article might have yielded under such considerations. That similar considerations are hinted at by Kassler as "stylistic rules" seems to me to place "style" [in his sense] at a rather too deep level of music-structural description, and, again, while I understand the possible notion of "maximum generality" motivating this, it seems to me preferable to "build in" such potential resources whose importance in composition we know quite well, and whatever "chances" it entails taking to do so. In fact, the risks seem especially worthwhile in contexts where sub-construct relations may consistently be asserted at levels of construction *prior* to those of which the supposed "syntactical conventions" [e.g., the "Schoenberg rules"] are assertible; for this assertion in no way *predetermines* the invocation of such "conventions" at any particular level in the particular analysis involved. That is, for any given piece, it might indeed be relevant to regard the unit-generated 12-tone set [as a *monad* set] as the "minimum partitioning" [or "minimum determinacy" of the structure], but such a determination could be made in the context of a syntax where smaller generating partitioning constructs *could* also be asserted in other cases [or as a more "general" determinacy in the given case]. But the procedure of *beginning* at the total monadic-ordered set level and then deriving any sub-partitionings by a kind of "stylistic quasianalysis" seems incongruent for those pieces where such sub-partitioning is relevant at very basic levels. See the remarks on centricity and tonality above, also, for "content-system" analogs to the same problem.

vidual acoustic interpretation. But as we shall see, the "12" is an important aspect of the system in more than one respect; the most important, however, is undoubtedly its "superabundance" (as pointed out by Babbitt), which in the tonal system has the virtue of restricting its "asymmetric partitioning cycles" (i.e., those whose cyclic application produces a partitioning such that the resultant set determined by that partitioning exhausts the elements of the partitioned domain). The fact that only two integers included in 12 (and their mod-12 complements) are "prime" to 12 seems significant (and reasonable to invoke as a "decision" factor) in the "choice of dimension" for the tonal pitch-class universe. (*Could* it have been otherwise? I hope the question no longer seems meaningful.)

A. First partitioning:
Having dimensioned the "pitch-class octave" at 12, we take as initial partitioning a particular pitch-class octave, in conformity with our notion of "pitch centricity" as an "ultimate" basis for the tonal system. Thus we construct a domain,

$$)0( )(12)($$
$$)0($$

where the pitch-class elements are assigned particular values with respect to a particular zero, rather than being regarded as "some value relative to some 0". This "fixes" the "centric" pitch-class element by its particular "octave partition" of the pitch domain.

B. 1) We then seek to construct (with polyphonic malice aforethought) a *maximum partitioning construct* through which to arrive at a *maximum referential collection.*

2) Since we have begun with a *pitch*-hierarchical notion, we seek to construct such a collection in one-pitch-at-a-time stages, such that each resultant relation is hierarchically defined with respect to the "preceding" stage and "subsequent" stages, and such that we maximize the *uniqueness of function* associated with *every relation at every stage* (multiplicity of function derives from associations among different stages) resulting, first, in a succession such that were we to stop at any point we would have a potentially coherent system (i.e., every *stage* of a syntax is a potential syntax, just as every level of a composition is a potential composition); second, in a succession that in fact is *maximal* for each of the transforma-

tions defined (this is clarified below); and third, in a succession which multiply defines, at different levels, the hierarchical relations of every pitch with respect to every other, on the basis of their commensurable relations to the pitch center. Thus we maximize, in particular, ways of asserting hierarchical degrees of similitude among differentiable, but comparably (content-) dimensioned subsets of elements.

C. Second partitioning:

To produce a construct, from a partitioning of the centric octave, such that that construct represents a determinate hierarchization of the partitioning element with respect to the centric element, the partitioning must be "asymmetric", i.e., one that partitions the octave into non-equivalent segments whose (complement-class) intervallic value is "prime" to that of the modular-interval; otherwise the determination of which is the *partitioning* and which the *partitioned* pitch-class octave would be non-unique. That is, if we choose 6 as the partitioning interval, the equivalence of (0, 6) and (6, 0) represents a non-unique basis for interpretation of the "reference octave". Similarly, 2, 3, 4, and their complements 8, 9, 10, are all extrapolable into non-unique partitionings in the same sense. Further, it may be said that any symmetrical partitioning in any domain of any size is non-unique operationally, in that the partitioning interval itself may be taken as an "octave" with internal isomorphism in structure to the "actual" octave (thus all relations assertible mod 12 are describable as relations mod 6, or 4, or 3, given reinterpretation of "complement", etc.).

The only intervals conforming to the criterion are 1/11 and 5/7. The partitioning by 1/11 has several points against it: 1) its maximal extrapolation by, e.g., transpositions and complementations in terms of itself, produces (at best) a subset of the pitch domain isomorphic to the domain itself (i.e., symmetrical in content-structure):

Second Partitioning by 1/11:

)0(
)1(
)0(

Maximal reference-set extrapolation by transposition and complementary transposition:[28]

"Prime":

```
                    1                            11
             0                                10
    11                              0
                    2                        11   11
          1     1                1
       0     0                0      0
       11                        1
```

collection: (11, 0, 1, 2)   "Complement":   collection: (10, 11, 0, 1)

Further "secondary" extrapolation only enlarges the dimensions of the collection without affecting the non-uniqueness of internal structure.

2) Beyond this initial extrapolation (which produces a "2-level" hierarchization), no further analogous partitioning is possible for 1/11, as the minimum pitch-class interval.

3) The notion of "polyphonic voice domains" defined linearly is impossible if the model for simultaneity contains intervals of minimum pitch-class adjacency while the intervals of succession include larger intervals:

  intervals of simultaneity (co-referential): 1/11, 0.

  primary intervals of succession (between reference construct and each of derived constructs, but not also within reference construct) 2/10.

  secondary interval of succession (between secondary constructs only): 3/9.

---

[28] The "maximization" of the reference set consists of generating new pitches (and intervals) by extending the relations implicit in the reference construct. At this stage maximization consists of generating, out of a pitch B in a central construct (A, B) wherein B *partitions* (the octave of) A, the pitch C such that C partitions B as B partitions A. Also, A generates a pitch D such that A partitions D as B partitions A. This is *maximal* by the centric criterion, since it places every member of the reference construct into every relational position determined by the reference construct. The next maximizing stage for the syntax ("partitioning something (x) as x partitions something else (y)") generates new pitches out of each of the constructs generated at the third stage. This notion accounts for the procession described below ("Third partitioning").

4) The resultant collection not only fails to exhibit a unique partitioning of the pitch-class domain, but also fails to exhaust the interval content of that domain, thus allowing "undefined" intervallic relations as "transposition relations" to arise, at every transpositional level.

This leaves 5/7 as the remaining "prime to 12" interval. We shall not at this point distinguish between 5 and 7, since at the level of two-pitch "models for simultaneity" they seem equally viable. (In this respect, consider the "4th"- or "5th"-referential polyphony of the earliest, even post-parallel-organum period. It is a question, with respect to this music, whether one wants to regard the following as in the "polyphonic" or "monophonic" domain, even though simultaneous variability in two dimensions could very well have been inferred from it:

```
C C D E F G G F D E E
C C C C C D D C D E E
```

But organal polyphony later than this "free" organum still exhibits a "5"-model for two-pitch simultaneity. Note that two-pitch music most often has as its "minimal norm of sonority" a "3-part" textural articulation, just as three-pitch music most often has a "4-part" one: not only does this enable the multiple "definition" of each presented element of a simultaneity—"syntactical" hierarchical interpretation and "doubling" interpretation—but it also provides a "complete" closure for the partitioning by asserting "both ends" of the modular octave, thus exposing the referential partitioning "within":

```
       )0(                )0(
       )7(     or         )5(
       )0(                )0(
```

as "presented", not just inferred, "final" sonorities. A connection with the *finalis* of the Schenker model seems evident.)

Another virtue of 5/7 is that it represents a maximal partitioning of the pitch domain in the sense that the two resultant "regions" are *minimally* distinct in dimension (i.e., number of intervening elements); no other partitioning that produces *any* differential in dimension produces *less* difference. This, of course, is an advantage in creating hierarchical "degrees of similitude", and maximizing the number and identities of "polyphonic voices".

Whether or not we could at this point assert a preference for 7 over 5 on the grounds that 7 produces the uniquely non-duplicating partition (is the *smallest* interval to do so, in fact), whereas 5 "repeats" within the octave, is an open question. Stronger considerations determine our later preference for 7.

Thus we can choose our second level of partitioning, and maximize the collection it can generate by the operations of transposition and complementary transposition. The complementary partitionings are constructed side by side:

```
                    )7(
                    )2(
              )0(              )0(
                                      )5(
                                      )10(
              )7(  )7(     )7(
        )5(                     )5(  )5(
              )0(  )0(     )0(  )0(
                                )7(
        )5(
```

collection: (5, 0, 7, 2)   collection: (7, 0, 5, 10)

Note that the collections resulting are transpositionally identical; the interval of simultaneity generated at this level is, after 0 at the "primary" level (and trivially), 7 or 5; and the primary interval of succession is 2. Note the relation between "level of generation" and "multiplicity in the collection" (in the ultimate diatonic collection) translatable as "associational range" with respect to collection-transpositions. Note, too, the restricted "defined interval" range of the resultant collection (3 out of a possible 6 intervals); compare this to the degree to which simultaneity in two-pitch-simultaneity-model music is defined (i.e., determinate) for "interstitial" passages.[29] Nevertheless, for elements within a given "mode", an in-

---

[29]Also, in the 7-model, the lower degree of determinacy with respect to construct elements at this level provides the lower-level basis for regarding the tonal system as a "major-minor" system, since (at this level) only the "fifths" are determinate, i.e., a chord containing (C, E♭ G) is an equally possible interpretation of a tonic C chord (defined only as "C, G") as is one containing (C, E, G). But at a higher level, the distinction becomes operative—and no one would want to deny that we can distinguish major from minor at some level. This lower-higher level relation conforms to my claim that "higher levels" are simply *more*

terpretation is possible on transpositional grounds, which creates a defined polyphonic structure in which "voice areas" are primarily defined as neighbor-note relations around the center construct:

$$5 - 7$$
$$2 - 0$$

or:

$$7 - 5$$
$$10 - 0$$

with transpositionally derived intervals forming "secondary neighbor notes":

$$t7S\ (5\ 0\ 7\ 2) = (0\ 7\ 2\ 9)$$
$$9 -)7(- 5$$
$$2 -)0($$
$$t7S\ (0\ 7\ 2\ 9) = (7\ 2\ 9\ 4)$$
$$9 - 7 - 5 - 4 - 2 - 0$$

This may explain the "hexachord" orientation, as well as the "indifferent" modal-centric interpretation of pretonal music, and even to a certain extent of triadic pretonal music; but this is a largely uneducated guess.

D. Third partitioning:

The restricted intervallic range noted above leads us to pursue the goal of maximization in projecting a partitioning "referential construct" out of which to generate a collection. Thus, if we partition 7 by the analogous "maximal complement" criterion ("smallest difference from midpoint") we partition the interval 7 into two maximal complements, as it partitions 12 into maximal complements, by 4 + 3/3 + 4. In our "complementary system", however, the result of "partitioning 5 as 5 partitions 12" are the constructs 025 (2 + 3) and 035 (3 + 2). But the interval 2 has already been defined as a primary interval, as a first-level primary interval of *succession*; thus this further partitioning sacrifices a significant functional distinction available in pitch systems: that of functional

---

determinate ways of "hearing"; and the "5th" level is a stage at which the "3rds" are *indeterminate*. Cf. the "perceptual randomness" of the between-reference-construct interstices of pretriadic music (e.g., 12th- and 13th-century motets), which we hear as relatively indeterminate *except* at the "5th" level.

uniqueness (and in fact the loss in uniqueness is a major loss in determinacy on other grounds too, for instead of increasing relational resources through the further partitioning, the determinacy "defined into" the interval by its being generated at its initial level is fatally weakened). Thus the 5-system is not capable of extension equivalent to that of the 7-system; this is the principal basis, as promised, for preferring the 7-system as the tonal system. Note, too, that the collection resulting in the 5-system is a *hexachord*, the "diatonic hexachord" (5 7 9 10 0 2), which also fails to include and hence define functions for all "chromatic" intervals.

To return to our 7-partition, then: the result here is dramatically different. The further partitioning of the previously constructed 7s, yields the following "complementary-systematic" results (intervals in square brackets):

$$
\begin{array}{cccc}
 & & & [3]\ 2 \\
 & & & [4]\ 11 \\
 & & [3]\ 7 & \ \ \ 7 \\
 & & [4]\ 4 & \\
0 & [3]\ & 0 & \\
9 & [4] & & \\
5 & & &
\end{array}
\qquad
\begin{array}{cccc}
 & & & [4]\ 2 \\
 & & & [3]\ 10 \\
 & & [4]\ 7 & \ \ \ 7 \\
 & & [3]\ 3 & \\
[4] & 0 & 0 & \\
[3] & 8 & & \\
 & 5 & &
\end{array}
$$

collection: (0, 2, 4, 5, 7, 9, 11)   collection: (0, 2, 3, 5, 7, 8, 10)

The two collections are, of course, transpositionally isomorphic, with the same "tonic fifth"; they represent, respectively, a "major-model" and a "minor-model" interpretation (generation) of the same collection. Notice that in "logical" structure, the major-minor isomorphism is complete, and no hierarchy could be asserted between them on internal grounds alone. But it seems nevertheless reasonable, on empirical grounds, to regard the major as the paradigm system, because of the alterations normally made in "minor-tonic" pieces to incorporate "major-model" features. A more internal (possible) reason for this is considered below.

At this stage, then, the "new" intervals generated are:

                     intervals of simultaneity: 3, 4
   (primary)   interval of succession: 1

and the single interval that does not occur either within the central "model for simultaneity" or between it and one of its two transpositions (the relation we have called the "primary interval of succession" relation), but only between the two "secondary" constructs, is the "unique interval" 6.

Now note that the (unique) multiplicity with which each chromatic interval occurs in this collection varies directly with its hierarchical position in the constructional chain, with all the intervals of simultaneity generated at each level occurring more frequently than the intervals of succession generated at the same level:

Levels:	Intervals of Simultaneity	Frequency of Occurrence	Intervals of Succession	Frequency of Occurrence
First:	0	7	—	—
Second:	7	6	2	5
Third:	3/4	4/3	1	2
"4th":	—	—		
("Secondary Interval of Succession"):			6	1

Of course, the significance of this unique multiplicity is the uniquely defined range of association (among collections) or uniqueness of identification (of a particular collection) characteristic of each interval. After total-collectional transposition is hierarchized and included in the construction, the number of occurrences within the collection of a given scale-degree interval will be seen to be equal to the total number of transpositionally related collections in which the pitches determining that interval in the reference collection occur. (This follows trivially from the transpositional isomorphism of the collections involved.)

E. Before turning to other properties of the present collection, let us consider why it constitutes a "maximum referential set". In order to demonstrate this, we may try to maximize the generating construct still further, producing a fourth hierarchical level (after the "0", "7", and "4/3" levels of polyphonic voice definition). Thus we partition the "major" collection once more, again by analogy to our previous efforts:

```
               7   7   7   7   7
           6               6
             5   5
4   ⟶   4 or 4 or 4 or 4 or 4 etc.
           3   3       3
                   1
0          0   0   0   0   0
```

But we need go no further: any of these partitions adjoins to our previous construction a confusion of definition, since intervals previously (uniquely) defined as intervals of succession are here reconstructed as also intervals of simultaneity, thus in effect producing a weaker system than was produced at a lower level of partitioning. Moreover, since every chromatic interval has already been defined at earlier levels, no further construction adding to the referential collection could but similarly weaken the determinacy of the system. And if we examine a normal-form arrangement of the collection we find that the uniqueness of intervals of succession (2, 1) and of simultaneity (7, 3, 4) is paralleled by the relation of "scale-degree adjacency"—for intervals of succession—and "scale-degree non-adjacency", for intervals of simultaneity. Here is an interesting confirmation of the way that the "linearity" criterion for voice relations is "built into" the system: compare successional-"closeness" (order-interval) in the successional normal-form representation to simultaneity-"closeness" (pitch-class interval) in the "models for simultaneity":

```
(0   2   4   5   7   9   11   0)
   2   2   1   2   2   2    1
```

But this criterion is violated by any new construct, which will produce conjunctions such as:

```
(0   2   3   4   6   7)
   ×       ×
   └─ 2 ─┘
           ×   ×
           └2┘
```

where the same intervals are produced by both adjacent and non-adjacent pitches—again in conformity with the simultaneity-succession result.

F. Collection transposition:

Thus, at the stage where we have defined a referential collection, and a function within that collection for every chromatic interval, we have still to define a multiple-hierarchical ordering of relations among all pitches in the pitch-class vocabulary, in terms of the "centric" pitch class. An obvious extension of the partitioning-construct transposition to a collection-transposition suggests itself (and it is obvious from the isomorphism of tetrachords in the normal-form representation that this property follows:

"t0S": (0 2 4 5)   "t7S": (7 9 11 0)).

Moreover, of course, it proves to be the case that transpositions by the "generative interval" 7 (and its complement) produce collections of maximum similitude (short of total identity) with the reference collection, in that they exhibit just one nonidentical component.* And in each of the complementary transpositions, the one-element difference involves the "replacement" of one of the two elements determining the "unique" 6:

```
              (0   2   4  (5)  7   9  (11)  0)
                            7   9   11  0   2   4  (6)  7)
(5   7   9  (10)  0   2   4   5)
```

The extension of this hierarchical chain (a "centrically interpreted" ordering of the syntactical content-array of which the reference set is a member) thus places every pitch class into multiple relation with every other in the pitch-class vocabulary. The exhaustion by the 7-cycle of the 12-pitch-class domain is operative in this hierarchization, which thus completes the "macrosyntactical basis" of the diatonic tonal system (what is generated is, in fact, a *complete* "syntactical content array" such as was defined in Section 2, above).

Earlier we considered how "chromatic intervals" are given "double meaning" by their additional syntactic definitions as "scale-degree intervals". But under transposition, each chromatic interval acquires multiple possible "scale-degree-interval" interpretations, familiar from such terms as "augmented second", "diminished fourth", etc. This phenomenon arises in the "first transposi-

---

*(1995:) This, of course, also follows trivially from the distribution of the members of the diatonic collection as seven adjacent positions in the 7-cycle which exhausts the 12-pitch-class domain.

tion" shown above, where a succession such as (E, F, G, B♭, B) would not be considered an erosion of the "adjacency-non-adjacency" distinction, but rather the "double representation" of "adjacencies to A and C" in two different scales. Thus the pitches that determine a chromatic "1" are, in one place, an "augmented prime" (B♭-B), and in another, a "minor second". The explanation for such weird interval types is that they arise as extensions of the notion of scale-degree interval within a collection to relations between distinct collections. And the succession E-F-F♯-G-A-B♭ can be regarded simply as the result of superposition of both 5th-related transpositions with the central collection (in the order $\binom{7}{0}\binom{5}{0}$). To illustrate the particular "scale-degree" dependency involved, consider the proposal to "hear" (notate) a pitch succession as (C♭, A). Now since, for all pairs of diatonic pitch-class collections, the minimum dimension of their intersection-sets in a 12 pitch-class system is 2, it will always be possible to "match" at least one scale-degree of each scale with an element of any other as a "0 prime".[30] Then, regarding "equal scale-degree interval" as "equal number of intervening scale degrees", we can correlate the "primes" to find the appropriate interval-designation (problems arising from the invocation of the supposed "fifth-*spiral*" are easily disposed of as pseudo-problems; enharmonic notation of a whole collection preserves everything relevant to the tonal syntax with regard to that collection):

(B♭ C♭ D♭ E♭ F♭ G♭ A♭ B♭)
(B♭ C D E♭ F G A B♭)

Counting from B♭, it is a 2nd to C♭ and a 7th to A; a 7th is a 6th larger than a 2nd, so the interval between C♭ and A is a kind of 6th, a "10-6th" (which conforms to the functional view of the "augmented sixth" as the superposition of the minor-collection "upper neighbor" of V with the "leading tone" of the V-major collection).

---

[30]Although the minimum *pitch-class* intersection is 2, the minimum *0-prime scale-degree* intersection is 1, because the 2 pitch classes may be in different scale-degree-interval relations in the two distinct collections. In such a case, *either* pitch class may be taken *as* the 0-prime intersection, but *not both*: F-B and E♯-B in the C and F♯ collections, respectively, represent such a case; if B is taken as the 0-prime, the F and E♯ represent *distinct* scale-degree distances from it, while if F is taken as 0-prime (changing the second collection enharmonically to G♭)., B and (what is now) C♭ represent distinct relative scale degrees.

To return to the diatonic collection itself: note that the entire collection is generated out of a single construct and its transpositions by its hierarchical principal components. Now (although the other plausible additional partitioning, by transposition in terms of the *tertiary* elements [the "3rds"] as well, would lead to the same double-definitional problems encountered before), the transposition within the collection by the "thirds" of the triads produces a set of inverses of the principal constructs of the *collection* (such inverses being defined, where the major form is primary, as "secondary triads"):

```
                           11
                            7
              4             4
              0
  9           9
  5
  2
```

(This is based on the (4 + 3)-cyclic representation of the collection as ((5 9 0) (0 4 7) (7 11 2)), and thus, also, as ((2 5 9) (9 0 4) (4 7 11)).)

The "triad" (11 2 5) is thus produced only "by analogy", since it is not transpositionally *or* inversionally isomorphic with the others, and in fact includes a "relation of succession", so that it is a definitionally "linear" event, bound to a "resolution" (see p. 234, above).

G. Tonal structure

Finally, two remarks about polyphony and succession: the derivation of the collection out of a hierarchical model for simultaneity defines three "structural voice" areas. Thus a "linear model" of the collection is assertible, wherein the entire collection is functionalized as "the tonic triad and the neighbor notes to its components", the neighbor notes being the "linear regions" for referential-construct component elaboration (or "structural-polyphonic voice regions"), according to the following model:

```
            9  -  7
            5  -  4
            2  -  0
           11  -  0
```

which exhausts the collection and suggests the "background" for the Schenker-linear (successional—i.e., "structural") model:

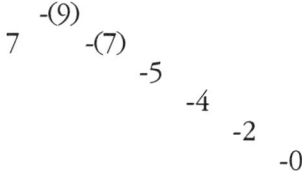

Now note that the tonic pitch is, in the "neighbor-note" model, assigned *two* neighbor notes, uniquely among the triadic components; they are functionally distinguishable as "upper" and "lower", and this distinction is identifiable by the different-sized 2nd that each represents. It is this functional distinction that might suggest a more internal reason for the primacy of the major model in tonal music, since the "leading tone" and "upper neighbor" are intervallically indistinguishable in the minor model. And as a justification, this seems more plausible than anthropomorphic yearnings of semitones for their upper neighbors or the greater "strength" of a dominant relation when the dominant is major, etc.

The fact that the triad is the "model for sonority" in tonal music means that every "linear" "polyphonic" embellishment is generated (at some determinable structural level) as a component of a resultant pitch conjunction modeled on the tonic triad (i.e., as a member of some determinate major or minor triad), as the familiar

$$\begin{array}{ccc} 7\text{-}9 & -7 & \\ 4 & -5 & -4 \\ 0 & -2 & \\ 0 & -11 & -0 \end{array}^{31}$$

---

[31] It seems plausible to regard 2 as displacing *both* 4 and 0, in which case it would be defined as a member of both the 0-voice and the 4-voice, assignable on some occasions to both (as both 11 and 2 are assignable to the single 0-voice), or otherwise to either one or the other depending on the context. Without this possibility of multiple assignment, it remains unexplained why in our model 4 is "suppressed" but not structurally "displaced" by the assertion of a (7 11 2) triad, such "suppression" requiring the introduction of what is in effect a new syntactical function.

On the other hand, the prevalence of the dominant seventh as a "cadential" articulator may be considered to be motivated in part by the explicit (the "four-voice" representation familiar as the basic "contrapuntal model" for tonal music has evident correspondence to the above; see the discussion of the question on p. 240ff., above). So every entity in a tonal structure is *initially*, at least (i.e., at its level of initial appearance), a member of *at least* one triad, and a component of a purely triadic succession.[*]

At the same time, the (interval-7) relation between the referential construct (I) and the principal secondary constructs (IV and V), from which the definition of "interval of succession" has emerged, is defined, as a "total relation (between constructs)", as the normative "model for succession" for background-structural simultaneities, as well as for local articulations. Again, the presence of such a model does not necessarily constrain *literally* any foreground successions; but where the sonorities presented in a foreground are non-triadic and the successions non-"fifth" the presumption is still of a consistent level-derivational *relation* of what does happen in the foreground to such a background model. Thus, too, the status of a local, or foreground, articulation may be partially determined as "more linear" or "more construct-successional" by whether the *presented* voice relations are more akin to the "linear model" or to the "harmonic model" of the tonal collection. Here the function of the "fourth contrapuntal part" is particularly significant, in providing the "fifth-outlining 'bass'" in conjunction with the "adjacency-outlining 'upper voices'".

At this point, the entire "syntactic" basis of the tonal system may be considered to have been sketched. Further considerations, including concepts of *"Ursatz"*, "tonicization",[32] etc., belong to the next, the analytic-compositional domain, and would be

---

voice displacement for the 4 this chord projects (as, 4–5–4), a displacement which must otherwise be "inferred" (given only (7 11 2) to go on). The question, it seems to me, remains open in view of the *intelligibility* of the seventhless (7 11 2) in the literature.

[*](1995:) It has seemed to me since shortly after this was written that the qualification "initially, at least" is unwarranted: every pitch sound in every tonal-syntactically construed structure is a member of some determinate triad(s)—theoretically, the number is limited only be the range of memberships of any pitch in triads of the total diatonic-collection array.

[32]Whose relatively universal applicability shows an extraordinary amount of "invariant precomposition" to characterize tonal music, the individuality of the instances of which entirely at the still higher levels is thus all the more remarkable.

beyond our scope here in any case. But the constructions suggested in this and the preceding parts, if carried out, would presumably provide a sufficient basis on which to rest the (Schenker-type) tonal and (Babbitt-type)[33] 12-tone systems as "normally", if somewhat variably, defined, with a minimum of additional patching required to effect the join.

---

[33] Or even Winham-type (see [41a]).

VI.
Part IV:
Analytic Fallout (I)

> In every activity, satisfactory performance requires meticulous care in some matters....What choices fastidiousness will dictate will vary with the individual....But if that were good reason for indifference, then variations in taste and belief would be good reasons for indifference about quality in art and about truth in science.
>
> —Goodman [55]

> ...clarity is more fruitful on the average than confusion, even though the fruits of neither are to be despised.
>
> —Quine [66], p. 123

1. ANALYSIS AND COMPOSITION

The purpose of an analysis (or a composition) is to reconstruct (or construct) a musical structure. We bother to reify "analysis" (and "composition") and "analytic methods" ("compositional methods" or "techniques") because of the conviction, reinforced by confirming practice, that, beginning from the simplest levels of intersubjective auditory experience, pieces are constructible most favorably up to a certain point through hierarchical functional paths that may be considered to be shared by all, then, beyond that point, through increasingly divergent, coherently subdivided paths, up, finally, to the singular stem: the individual piece. Now what these shared aspects are is not best understood as a "common practice" or "common language", because that viewpoint is more appropriate to a construction where the individual's importance is mainly that of an *instance* of structure in a domain of such structures. Here, the domain itself, and its model, are reified mostly as a map that juxtaposes (and superposes) the individual maps of individual pieces, resulting in a composite map that shows as single entities the intersections among all the maps that are nondivergent at the places where those entities occur; and, of course, any place where just one map is so nondivergent (i. e., from itself), contains whatever is associated uniquely with one piece. Principally, the value of this association is to make it unnecessary to reconstruct each piece as a phenomenon utterly *sui generis* beyond its characteristics as an "auditory object" at the purely "discriminative-perceptual" level. By deciding that certain predicates (terms) defined in certain ways and in a certain hierarchical order are correspondingly useful in the construction of a more or less long list of phenomenal objects, we reify, in turn, (e.g.) "music", "content music", "construct-centric music", "pitch-centric music", "tonal music", then perhaps some sub-categories determined by transposition-structural or intertriadic linear-structural characteristics (the first of which might distinguish, say, Mozart from late Beethoven and Schubert, and the second, say, Brahms from Wagner), and then, finally, such "categories" as "Beethoven's Sixth Symphony". In short, we find it useful to have each such predicate generalized to the maximum degree possible, consistent with the essential particularities that capture the sense of the intuitive concept involved, precisely because we want to know the maximum extent to which we can regard a given composition as *individual;* and by inferring the maximum set of *shared* characteristics it exhibits (along with some idea of the range and extent of the set of compositions with which each such characteristic is shared), we can, thereby, focus on that which is, in just the same sense, unique to the music in question. But it should be borne in mind that one of the most strongly identifying characteristics of this conceptual picture of music is the notion that we can in principle consider the total constructional hierarchy of each single piece to be inferable from its data alone, without recourse to a conventional lexicon or grammar (which, of course, does not mean that we do not wish to make *any* assumptions, only that it is conceivable that anything assumed *might* have been inferred without necessary reference to any other contexts "of the same nature"). Were it not for this radical contextuality, the generalizing kind of activity would be more "scientifically interesting" than "musically crucial", for our *musical* stake is in discovering as many *respects* as possible in which pieces can exhibit particularity of choice among alternatives, as many dimensions as possible of significant variability (where, hence, choices make a difference) and, thus, of individuality of identity.

Thus our interest in *comparing* pieces is not like our interest in comparing sets or passages within pieces, nor like our interest in comparing the behavior of rats in one controlled experimental environment with their behavior in another. In one sense, of course, the composer is somewhat like the scientist who wants to *predict*, on the basis of a particular observational path through a complex of data, what is likely to result, as observable relational behavior, from a different, as yet untested, data-complex, which is to be first hypothesized, then realized in the form of a set of instructions for the physical conjoining of available entities into prescribed relative dispositions. Nevertheless, the concept of a theory of music as predictive or post-dictive in a *normative* sense (as a way of sorting pieces into, say, "coherent" and "incoherent") seems hardly fruitful as compared, simply, to a maximal commensuration among explanations to further their cognitive content by giving them an ample comparison-domain for context, and thus also increasing the degree of individuation that they are able to confer on their subjects.

So, again, we compare individual pieces only to infer some terms whose interpreted transfer from one context to the other gives the attempt to "understand" a particular piece the benefit of discoveries and insights that have emerged in the course of "understanding" another (both "understandings" being simply equivalent to "reconstructing" or "constructing"). In previous sections, by considering reconstruction from "bottom" to "top", I distinguished among those predicates whose theoretical definitions were identical for all music, and some extrasystematic concepts which could be correlated with disparately defined theoretical terms in different systems ("polyphony", "counterpoint", etc., are concepts of this latter type). These, however, arise at the very point of first divergence in the foundation system. The question, then, is, can we in fact make use of super-syntactical structural observations in one systematic domain to assist cognitively the explication of structures defined as being in another? That is, beyond the shared systematic level, can the analytic reconstruction of a tonal piece help us to understand or to compose a twelve-tone piece or any other piece of a non-tonal kind? The answer would appear to lie in the analysis of some extrasystematic structural concepts that might be generalized at a high descriptive level, independent of, and variably but precisely correlated with, actual syntactic models themselves.

Frequently, such identification is attempted through a simple confusion of categories in which a structure otherwise undefined in terms of a system in which some single predicate occurs is assigned that predicate without further interpretation, or in effect treated in a very partial sense as an instance of some system, without consideration of the remaining aspects of either the piece or the system; as, the assignment of words like "cadence" and "phrase" in their tonal sense (or without specified alternative sense) to nontonal pieces. This practice, and uses of such terms as "polytonal", "quasi-tonal", "freely tonal", or "pan-tonal", produce a similar indeterminacy of reference that results from the apparent incompatibility of a defined functional term with an associated one, where the latter either 1) is represented by the same name as the familiar one, but is simultaneously defined in some new, inconsistent, sense, or 2) is a term conjoined to the familiar one that either denies some fundamental characteristic of the original, or is simply left undefined. The narrowness that such a critique may suggest to some readers wishing for a maximum latitude in the use of theoretical terms is simply an unavoidable result of the belief that only maximum cognitivity yields maximum musical "characteristicness". Consider the cognitive consequences of such "freedoms" as the supposed "mixture" of separately well-defined systems which, however, simultaneously interpret the same "acoustical" events in ways that are not simultaneously tenable. For even where every element in a composition is a member of many subset-successions, even of different types at different levels, these interpretations are compatible as long as there is a *single* ultimate background system that subsumes all of them as a medium for their coherent interrelation. But they are *incompatible* where the background system employed to obtain one interpretation must be replaced by another background system—one for which no correlation to the first is established—to generate the other. Similar cognitive problems arise with the mixture of well-defined with undefined or ill-defined systems ("degree of definedness" should be understood as signifying "extent of *discoverable definability*"). In both cases, the result is a net *loss* in "freedom" or, what amounts to the same thing, understandability, the cognition of *how* a piece "is itself".

For maximizing understandability maximizes the numbers of different ways in which things can be distinct entities; hence it leads to the existence of a maximum number of things among which there is freedom to choose. Otherwise, we get the paradoxical result that greater freedom is associated with a *reduction* in the *number of distinct choices available* in the world.

The possible suspicion that this argument is "mere semantics"—"why should the *music* be affected by differences over terms and definitions; isn't it all just a question of what *names* are given to the *same things?*"—will, I hope, have been adequately intercepted by what has preceded; but perhaps it deserves special consideration with respect to the "mixed-system" question. Here an example cited by Goodman (in [55]) in connection with a similar problem in philosophic systems may be useful: "Suppose that in a certain game a player is to begin by dealing each card from his hand onto the table at either his left or his right; he may put any card on either side and may move a card from side to side if he likes. Then while it is quite true that he is free to put any card on either side, he can never get a left-hand card on the right-hand side; for a card is a left-hand card or a right-hand card according as it lies on his left or his right." And thus, to paraphrase Goodman's conclusion, we can construe *any* sound-succession as a tonal or a twelve-tone structure; or as a manifestation of one key or any other key; but we can no more construe a twelve-tone trichord as *also* a tonal triad in the same piece under the same explanation, or a two-triad complex *as at the same time* (i. e., at the same level of the same ascription) two equivalent and simultaneous but distinct *tonic triads;* or a single one as equivalently and at the same time a tonic and a dominant triad (n. b. *equivalently*), any more than we can, in Goodman's game, get a left-hand card on the right-hand side.*

And with respect to "interpretative freedom", and the plea for "semantic tolerance" urged by many writers, presumably to maximize flexibility in subsuming pieces under "music", I would say that the more fastidious we are regarding the cognitive status of the *theoretical grounds* on which, and the *sense* in which anything is admitted to the category "music", the more such an admission when it does take place is worth, because of the far greater chance

---

*(1995:) Although one can imagine (and have experienced) cotemporally several "incompatible" constructions *amgibuating* one another, like two Goodman-games going on in an imagined spatiotemporal simultaneity.

that it actually confers some meaningful conceptual-perceptual status (in the sense of "what", not "how worthy") on the thing admitted. In other words, the more explicit the grounds of admission, the more generous we are, in the end, with respect to the consequentiality we ascribe to such an admission. Of course, each individual must choose his own standards of what he counts as relevant musical cognitiveness. But theorists and analysts are supposedly devoted to the maximum elucidation of what is intersubjectively cognitive about pieces, and thus, on their part, taking tolerant attitudes toward variable standards of musical cognitiveness is not only intellectually unbecoming, but hardly serves their presumed musical self-interest. For a theorist may be tolerant of any listener's music-cognitive awareness or demands, and even of his own or other theorists' "musical tastes"; but he can hardly afford to be equally tolerant of his own or other theorists' standards of music-theoretical adequacy or cognitiveness, or else he has very little motivation to offer himself as a theorist, analyst, or other kind of explicator of "music" instead of as an appreciationist or enthusiast.

The question of *what is admitted* as music is itself quite variable depending on the context of admission. The listener, or the theorist himself as a listener, can be as capricious and cavalier as he likes in making admissions; but *as* theorist or analyst, he may admit whatever he likes only as long as his tolerance regarding *what* he admits is accompanied by an equivalent intolerance in the application of *his own standards* of what constitute adequate grounds for such admission, and what constitutes an adequately cognitive account of how such an admission is to be understood. Whether these standards, in turn, will prove acceptable to other theorists, analysts, and listeners, is, of course, subject to all the same considerations. Again a remark of Goodman's seems apt here: "I admire the statesman tolerant of divergent political opinions, and the person tolerant of racial and educational differences, but I do not admire the accountant who is tolerant about his addition, the logician who is tolerant about his proofs, or the musician who is tolerant of his tone" (*sic:* we cite Goodman for philosophical, not musical aptness).

Some writers, especially in the field of contemporary music, have demonstrated an awareness of these problems by using, for the "structural concepts" to be transferred from one system-domain to another, "neutral" terms like "event" and "continuity" as general structural terms; but most often these terms are applied on the apparent basis of a vague synesthesia that gives them little cognitive value beyond the simple avoidance of the more blatant confusions mentioned above. But, their employment usually has at least the virtue of being vacuous with respect to *any* theory, rather than positively destructive of what may be mildly cognitive in the customary applications of some particular theory or other.

So it will be my effort in what follows to demonstrate some of the direct analytic applications of the general view of music I have been developing in this essay, and specifically of the general model for music sketched in Parts II and III. An attempted explication of predicates such as "continuity" and "event" as high-level "communicants" among pieces having distinct syntactical bases is the substance of the later sections. In the parts that immediately follow I consider the implications of the availability of our model in dealing with problems in analysis that have appeared heretofore to require very elaborate adjustments of familiar systems or special constructions of new general syntaxes, in order to explain their objects and either associate them with an existing literature, or reify a new one for their (collective) benefit. A prime normative criterion used as a guide in this consideration is that of analytic simplicity.

2. ANALYTIC SIMPLICITY AND SYSTEMATIC GENERALITY

In the absence of a background music-syntactical model such as has been proposed herein, analysts have tended to deal with "problematic" pieces, or chronologically proximately composed groups of such pieces, by one or more of the following expedients:

1. They accept a standard of "total-structural" explanatory adequacy far below what they would accept for "known-systematic" music. (See my remarks on Perle [29] in [7].)

2. They plug such problematic pieces into existing general-systematic models whose normal justification and motivation for construction and application is the high degree of uniformity they confer on particular literatures, even though such plugging in requires the acceptance of a considerably reduced standard of uniformity at many levels of structure, even with respect to the very number and status of the levels of structure on which such

uniformities can even be asserted. Examples of this phenomenon abound in the literature; some of the most sophisticated examples are to be found in the analyses of 20th-century compositions in Salzer's *Structural Hearing*, in Forte's *Contemporary Tone Structures,* in Imbrie's "Roger Sessions" (*Perspectives of New Music* I/1) and in Mitchell [28].

3. They construct an uninterpreted system which is explicated as determining a correlation of the data of problematic musical structures with analyses of structure in other, non-musical, domains, with questionable effectiveness in accounting for the music-epistemic significance of the correspondence involved. Numerous examples from European literature, including several of the principal articles published in *Die Reihe,* may be cited in connection with this technique, but it seems also to inform much of the literature concerned with connecting music with stochastic, statistical, or psychological processes, as well as many efforts at constructing a verbal-linguistic model for music.

4. Finally, there is the attempt to construct an entire new general-syntactical model to reify a group of problematic pieces *as* a neo-literature of a sort analogous to the existing "unproblematic" literatures. One such account of a background model for the "literaturization" of "motivic" music (my preferred name for what Babbitt calls "contextual" and almost everyone else "atonal" or "freely atonal") that correlates musical relations with set-theoretic operations in a way that accounts for music-epistemic factors in just the domains of pitch-class and interval-class relations (but not in the domain of order-class relations) is to be found in Forte [15], some aspects of which are considered more particularly below.

Now the motivation for these variant explanatory maneuvers is clearly that, in the absence of either a general background theory for music, or a general syntactical model for a "literature", there remains a relatively large number of pieces that a relatively large number of people care about having as part of music, which cannot in any known cognitive sense be so included, because no one has yet found an acceptable way to describe them as musically coherent. But with an all-musical background theoretical model, such as the one developed in Part II, the situation is materially altered: the compulsions to reify a literature, to find some general structural paradigm at some *particular* structural level that makes every composition a member of some group of a certain kind, to force everything into some *existing* model of musical structure, or to accept a greatly reduced standard of musical coherence, are considerably relieved when musical coherence is regarded as a *direction* on a relativistic scale rather than an absolute *attribute,* and when, as is possible with such a background theory, everything likely to be regarded as a potential piece can be shown to be coherent to at least a certain degree if it is admissible at all—and all it has to be to be admissible is a finite succession of discriminable (and discriminated) auditory phenomena that someone wants to regard as music. Whether after observing the degree of coherence that can be ascribed to it under the best reconstruction we can produce we will not think it more useful to take our piece to another domain is dependent only on, again, how much coherence we require in those things we are willing or eager to regard as "usefully regardable as music", and, of course, how hopeful we may be that by using the yardsticks of some particular other domain we are likely to arrive at some more satisfactory ascriptive results—such greater satisfactoriness being dependent both on the scope of the ascription derivable from such another domain and on our willingness to accept the normative or epistemic implications of the association of our piece with the other entities in that domain as well as with the legend on the sign on its door.

Now since the lowest possible degree of correspondence to the definitions offered herein, by anyone's criterion of musical admissibility, must still be greater than zero, all things presented as candidates for music that have *just zero* correspondence to those definitions are not—*as music*—ever anything that could be called "negatively coherent music" (or "positively chaotic music"), or in some way "negatively distinctive", whatever that might mean, but simply are—*as music*—all alike, insofar as they all share a *lack* of the *same totality* of music-identifying characteristics (insofar, in turn, as our music-identifying capacities can tell). What they are alike *in* is, in fact, just being "something else". For our definitions are predicated on the notion that any specified finite set of auditory phenomena may be regarded, and regarded in a virtually inexhaustible number of ways, "as music". It is true, however, that neither a goat, say, nor a heat wave, are admissible under this restriction (to auditory things). And where *they* would be presented as "two distinct candidates for admission as music", they would indeed be "identical as music in being something else". But although such entities have been, and are increasingly being, presented as music, there are also strictly *auditory* entities being presented as music which, we are told, are in fact (partly or wholly) "chaotic". Here someone is fooling himself, because, first, if we *do* regard something as *relatively* chaotic (some or all of it as somewhat chaotic, not some part of it as wholly chaotic) as music, that just characterizes the *negative* circumstance that we have been able to attribute to it only a *low degree of coherence*. (If we *choose* to regard it as *utterly chaotic as music,* we would simply be converting it, at the perceptual end, into something musically characterless *for us*; or, in other words, it would be *identical as music for us* with heat waves and goats. But it seems a virtually empty possibility that we would ever *have* to so regard any succession of auditory things.) But, second, it seems (and has proved in practice) that what is far more likely to happen with something presented as music that its maker has designed in a way appropriate to his notion of "chaos", is that it will tend to break down into trivial, commonplace, or gross kinds of coherences in its audition by reasonably experienced receptors. The trouble is that the desired chaos, no matter how bad a boy the would-be perpetrator thereof is willing to be, is simply unavailable (except by extramusical agreement) because it is an empty notion in the first place; and what he perpetrates is far less likely to appear destructive or nihilistic than just commonplace.

And since a background theory thus relieves us of the worry with respect to most pieces we care about that they will not be "admissible as music", we can all the more firmly hold to adequate cognitive standards (the ones we care about with respect to most pieces) in the explication of, and for the admission of, *any* piece that is so admissible. For we are able to sustain a crucial distinction between *what something is as music* and *whether something is music*; and it *is music* just because what we are going to make of it depends on what we make of any array of relational qualities obtained through determinate observational headings on an array of auditory things with respect to such matters as pitch characteristics, interval characteristics, modular-equivalence characteristics, registral characteristics, "earlier than-later than" characteristics, etc.—in other words, the things whose interrelated definitions and applications to auditory phenomena are just what constitutes our *making music of those phenomena*. Our efforts beyond the point of simple admissibility of something, then, can be directed to the construction of a model that makes the *most* music possible out of that thing, by discerning the *most* instances and kinds of coherence that can be ascribed to the data-array with the *least* inferential complexity (in the form of elaborate rules of inference based on concepts relatively remote from observables) between the *model* of the data and the observable data itself, on the one hand, and between the model of the *data* and the model of the *theory,* on the other (cf. Part I, pp. 21–23).

Thus, it might turn out that the "contextuality" of a piece is in fact sometimes associated with a relatively low degree of coherence in our *best* model of it.[1] This may arise as a consequence of our being unable to come up with, say, a primitive basis whose simplicity is comparable to that (those) available for traditional literatures. And such a complex primitive basis may underlie relatively few higher structural levels beyond itself in our best model, or perhaps the interlevel inferences we are able to make are themselves complex and require the subsumption of relatively many disparate discriminables within one complex generative step.

On the other hand, since every piece is ultimately just one-to-one with its own "system", it might happen that some pieces appear to instantiate systems that, for most of their upper reaches, intersect with those of no other pieces. Isolation of this sort may be due to a virtual exhaustion of the differentiating resources of the system at those higher levels by those single instances, or it may be a result of the non-extensibility of the system's high-level resources to a sufficiently wide range of different "musical events" or "compositional ideas". Or, it may be the case that there are more ambiguities in the system and its modeling of the associated data than seem desirable in a system that one would want to try to transfer to other instances. In any case, the observation will be merely a biographical one in the long run; if what we can "make of" pieces is what they "are", then certain systems are "shared by" *more* pieces than are others, and some are apparently unique to *single* instances.

---

[1] It follows from our discussion in previous chapters that we are never in a position to speak absolutely in a negative sense about the "incoherence of a piece", only about 1) "the coherence we can ascribe to it", and 2) "our relative incoherence with respect to it".

Here, then, we may consider two possible ways of viewing "problem" pieces: 1) as individuals, or literatures, that are clearly music but where general syntactic systems, old or new, are not of much help because the syntactical and articulative levels in these pieces seem virtually identified, by which I mean that the "individual pieces", their actual presentation of particularities of projection, *begin* right at or just after the level at which one's basic model for any music terminates, at a point where most traditional pieces are still further constructible in terms of shared or contextual (unshared) reference collections; 2) as individuals representing high-level articulation through elaborate syntactical ascensions which, however, must be uniquely inferred for these individuals, since they are not evidently shared by the members of any literature or any other instance of music.

The acceptance of these two approaches as legitimate analytic possibilities may, if they produce adequate ascriptive results, save us from having to construct enormously elaborate systems to "syntacticalize" and make "part of a literature" pieces whose rendering as rather more simplistic varieties of music may actually yield a structure of greater "significant coherence" (see Part II, pp. 94ff.) than anything yielded by those systematically higher-powered efforts. For by sacrificing "number-of-levels" criteria which require for their implementation a "complexity of primitive" characteristic and perhaps also a "high interlevel opacity" characteristic (both of which reduce sharply the *effective* complexity of the resultant structure), we may gain a great deal in lucidity by constructing a simpler, but relatively ambiguity-free model. And in calling some of the music to which a model of this kind seems applicable "motivic", I do mean to suggest a relatively immediate connection between the motivic level—that articulative surface whose correlate in traditional music is normally rather elaborately generated through many intervening levels from a deep-lying referential background—and the assertible background itself. The resultant model might indeed lead one to conclude that the music it modeled was in fact less richly and elaborately coherent music than the most esteemed instances of tonal or twelve-tone composition—which might also explain why this music troubled its own composers to the degree that the most accomplished of them abandoned composition for a while to think of a more satisfactory way of going about it, why, too, it had such a relatively brief history, and why it found so few eminent champions in the form of practitioners after the twelve-tone system was developed. On the other hand, having a model of our kind for "motivic" music not only would confirm that it is in fact reasonable to regard these pieces as music in an intelligibly traditional sense, but that at their relatively few, shallowly generated, levels, they do exhibit individual syntactical and structural characteristics that give us at least a tenuous hold on individuality for them. Parenthetically, it should be noted that a predictable consequence of shallowness does seem to show up in analyses of such pieces: namely, that the assertible range of functionally unambiguous development is rather narrow, so that the most fully coherent models will tend to be of pieces of relatively limited extent. In longer pieces, the model derivable for an individual segment of the piece will tend to be more maximally coherent on a more atomic basis than the models subsuming several segments, or those of the "total structure", a relationship (among the models) that is relatively "inside-out" by comparison with the situation normally encountered in traditional-systematic music. (How and why such music came to be composed at a time of such apparently high compositional development may become more clearly understandable in the light of a similar re-examination of the music of late tonality, where the extension of the tonal reference appears to result both in a "motivicism" with respect to *local* coherence which is perhaps incompatible, or non-commensurable, or at any rate discontinuous with the tonal global structure, and in a fragmentation of that global structure and even of its larger articulated segments. But this question will be further considered in due course.)

The second of the suggested approaches, in particular, may save us from the necessity of Procrusteanism with respect to some pieces we have cared enough about to be willing to force them into some system or other, often by ignoring certain kinds of evidence that we normally regard as crucial signalogy for the invocation of the particular systematic-model-type involved, and by accepting a degree of interlevel opacity that, especially when it occurs at lower levels, would be decidedly unacceptable to us in an analysis of almost any of the other pieces we have subsumed in that literature. These equivocations produce a rather coarse fit of piece to model that may be to the detriment of the piece or result in an unfortunate weakening of coherence over the whole literature, or both. If we do care enough about the piece, however, it may still be possible to construct a special syntactical model to get the most out of it; otherwise, we may be content to regard it as a rather coarsely coherent instance of some known system (to save the virtues of the rest of a literature at their maximum virtuousness—this may have been Schenker's Paladinate), and thereby simply resign ourselves to its exclusion from the repertory of Ultimate Musical Masterworks.

3. THE *TRISTAN* PRELUDE

We do, evidently, care enough about *Tristan* to probe it a great deal; it has not been notably cooperative, as any even casual student of the literature knows. The most successful attempt I have seen to explain its Prelude by means of the Schenker-model version of tonality is Mitchell [28]. But even there, the amount of direct evidence that is, in one way or another, suppressed—or, better, treated in a highly non-standard way—leaves one feeling that the piece ought to come out looking better than that with respect to the relation between its most prominent features and our most explanatory model; otherwise, perhaps, one oughtn't after all to think so well of it, by comparison to other pieces that manage at least as much tonal subtlety as the *Tristan* Prelude of Mitchell's account with a great deal more compositional grace in the relation they embody between syntactical importance and articulative prominence. And the "A-major" notion of the analysis, with its accompanying virtual non-consideration of one of the most interesting questions about the Prelude, namely that of the structural "meaning" of the Gs that end the piece and connect it with the first scene, is at best an explanation of the "concert version" which is not, I believe, the piece that most of us care about. I tend, in fact, to regard the concert version as providing strong intuitive confirmation that the (Schenker) tonal system is *not* the best place to look to find a good way to reconstruct the Prelude itself, whatever Wagner thought. Thus I would rather not hear the Prelude as the piece to which the "concert ending" is an appropriate one, because that piece seems a good deal less interesting to me than the one I believe *Tristan* as a whole, and the Prelude as a significant chunk of it, can be. So among the really crucial questions that Mitchell's analysis leaves unasked are the following: Is the *Tristan* Prelude part of *Tristan?* And if it is, *how* is it? I will try to suggest some directions from which answers to these questions might be essayed.

Let us consider first some of the "evidence" with which *Tristan* confronts a "naive" observer, let us say one examining it in our own time who hasn't a very good idea of when it was composed. If he knows the "Schenker model" but doesn't consider its invocation in every case a moral imperative (so that for him, something can be "music" on other grounds, and even equally "highly developed" music), how likely is he to find it advantageous in interpreting this evidence? First, he may notice that virtually all the melodic contours in the piece are framed not in triadic fifths or octaves as in most tonal music, but in minor thirds, tritones, or minor sevenths. Triads, the models of sonority for tonal music, even most elaborately elaborated tonal music, appear rarely; in fact, the presented sonorities of the piece more often contain four distinct pitch classes than three; and although a familiar phenomenon, the intervallic conjunction whose homonym is the dominant seventh of tonal music, does occur frequently, its behavior *as* a dominant seventh is consistently curious.[2] Even the big "structural dominant" itself appears (in Mitchell's charts) after a "dominant preparation" that overlaps in the "basic structure" the basic "neighbor-note" prolongation whose "resolution" happens *inside* the initial *tonic* prolongation, which then proceeds directly to the cadence—except that the resolving tonic of that cadence is found only in another piece, the one with the concert ending. Altogether, this seems a pretty confused bit of tonal composition, and our observer is dissatisfied that he has to regard most of its peculiarities as *barriers to* rather than *particularities of* its coherence (in fact he is even sometimes obliged to regard them as things that have to be suppressed altogether in the explanation and hence rendered conceptually non-existent in the contemplation of the piece). And that

---

[2]Of course, any or all of these assertions could be true of a piece which was nevertheless favorably explicable as tonal, even as highly subtle tonal; the choice would depend on whether all the characteristics noted were generated in a consistent and significant way out of a triadic structure. The question here, however, is just whether their conjunction (and in particular their conjunction as it occurs in *Tristan)* would *predispose* one to conjecture that the Schenker-tonal model was the *obvious* leading model-candidate for the reconstruction of the piece in question. And the appeal of the *results* of its application (in case the answer were "yes") would in any event be the principal motivator of any ultimate *analytic* determination.

final G, coming right out of an obvious horizontalization of the first presented multiple-pitch sonority in the Prelude, leaves a disturbing question of just how capricious a composer Wagner could, plausibly, have been.

For the consistency with which the non-tonal tritone is in fact *the* interval, or *a* prominently articulated interval, of both simultaneity and succession in the *Tristan* Prelude suggests considerably more structural integrity than the tonal analysis reveals. Enough to make a doubter of, at least, our observer—who, still caring enough to try it himself, might decide to begin just by noticing what is actually *presented* as context by the piece, and what more general coherences might be suggested by such a contextual survey of the actual events and successions, undertaken with a minimum of prior structural bias.

Here is one path he might follow:

Consider the very opening of the Prelude. There are presented, initially, two almost exact-transpositionally related fragments separated by intervening silence, followed after a second silence by a third fragment, more complexly related to the first two than they are to each other, the end of which seems to generate a fourth-fragment "transition" to the continuously unfolding "principal section" of the Prelude. An obvious place to start, then, is with the fragments that are minimally differentiated from each other—the first two—to determine something about their internal characteristics, their interrelation, and their totality. If, for the moment, we regard the opening A as an anomaly (although it will soon enough be considered), we may notice the "minor third" parallelism in the "spans" of three of the four registral lines in the opening fragment.

```
              G♯ -A-A♯-B
       F-E-D♯ - D
           B  - G♯
          (F  - E)
```

with the lowest line cooperating with the second highest one to associate its first two pitches as simultaneity with its last two, as the second from lowest associates the first two of the highest with its last and the last two with its first; the effect of the F-E imitation, moreover, is that the total pitch-class content of the entire three-measure segment (including the A) is also unfolded within just the two-measure subsegment of it consisting of mm. 2–3. The F-E/D♯-D foldover is, moreover, delineated orchestrally by the joint between strings and english horn at the point of crossover; and the exchange between the next-to-lowest line B-G♯ and the upper-line G♯-B gives the two measures of the two-measure segment their only pitch-class intersection.[3]

Thus the two-measure segment, mm. 2–3, articulated as the span from first simultaneity to first silence, may be regarded as a partitioned-off unit itself internally partitioned into one-measure segments by the pitch-class intersection exchange of B and G♯, aside from the other "justifications" for this latter partition noted herein. For on examination, this two-measure segment turns out to exhibit some interesting internal symmetries as well: m. 3, in fact, is the exact retrograde inversion of m. 2, when regarded as follows:

$$(\text{where } C = 0)$$

measure 2	measure 3
8 - - 9	10 - 11
3 - - -	2 - - -
11 - - -	8 - - -
5 - - -	4 - - -
(m. 2: (8 3 11 5),	(9 3 11 5) = T0S)
(m. 3: (11 4 8 2),	(10 4 8 2) = T7I)

A nicety is that the inner chords are internally symmetrical also: T8S or T2S (9,3) = (11,5)); and T2I or T8I (9,3) = (11,5)) so that the first chord of m. 3 is a transposition of the second chord of m. 2 as well as its inversion (and that the interval of transposition is 1/11 significantly associates with an important transpositional characteristic of our eventual analysis). And, of course, it now emerges that the notoriously "ambiguous" Tristan chord, so elusive or anomalous in most tonal explications of the piece, and the familiar "dominant seventh", so crucial to these same tonal explications, are here just exact, balanced, simple inverses of one another, with very

---

[3]The entire pitch-class content of the fragment is still more compactly unfolded in the succession of the two innermost chords (F B D♯ A and E G♯ D A♯) alone; see note 13, below.

little local evidence to support their consideration as anything but equivalents in this sense. Moreover, these two chords also share a common relation to the complex made up of the pitch classes that determine the spans of all the registrally defined lines:

$$\begin{array}{cc} G\sharp & -B \\ F- & D \end{array}$$

$$\begin{array}{cc} B & -G\sharp \\ (F) & \end{array}$$

namely, D-F-G♯-B; each of the outer chords of the two-measure segment contains just three of its four pitch classes, with one pitch "contrapuntally" displaced by a semitone; for only the D♯ "spoils" the first chord of m. 2, and when it "resolves" to D, the F of the complex is "displaced" to E.[4]

Now how is *this* framework for hearing this passage supported or weakened by the characteristics resulting from the presence of the other pitch-class elements therein? Here is the pitch-class map that results from the use of D-F-G♯-B as an intervallic model on the basis of which the other pitches are sorted as well:

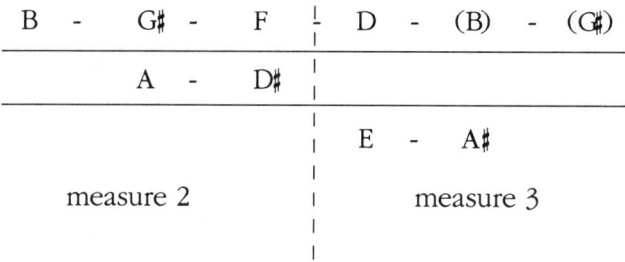

There are eight distinct pitch classes all together; five distinct ones in m. 2 and five in m. 3. The five in m. 2 include *three* of the four members of the (D F G♯ B) complex, and *two* members of a trans-

---

[4]The pair of semitone dyads F-E and D♯-D, articulated both as a sequential succession (F-E-D♯-D) within a voice, and as an imitative superposition (D♯ D) (F E), may be heard cross-rhythmically as at once a *parallelism* (of commonly descending semitones) and a *complementation* (of inverse (0 3 6 9)-displacement patterns).

position of it, the two presenting the more determining of the two intervals of the complex, the tritone. The five in m. 3 again include three from the (D F G♯ B) complex (reiterating the G♯-B as noted and exchanging F and D), and also a tritone-related pair from the remaining distinct transposition of the (D F G♯ B) complex. The A at the very opening, then, can be regarded as being like a "voice displacement" (to produce a motivic linear contour that is, structurally, "between polyphonic voices"), in which the A "voice-displaces" an F♯, for, as presented, each of the first three pitches of the piece belongs to a distinct one of the three possible (0 3 6 9) complexes, and the tritone-related pitch class of each is present in the ensuing fragment (a subtlety of the substitution is, of course, the contour isolation of the "syntactical" span F-D in the "alto" voice). The articulation of these three pitches is isolated by the simultaneous entrances of all the other voices on the first beat of m. 2, and by the verticalization of the relationship by the F-E in the "bass" of the multilinear complex after the monolinear F-E of m. 1.

The second fragment transposes everything in the first except the opening A (but the B of the opening of the second fragment may be regarded as a long-range realization of the A-B *span* from first (isolated) to last (isolated) pitch of the opening fragment) by the (0 3 6 9)-chordal interval 3. The result is that, naturally, (D F G♯ B) maps into itself, while A-D♯ and E-A♯ map into the pitch classes that *complete* their respective (0 3 6 9) complexes, F♯-C and G-C♯, respectively. Here, B and D are the intersection between the two halves, while F and G♯ are exchanged; and, of course, the number of distinct pitch classes, and the relative number of members of each (0 3 6 9) complex are held invariant:

G♯ - D - B	F - D - B
F♯ - C	
	G - C♯
measure 6	measure 7

Here, the "displacing" pitches in the Tristan chords are F♯ and G, as before they were D♯ and E. And the appearance of the bass succession E-G both as a long-range succession in the Prelude and as a local succession at prominent articulative changeover points in it, might be associated with the appearance of those two pitches here as the members of the opening end-point bass-succession. If, moreover, we look ahead to the end of the "introduction", we find not only that the last configuration of the upper line is framed in E♯-G♯-B, with the G♯-B at the end giving the *whole* upper-line span as a temporally immediate succession of its first to its last pitch classes in the intervallic relation they have as the first and last pitches of the *first* upper-voice span, but we also find that the final A (in the upper voice) associates with G♯ in the same way that those pitches were associated as the first to second pitches of the initial upper-voice span (see Ex. 1), suggesting an analogous G♯-A macro-succession in the passage as a whole.

Ex. 1

So we are presented with two sets of eight distinct pitch classes each, partitioned to produce a collection most simply described by reference to the (0 3 6 9) complex. The Tristan chords and their inversional equivalents all contain "neighbor-note" displacements and each contains three elements of a *single* transposition of the (0 3 6 9) complex:

measure 2:   8 | 11   measure 6:   11 | 2
            (3) -|- - 2   (6) - |- - 5
             11 | 8   2 | 11
             5 --|-- (4)   8 -- |-- (7)

These represent three of the four possible three-out-of-four combinations with respect to the (2 5 8 11) complex, and the fourth [(5 8 2)] appears immediately following them, in m. 10. Also, the inner chords each contain two tritones from different (0 3 6 9) complexes, with the "referential" one [(2 5 8 11)] completing in their union:

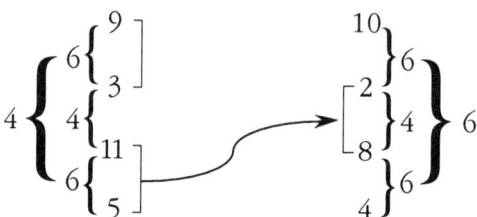

Note the "linear counterpoint" conceit that "inverts" the tritone relations on the model of the way that adjacent fifth-related triads are linearized in their presentation in tonal music and produce "inverted presentations" of their interval content, as:

$$5\left\{\begin{matrix}3\\4\end{matrix}\right.\left\{\begin{matrix}G\\E\\C\end{matrix}\right.\qquad\left.\begin{matrix}G\\D\\B\end{matrix}\right\}\left.\begin{matrix}5\\3\end{matrix}\right\}4$$

Here, adjacent 6s separated and spanned by 4s are "inverted" into adjacent 4s separated and spanned by 6s (see example above).

And, by the nature of all these relationships, the union of these two eight-pitch-class groups is the set of all twelve pitch classes, and the four duplicating pitch classes are, of course, the "reference set" (D F G♯ B).[5]

---

[5]Another respect in which fragment 2 "completes" something initiated in fragment 1 is due to the internal transposition by 3 of the (D F G♯ B)-forming tritones:

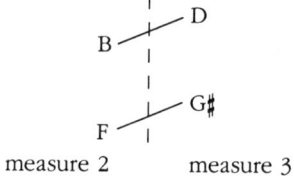

measure 2   measure 3

Thus fragment 2, transposing the whole of fragment 1 by 3, immediately repeats

Now the third fragment is not a total intervallic transposition of the first two, although it opens similarly. The first deviation is the addition of a fourth isolated pitch before the first chord attacks, and this is echoed by the "extra" pitch in the upper-voice line.

What, our observer considers, do these differences represent with respect to the relationships already determined?

First, in transposing by yet another 3, the pitch-successional areas of fragment 1 are re-engaged in different registral voices. Thus the (B-B♭-A-G♯) in the "alto" is the retrograde of the upper voice of mm. 2 and 3; the "tenor" (F-E-D♯) duplicates part of the "alto" voice of mm. 2–3; in fact, the comparison of the passage to an *exact* pitch-class retrograde of mm. 2–3 is interesting both for some striking correspondences and some significant noncorrespondences (see Ex. 2).

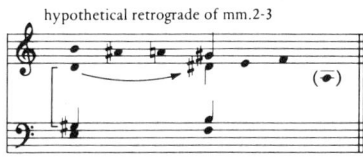

hypothetical retrograde of mm.2-3

Ex. 2

(D G♯) in its first half, and arrives at (F B) in its second half:

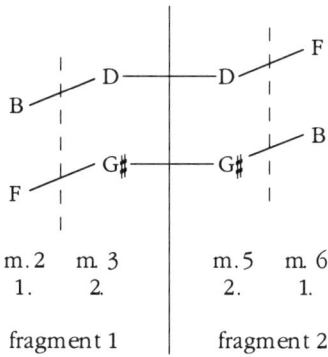

In this passage, especially, the role of A at the opening as a "substitute F♯" is made particularly plausible: the complex E-F(E♯)-F♯ is harmonically associated with an A, the structural significance of which will become clear in the sequel. And in fact, one of the peculiarities of the passage is the G♯-A succession in the "alto" and the E♯-F♯ succession in the upper voice; and we shall return to these as well. Otherwise, note that the Tristan chord of m. 10 is intervallically inverted from the earlier Tristan chords in mm. 2 and 6:

```
                 D                              G♯
                      6                              5
measure 10:      G♯            measure 2:     D♯
                 F                              B
                      5                              6
                 C                              F
```

Actually, of course, the chord in m. 10 is a pitch-class transposition (by 9) of the chord in m. 2; and, although the presentation of the pitch classes that determine the tritone inverts the registral position they would have in an exact interval exchange of this nature (i. e., G♯ would appear *above* D; see Ex. 3 for a hypothetical such construction of the whole fragment), the counterpoint, subtly, does actually produce the C-B "bass" line that would result from such an exact exchange.

Ex. 3

But a content-examination yields even more interesting results; there are, to begin with, *ten* distinct pitch classes rather than eight:

```
D - F -   G♯ - B
A - F♯- - -D♯ - C
B♭- -  E
```

And the "chord-area", by itself, presents just nine:

```
D -G♯ -F -B
E
C -D♯ -F♯ A
```

Thus the transposition T1S of (D-F-G♯-B) is given "equal weight" (i.e., representation) with T0S, and in fact the two "outer" chords balance T0S and T1S in just this way, while the upper voice proceeds *through* the last three of its (0 3 6 9), or the D-F of the overall (G♯-B-D-F), and then goes one semitone "step" further, to the F♯ that belongs to the T1S "neighbor" (0 3 6 9) complex (C D♯ F♯ A):

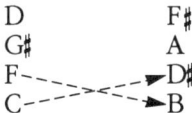

This progression, in both its immediate and its long-range spans, in fact, yields a view of the Tristan chord as a *means of interlocking linearly adjacent (0 3 6 9) complexes*; especially since the "upper line" explicitly traces such an interlock between (D F G♯ B) and (D♯ F♯ A C) (see Ex. 4).

Ex. 4

And the procedure observed here is a means of interlock of the same kind throughout the Prelude. The repetition of this "modulatory" fragment in a higher register, followed by isolations of just the two-pitch "fulcrum" of the "modulation" itself, the F-F♯ of the upper line, seem significative in the light of such a background function.[6]

The last fragment of the introduction carries this linear-harmonic succession into the passage beginning at m. 17, which by its sharply differentiated (from the preceding) continuity and registral characteristics, "isolates" the opening 16½ measures *as* a "section", and, by virtue of the continuousness of unfolding thereafter, as an "introduction" (or perhaps an "exposition", since it encompasses the assertion of the central collection (the 3 (0 3 6 9)s centered on (D F G♯ B)) and effects a centricization of a secondary construct (C D♯ F♯ A) therein).

In any case, in the final fragment of the introduction, in mm. 16–17, the "modulation" to (C D♯ F♯ A) is "prolonged" through a local return to (D F G♯ B); and the exposure of the pitches F♯, A, C, and E is notable, since their "arpeggiation" as an upper-line succession may be expressly inferred from the immediately following passage, and can be regarded as constituting the next interlocking linearized Tristan chord (but with *lower-level* structural significance, as will be seen)[7] (see Exx. 5 and 6).

---

[6]Note, too, how the counterpoint in this fragment projects the equal weighting around the midpoint of the two distinct (0 3 6 9)s (D F G♯ B) and (D♯ F♯ A C), in contrast to the single-chord (D F G♯ B)-weighting of the two preceding fragments:

1) The "spoiling" C in the lower voice of the first Tristan-chord connects with the (A D♯ F♯) of the end-chord, complete T1S, just as the B which displaces that C, spoiling the T1S of the end-chord, completes a (D F G♯ B) with the (D F G♯) of the initial chord; see the arrows in the example, above.

2) The "new" first inner chord (C F G♯ D♯), like its predecessors, equally weights two (0 3 6 9)s by superimposing an equivalent interval from each; but here the superimposition is of two 3s rather than as before of two 6s. The (0 3 6 9)s so weighted are T0S (F G♯) and T1S (C D♯).

3) In the previous two fragments the balanced halves are disjunct, the first crossing directly into its successor by the immediate juxtaposition of the two inner chords. Here the two inner chords are separated by a "new" midpoint chord (C G♯ E), which alone among the chords of the introduction projects, and equally weights, *all three* possible (0 3 6 9)s; thus the lone pitch of T2S (E), which occurs in this fragment at this place, functions singularly as the midpoint "extra" pitch of the upper line (regarding which more below), and as the "balancer" of

Ex. 5

Ex. 6

the central chord—a singularity underlined by the "functional-voice" octave doubling it is given, uniquely within the introduction.

4) The inner chord just past the midpoint, through which the fragment passes directly into the new T1S weighting, exactly duplicates the pitch-class content of the first inner chord of the Prelude: (B F A D♯), balancing T0S and T1S, passing *out of* T0S in its first appearance, and passing *into* T1S in its second. Accordingly, the entire counterpoint may be rendered as follows:

		D	D♯	E	F	F♯
		G♯	G♯	G♯	A	A
		F	F	E	D♯	D♯
		C	C	C	B	B
no. of	T0S:	3	2	1	2	1
p.c.s	T1S:	1	2	1	2	3
from	T2S:	0	0	1	0	0

But in the long-range upper-line outline, the F♯ appears, as noted, as the "extra" pitch in this fragment (extending the completion of the third overlapped 3 of a G♯-B-D-F succession by one more semitone: D-F *plus* F♯). This way of constructing the rhythm is nicely supported by the "alto"-voice outline of the entire descending 3 (B-G♯) at the opening of the fragment, so that the "modulatory" A which completes the register in the counterpoint may be regarded as *that* register's "extra" pitch. Hence a sharp, deep-structural cross-rhythm may be observed

On the basis of these and further observations on the data of the Prelude as a whole, we might hypothesize, as a data-basis for analytic inferences, a charting of the structure of the Prelude in terms of a simple partitioning of the (twelve) pitch-class "octave" by the (0 3 6 9) construct and its complementary mutually pitch-class exclusive transpositions (1 4 7 10) and (2 5 8 11), regarded as both internally and externally unordered, while using the Tristan-chord connection as the basis for asserting transition among the reference constructs, and "associative" criteria (such as the "phraseological" considerations invoked above) for determining "prolongation"-structure (for determining, that is, on each pro-

---

to unfold across a single line, by regarding that line as referring to, and diverging from, the prior contextual (0 3 6 9) setup at two distinct levels (i. e., in two distinct ways):

Rhythm 1:

				G♯	(A	A♯)	B		fragment 1
		F	(E	D♯)		D			
				B	(C	C♯)	D		fragment 2
	G♯	(G	F♯)			F			
				D	(D♯	E)	F	[F♯]	fragment 3
B	(B♭	A)		G♯			[A]		

Rhythm 2:

				G♯	A	/	A♯	B	fragment 1
	(F	E)	D♯		/	D			
				B	C	/	C♯	D	fragment 2
(G♯	G)	F♯			/	F			
				D	D♯	[E]	F	F♯	fragment 3
(B	B♭	A)	G♯				A		
				F		[E]	D♯		

---

[7] Two further inflections: 1) The fourth fragment, like the third, begins with a four-semitone span articulated through a five-*element* succession, overlapping (on F-F♯) with the end of fragment 3. But this, in turn, is overlapped (beginning on G♯) with another four-semitone span, this time articulated through a *four*-element succession. Now the three-semitone spans contained within this latter four-semitone-spanning figure are each unfolded in *three* elements; following which,

posed level, which of the partitioning constructs is to be regarded as *being inflected* by, in turn, which of the others).

Adopting this (still, let me emphasize, quite weakly determinate) referential model, and deferring for the moment the stickier systematic questions it raises (especially concerning the basis for the "centric" assumption implicit in the (transferred) notion of *prolongation,* and the "order-determinate" implications of the pitch-class content identity of the referential collection with that of the twelve pitch-class octave), we will also adopt a *Grundgestalt* (successional) model to order the "prolongation structure"; here the succession unfolded in the opening chromatic tetrachord G♯-A-A♯-B will be regarded as the "principal upper voice" for the Prelude as a whole (up to its final "centricization"), and the F-E-(G) succession in the "bass" will be considered as the "structural bass", in which the F-E is regarded as "more background" than the G (which is, again, associated with the final construct-shift). (Here as elsewhere, conceits of tonal *analogy* constantly suggest themselves—as the "center" (0 3 6 9) with its equirelated "subsidiary" transpositions creating the twelve pitch-class octave partitioning

---

the next presented four-semitone span (E-F) unfolds in just three elements on *that* model, all in close temporal succession:

D D♯ E F F♯ ──────▶(F F♯) ──────▶ F F♯ G G♯ (B)   A
                                  G♯   A B C ──────▶C D E

Each of the four-element groups to this point may be regarded as a conjunct pair of trichords, a (0 1 3) trichord plus an inverse thereof.

    2) The next four-element group (in register D E F G, foreshadowed by the just preceding biregistral A B C D, in which the double attack on C creates a four-attack framework which the three- and four-element groups inflect variably) also overlaps two 3s, partitioned by a (0 1 3) and an inverse as above; but this group spans a total interval of five semitones:

               D E F G

Thus to this point can be observed a progression among successive four-element groups consisting of overlapped inverse (0 1 3)-pairs, proceeding "stepwise" from the smallest interval spannable by such a group (three semitones) to the largest possible (five semitones):

⌐ ¬	⌐ ¬	⌐ ¬	⌐ ¬
G♯ A B	G♯ A B	A B C	D E F
G♯ A♯ B	A B C	B C D	E F G
mm. 2–3	mm. 16–17	m. 17	m. 18

267

set, the "prolongation" notions that this sub-collection hierarchization enables, and the "principal-voice" *Grundgestalt*, all of which can be regarded as a kind of sub-surface counterpoint to the surface conceits of traditional phraseological appearance and traditionally interpretable sonority; but as these are mostly not only fairly transparent but perhaps would tend to confuse perspective at such a tenuous analytic stage, it seems to me preferable to let them drop unmarked in our discourse, as unaffirmed as undenied, to be observed by the reader at his discretion.) A general reading of the data of the Prelude grouped according to the (0 3 6 9) partition and the proposed *Grundgestalt* model is offered in Exx. 7 through 10.

The long "delay" of (C♯ E G B♭) exhibited in Exx. 7 through 10, after several "arrivals" on C♯ (m. 24, m. 44), and then the short duration of the "assertion" of (C♯ E G B♭) from m. 50 to m. 60, and its even shorter duration and more "passing" character at m. 79 is particularly interesting in view of its eventual centricization at the close of the Prelude and its (probable) consequent centrality in Act I (but we haven't yet envisaged a way of regarding the opera beyond the Prelude as interpretable by means of (0 3 6 9) relations). The "harmonic structure" underlying these observations is given in Ex. 10b. Note the "bass line" just before the shift to (C♯ E G B♭) in m. 100: D♭-A-A♭-G—the opening "exposed upper line", in a transposition which is "centered" on the new (0 3 6 9)—namely (C♯ E G B♭)—by virtue of its *not* proceeding the further downward step to F♯ (on the model of m. 2) that would "center" the line analogically on (C E♭ F♯ A); a nice bit of motivic "identity/nonidentity" composition. The B♭ in the middle register over the D♭ assists this interpretation as well. And note also the upper line in mm. 89–90; whereas the parallel passage at the opening (m. 11) has F-F♯, which represents the "T0-T1" (0 3 6 9) succession (i. e., (D F G♯ B)-(D♯-F♯-A-C)), here F-E produces the complementary "T0-T11" succession (D F G♯ B)-(C♯-E-G-B♭). A motivic significance may also be attributed to the transference into the lowest register at the "climactic" passage beginning at m. 79 of the "upper-line" A♯ (B♭) to produce a presented "5th"-succession B♭-F. This succession is also projected in m. 97, where the "transition to (E G B♭ C♯)" begins: (D♭ G *B♭* F), the Tristan chord that opens Act III, here first is succeeded by its inverse (D F G B), then (m. 99) initiates the immediate centricization of (E G B♭ C♯).

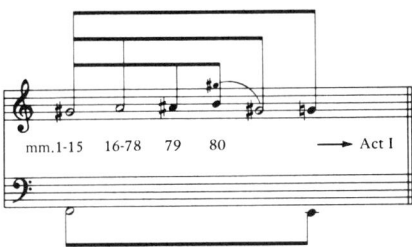

Ex. 7a

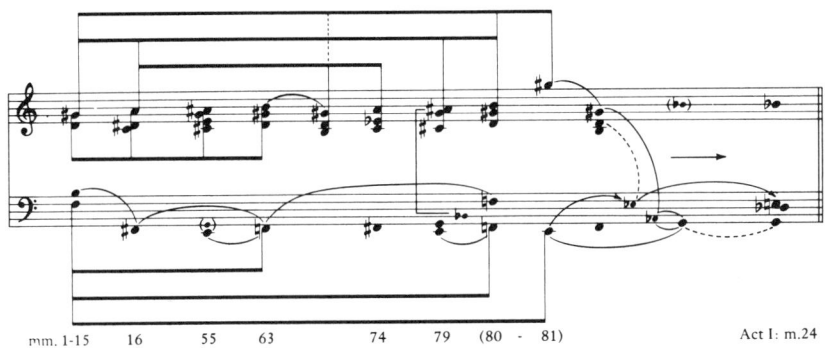

Ex. 7b

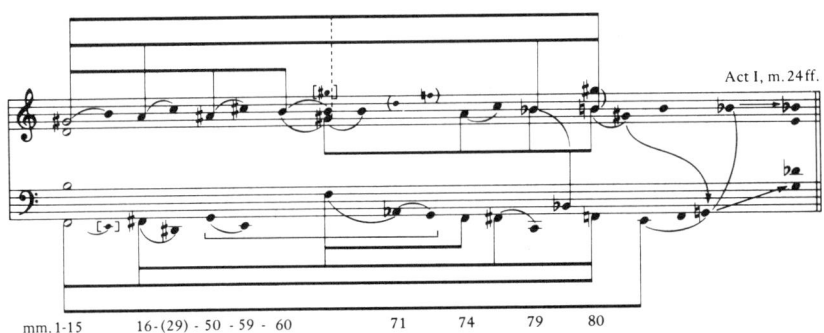

Ex. 8

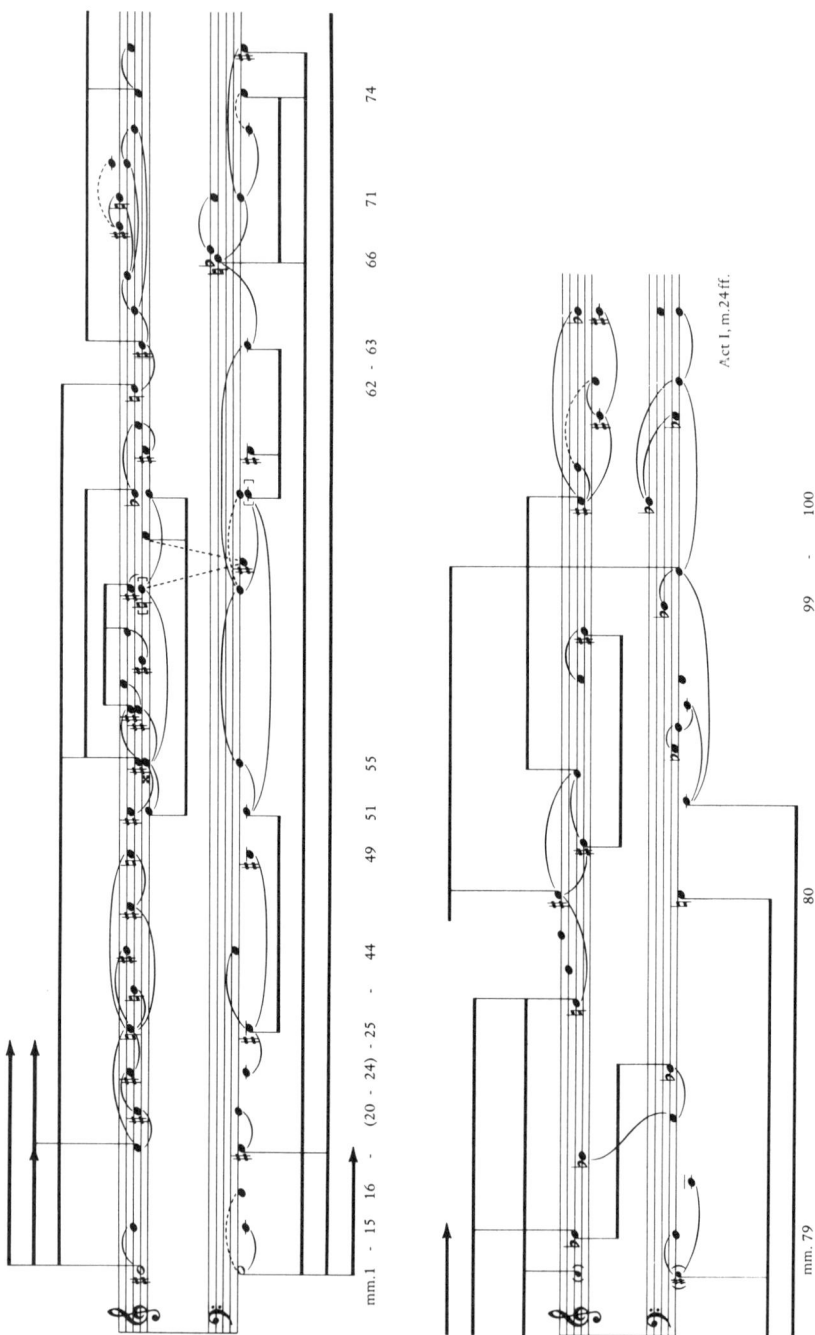

Ex. 9

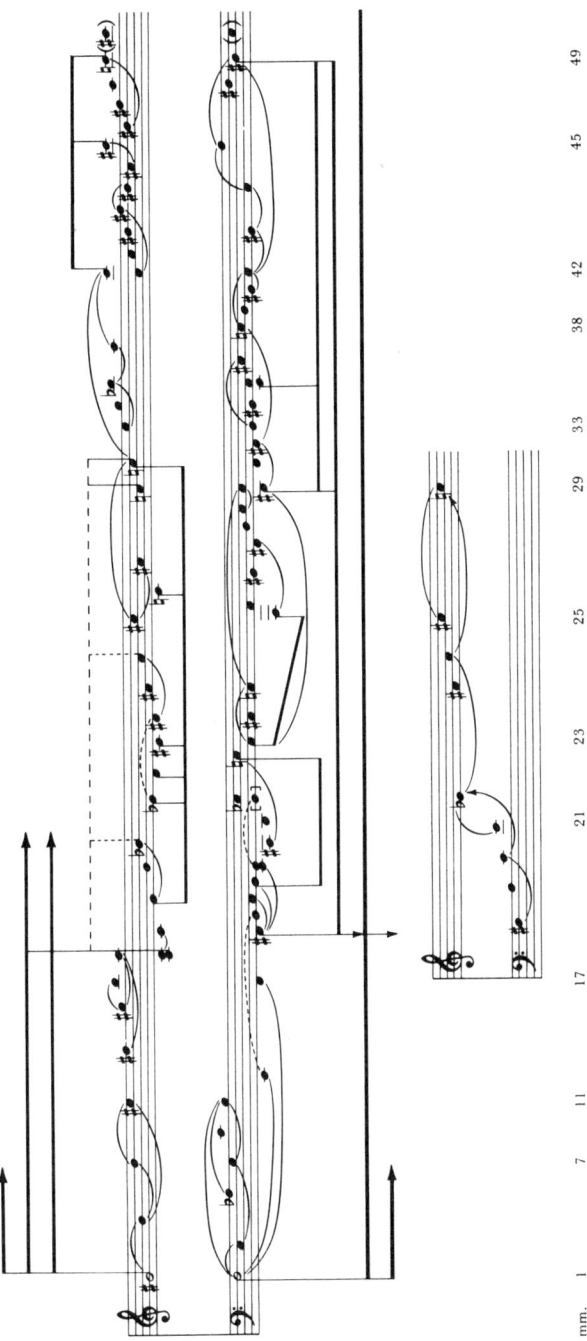

Ex. 10a (beginning)

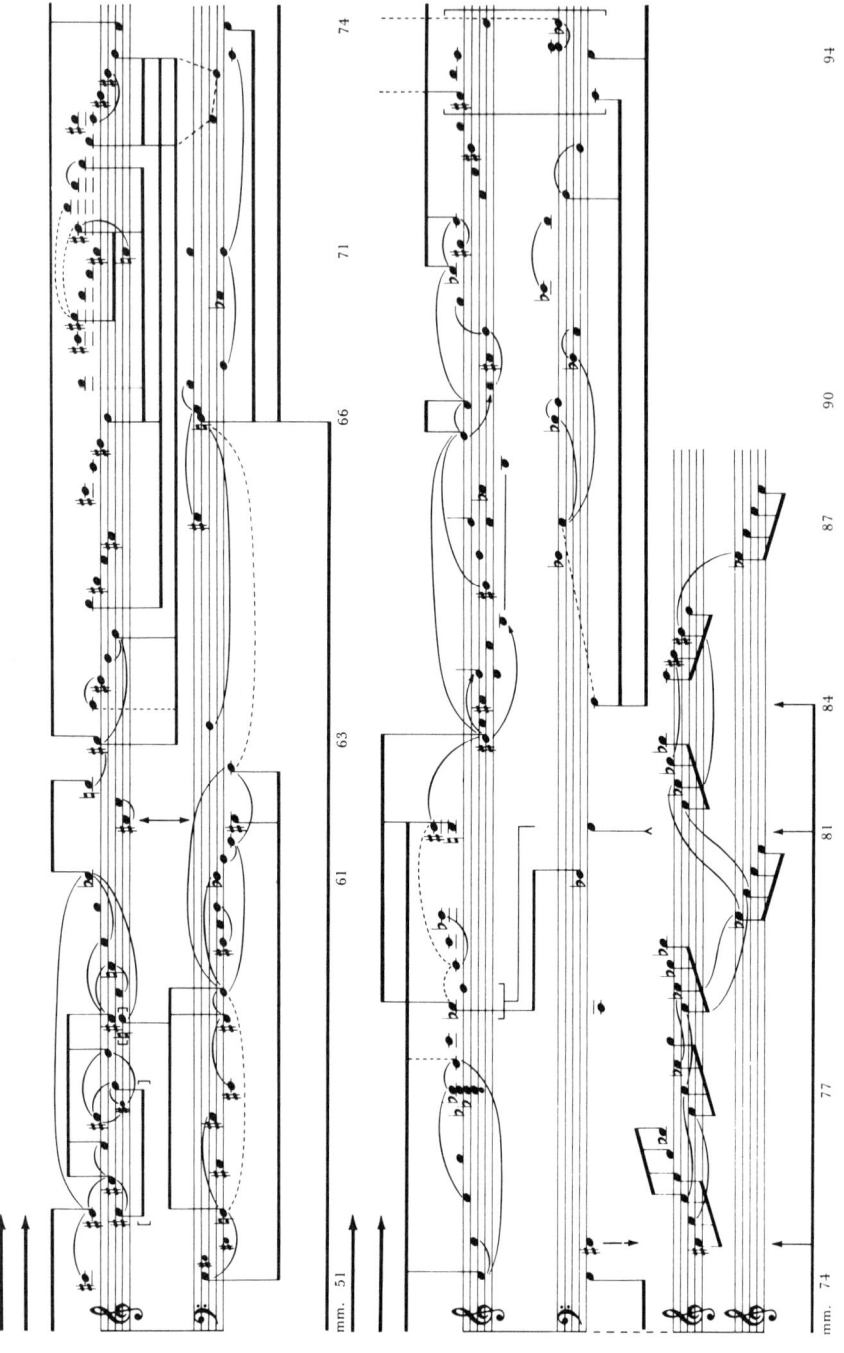

Ex. 10a (continued)

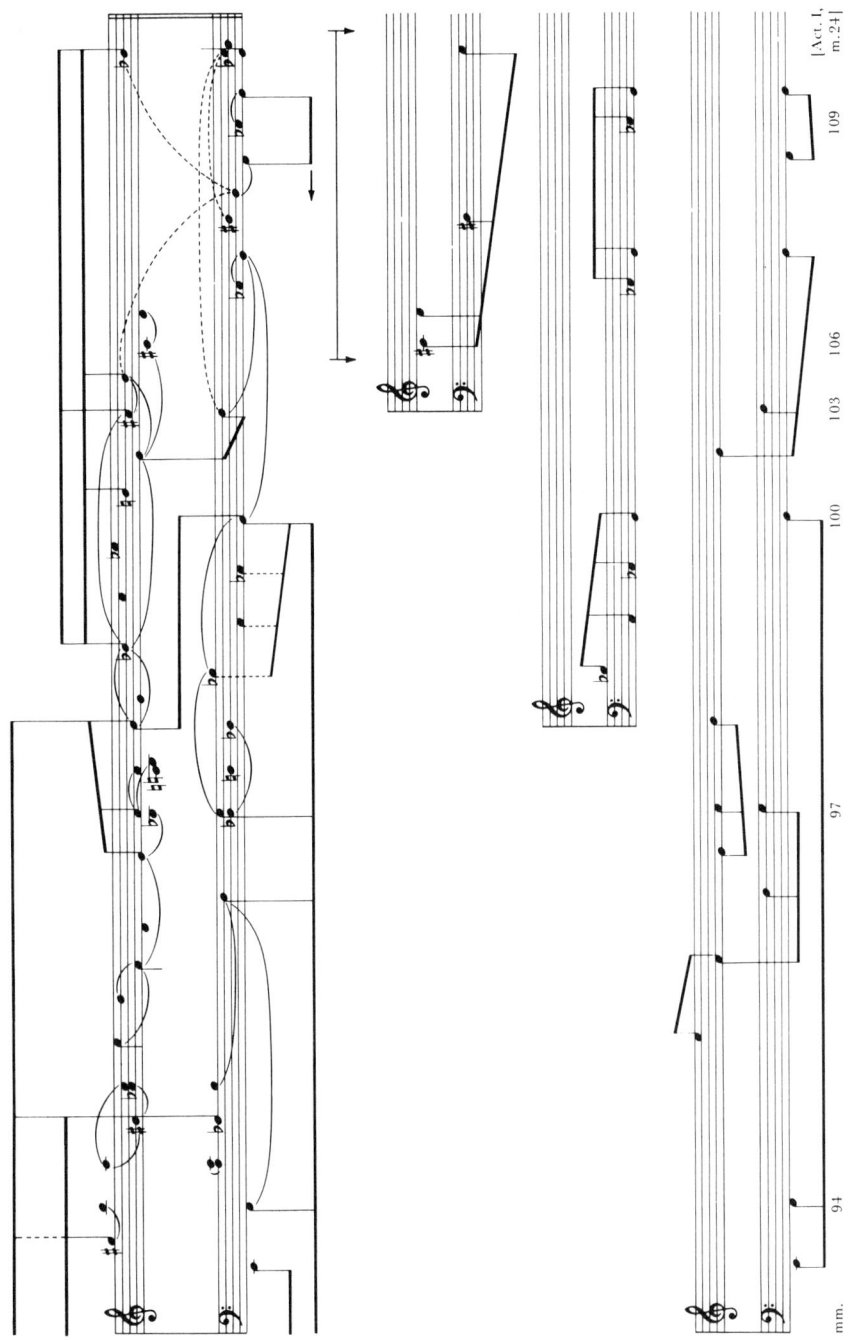

Ex. 10a (concluded)

Ex. 10b

Now such a B♭-F succession is, first, a reasonably assertible "framework" for the first bass line of Act II, but, more particularly, it is the directly asserted bass line of the "diatonicized" replication of the opening of the Prelude that opens Act III. There, the convenience of a "tonal" notion of the opera is particularly counter-supported, despite the "triadic-diatonic" surface, by—at least—the long-range relation of this succession to the final one of the opera, on the 6-related E-B (which is thus also motivically identifiable as a "total transposition", making reasonable an emphasis on the *interval of transposition* (6) as a strong basis of association). Again, we have not yet produced any evidence of relation between the structure or even the referential basis of the Prelude and those of the whole opera, but—assuming we can—it might be revealing to regard the final B as completing a total-opera G♯-B upper-voice/F-B lower-voice span (that adding a B to the Prelude's overall bass produces E-G-B seems potentially explanatory too regarding the last sonorities of the opera), as well as a "total last-segment" (from the beginning of the *Liebestod*) span A♭-B. The *Liebestod* itself in a number of more or less local-successional ways reinforces the feasibility of making such an association. And once again, the two "ends"—here of the Act as before of the "phrase"—exhibit an analogous combination of transpositional and inversional symmetries (C=0):

```
opening of Act III:   7 10 1 5  (7 10 1 5)    0 5 8 0    (T0)
close of Act III:                  1 4 7 11   6 11(2) 6  (T6)
                       4 1 10 6              11 6 3 11   (T9I)
```

But our account thus far has not, as we have noted several times, given us an adequate way to ascribe particular function to the sonority-successions that predominate in the opera as a whole, namely "triadic" ones, in a manner preferable to regarding them as directly significant in a "tonal-referential" way; nor, indeed, have we particularized among such sonorities (and all other non-Tristan-chord ones) as they appear in the Prelude itself, beyond subsuming them as "contrapuntal chords" in a larger, defined reference-sonority structure. Thus, to begin with, let us consider the status of such "triadic" configurations in the Prelude. If the (0 3 6 9) construct is a "center", its intervallic structure is thereby the "model for sonority" in the piece (which doesn't mean it need appear as a presented sonority with any particular frequency (a frequent analytic error) but rather that the sonority-structure of the piece can be placed into some sort of consistent and evidently revealing relation to it—as consider those advanced tonal pieces (Chopin, Brahms, etc.) where triads hardly appear at all as presented sonorities but where the most deeply sense-conferring references for what is presented are triadic successions). So the "triad", like the Tristan chord of which it forms a segment, is a "between-construct" (i.e. "dissonant") relation in the *Tristan* "system", and triads in the Prelude are always "resolved" to literal (0 3 6 9) segments.

As noted, this is particularly emphasized by the almost invariable "interlocked Tristan-chord" framework for linear succession, on the model: 0 4 7 10 1 5 ("ascending") (the harmonic hexachord of our eventual Tristan system). But in the opera itself, "triads" appear in much less obviously interpretable ways; and, to be consistent with our insistence on "noticing what's there", can we be as careless in our dismissal of triads as we protested that others have been about (0 3 6 9)s? Of course, we could regard them as a "conceit"—a historically obvious one, and a particularly nice one, in that one can speak of there having been composed, in the midst of an age of tonal music, a piece in which triads can be regarded as "dissonant". But further, the conditions of a "system" which has the (0 3 6 9) construct as its generator and model for sonority will also have the problem of the non-uniqueness of transposition, by contrast with the "asymmetric" (0 4 7) partition of tonal-systematic reference, since the (0 3 6 9), transposed by any of its own intervals (3, 6, 9), yields the identical pitch set as well as the identical interval set. So the "triadic" configurations in the opera could be regarded as a plausible expedient to articulate such otherwise indistinguishable transpositions by means of a "mixed system" in which the (0 3 6 9) would provide the "model for transposition", and the triad (whose twelve transpositions and their twelve inversions *are* content-distinct), the differential pitch-content "identity" of the transpositional level involved—again, the particular appropriateness of the "triad" to this task might still have to be mostly the force of its associative familiarity in the ear of the contemporary beholder. But, to regard its function in terms of a "given" of this kind would seem to entail a serious net sacrifice in the "coherence"-producing power of the new system, by comparison with tonality itself; and this alone might justify strenuous efforts, however awkward, to reclaim the opera for tonality after all. On the other hand, such a flaw might be adduced as a reasonable explanation of "why" *Tristan is* a unique piece of its type, why it had no obvious consequences in the sense of a literature (rather than a surface progeny) of "(0 3 6 9) pieces".

A solution, however, seems to me to be available that is rather less superficial than the foregoing might predispose one to expect. Through it, in fact, not only can "triads" be generated as *integral* consequences of the systematic construction, but they can be considered an indispensable component thereof; for they may be regarded as the *minimum* (in dimension) pitch configurations that arise as *constructs uniquely identifying* "positions" on a hierarchical transposition cycle,[8] whose totality (as interlocked or adjoined on that transposition-cyclic chain), *exhausts* the pitch elements of the system.[9]

---

[8]That is, a cyclic ordering of the transpositions of the elements of a system that are taken as *syntactically* hierarchized, against which the particular transposition cycles of given musical *structures* are measured. Thus, in the tonal system, the 7-cycle is the syntactical transposition cycle for *single pitch elements, triads,* and *diatonic collections.* Because of the internal transpositionally self-reproducing symmetry of the (0 3 6 9) construct, the normative *interval of transposition* in a (0 3 6 9) system cannot be an interval contained in (0 3 6 9) itself (i. e., neither 3 nor 6); hence, the syntactical "transposition cycles" of the (0 3 6 9) system are cycles of constructs and of collections, not of single pitches.

[9]Thus, the dyadic construct (0 4) is equally unambiguous in position-reference on the (0 3 6 9) transposition cycle, but its compositions (whether conjoined or adjoined) cannot exhaust the twelve pitch-class octave, and hence it is unsuitable as a "harmonic" construct for a (0 3 6 9)-systematic composition.

To see how this may be, let us now consider those "systematic" questions that were earlier deferred. What, up to here, have we produced by way of a "syntactical reference"? Essentially, a "twelve-pitch-class system" where the twelve pitch classes are "normatively" partitioned by the (0 3 6 9) construct and its mutually content-exclusive complementary transpositions (1 4 7 10) and (2 5 8 11). On the sub-collectional level, the constructs are content-differentiated—hence the possibility of our "centric" map of the Prelude, where the constructs are hierarchized "articulatively" by such characteristics as pitch-class "weighting", contour shaping, etc. But at the "collection" level, no such "centricity" is available, on two grounds: first, that a *single whole collection* encompasses all members of the twelve pitch-class octave, and hence no transposition of it is *content-distinguishable* from any other; and second, that the *constructs within the collection* (the (0 3 6 9)s) are themselves *internally symmetrical,* and hence simply map into each other or themselves under every transposition; that is, the symmetrical nature of the (0 3 6 9) construct guarantees the content-identity of any transposition by any internal interval, while transposition by any other interval merely reproduces the content of one of the other two such constructs already content-identified in the reference collection. In either case, all transpositions are non-unique with respect to content-identity, in the second case at the *collection,* and in the first at the *construct,* level. So, unless we wish to regard the single (0 3 6 9) as "the" reference *collection,* of which a single-functioned representation of each member of the twelve-pitch-class octave is the maximal transpositional extension (which would drastically curtail the complexity-coherence extension through which we have striven to keep *Tristan* compositionally transcendent), we have to commit ourselves to a "reference collection" containing all the twelve available pitch classes in our "octave"; and in that case, content-determinacy *cannot* extend beyond the sub-collectional, construct level. In other words, at the reference-collectional level itself (or themselves—the levels, that is, at which the sets being compared are dimensionally equivalent to the maximal reference set rather than to any proper subset of it), content cannot be the functional determinant inferred as syntactical (rather than articulative). So *ordering,* of some kind, *must* be (there exists no third alternative). Yet the *time* order of elements seems plainly *not* a comprehensible determinant for any kind of syntactical coherence in the *Tristan* Prelude, let alone for the opera as a whole. Thus, we are confronted with the question of how and what kind of order can be so regarded (as, that is, such a determinant). Now the problem, as we have noted, is heightened when the extension of the "collections" by transposition is projected, since not only the "whole collection" but also its internal (0 3 6 9)s display no content-unique characteristics; for even though the "content" of each construct is determinate within a single collection, every transposition of the whole collection merely reproduces the same construct, as well as the same collection, pitch content. So, again, without an order-referential basis, no transposition of a construct is distinguishable from any of the other (content-identical) ones.

But a non-time-referential ordering criterion is, in fact, an integral constituent in our traditional consideration of all music. The peculiar identity of a presented triad in tonal music is determined not only by pitch-class content, but also by such phenomena as the relative placement of the constituent pitches, particularly which of the functionally defined elements appears in the lowest register—i. e., by observations of *registral order* (and note that this is more to the *structural* side of our observational hierarchy in tonal music than the more *articulative* matter of the time-order of unfolding of a triadic complex). Evidently, we assume pretty fundamentally a capacity to discriminate the "bottom-to-top" locations of all the elements of a presented pitch complex, which, then, gives us a kind of "ordering" as unambiguously assertible as temporal ordering, and quite independently variable.

Now if such a registral layering as presented in a given piece were itself the actual syntactical determinant in question here, it would considerably reduce the articulative-level resources available to our (0 3 6 9)-systematic reconstruction. And in any case, no observations on the data of *Tristan* seem to point toward the fruitfulness of any such drastic revision of a presentational surface function as a background one *as well*. What, then, might a "syntactical registral ordering" consist of? To answer this, let us first consider an analogy to "voice leading" in its syntactical and in its presentational senses, where, e. g., a functionally defined "upper neighbor" may perform its function unambiguously although presentationally actually appearing "below" its "reference". In other words, some identifying characteristics are regardable as establishing a *syntacti-*

cal upper-neighborness *independently* of the articulative unfolding. Thus, similarly, we would wish to establish a *defined syntactical registral ordering* of the member pitch *classes* of the entire (twelve pitch-class) referential collection of the (0 3 6 9) system, such an ordering being taken to identify the *referential transposition* of the collection (and, of course, hence of its internal (0 3 6 9) partitioning constructs and of their interiors). Now the construct-transformations in the tonal system that retain but registrally permute pitch content are the registral-interval-order-distinct (but content-identical) "inversions" of triads; and thus such transformations function as construct-level distinctions within collections. But since what such "inversions" would produce in the (0 3 6 9) system are constructs that, even if "ordered", would be identical with the constructs resulting from given *total transpositions* of the collection (that is, transpositions and permutational "inversions" of the (0 3 6 9)s would not be *interval-order* distinct from one another at all), the level at which this consideration operates effectively is that of the *reference collection* (a deep-syntactical level) rather than that of the *construct* (a relatively more articulative level). Thus, a complete unfolding of the (0 3 6 9)-systematic transposition cycle produces a *multiple* partitioning (exhaustion) of the pitch-class octave, a partitioning in which each construct is *internally* pitch-*class ordered*, and in which all the resultant constructs are consecutively ordered, in both cases by means of such a "syntactical registral" ordering criterion. And precisely because no new interior content is produced by transposition in either the constructs or the collections, its (transposition's) function as a *syntactical-order* determinant may be unambiguously inferred.

Let us see how the system can be constructed along such lines, and how the *contents* of those maverick (non-(0 3 6 9)) sonorities can be considered the *crucial* means for creating the requisite functionally unambiguous *order* identity independent of presented register or even presented registral order. First, the generating partition is the symmetric "interval-halving" one, represented at the first partitioning level by the half-octave interval 6 (in appropriate contrast to the asymmetrical tonal 7); this symmetry, as we have noted, underlies many of the special characteristics of the system's transposition cycle—which as we have also noted is to be regarded as primarily a "cycle of constructs" rather than one of single intervals (which accounts for the disparity of the "intervals

within" the construct and those "between" the construct and its transpositions). This is necessarily so because neither of the generating-interval cycles of the (0 3 6 9) exhausts 12. Moreover, since the collection itself is to contain all the available pitch-class elements, *any* interval not internal to the (0 3 6 9) may be regarded as the "collection" generating one that defines "between-construct" relations, especially since "polyphony" (i. e., relations within and between voices *of* the constructs) is *identified* with the "model of whole-*construct* succession" itself in the (0 3 6 9) system (rather than with a particular *pitch*-successional model as *well*, as in the tonal-systematic *Ursatz*). And complementary transpositions, as (T1+T11); (T2+T10); (T4+T8); or (T5+T7); or indeed transpositions by any two distinct non-(0 3 6 9) contained intervals not 3- or 6-related, will produce the same (content-identical) partitioning-construct (0 3 6 9) characteristics as any other. We, however, choose the (T4+T8) transposition as our *basis*, to account for the role of the Tristan chord as the principal articulator of (0 3 6 9) succession, since 4 is the interval that separates the "top" one of the three 3- and 6-related pitches of the "base" (0 3 6 9) from the "displacing" pitch (as, 2 5 8̲ 0̲ (3 6 …)). Here is the initial octave
        4
partition, on the model of our construction of the diatonic collection in Part III.

1. Symmetrical octave partition, transposition, and complementary transposition:

$$\begin{array}{ccc} & & 4 \\ & 0 & \\ 8 & & 10 \\ & 6 & \\ 2 & & 4 \\ & 0 & \\ 8 & & \end{array}$$

The "half-octaves" thus defined are partitioned analogously, i.e., in halves, to produce an entire (0 3 6 9)-generated collection containing all twelve pitch classes:

2.

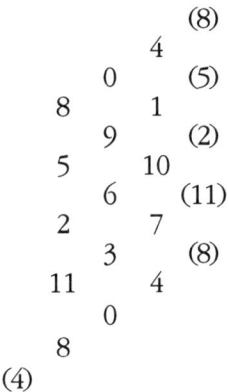
```
                    (8)
                 4
              0     (5)
           8     1
              9     (2)
           5    10
              6     (11)
           2     7
              3     (8)
          11     4
              0
           8
        (4)
```

The above may be regarded as a "harmonic" model of the partitioning, while the following represents a "polyphonic" (linear-interval) model, or "order" model:

3.

```
        (7)  8  9  10 (11)
             5  6  7
             2  3  4
       (10) 11  0  1  (2)
```

Now the "order" model may be regarded as joining "adjacent" (0 3 6 9)s through the Tristan chord; the "common-tone" connection of analogously adjacent triads (e. g., IV-I-V) in the tonal-collectional model is replaced here by the *disjunct* "non-common-tone" connection, which is compositionally projected by the Tristan chord, the (0 3 7 10) chord, the (0 3 7) chord, and the dyads (0,1), (0,4), and (0,5) (and their complements). By means of the Tristan-chord connection, we may represent the "order" model as follows:

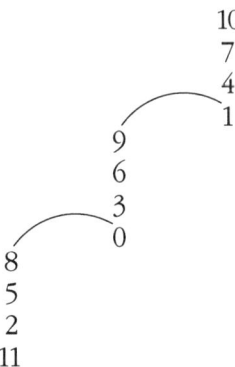

which incorporates our "ordering" criterion in *pitch-class* terms, a matter of indifference in the derivation of the exclusively content-determinate tonal syntax. (Note also, in connection with the "4"-connected model above that a 1, 2, 4, 5, 7, or 8-connected model would have provided an equally unambiguous "interlock" chord in place of the Tristan chord of *Tristan* (which also indicates non-triviality for *its* appearance in an (0 3 6 9)-systematic piece).

Thus, whereas our present model yields (2 5 8 0) as the (lowest) interlocking four-pitch adjacency, a 1-connected model would yield (2 5 8 9), an 11-connected one (2 5 8 7), and an 8-connected one (2 5 8 4). This is, in fact, an exhaustive list (to within inversion), since (0 3 6 9) arrays whose intervals of connection are 6-complementary to one another yield *equivalent* four-pitch interlock chords: both the 4-connected and the 2-connected models produce Tristan chords and dominant sevenths as interlock chords; Tristan chords always associate their "center" (0 3 6 9) with its 1-related transpose; and dominant sevenths always lean to the 11-related side—though the "ascending" and "descending" order positions are reversed in the two systems:

4-connected system:

ascending T1-wards: Tristan chord

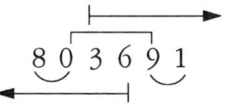

dominant seventh: descending T11-wards

2-connected system:

ascending T11-wards: dominant seventh

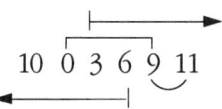

Tristan chord: descending T1-wards

That the distinction between the two systems is more than metaphorical, however, is observable from the difference in content of interlock segments of the *three-note* variety: whereas they are *triads* in the 4-connected system, they are (0 2 5/0 3 5) chords in the 2-connected one; so that the three-note interlock chords in the array more uniquely identify the system than do the four- (or more) note ones, yet they do so with no less internal selectivity: just as the four-note-chord evidence in *Tristan* leads us to the 2/4-connected array-family, so the three-note chord evidence would seem to lead us to the 4-connected one in particular. And that the homonym of the *minor* triad is a subset of the Tristan chord, while that of the *major* triad is a subset of the dominant seventh means—with some evident interest for our *Tristan* observations—that the *modality* of a triad in *Tristan*-systematic music is an invariable index of its "modulatory" lean.

But even as one of a number of possible four-element interlock chords, the Tristan chord is not without its own unique strategic advantages. In particular, as the only interlock chord that contains no semitone, it is the only one able to reflect a (0 3 6 9)-member displacement simultaneously in the *harmonic* and the *linear* dimensions, insofar as the note which harmonically displaces a (0 3 6 9) member (as a "next pitch in order" to the whole (0 3 6 9) in the (0 3 6 9) array) also displaces that member linearly (as a "next pitch in order" in the chromatic scale—since successive (0 3 6 9)s in the array are T1-related). Since no other (0 3 6 9) system can reflect this dual functionality in its interlock chords, it is in at least this respect inferior to the Tristan system. And that *Tristan* heavily exploits this particular depth of its system may be inferred from the virtual saturation of the introductory fragments of the Prelude by Tristan-chord-producing semitone inflections.

If we now expand our "order model" to its *maximal* extension, we generate a *chain of (0 3 6 9) transpositions*, which may be sliced into twelve *distinct* twelve pitch-class collections, each with a particular (0 3 6 9) at its "center":

4. Cycle of (0 3 6 9)s:

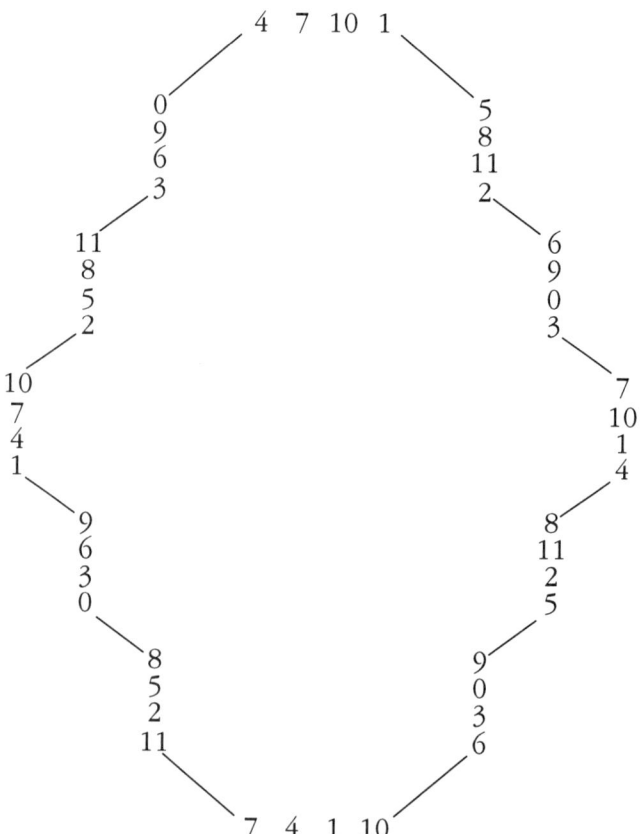

Each possible Tristan chord occurs *just once* in this array as a relation amongst pitch classes defined as "syntactically adjacent". Thus each one, relative to any inferred (0 3 6 9) "center", represents *one and only one* possible "hierarchical position" in the "transpositional cycle", even though the transpositions themselves map every (0 3 6 9) into itself at every third transposition-position, and every three consecutive (0 3 6 9)s into the twelve pitch-class set. Thus there are just 24 possible Tristan chords; every other four-pitch-class adjacency is either a (0 3 6 9) or a (0 3 7 10) (the latter being the relation between adjacent "half-constructs"—concerning which see below). Since the (0 3 7 10)s (unlike the Tristan chords), invert into themselves, there are just twelve of them—like the number of distinct (0 3 6 9) transpositions; but unlike the (0 3 6 9)s, *no two are content-identical.* Thus, with the Tristan chord and the (0 3 7 10) construct, we have secured an unambiguous "syntactical order" identification within our array by means of the *content* they project as subsidiary, "between-construct" constructs.

Here are the twelve distinct (0 3 7 10)s, in "order":

(4 7 11 2) / (5 8 0 3) / (6 9 1 4) / (7 10 2 5) / (8 11 3 6) /

(9 0 4 7) / (10 1 5 8) / (11 2 6 9) / (0 3 7 10) / (1 4 8 11) /

(2 5 9 0) / (3 6 10 1)

But then, on examining the "interiors" of these (0 3 7 10)s, we find the heart of the "triad" matter as well: for the interlocking 12 (0 3 7 10)s produce, by virtue of their partitionability as two "overlapping-triads" each, {(0 3 7),(3 7 10)}, just the 24 possible distinct "triads" (and like the Tristan chords, but unlike the (0 3 7 10) chords, "biased" toward *particular* (0 3 6 9)s by their "weighted" content); but of course they are generated in a hierarchical order that has nothing to do with "tonal transposition", yet is totally unambiguous in fixing the identity of a particular position in a particular (0 3 6 9) transposition cycle, since each occurs uniquely in its defined position:

5. How "triads" arise in the (0 3 6 9) system. Exactly twelve transpositional forms of the (0 3 6 9) construct produce the following chain; triads are outlined by brackets:

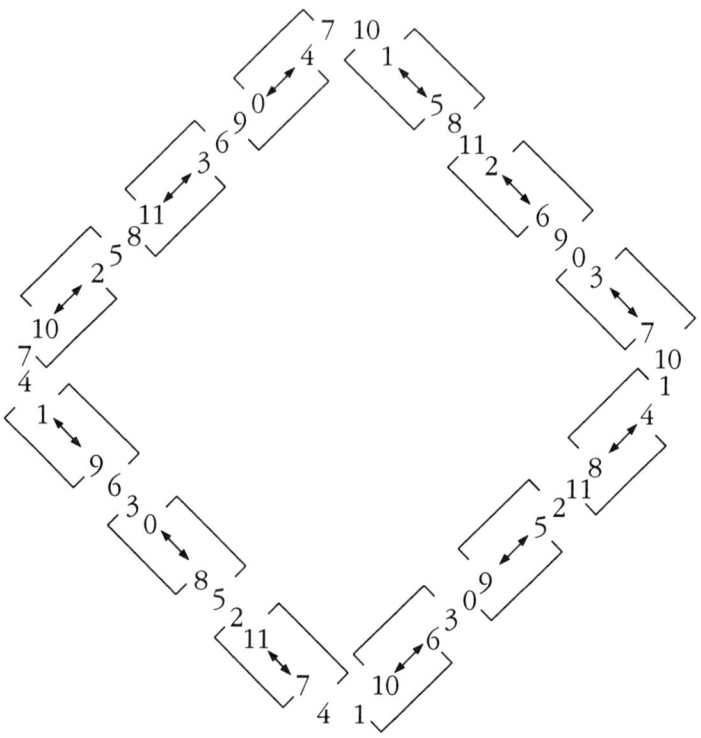

Inside brackets = "minor triads"
Outside brackets = "major triads"[10]

---

[10] A psychoacoustic, or ear-training, demonstration may be interesting here: compare the experiential "feel" of successions of pairs of triads represented as adjacent in Figure 5 as screened tonally, by the cycle of fifths:

G B♭ D   A C♯ E

with that of the "same" triads as screened by the *Tristan*-systematic (0 3 6 9) array:

A C♯ E   G B♭ D

In our "centric" interpretation of the *Tristan* Prelude, each passage is regarded as "centered on" a given one of the three (pitch-class) (0 3 6 9)s, with the others present as locally subsidiary "members" of the polyphonic "voices" defined by the "center" (0 3 6 9). Now it turns out that if any one group of three consecutive (0 3 6 9)s from our "cycle of (0 3 6 9)s" is regarded as such a referential partitioning, with the (0 3 6 9) at its "center" taken as the "referent" for its "polyphony", then *all* the content-identified "order" relationships obtainable within such a set are obtainable from just the *"center" hexachord* of that set; i.e., the "center" (0 3 6 9) plus the nearest member of each "subsidiary" (0 3 6 9). This is the configuration called "the harmonic hexachord" above:

(1)   {11 2 5 [8 0 3 6 9 1] 4 7 10}

"harmonic
hexachord"

Note that this hexachord is distinguishable as the segment consisting just of the two *disjunct adjacent* "triads" represented in a single such set (i. e., as partitioned off from the rest of the "cycle of (0 3 6 9)s"). And note, too, that moving to either of the *other* triads exhibited within the single set produces a subset of the "harmonic hexachord" of a *different* (0 3 6 9) set, one whose center is either one or the other of the "outer" constructs of the original set—hence, one related to the original as one of two complementary transpositions of it, either "T1" or "T11". The analogy to "tonal transposition" by 7 and 5 is interesting: in our example, the two "other" triads are (5 8 0) and (9 1 4). If the set labeled "(1)" is called "T0S", a transposition-cycle segment including T0S, T1S, and T11S may be represented as follows:

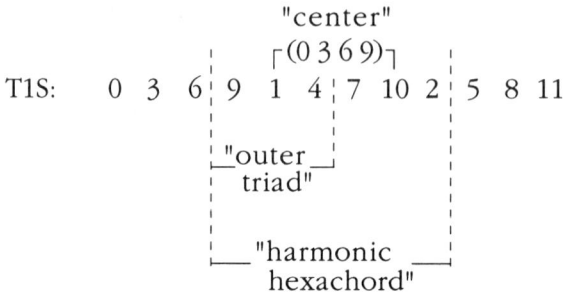

As in tonal transposition by 5 and 7, the representations of the "tonic" in these three transpositions "exhaust" the three "principal-construct functions" exhibited in any *one* of them (on the IV, I, V model). But in particular, each transposition is uniquely characterized by its disjunct-adjacent triad pair (and indeed by *each triad* as its "representative"), which enables the *invocation* of the complete twelve-pitch-class reference, with its unique *ordering*

of (0 3 6 9)s respectively and internally, without a complete presentational statement of that reference—simply, in fact, on the basis of the actual presence of as few as *three* pitches. Thus each triad not only represents a unique position on the (0 3 6 9) transposition cycle, but also identifies uniquely a particular 3-(0 3 6 9) set, with a "center" (0 3 6 9) that may be regarded as "generative" on the tonal-systematic model without necessitating any crossing of the "order"-"content"-reference barrier.

Similarly, all the remaining significant "harmonies" of *Tristan,* including the Tristan chord, are derivable from relations on this harmonic hexachord, sometimes uniquely identifying a single reference set, sometimes associating two determinate reference sets. The latter function, a characteristic notably of the "symmetrical" (0 6 2 8) chord, is particularly significant in our "set-structural" analysis below. For the two measures of the "first phrase" of the Prelude are "balanced" between the T0S set and the T6S set that lies "halfway around" the (0 3 6 9) set transposition cycle, a characteristic determined for those two measures by their component Tristan chords ((F G♯ B D♯) in m. 2; (E G♯ B D) in m. 3). But the "symmetrical" chords at the "crossover" between the two measures discussed above *both* arise *uniquely* from the *conjunction* of T0S and T6S (see Table 10, below).

Here is a model of the entire set-transposition cycle, followed by a model of the transposition cycle of the set-identifying harmonic hexachords alone. I give both "T" and "I" numbers here, corresponding to "0 3 6 9-step distances on the 'cycle'"; but note that while, where "T" is concerned, this purely "order"-based tabulation gives the same subscript identity as would the corresponding "pitch-class" tabulation, the "I" numbers resulting from complementary order transpositions with respect to the given "T" numbers are, in fact, the mod-12 complements of their pitch-class-operational equivalents. For contextual reasons, I regard the transposition cycle as a "revolving" juxtaposition of two "complementary" cycles whose "0"-positions are "T6"-related sets:

6. Hierarchical (0 3 6 9)-set "S" and "I" Transposition Cycle (the "TnS" succession may be thought of as an "ascending", and the "TnI" succession as a "descending", reading of the (0 3 6 9) cycle given in Table 4):

S →   ← I

T0S: (11 2   5   8)(0   3   6   9)(1   4   7 10) : T6I
T1S: (0 3   6   9)(1   4   7 10)(2   5   8 11) : T5I
T2S: (1 4   7 10)(2   5   8 11)(3   6   9   0) : T4I
T3S: (2 5   8 11)(3   6   9   0)(4   7 10   1) : T3I
T4S: (3 6   9   0)(4   7 10   1)(5   8 11   2) : T2I
T5S: (4 7 10   1)(5   8 11   2)(6   9   0   3) : T1I
T6S: (5 8 11   2)(6   9   0   3)(7 10   1   4) : T0I
T7S: (6 9   0   3)(7 10   1   4)(8 11   2   5) : T11I
T8S: (7 10   1   4)(8 11   2   5)(9   0   3   6) : T10I
T9S: (8 11   2   5)(9   0   3   6)(10   1   4   7) : T9I
T10S: (9 0   3   6)(10   1   4   7)(11   2   5   8) : T8I
T11S: (10 1   4   7)(11   2   5   8)(0   3   6   9) : T7I

7. Hierarchical harmonic hexachord "S" and "I" Transposition Cycle:

S →   ← I

T0S: (8 0 3)(6 9 1) : T6I
T1S: (9 1 4)(7 10 2) : T5I
T2S: (10 2 5)(8 11 3) : T4I
T3S: (11 3 6)(9 0 4) : T3I
T4S: (0 4 7)(10 1 5) : T2I
T5S: (1 5 8)(11 2 6) : T1I
T6S: (2 6 9)(0 3 7) : T0I
T7S: (3 7 10)(1 4 8) : T11I
T8S: (4 8 11)(2 5 9) : T10I
T9S: (5 9 0)(3 6 10) : T9I
T10S: (6 10 1)(4 7 11) : T8I
T11S: (7 11 2)(5 8 0) : T7I

8. Tristan-Chord Distribution

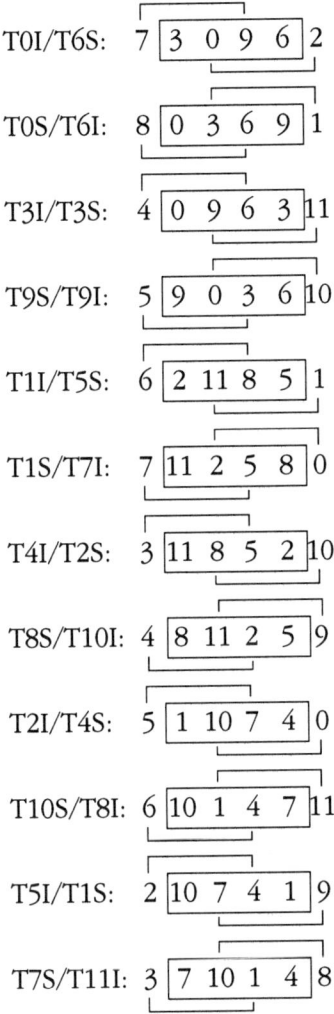

```
T0I/T6S:    7 | 3  0  9  6 | 2
T0S/T6I:    8 | 0  3  6  9 | 1
T3I/T3S:    4 | 0  9  6  3 | 11
T9S/T9I:    5 | 9  0  3  6 | 10
T1I/T5S:    6 | 2 11  8  5 | 1
T1S/T7I:    7 | 11 2  5  8 | 0
T4I/T2S:    3 | 11 8  5  2 | 10
T8S/T10I:   4 | 8 11  2  5 | 9
T2I/T4S:    5 | 1 10  7  4 | 0
T10S/T8I:   6 | 10 1  4  7 | 11
T5I/T1S:    2 | 10 7  4  1 | 9
T7S/T11I:   3 | 7 10  1  4 | 8
```

9. (0 3 7 10)-Chord Distribution

T0I+T1I:	9 6 2 11
T0S+T11S:	0 3 7 10
T1I+T2I:	8 5 1 10
T11S+T10S:	1 4 8 11
T2I+T3I:	7 4 0 9
T10S+T9S:	2 5 9 0
T3I+T4I:	6 3 11 8
T9S+T8S:	3 6 10 1
T4I+T5I:	5 2 10 7
T8S+T7S:	4 7 11 2
T5I+T6I:	4 1 9 6
T7S+T6S:	5 8 0 3

10. The (0 6 2 8) chord (generated as a relation between outer dyads of T6-related harmonic hexachords; the (0 6 2 8) results from the conjunction of the dyads at *corresponding* "outer" ends; the *opposite* outer-end conjunction produces the (0 4 7 11) chord which appears more conspicuously in the opera itself (e.g., the chord that opens Act II) than in the Prelude to Act I):[11]

A. Generating Relation:

T0S:	8 0	3 6	9 1
T6S:	2 6	9 0	3 7
Resultants:	0	0	0
	2	3	2
	6	6	6
	8	9	8

---

[11]Significantly (0 4 7 11) may be regarded as in a special sense an *inverse* of (0 3 7 10), insofar as both may be regarded as determined by an overlapped (0 3 7)/(0 4 7) pair, which in the (0 3 7 10) emerges from a configuration of two 3s "surrounding" a 4, and in the (0 4 7 11) emerges from two 4s surrounding a 3.

(The relation between (0 2 6 8) and (1 3 7 9) in this example is the same, pitch-transformationally, as that between the two (0 2 6 8)-type chords at the last eighth of m. 2 and the first beat of m. 3 of the Prelude to Act I.)

B. The (0 2 6 8) Chord Array:

T0S/T6I:	8 0	3 6	9 1
T6S/T0I:	2 6	9 0	3 7
T3S/T3I:	11 3	6 9	0 4
T9S/T9I:	5 9	0 3	6 10
T5S/T1I:	1 5	8 11	2 6
T11S/T7I:	7 11	2 5	8 0
T8S/T10I:	4 8	11 2	5 9
T2S/T4I:	10 2	5 8	11 3
T4S/T2I:	0 4	7 10	1 5
T10S/T8I	6 10	1 4	7 11
T7S/T11I:	3 7	10 1	4 8
T1S/T5I:	9 1	4 7	10 2

In the above table, each (0 2 6 8)-chord occurs twice, but no pairs of (0 2 6 8)-chords occurring in a given hexachord-pair conjunction recur together in any other hexachord-pair conjunction. Each "side" of the list contains just one occurrence of each transposition of the (0 2 6 8) chord:

```
0  2  6  8  = T0(T6)    T1(T7)   = 1  3  7  9
9  11 3  5  = T9(T3)    T4(T10)  = 4  6  10 0
5  7  11 1  = T5(T11)   T0(T6)   = 0  2  6  8
2  4  8  10 = T2(T8)    T3(T9)   = 3  5  9  11
4  6  10 0  = T4(T10)   T5(T11)  = 5  7  11 1
1  3  7  9  = T1(T7)    T2(T8)   = 2  4  8  10
```

Now none of the above is construable as the "analysis" of anything—in the sense of its integrated construction; rather some promising-looking tools of measurement are offered, as perhaps capable of producing high-level "theoretical data" (by slicing the relatively "observational" data in particular ways), from which analytic construction might fruitfully proceed. Nevertheless, it might be useful to undertake some brief, partial- and quasi-analytic examples to test the plausibility of the thesis that these particular syntactical referents, in application to *Tristan*, would in fact produce something that looked like a significant musical construction. Let us, to begin with, reconsider the introduction of the Prelude (mm. 1–17) from this point of view. On the basis of our previous discussion, we might regard the collection as "centering" on the (D F G♯ B) construct; since the first Tristan chord is (F G♯ B D♯), let us call the (D F G♯ B)-"centric" collection in which that occurs "T0S". This gives further the pitch-class-space partitioning constructed on p.284 as follows:

T0S: $\{\{((C\sharp\ E\ G\ A\sharp)\ (D\ F\ G\sharp\ B\ )\ (D\sharp\ F\sharp\ A\ C\ )\}$

T3S: $\{(E\ G\ A\sharp\ C\sharp)\ (F\ G\sharp\ B\ D)\ (F\sharp\ A\ C\ D\sharp)\}$

T6S: $\{(G\ A\sharp\ C\sharp\ E\ )\ (G\sharp\ B\ D\ F\ )\ (A\ C\ D\sharp\ F\sharp)\}$

T9S: $\{(A\sharp\ C\sharp\ E\ G)\ (B\ D\ F\ G\sharp)\ (C\ D\sharp\ F\sharp\ A\ )\}\}$

Here the bracketings are determinate not only of (0 3 6 9) orders but of principal twelve-collectional boundaries as well; this is effectuated by a new interpretation superimposed on that of the previously given "open" (0 3 6 9) cycle in which adjacencies are defined only as "within-construct" or "between-construct", while here they are further identified as either "within-collection" or "between-collection" (each collection having thus a unique adjacency-construct-content identity). This is a further "syntactical" distinction at a more "foreground" level than our previous, "open" (and thus more general-systematic) one; our new distinction is just as unambiguously and consistently applicable as the former one, and is compatible with it not only in the sense that it is sustainable without prejudice to the earlier-formulated one, but also in the sense that it is based on a large-scale application of the same (pitch-) transposition principle as was applied, with respect to single pitches, to generate the (0 3 6 9) cycle. (And this "application" of the transposition-by-3 relation to successive twelve-pitch-class *collections* arises naturally as a result of our having created the collections just by slicing the "cycle" as we have done.) This, too, makes meaningful the extension of the cyclic set (T0S), (T3S), (T6S), (T9S) into a complete transpositional complex—since by our new distinction, we have not only been able to create a fourfold *unique* partitioning of the twelve pitch-class octave, but have opened the way to a threefold extension thereof wherein the complete "within-collection"/"between-collection" identification is expanded:

$$\left\{ \begin{array}{llll} \{T0S & T3S & T6S & T9S\} \\ \{T1S & T4S & T7S & T10S\} \\ \{T2S & T5S & T8S & T11S\} \end{array} \right\}$$

in content:

T1S: {(D   F   G♯   B) (D♯ F♯   A   C) (E   G   A♯   C♯)}
T4S: {(F   G♯   B   D) (F♯   A   C   D♯) (G   A♯   C♯   E)}
T7S: {(G♯   B   D   F) (A   C   D♯   F♯) (A♯   C♯   E   G)}
T10S: {(B   D   F   G♯) (C   D♯   F♯   A) (C♯   E   G   A♯)}

T2S: {(D♯ F♯   A   C) (E   G   A♯   C♯) (F   G♯   B   D)}
T5S: {(F♯   A   C   D♯) (G   A♯   C♯   E) (G♯   B   D   F)}
T8S: {(A   C   D♯   F♯) (A♯   C♯   E   G) (B   D   F   G♯)}
T11S: {(C   D♯   F♯   A) (C♯   E   G   A♯) (D   F   G♯   B)}

This is a maximal extension of the principle, since none of the systematically defined "harmonic" constructs appears *uniquely* as a "between-cycle" one.

A charting of the sonority successions in the opening measures against this background proceeds from the (F G♯ B D♯) (of T0S) to the "neutral" (F B D♯ A) and (E A♯ D G♯), both equally weighted between T0S and T6S, to, finally, the (E G♯ B D) of m. 3, found in T6S: the "balanced" (T6-related) transposition, *"halfway"* across the partitioning cycle (where, as noted in the charts above, T6S = T0I); while the *construct* shifts to the non-transpositionally equivalent inverse in leaning from the (D♯ F♯ A C) side in m. 2 to the (G A♯ C♯ E) side in m. 3—a neat "structural-level" compositional distinction.

In the second "phrase", the first Tristan chord is (G♯ B D F♯) of T3S, and the last is (G B D F), of T9S, completing the cycle of references at the point where also are completed the twelve pitch-class cycle, the (0 3 6 9)-cycle assertion, and the (D F G♯ B) weighting.

The third "phrase" begins with the Tristan chord (D F G♯ C) of T9S (the "inverse" of the preceding "T-chord" (G B D F) within the *same collection,* which signals the longer-range differentiation involved here). The phrase concludes with (B D♯ F♯ A), a (D♯ F♯ A C)-based T-chord found in T0S, but suggesting, by the associative (articulative) means discussed before, a "linkage" with T1S, in the (D♯ F♯ A C)-centered collection cycle. This inference of T1S would, of course, be more particularly entailed by the assertion of constructs which appear *only between* Ts; but this remark in itself sounds like talk about degree-of-assertion distinctions which are a rather rich source of compositional coherence, and hence would tend to increase one's bias in favor of a system in which such differentiations of degree were available.

As to the final phrase, note that both (E G♯ B D) and (F A C) occur in T6S—"balanced" by 6-relatedness with the T0S reference of (B D♯ F♯ A), the "shift" from (D F G♯ B) to (D♯ F♯ A C), and the "same-set" relation of the end-point of phrase 2 and the beginning-point of phrase 3.

But by the opening of the "principal section", the overall transpositional shift *is* entailed by the conjunction of (D F♯ A C) and (C E G), since the latter does not occur *within* any collection of the (T0-T3-T6-T9) cycle, and they *both* occur within only the (T1-

T4-T7-T10) cycle, as constituents of T4S and T1S, respectively, and since this partitioning cycle is centered on just the (D♯ F♯ A C) construct on which we, for contextual reasons, have already decided to center this section, this seems an admirable point at which to leave the remainder of the task as an exercise for the reader.

How about the whole of the music drama? Some indication of an answer to this question may be given by the following observations on the first few measures of the *Liebestod,* measured against the (0 3 6 9)-systematic metric, with particular reference to similarities observed to our previous observations regarding the Prelude.

First, a bit of derivational tune-detective analysis: we have already noticed the "diatonicization" of the "chromatic tetrachord" at the opening of the Prelude to Act I in the opening of Act III; and we have also noticed the *Grundgestalt* F-B spanning the entire third act. Here we may begin by noticing that the Prelude's upper-line *Grundgestalt* A♭-B may be described as characterizing the macrospan of the *Liebestod* (thus lying as a sub-span within the overall F-B span of the act as a whole).

But the motivic-derivational chain leading from the wholly "chromatic" line that "fills in" the A♭-B span both locally and globally in the Act I Prelude to the "diatonic" lines in the later portions of the opera may be regarded as considerably less "general" or "casual" than such large-scale observations alone may suggest. Here is a possible associational path:

Start by imagining the following contrapuntal transformation:

1) Consider the outer chords of mm. 2-3 as balanced by an interchange of displacements of reference (0 3 6 9) pitches in two registral voices—each displacing pitch being a member of a different one of the two other possible (0 3 6 9)s. If the *displacing* pitches are represented as encircled, and the pitches they displace (call them *resolving*) are represented ensquared, each side of a diagram of the counterpoint will contain just one encircled and just one ensquared pitch:

1:

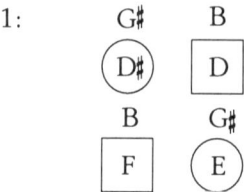

2) Suppose the balanced succession unbalanced by placing *both* displacing pitches first, and both resolving pitches second, so that the balanced succession becomes a progression, from a displacement-bearing to a displacement-free chord; thus our diagram will contain two circles on the left-hand side and two squares on the right-hand side:

2:

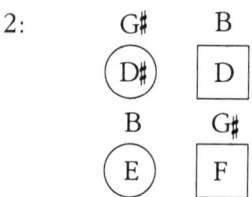

3) Now suppose the succession a) transposed on the model of the end of the Prelude to Act I; i.e., on to the (0 3 6 9) (C♯ E G B♭), or T11; and b) with the first chord altered to contain just a "verticalization" of the opening three-note figure, retaining both encircled notes, and projecting in particular the aspect of asserting one pitch from each possible (0 3 6 9):

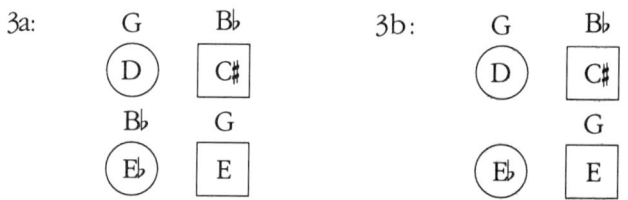

3b may now be read as a map of the two-chord counterpoint that opens Act II, as well as one which juxtaposes the opening three-note figure of the Sailor's Song at the beginning of Act I with the first orchestral chord of the act. And, transposed by seven semitones, the first chord of 3a may be heard, horizontalized, as the initiating four attacks of the bass tune beginning at m. 21 (regarding which see below):

<pre>
         F   A   B♭   D
</pre>

4) Moreover, if we were to transpose the opening of the Act I Prelude on the model of the first chord of Act II, we would arrive at the following counterpoint:

<pre>
     4:                F♯

            G   E♭ D   C♯

                A

                E♭
</pre>

5) If we *delay* the arrival on this first Tristan chord by first asserting the entire (0 3 6 9) chord of its "spoiler" note C♯, and then *extend* the counterpoint by "resolving" the spoiling C♯ to its (0 3 6 9)-completing reference pitch, the result would look as follows:

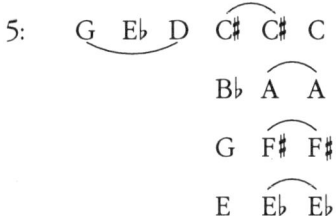

5 may also be read as a map of the first eight measures of Act II of *Tristan*.

Further, consider the opening "alto line" of the Prelude to Act I as a conjunction of two distinct "motivic segments", both phraseologically "isolated" as noted earlier; the first is the (A F E) (0 8 7) trichord that opens the Prelude and the Sailor's Song, and the second is the (F E E♭ D) "chromatic tetrachord".

Now if we look again to the opening of the second act, the first continuous "theme" in the bass of the Act II Prelude (at m. 21) unfolds as follows:

F   A   B♭   D   E♭   E   G   F

This may be "derived" from the opening of the Act I Prelude as, first, the "inversion" of the opening (A F E) into the two-pitch-class-preserving trichord (F A B♭), interlinked with a second "inversion" of (A F E), (B♭ D E♭), which, in continuing in exact complementation to the (A F E) line at the opening of Act I, through E and F (as B♭ D E♭ E (G) F)), reproduces the entire "chromatic tetrachord" at its original pitch-class level, but unfolded in retrograde (as the same tetrachord was unfolded in mm. 10–11 of the Act I Prelude). But the (F A B♭) inversion of the (A F E) trichord is also "filled in" in the passage by the "cambiata" G that intervenes between the E and the F of the "chromatic tetrachord". Thus is derived that "diatonic tetrachord" that we have already noticed in connection with the "upper line" at the beginning of Act III:[12]

G   A♭   B♭   C

which represents an exact *inverse* of the second-act (F G A B♭), and hence reproduces the motivic trichord in its original form as (0 8 7) (here (C A♭ G), *T3-related* to the opening (A F E)).

---

[12]The Act III english horn tune also begins with this tetrachord, 5-transposed, intervallically camouflaged, and retaining the (0 8 7) rhythm of the opening phrase of the Act:

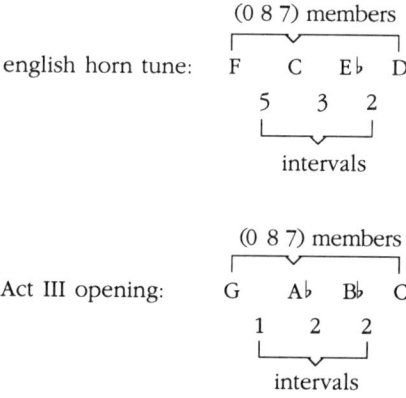

As to the Act II Prelude, the "continuation" of the bass tune on B♭ at m. 25 permutes the pitches of mm. 21–22, phraseologically "placing" the "diatonic tetrachord" where the "chromatic" one previously appeared, and thereby adjoins to that diatonic tetrachord the "linked"-7 C (as (F G A B♭ (C)), which becomes motivic in the third act as well, as:

G   A♭   B♭   C

(opening of Act III:)

(F) (G   A♭   B♭   C)

which is still an exact inverse of the Act II cluster, but also preserves invariant the F-C extrema. The third version of the "bass tune" in Act II, at m. 27, interlocks the original "diatonic tetrachord" (F G A B♭), via the linked-7 C, to a new "chromatic" tetrachord (C C♯ D E♭), a conjunction which juxtaposes the (0 4 5) / (0 8 7) trichords (G E♭ D), (F C♯ C), and (F A B♭), the union of which is, in fact, the entire pitch-class content of the passage from m. 27.0 to m. 29.0. And the "soprano" counter-melody at m. 29 begins with a descending line which unfolds, in presented "normal form", an exact inverse of the pitch-class contents of the m. 21 bass tune. This inverse preserves invariant the "chromatic tetrachord" (F E E♭ D), but adjoins it to a different "diatonic" one (D C B♭ A), whose earlier appearance in the passage at mm. 25–28 may thus be regarded as "linking" the mm. 21–22 pitch complex with its m. 29 inverse. Note, too, that the difference between the m. 21 bass tune's pitch-class content and that of the m. 29 "soprano tune" is just one element of each (G and C, respectively); the G "missing" in the m. 29 passage is immediately supplied in m. 30, and the motivic associations projected by the ensuing passage should be evident.

Here are the pitch-class contents of the m. 21 bass tune and the m. 29 soprano tune compared:

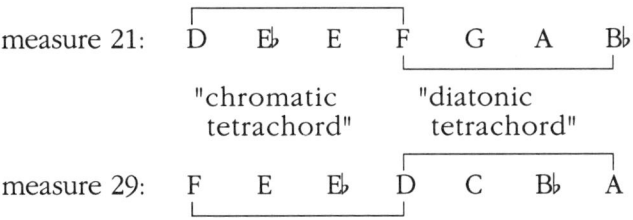

A final observation: the "repetition" of the "soprano" tune at mm. 33–38 is accompanied by a slowly unfolding bass line whose outline is (D E♭ E F).

In the *Liebestod*, the explicit phraseological connection to the Act I Prelude of the successive rising T3s, both within and between phraseological articulations, continuing through an entire (0 3 6 9) span, is supported melodically by just the motivic connections we have noted. Thus the opening "*Liebestod* motto" (E♭ A♭ G) is an obvious permutation of the (A F E) trichord that opens Act I (transposed, of course). And comparing the referential pitch levels of the presentations of this trichord (and its inverses) at the beginning of the Act I Prelude, the beginning of Act III, and the beginning of the *Liebestod*, we may observe a (0 3 6) relation linking them:

Act I Prelude:	(A	F	E)	(T0S)
Act III Prelude:	(C	A♭	G)	(T3S)
Liebestod:	(E♭	G	A♭)	(T6I)

Note the preservation of A♭ and G between the second and third trichords, which suggests a long-range relational analogy to the relation between the (F A B♭) and (B♭ D E♭ E F) of the Act II Prelude and the (A F E E♭ D) of the Act I Prelude. And of course, the *Liebestod* itself carries out (and thereby presumably underlines) this long-range relation as, also, a short-range one in transferring (E♭ A♭ G) immediately onto (F♯ B B♭), which latter would "complete" an (0 3 6 9) cycle of trichord-transformation forms in our table, above. As a local relation, of course, the 3-transposition directly reflects the corresponding passage in the Act I Prelude.

But the continuation of the *Liebestod* line past the opening (E♭ A♭ G) establishes an even more "connective" association, as the (E♭ A♭ G) merges into an overall line that overlaps a "diatonic" with a "chromatic" tetrachord. This overlap is arranged such that the "completion" of the chromatic tetrachord (A♭ G G♭ F) is "delayed" (as in m. 22 of Act II) by the intervention of the diatonic one (G♭ A♭ B♭ F), so that they both "complete" on the same attack, on F, which thus underlines the phraseological "break" following that point of convergence:

E♭	A♭	G		[F]	((0 4 5) trichord)
	A♭	G	G♭		F	(chromatic tetrachord)
			G♭	A♭	B♭	F	(diatonic tetrachord)

Also, the four attacks on the three pitches (E♭ A♭ G) perhaps suggest the "tetrachordal" framework as well (the F also completes a "diatonic tetrachord" with respect to that (E♭ A♭ G): (A♭ G F E♭), which is an inverse of (F G♭ A♭ B♭)). Note, too, the 3-related pitch classes (E♭, G♭) linking the two interlocked, inverse (0 8 7) / (0 4 5) trichords (E♭ A♭ G) and (G♭ B♭ F), a relation that is of course generative for the second-segment transposition of the whole tune "on" E♭ to a version on G♭.

But most interesting of all from the total-structural point of view is the fact that this conjunction of diatonic and chromatic tetrachords can be generated entirely (that is, the entire pitch-class content of mm. 1 and 2 of the *Liebestod*) as a conjunction of three ((0 4 5)/(0 8 7)) inverse pairs, with respect to three "0"s, namely, B♭, E♭, and A♭. This generation requires taking into account the F♭ that occurs two measures before the beginning of the *Liebestod* proper, but the (F♭ E♭ A♭) trichord is so explicitly unfolded in register that the *possibility* of its inclusion in the generative scheme seems more significant (that is, as a structural *advantage*) than its *necessity* (as an analytic expedient).[13]

Thus the (B♭ D E♭) trichord, formed by the (E♭ D) bass succession, seems especially interesting as both the "longest-range" trichord of the passage (in terms of total time of unfolding), and the one most directly associated with the bass tune of the Act II Prelude. For it turns out that that bass tune, too, can be generated entirely as the intersection of three (0 4 5) trichords (without, however, their (0 8 7) inverse counterparts), a condition which is representable as an interlocking (1+4) intervallic chain whose (0 4 5) members are T5-related, like those of the *Liebestod* passage:

Act II, mm. 21–22:   E   F   A   B♭   D   E♭   G

---

[13]That the (0 4 5) trichord has intrinsically special syntactic significance may be gleaned from the fact that it is the only non-symmetrical trichord (i. e., the only one containing three *distinct intervals)* each of whose members belongs to a *distinct* (0 3 6 9); so just as *each* (0 3 6 9) is represented by a distinct *pitch-class*

And the three ((0 4 5) / (0 8 7)) pairs of mm. 1–2 of the *Liebestod* (with the F♭ "upbeat") are representable as *two* similar chains, inversely related:[14]

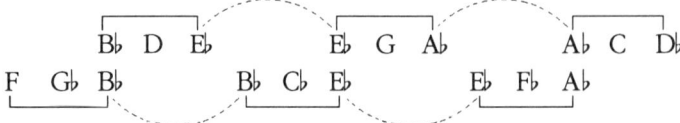

element, each *relation between pairs* of (0 3 6 9)s is represented by a distinct interval-class element. Its special place in the (0 3 6 9)-systematic array may be discerned from the following filtration of some strands of the opening of the *Tristan* Prelude through the harmonic hexachords of T6S and T0S:

linear successions:

A - F - E - G♯ - [A]
            D♯ - D
                 A♯ - B
m. 1   m. 2   m. 3

simultaneities:

$$\begin{bmatrix} D♯ & - & D \\ B & & A♯ \end{bmatrix}$$

$$\begin{bmatrix} A & - & G♯ \\ F & & E \end{bmatrix}$$

m. 2 m. 3

harmonic hexachord, T6S:

E G♯ (B D) F A

harmonic hexachord, T0S:

A♯ D (F G♯) B D

(0 4 5)s:

$$\left\{ \begin{array}{l} (A\ F\ E) \\ (E\ G♯\ A) \end{array} \right.$$

$$\left\{ \begin{array}{l} (D\ B\ A) \\ (A♯\ D\ D♯) \end{array} \right.$$

[The passage also embeds F A B♭ D, as:

A	A♯	T6S: (E G♯ (B D) F A)
	D	
F		T0S: (B♭ D ((F G♯) B D♯)
m. 2	m. 3	

which may be taken as a connection with the "bass-line" tune at m. 21 of Act II. In an even more direct way, the embedding in the opening "upper line" of

304

Here is a "rhythmic-registral" representation of the same passage:

```
                                    F♯         B♭  F
              E♭      A♭  G
    F♭        E♭      A♭
             ⎧ A♭     D♭  C
             ⎩ (C)
                                   ⎧ C♭
                                   ⎩ (E♭)        C♭ B♭
    (E♭)      E♭                                   D ⎫
                                                   B♭⎭

              m. 1                  m. 2
```

(13) E G♯ A refers to the registral and intervallic position of the voice-part trichord in m. 1 of the *Liebestod*, where it is transposed so as to preserve one key pitch-class intersection:

```
           E    |  G♯  A
                |                Prelude
          m. 1  |  m. 2

         | E♭  A♭  G |
         |           |           Liebestod]
         |    m. 1   |
```

As noted, the eight pitch classes involved, which comprise the entire pitch-class content of the fragment, are completed within the whole fragment, within mm. 2–3, and by the two chords around the mid-point of mm. 2–3.

The special *Tristan*-systematic significance of dyads determining the interval 4 is discussed in note 9, above.

[14] A pair of interleaved, T5I-related (0 4 5/0 8 7) chains such as this one, extended to eleven entry positions, such that no pitch-class element appears in more than one entry position (and where 0-related pitch-class elements occurring in corresponding places on the two chains are considered to determine one entry position, so that (0, 1, 5) and (0, 4, 5) together determine just four entry positions, occupied by 0, 1, 4, and 5), is in fact the *maximal* (0 4 5/0 8 7) chain-pair in which such a uniqueness of entry-position/pitch-class element correlation is conserved: 1) any other interval of inversion between the chains produces a *shorter* possible non-duplicative chain-pair, and 2) the extension of the T5I-duplication. In this light, the eleven-out-of-twelve pitch-class content of the first phrase of the *Liebestod* can be regarded as motivically "selective", insofar as it is

(Note that to carry this scheme forward into mm. 3–4, the G of m. 1 (two measures before m. 3) must be invoked. But despite the exact parallelism of its "metric" position, two measures before its referent "downbeat", with the F♭ before mm. 1–2, and despite its equally parallel function as "leading" to G♭ with a direct registral succession (in mm. 1–2) as F♭ "leads" to E♭ in the preceding passage, this G is distinctly different in its relation within the passage from that of F♭, in a number of evident respects. But so are mm. 5–7 "different" from mm. 1–4 in the Act I Prelude, in particular because of the "common-tone" linkage of the first pitch of the second passage with the last pitch of the first passage, nearly as the two *Liebestod* passages differ.)

Through this loosely associative chain, then, we can connect the (0 3 6 9)-outlining openings of the Prelude and the *Liebestod*. But so far, it remains an open question whether the deployment of our (0 3 6 9)-systematic array can materially deepen the structural integration of these associations. A first line of observation to this end might be a direct (0 3 6 9)-referential matchup of the openings of the Prelude and the *Liebestod;* for the sequence of (0 3 6 9) references is, to begin with, virtually parallel:

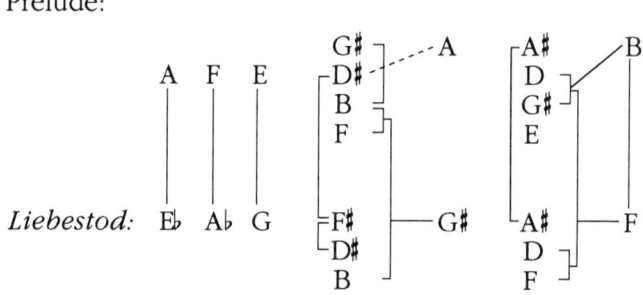

---

distinguishable, as a motivated *choice*, from any set of, say, ten pitch-class elements, or from the set of all twelve.

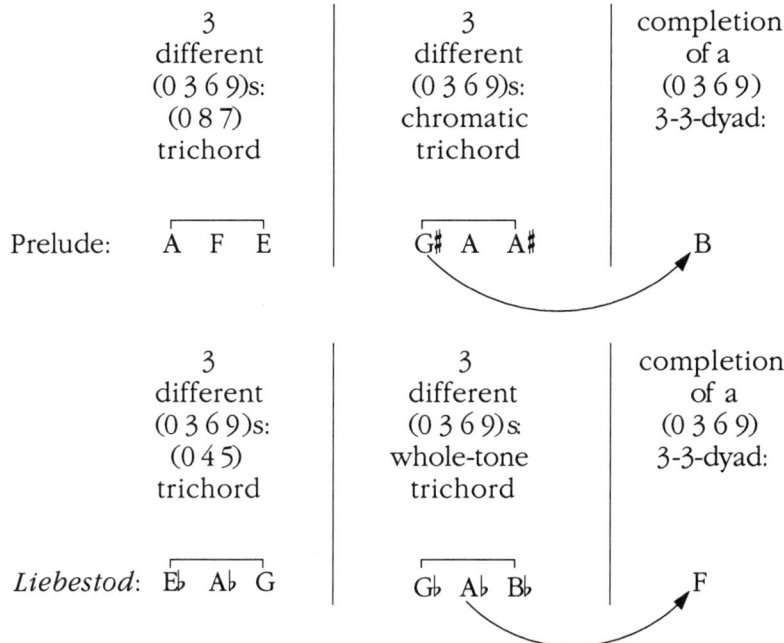

And the pattern of displacements is parallel, too, but in the significant sense that what we may hear as single pitch-class *leanings* within single chords in the Prelude may be matched with successive chord-weightings (and balances) in the *Liebestod*:

"T0" refers to the (0 3 6 9) (D F G♯ B),
in any permutation:

Prelude:	G♯	A	A♯	B
	D♯	D♯	D	D
	B	B	G♯	G♯
	F	F	E	E
		m. 2		m. 3
leaning:		toward T1		toward T11

Liebestod:	E♭	A♭	G	G	F♯	G♯	B♭	F
	C		D♭	C	B	B	B♭	
	A♭		B♭	B♭				F
	E♭		E♭	E♭	E♭	E♭	D	
		m. 1				m. 2		
weighting:	T0		T1	T0̲ T1	T0	T11	T11	

The leanings of successive T0-weighted chords in the Prelude first to T1 and then to T11 is "transformed" in the *Liebestod* into the successive weightings of the chords of two passages, first from T0 to T1 and then from T0 to T11, a parallelism preserved by the parallel 3-transpositions of the second articulated stretches of both Prelude and *Liebestod*. But whereas the two fragments of the Prelude complete a simple set of collection references, exhausting the going "tonic" cycle, those of the *Liebestod* are considerably more complex:[15]

(names of collections *weighted* are unparenthesized:
names of collections *leaned* toward are parenthesized:)

E♭	G	G	F♯	G♯	B♭	F♯	A♯	A♯	A	B	C♯
C	D♭	C	B	B	B♭	D♯	E	D♯	D	D	C♯
A♭	B♭	B♭			F	B	C♯	C♯			G♯
E♭	E♭	E♭	E♭	E♭	D	F♯	F♯	F♯	F♯	F♯	F
T10S	(T4S)	T4S	T1S	(T1S)		T1S	(T7S)	T7S	T4S	(T4S)	
	T5S	T5S			(T11S)		T8S	T8S			(T2S)
(T9S)			(T0S)	T0S	T0S	(T0S)			(T3S)	T3S	T3S
	m. 1			m. 2			m. 3			m. 4	

---

[15]The (0 3 6 9) identification of the "centric" transposition cycle as (T1-T4-T7-T10) gives a special significance to the $^6_4$ representation of the initial triads of these "phrases", in that the (0 3 6 9) outlined at the lowest registral extreme is the "center" (D♯ F♯ A C), with the "spoiling" (A♭ B D F) always appearing "within" a "tonic" (0 3 6 9)-framing interval span, as the first A♭ of m. 1 appears registrally *between* E♭ and C. This intervallic disposition perhaps also clarifies the Tristan-chord-like status of the "triad", as half of an (0 3 6 9) with a 1-related "neighbor note" to a third (0 3 6 9) member. And taken as a crypto-Tristan chord, the

[The "stronger" modulatory weighting in the second sub-phrase of each phrase corresponds to the longer-range articulations they conclude: both T0S in m. 2 and T3S in m. 4 are expressed in three progressively modulatory stages (on the model suggested on p. 307, above), progressing from two chords shared with the tonic-cycle collections (the first lying within the harmonic hexachord of the tonic-cycle collection, the second within that of the new collection) to a third chord, *not* shared by a tonic-cycle collection (which conjoins with the second chord to complete the entire harmonic hexachord of the new collection):

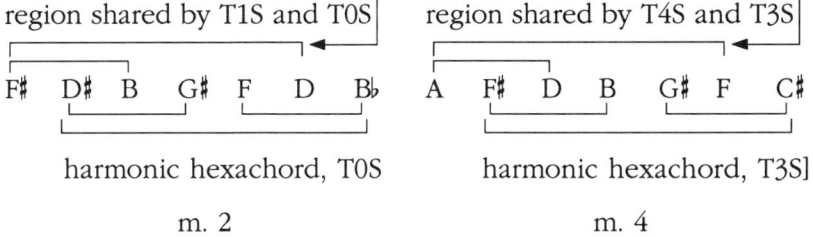

A clue to a less inscrutable collection-referential connection between the Prelude and the *Liebestod* may be available from our earlier construction of a parallelism of (0 3 6 9)-displacement rhythms by transferring from the relatively immediate *pitch*-class-content (0 3 6 9)-*leaning* shapes of the Prelude onto the syntactically deeper *set-referential* (0 3 6 9)-*weighting* shapes of the *Liebestod*: recall that we derived a pattern of (0 3 6 9) *completions* in each fragment of the Prelude by observing the pitch-class contents of each sub-fragment: each measure contained three (D F G♯ B) members, and two "displacing" non-(D F G♯ B) members, such that each whole *fragment* completed one whole (D F G♯ B) and one half each of the other two (0 3 6 9)s. In the *Liebestod*, the weighting patterns transfer, onto *collection references* (rather than *pitch-class assertions*) *over two phrases* (rather than *within one fragment*), just this pattern of (0 3 6 9)-

---

(A♭ C E♭) triad of m. 1 is "completed" by the F♯ in m. 2, while another Tristan-chord is supplied by the association in m. 2 of the A♭ with the (B♭ D F) triad. Then, in m. 3, the (C♭ E♭ F♯) of m. 2 is associated with the A of m. 4, as the B is with (C♯ E♯ G♯). And the only *presented* Tristan chords in these four measures are associated with the "tonic" cycle (T1-T4-T7-T10).

weightings: each phrase of the *Liebestod* contains chords weighted toward (or balanced with) *three* tonic-cycle collections (overlapping to complete a set of references to the entire tonic-cycle array), and chords weighted toward *two* non-tonic-cycle collections (such that *half* of each non-tonic-cycle array is referred to by weighting (or balancing) over that same two-phrase span).

That the three-plus-two, within-a-measure, rhythm of the Prelude, where each "two" belongs to a single "displacing" (0 3 6 9), is altered in its transference onto the within-a-phrase scale in the *Liebestod*, where the displacement references are alternated, is a function of the multiple scaling of parallelisms—the *displacement* patterns are one-to-one, fragment to phrase, whereas the weighting patterns, two fragments to one phrase, are part of what gives the *Liebestod* its greater phraseological breadth, in correspondence with its deeper and more-leveled syntactical functionality and developmental complexity, as a rerealization of the Prelude.

The maneuver that crucially creates the room for this greater depth and breadth is the T3 collection-reference relation *internal* to each *Liebestod* phrase, which anticipates at short range the successive T3 transpositions of the whole phrases. (A new complexity here: in this respect the rhythm of the *Liebestod* is *contracted* relative to that created by the exclusively between-fragment T3 relation of the Prelude.) As a result, whereas the T6 collection-reference relation internal to each of the Prelude fragments creates a cycle which returns on itself after a span of just two successive 3-related transpositions, the cycle created by the internally contracted phrases of the *Liebestod* can spread out over four such transpositions before retrieving its beginning. This resource, directly exploited in the opening phrases of the *Liebestod*, is extended onto a still larger phraseological and temporal scale by the T3-related parallelism between m. 1 and m. 12, the beginning of a "second macrowave" in the *Liebestod*; in this sense mm. 1–11 have, relative to the passage beginning at m. 12, the relation of "first" to "second fragment". The development, after m. 4, of the T3 idea, may be charted in a way that seems interestingly suggestive of and for the phraseological cut of the passage:

(The following chart may be read as displaying a series of six continuously unfolded phrase-segments, each initiated by a tonic-cycle (T1S-T4S-T7S-T10S) reference and displaced by references, over the first three measures (mm. 5–7), to collections from the T1-related cycle (T2S-T5S-T8S-T11S); over the next three measures (mm. 8-10), to collections from the T11-related cycle (T0S-T3S-T6S-T9S); and, in the last measure (m. 11), before the new large-phrase beginning, to one collection from each non-tonic cycle; reading the upper line of the chart will reveal the tonic-cycle transposition pattern, first by T3, and then, in mm. 9–11, where the referential alternation is expanded into a 2-measure (rather than, as elsewhere, a 1-measure) rhythm, by T6; the T3 and T6 patterns of the tonic-cycle references are shadowed within each 3-measure group (and in their relation to the last one-measure group in m. 11) by the sequence of "displacing" collection-references, which may be read on the second and third lines of the chart.)

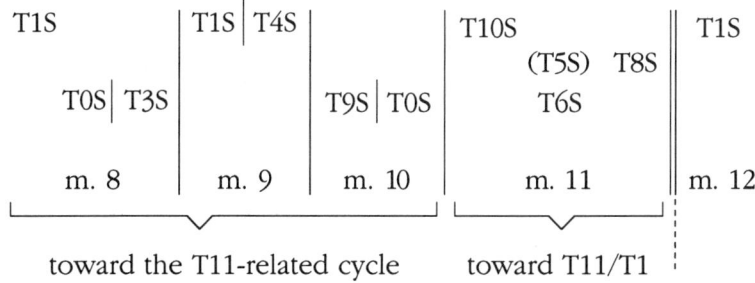

Should our persistent observer have endured thus far, he might be struck by the reflection that this entire network of rhythmic-motivic developments and associations is, for the very possibility of its existence as an experienceable musical phenomenon, wholly consequential on the construction and invocation, in full hierarchical elaboration, of the (0 3 6 9)-cyclic reference-set array which we have been calling the *Tristan* system.

CONCLUDING REMARKS

The "systematic" status of the *Tristan* syntax proposed here can be likened to that of a *primary order-generated* system where the maximum determinacy is located in the order relations among internally ordered tetrachords. For the *content* of the referents remains unaltered from transformation to transformation (e. g., among *transpositions* in the *Tristan* system) of the collection; what is varied, and thus syntactically generative, is the "order" for (and within) each reference construct within the collection in each transformation. The determinateness of such an ordering, and hence the determinateness of its variability, depends on its generation of content-unique pitch sets as relations between reference constructs defined as order adjacent. Ordering, thus, is not necessarily interpreted in musical systems as "time order", as in the usual interpretations of the "classical" twelve-tone system. In fact, a single "chord" (in *Tristan*) represents a potential "ordering" partition of the pitch domain quite different in its signification from the polyphonic-triadic, register-independent, "voices" (and from the partial-content reference-set identifications), crucial to the tonal syntax. So that "serial" music, in presenting an ordered set, may *interpret* its orderings in terms of simultaneity, leaving *immediate succession* as an *articulative level* of structure. (This, essentially, is what seems to be involved in some recent self-declared "non-serial" music, such as Arthur Berger's "registrally determined" Six Piano Pieces.) Thus the usual notion of "serialism", even as sustained in sophisticated quarters, might yield to a more relativistic explication through the admission of possible ranges (i. e., variable domains) of interpretation of the "ordering" of the referential set (even, possibly, within a single piece). For in these terms, *Tristan* as we have described it is not only "twelve-tone" in a special sense but also "serial" in a special sense,[16] as radically precompositionally unique a work as any in the explicated literature. And its connection not only with the "motivically" expanded tonality of Mahler and early Schoenberg, and with the eventual "atrophy" of the tonal superstructure that produced purely "motivically" generated music, but with the Schoenberg twelve-tone system itself, seems in the light of our inquiry more than just a matter of "chromaticism", the "emancipation of the dissonance", or the deployment of nontraditional successions of triads.

4. WEBERN: OP. 5, NO. 4

Confirming evidence for the claims just advanced for *Tristan is,* it seems to me, available from this piece of Webern. That this is so I find particularly satisfying in the alternative that it may represent to the practice, in the analysis of twentieth-century music, of deriving bases of musical relatedness largely from textural-articulative characteristics, which seems to me unduly to minimize the structural range attributable to this literature. And if this early Webern piece is, as it seems to me, far more fundamentally *Tristan*-Wagnerian than anything I know in, say, Berg, where does that leave the facile dichotomies of "traditionalism" and "radicalism", or notions of "voluptuosity" and "asceticism", "sensuousness" and "austerity", as reflectors of musical distinctions of any considerable depth?

But there is what seems to me to be a rather worthier persuasive purpose in the presentation of the present speculation than the mere casting of aspersions, however diverting, on the fragment manifestations of music-appreciative discourse. For considerable efforts have been invested by some of the most sophisticated contemporary music theorists to generate a "syntactical model" that would be adequate to account for, and to reify as a literature, the music commonly called "freely atonal", written mostly between 1910 and 1925 by the members of the "Viennese School", but possibly also including a considerable number of subsequently composed pieces (by, e. g., Sessions, Carter, etc.). The most

---

[16]But the "special sense" is primarily that *Tristan stratifies* its serial-motivic surface relative to its ordered-collection references, and thus represents a more deeply and subtly layered—one might say more "advanced"—use of the "classical" twelve-tone system than almost anything that has appeared subsequently.

considerable of these efforts is undoubtedly that of Allen Forte, whose most recent important article in this field, [15], attempts to deal with what I have called "motivic" complexes as syntactical sets by defining transformation relations among them not previously recognized in music-structural analysis. These transformations, so far, do not appear to produce an extensive "structural-level" nest for the pieces involved, largely because they are conceived as relations among successively *presented sets*, rather than as ordered successions of transformations of a "background" referential set. Moreover, while the transformations appear to interrelate sets of various cardinalities, whatever their relative order positions within the presented succession (in which respect they are unique among music-analytic resources and perhaps most potentially fruitful), no "principal" cardinality appears to be inferable as the source of "background" rhythmic, and, hence, total successional, structure in any given piece. But a number of kinds of relatedness among pitch complexes are displayed that involve novel and coherent extensions of the notions of transposition and complementation in terms of operations on the *interval* contents of sets. Such operations are Forte's principal means toward the construction of models for this group of compositions—the implementation of which is, presumably, what the realization of a "literature" consists of.

The only "analytic" example presented in Forte's article is Webern's Op. 5, No. 4. Some other remarks on the piece and on Forte's analysis, with suggested analytic revisions, appear in Howe [16]. The following is an attempt to account for all the pitch-set relations in the piece by means of a much simpler "syntactical model" than is proposed by either Forte or Howe. Its evident relation to the *Tristan* model, if taken as more than historically intriguing, is, nevertheless, not intended here to be taken as asserted evidence for the reification of still a different new "literature" basket, but rather is intended to suggest the shared resistance to "literaturization" exhibited by the works of music composed during a particular compositional-developmental period. These works, I have already suggested, are perhaps mainly interrelatable by means of their "closeness" to the foundation-levels of musical structure at which, in contrast to "traditional" literatures, their significantly particularized "precomposition" begins, and by the relatively "shallow" level-succession from that point to the derivation of their actual articulative surfaces. Of course, "twelve-tone music" shares in this "contextuality" to a far greater degree than does "tonal music", in that pieces we associate in the twelve-tone literature we regard as proceeding from uniquely constructed reference sets (as compared with the invariance of the diatonic collection in tonal music), uniquely determined principal partitionings thereof (as distinct from the common triadicity of tonal music), and highly contextual interpretations of pitch-contrapuntal dimensions through variable correlations with temporal adjacency, registral adjacency, dynamics, timbre, and duration-contour (compared with the conjunction of those aspects with a basically registral counterpoint in tonal music).

The proposed model for the pitch structure of the Webern piece is based on a partitioning of the pitch domain by interlocking sets of equivalent dyads (of interval 7) that identify a twofold "exhaustion" of the "total chromatic". This 12 × 2 "norm" is possible since the identifying elements are members of "ordered couples", so that each pitch-class element is represented just twice, once in each "position" of the ordered couple (for (x, y), each pitch class represents just one value of x and one of y). The "partitioning cycle" may be represented as the following series of twelve 7-dyads in 1-transpositional sequence (a "circle of 1-related fifths").

(C = 0)
{(0 7) (1 8) (2 9) (3 10) (4 11) (5 0) (6 1) (7 2) (8 3) (9 4) (10 5) (11 6)}

(Compare these twelve "distinct dyads" to the twelve "distinct (0 3 6 9)s" of the *Tristan* system.)

As in *Tristan*, the "harmonic" identities are derived as unambiguous representatives of "positions" on the transpositional chain with respect to a stipulated "midpoint": ((4 11) (5 0)); first, each parenthesis-enclosed dyad is content-unique, as is each consecutive-pitch-class trichord, each such tetrachord, each pentachord, and each hexachord. Dyads of adjacent members of disjunct enclosed dyads do, however, recur, e. g.:

(7 2̲) (8̲ 3)   (1 8̲) (2̲ 9)

This recurrence is a principal associative factor in the harmonic articulation of the piece. Thus, there are two kinds of "degrees of similitude": partially shared pitch content with identical interval content, and partially shared interval and pitch content, both determinable by reference to "position relations" on the "cyclic" chain; the first resulting from "whole dyad", and the second from "half dyad" transposition, as:

(violins) m. 1:   4   11   5   0
m. 2:   11   5   0   6

The contents of the first of these ((4,11,5,0)) uniquely asserts a single two-dyad adjacency span in the given order-circle, while the content of the second ((11,5,0,6)) occurs *twice* in the order-circle, so that this second chord tends to *associate* the dyad area uniquely *fixed* by the first chord with the dyad area *halfway across* the circle. A complete pitch-modeling of the piece in terms of this syntactical reference appears as Ex. 11. Note particularly the "development" first in terms of "associated" areas (mostly by the (0 6) joint mentioned above), then at m. 6, in terms of "simultaneous distinct areas", and then the non-literal "recentering" at mm. 11–13. A particular measure of relatedness among simultaneous events is the symmetry of "interval distance along the pitch-partitioning chain"; note, especially, how the rhythmically stretched passage at mm. 7–9 asserts a correspondingly extended dyad-span, such that the "complementary" dyad-spans traced by the surrounding pitch successions are interlocked. Here connection with the results of the recent Schoenberg analyses in Lewin [26] and Lester [23] are interesting, particularly in suggesting that the identification of a functional "inversional balance" may not be limited to the level of actually presented registral dispositions.

In the light of this model, and its relation to the Forte "general-syntactical" one, the question is raised of the value of a "general-syntactical" model that produces explanations of greater complexity though not necessarily of greater depth than "individual-syntactical" models of some of its supposed applications. Is it worth it, for the sake of gathering some pieces into a "literature", to do so at the cost of such analytic-systematic complexity? And is it not consistent in any case with the "motivic" aspect of the music involved (symbolized in our model by the "close-to" relation of "background" ordering to presented "melodic" and "harmonic" events) that individual cases *would* tend to reveal more, and more

Ex. 11 (beginning)

Ex. 11 (concluded)

basic, non-correspondences with "other instances" than other "members" of other "literatures" exhibit toward one another; and hence, might not the effort to "syntacticalize" this group be likely to lead to a *net loss* in the coherence of *each member* individually? And would not that be a basic analytic disadvantage (see pp. 240ff. above)? These are the questions that seem to me to arise from the disparity between my model of Op. 5, No. 4 and Forte's. I do not presume them to have been answered, even implicitly, in the present essay, for this "mapping" of Op. 5, No. 4 does not yet constitute specification on the level of "analysis" that has been proposed; rather it is a set of measurements on the data of the piece which could presumably be organized into a particular temporally unfolded musical structure that would be worth acknowledging as "that" of Op. 5, No. 4.

VII.
Part IV:
Analytic Fallout (II)

5. ABOUT COMPARISON

The construction of musical systems is describable as the result of comparing the constructions of individual compositions, and "closing", as "system-bound", those aspects of reference that represent their most pervasive intersections, while "leaving open" (as "contextual") those aspects which are to be counted as individuating the singular structures in question with respect to their system-fellows. Such an approach leads to the extension of a "literature" just to the point where it appears that admission of various additional candidates would require the opening of significant aspects of the system that are closed for all other members, thus "weakening" the defining capacities of the system, and reducing the coherence of the relation between the various models of the data and the model of the system. So it makes sense to exclude such pieces as bona fide members of the literature, since the convenience of having the system for the benefit of the other members would be seriously impaired by their admission. Or, from another point of view, their fit in the system does scant justice to the potential coherence that could be asserted for them by the construction of another system. As we noted, some cases may not be sufficiently interesting to us to do so, whereby our likely strategy is just to beg off maximizing coherence for such pieces and declare ourselves relatively incoherent with respect to them. I think Schenker's "bristlingly normative"[1] rejection as "not music" of post-triadic-tonal works had some systematic justification on the strength of such considerations—if, of course, "music" is just regarded as mutually substitutable with "tonal-systematic music". But we, too, might find it inconvenient to admit as "music" some auditory artifact or other, however enlivening its appearance, because admission would require such fundamental revisions in our recon-

---

[1] To paraphrase a remark of Babbitt.

struction of everything *else* we want to call music that we might prefer to construct some new, "extramusical", category of "linguistic-type auditory structure" to account for the new phenomenon if we cared enough about it. We might, that is, unless its admission to "music" would engender revisions that actually *deepen* our insight into everything else we wish to call music. In the latter case, of course, the result is a net gain for all music, on the order of what does in fact happen when one re-examines, say, tonal music in the light of our knowledge of the characteristics of 12-tone music, or such pitch-redefining musics as those by Debussy, Ravel, Varèse, Partch, or Penderecki, with the objective of investigating how and why we are able to call it all music; such an investigation has been, in fact, the motivation for Part II of the present essay.

Thus we have a way of understanding "analytic comparison" as the general procedure that results in the progressive sorting into narrower classes of the members of the total set of "musical compositions". But this leaves out of account a significant additional motivation for comparison, namely, the consideration of the respects in which compositions in different "systems" manifest "comparable" (not necessarily meaning "similar") approaches to musical structure. I noted earlier how words like "event" and "continuity", are made use of in this domain, and suggested that they might be given cognitive force under some explicative cover.

For instance, we can explicate the notion of "event" as an association connecting at least two atomic elements in terms of a syntactically defined relation. Obviously, "events" on "more background" levels will "enclose" relations among "more foreground" elements so that *one* background event may be *articulated* through a multiplicity of foreground events. Such a syntactically defined "event" might be, in tonal music, the assertion of a single triadic interval, a single triad (on whatever level), a succession of two triads, or the unfolding of a diatonic collection or a set of transpositionally ordered collections, etc. And in 12-tone music, the "same" concept might be interpreted as the unfolding of a dyad, a trichord, a hexachord, a set, a cycle of sets, etc. One would not claim "correspondence" for the notion of "event" between pieces in different systems *in the same sense as* for it between those in the same systems; but the notion of a "syntactically defined presented unit of structure" is a better than metaphorical basis for analogy.

But in order to evidence it as such, it will be necessary to find a "neutral" dimension, a "medium" common in all relevant respects to the two contexts, in which their *relations of events* can be compared. (Comparisons of the "natures" or "interiors" of the events themselves cannot, I believe, be made except metaphorically; but that represents no particular disadvantage since our concern is precisely *not* with pieces commensurable at every level, but only with the commensurability of internal *relations* among events taken in this sense as equivalent "givens" within otherwise systematically *distinct* pieces.) Now relations among events are of two kinds: those that arise between "more background" events and the "more foreground" events "within" them; and those that arise between events at the same levels, which are therefore relations of *ordered successions of events*. And the "shapes of succession" for events constitute just what we call "continuity". Thus if we can compare "shapes", we can compare "continuities". So we need 1) a basis for shape-of-relationship comparisons when the shapes are shapes of relations in different systems and 2) a medium whose characteristics are neutral with respect to all syntaxes concerned. The second requirement is met, and met only (in the context of our normal view of the musically significant auditory dimensions), by *time*. Since "shape" is a measure of "change"—whether the "change" from a presented pitch to another regarded as its "displacement", from a "succession of two pitches" to a next such succession, or from a "sonority" to another, a "collection unfolding" to another, or a "section" to another—all the paths traced as "pitch-relational successions" through a pitch-presentational complex are *time-orders of change.* The neutrality of time as a dimension of change is noted in Goodman [53], p. 374: "change is concomitant variation in time and some other respect. Since time is always one of the variant factors in change, we speak of *change in* whatever is the other variant factor in the given case. Thus although there is no change that does not involve time, there is no change in time...there is no temporal change to be distinguished from temporal size".

But how can we construct "comparable" time-shapes of event-change to produce our desired comparison? Here we reify a concept implicit in the notion of a defined "event" itself, namely that our "event" has an "extent" (that is, a "functional extent") in its *content as an event* which *is articulated over a particular time-extent*. This "functional extent" answers to the description of our Need No. 1, above. Now the "same" event-content may at different places be articulated over different time extents, so that the criterion for the determination that a given event has been *displaced* (i.e., *succeeded by a next event*) is just the observation that it has been *completed*—such "completion" being determined by the operation of the syntactical referents at the relevant structural level. And, for any pieces in any system, there will be a "minimum" event—the "maximum" event being in every case just the entire piece—so that at every level the *temporal shapes* (time-length-and-content patterns) of the successions of events of relatively the same structural order in different pieces may be compared. And we may also compare temporal shapes *within* such events—the first event-relation-type mentioned above. If we think of "event-content" as a "syntactical function" determined independently by whatever the relevant pitch-syntactical referent is for the piece under consideration (the analog is a "propositional function"), and time-extent as "proportional relation to a time-unit", we might represent the notion of "rhythmic structure" for a given composition as follows:

Let F = "defined syntactical function"
T = "time-extent for a completion"

then we can assert the necessary value of a function that would map

$$(F_1, T_1) \rightarrow (F_1, T_n) \text{ for any } n,$$

where "F_1" stands for the *minimum* functional event-extent unit at a given structural level, and "T_1" is "referential time of unfolding", defined as the first (or, whichever is taken as referential) temporal extent over which the total content of the "function" is unfolded. But also, we would need to be able to perform the mapping

$$(F_1, T_1) \rightarrow (F_n, T_1)$$

In the first case, we observe the pattern of variation in "time per unit function", and in the second, of "functional content per unit time".[2] Now if we correlate such an observational path with the

---

[2]This view of "rhythmic structure" and the subsequent remarks on "continuity" structure account for the phenomena sometimes viewed, in various ways, as "strong-weak", "upbeat-downbeat" characteristics of large-scale rhythm as corre-

"*degree*-of event-difference" structure (thus correlating *rates* of change with *degrees* of change, and also creating larger rhythmic categories from "complexes" of event-complexes where change *within* is of a lesser degree than change *between*), we have a measure of what I believe corresponds best to the notion of "continuity structure"—which places a very high *individuating* value thereon, at the same time as it makes it possible to use the notion as the basis for comparing the most individual characteristics of pieces of different "systematic" background.

The "comparative" questions thus suggested would not most favorably take forms such as "What is the continuity-structure of piece A relative to that of piece B?", although some way might be found to answer this question. Rather, it seems fruitful to generalize such "structural" notions as we have outlined so that a description of *the* "event structure", *the* "rhythmic structure", and *the* "continuity structure" can be explicitly hypothesized for each explicated piece with some confidence that the descriptions are cognitive, and that they are correlatively related to the terms employed—in short, that they are about corresponding aspects of different pieces. I give hereafter three brief analytic speculations to illustrate some results, obtained by the application of such a choice-driven, relativistic "metric".

---

sponding to the different fore-and-aft event-boundaries at different structural levels. For expositions of these "qualitative-rhythmic" notions, see Cone [9] and [10] and Westergaard [40]. But their views still leave me uncertain as to the meaning of "*the* structural downbeat" without a specification of the level involved; for it is never stated that the first *presented* event that corresponds in pitch content to the *inferred* event-boundary at some prior level is a "moment of structural truth" having a privileged analytic status. If this is a fair observation about the views of Westergaard and Cone, it would be valuable to have the notion more fully explicated, by a specification, first, of the basis for choice of "referential level", second, of the difference between the "influence" of that event at that level over *all* the "foreground" events up to this *moment critique* (which would actually render questionable its isolation from its precedents) and over those *of* the moment itself and its consequents within the event, and, finally, of what is regarded as the structural information added beyond that already contained in an elucidation of the pitch-content and "proportional-duration" characteristics of the structure at all its levels alone—since the convergence of some number of event-boundaries on some number of distinct levels at the single given time-moment is an implicit rhythmic-structure weighting of that time-moment in that piece.

6. THE FIRST EIGHTEEN MEASURES OF BRAHMS'S FOURTH SYMPHONY

Schenker's analytic sketch of the first 20 measures of Brahms's Fourth Symphony (*Freie Satz*, Ex. 81, 2) deals with the "sehr gedehnten Terzzug" from G to E through a linear "octave descent" (81, 2b) as a "principal-voice" III–I Urlinie (81, 2a), and indicates the various local third-cycles from mm. 1–4, 5–8, 9–15, and 15–18. He does not, according to his custom, explicitly discuss the rhythmic structure either in the small or the large. But in fact, these 3rd-cycles, by their variable dispositions, produce a defining framework for the "time structure" of the whole passage that seems at least as unique a structural determinant as the facets to which Schenker's sketches are confined. For the first 3rd-cycle of four measures, "splinted" by a fixed E in the bass (in a way that associates covertly with the opening of Mozart's 40th Symphony), unfolds as upper voice a "complete" diatonic collection of E minor, whose inner "events" are the "complete" triads I, IV, V—represented durationally not as "sequential" parallels but through the temporally "displacing" intervening pseudo-triads II and VII; the "completion" of the unfolding of the intervening II and VII actually "completes" the set, but is linked also with the "cyclically" restated B at the beginning of m. 4 (Ex. 12). The "harmonic" association of the C-A-F♯-D♯ (realized through the superposition of the pitches of IV and V over the bass I) results in a "temporal shape" for the passage which may be described as 1:2:1 (Ex. 13), characterized by "tonic-triad" pitches (1), "neighbor-notes-to-tonic-triad" pitches (2), then "tonic-triad" pitches again (1). This durational contour is reinforced by the microrhythm of the woodwind accompaniment, which partitions the temporal extent of each measure by the same proportional temporal shape (Ex. 14).

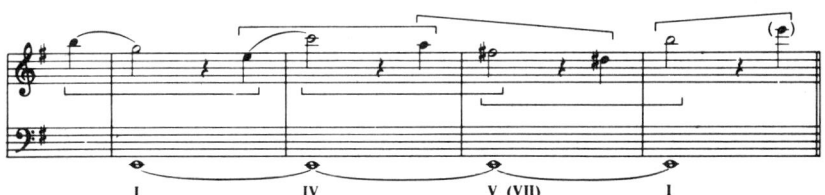

Ex. 12

Ex. 13

Ex. 14

Now the second 3rd-cycle (Ex. 15) "inverts" the first, but differs from it in several other significant ways as well. First, the

Ex. 15

diatonic collection unfolded in mm. 5–8 is not the *tonic* collection but that of IV (A minor), and thus can be assimilated as an elaboration of a *portion* of the original "function" (the tonic collection) through a 3rd-cyclic articulation whose surface (and pitch content) is parallel to the *entire* original one. Here the bass passes through a fifth-cycle whose boundaries are C and A while the upper voice spans E-C; the two spans together are interpretable as a third-prolongation of the A minor triad. The C-A in the bass of the four measures is, in fact, just the same as the span of the upper voice in just one measure of the opening 3rd-cycle (m. 2). And the upper-voice 3rd-cycle is just an unfolding of the diatonic collection associated with the triadic sonority of m. 2, A minor. Thus we seem now to have an "expansion" of the unfolding within mm. 1–4 in which mm. 1–4 themselves are regarded (at this new level) as the correlate of m. 1 alone, as the "tonic measure", and mm. 5–8 create a successional structure with mm. 1–4 parallel to that which m. 2 creates with m. 1. Rhythmically, this suggests the beginning of the projection onto a still broader temporal scale of the 1:2:1 relation, based on "completion" of the initial diatonic collection through a particular partitioning (i.e., first the scale-degrees and triads of the E minor collection, then the collections associated with those triads). Thus what the connected unfolding of the pitches of the A minor collection constitutes is an elaboration of a *part* (the IV-part) of the tonic collection, hence, a *part* of an elaborated assertion *of* the tonic collection itself, unfolded over the same (4-measure) time span over which an "entire" (unelaborated) assertion of the tonic collection, the referential "function", is initially unfolded. Here, too, the "prolongation" produces an internal 1:2:1 partition, the C-A succession partitioned by the fifth-related G-D, as

```
C  /  G  D  /  A
1       2      1
```

On this model, the next four measures do indeed "outline" the contents of m. 3 (Ex. 16). The bass span D♯-F♯ again corresponds to the upper voice succession in m. 3, F♯-D♯ (reversed), and the chromatic articulation between D♯ and F♯ is the "semitone analog" of the 7-cycle of mm. 5–8, producing again a finely modulated

Ex. 16

differentiation in the articulative surface. The upper voice here, too, is quite different; instead of a complete 3rd-cycle, there is a reiteration of the third C-A in two registers (Ex. 17). And here the internal 1:2:1 is projected, first, by the "separation" by two mea-

Ex. 17

sures of the D♯ and the F♯, and also by the intervention in these two inner measures of the collection of A minor (E-F is of course the characterizing V-VI semitone of A minor). So the B-D♯-F♯-A-C of m. 9, the "V" fragment of the E minor collection, is "displaced" in mm. 10–11 by, first, A-C-D-E, then F-A-B-C(-E♭) (which latter pitch in context seems to be the D♯ of the augmented sixth of A minor) and, then, the "diminished seventh" reappears in m. 12.

But m. 13 does not complete the 1:4-expanded parallelism by asserting "V"; rather what may be found is that the "differentiation" between mm. 5–8 and mm. 9–12 is actually the "intervention" of still another elaborating 1:2:1, this time with mm. 5–8 as its initiating "1", so that the "2" of the 1-4/5-12 "1:2:(1)" model becomes extended by an *internal* elaboration. The difference between the fifth-cycle in mm. 5–8 and the linear ascent in mm. 9–12 articulates this development, again, in a way analogous to the initial differentiation by "registral direction" alone in the unfolding of the tonic collection in mm. 1–4. Here we may consider the entire interior of mm. 9–16 as the extension of m. 3 through the leading of the bass through the entire D♯-F♯-A-C succession "under" a reiterated and variably articulated C-A in the upper register, the articulation in mm. 13–14 reinterposing the "IV" aspects of the succession, and the succession in mm. 15–16 elaborating the "V" aspects. But the total succession is two measures "short" of what would be produced by a literally complete 1:2:1 from mm. 5–8, which would extend to m. 20, as, 5–8 = 1; 9–16 = 2; 17–20 = 1. So we may suppose that an "elision" within the "2" part is observable. This 2-measure "elision" may be "composed in" in either, or both, of two ways: the "doppio movimento" articulation of mm. 13–14 may be conceived as "compressing" four measures into two, or mm. 15–16 may be regarded as an "overlap" between the "IV"-articulated part of the "neighbor-note" segment of the collection, and the "V" part realized as a full V in mm. 17–18. The completing "1" that balances the mm. 1–4 beginning is, thus, the "reprise" of those measures beginning at m. 19, which is also the initiation of a new articulation (Ex. 18). The entire 1:2:1 nest is shown in Ex. 19. Note also the "augmented" counterpoint to the woodwind measure-by-measure

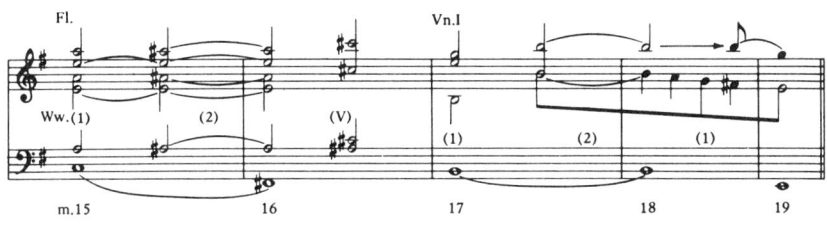

Ex. 18

1:2:1 which follows the "diminution" represented by mm. 13–14, perhaps mirroring the "two time scales" relation in which, at the time scale of 13–14, 15–18 would "take" two measures rather than four; or, inversely, that mm. 13–14 would take four measures on the time scale of mm. 15–18 (see Exx. 20a and 20b).

These results exhibit what seems to me a remarkable degree of embedding of significant and significantly nonliteral "uniformities" in the realm of the unfolding of events on different time scales. I prefer to construe this passage as just two presented unfoldings of the entire E minor collection, once in mm. 1–4, and once in mm. 1–22. Thus I do not assert an "additive" durational structure but a "level-dependent" one, which is consistent with the other tonal-structural things we care about in the piece. Now it has been suggested, on the other hand,[3] that they were just "what one would have expected" on the basis of the Schenker analysis and Schenker-analytic-type experience with tonal music. But I would regard this as an encouraging rather than a disparaging observation. For if the Schenker model, or a Schenker-derived model, is a truly "empirical" one capable of full cognitive articulation (as I think there is every good reason to suppose) then our "metric" is capable of generating *unique* observational data in a correlatively quantized form which would thus seem to confer a still higher degree of

---

[3] By Randall.

power on the "core theory" itself—the Schenker model. This is a result that should be highly desirable to enthusiasts of the core theory. And at the same time, by their very power to be "seen to" indicate such correspondence with that theory, the generated strings of information give strong evidence of their own analytic nontriviality. Further, if this is conceded to be the case, the fact that this particular set of measurements on the data of a piece is not available from any other analytically employed data-slicing mechanisms is further evidence for the virtues of the metric as a music-ascriptive tool, providing that there also seems a high probability that its measurements will be relevantly accurate under all significant conditions. In this way, one might compare it to a new experimental complex devised to provide crucial, or at least meaningful, tests of a theory by detecting and measuring evidential data not available by any previously known test means.

Ex. 19a

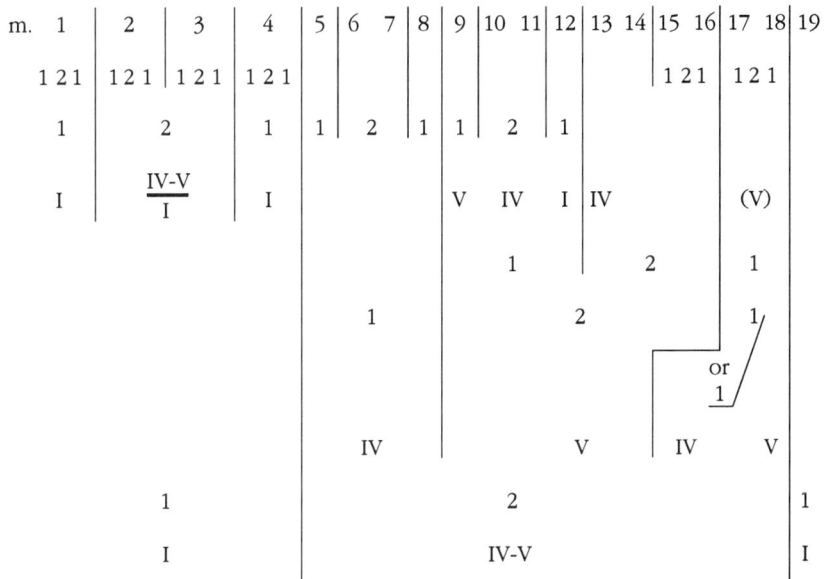

Ex. 19b

Ex. 20a

Ex. 20b

7. *PETROUCHKA*: FIRST SCENE

In deriving "rhythmic structure" in my Brahms speculation, I was able to proceed with a reasonable "syntactical" presumption—implicit in my own and Schenker's analytic sketches—of a "tonal-systematic" basis. But is there any way in which such a procedure can help to locate a relevant syntactical basis itself when one is not contextually evident? I take two 20th-century passages through which to investigate this question: the first is the opening scene of Stravinsky's *Petrouchka,* the second the introduction to the first song of Schoenberg's Op. 15.

If we proceed strictly on the basis of articulative cues to investigate pitch-structural questions, we may begin by contemplating some convenient-appearing time-extent as provisionally referential, perhaps on the basis of some outstanding presentational characteristics, with the idea of staking out a *likely* framework within which to investigate the possible pitch-functional generators of that and every other articulation. We do not reify "phrases", but just regard these framework-areas as reasonably promising candidates for reification as the confines of completions of some sort. And before we qualify them as such, we require of our analysis an adequate account of the *process* of their pitch-functional generation, as well as of the levels of structure at which they arise.

With respect to the *Petrouchka* passage, a close and minimally prejudiced scrutiny on the lines of the above appears to shed some light both on the "duration contour"[4] structure of the chosen articulations, and on the question of whether its "diatonic surface" is most favorably heard as referring to a syntactical "tonality". At the very opening, a desirably simplistic view of the data is facilitated by the neatness of the presentation: an invariance of 4 pitches from mm. 1–33 (D E G A) provides a relatively protracted framework for the investigation of degrees and kinds of differences among presented (and among presentations of) pitch collections. I use the 1911 score, noting some divergences in the 1947 version which are not always helpful to the furtherance of the views to be advocated here, a circumstance which could be taken as evidence either that by 1947 Stravinsky had forgotten or misunderstood some things about his work of 1911, or that my analysis is based on inadequate insight into "the composer's intentions". But since I am

---

[4]The configuration of relative durations between attack points.

bound to prefer my *Petrouchka* to other candidates offered for *Petrouchka*hood, I prefer to regard some of the 1947 revisions as introducing net losses in coherence.

The presentational characteristics of mm. 1–5 (those, that is, that I will focus on) may be regarded as symptomatic of a general "model of presentation" for events throughout the example. In contrast to the Schoenbergian note-to-note contrapuntal parsimony, there is here a generous unfolding over a complexly partitioned (and thus perceptually "extensive") time span of a single pitch-class collection, stated totally in the very first distinguishable "event", and articulated "laterally" as well as harmonically, in each dimension, however, by means of different intervallic symmetries. Thus the "two 2s" aspect of the collection is isolated by the (A-G) (D-E) "contrary motion trill" in the horns and clarinets, while the "three 5s" aspect surfaces in the one-pitch-at-a-time, "lateralized" and thus registrally contoured, unfolding in the flute, which may be summarized as E-A-D-G, but is presented so that the adjacent 5s are linked by linear 2's, as

$$
\begin{array}{c}
\overset{5\quad\;\; 5}{(A\text{-}D) - (E\text{-}A) - (G\text{-}\; D\text{-}A)} \\
\;\;5\quad 2\quad\; 5\quad\; 2 \\
\quad\quad\quad\quad\quad\quad\quad\quad E\text{-}\;\; A \\
\quad\quad\quad\quad\quad\quad\quad\quad\;\; 2 \\
\quad\quad\quad\quad\quad\quad\quad\quad\;\; 5
\end{array}
$$

In m. 6, the cellos' E-D-C♯-B adds another 2-dyad (C♯ B), and another 5-dyad (E B), but, also, completes thereby a non-symmetrical hexachord (G A B C♯ D E) in conjunction with the preceding tetrachord (D E G A), a non-symmetry resulting from the introduction of a 1- and a 6-dyad as well ((D C♯) and (G C♯)). The resultant hexachord (whose auditory identification is assisted by the flute's Bs) contains just 6 of the 7 members of the diatonic collection—not, however, "the" diatonic hexachord—partitioned into 2-dyads (see Ex. 21a–e). The harp-wind sweep of m. 11 begins the passage in which the 2-dyad (B♭-C) is introduced (first in m. 12), in particular as a constituent of the tetrachord (G A B♭ C), which together with the invariant (D E G A) yields the inverse (E D C B♭ A G) of the initial hexachord (Ex. 22), as well as the inverse (G A B♭ C) of the cellos' E-D-C♯-B (each of the two tetrachords "departing" from a distinct one of the 2 disjunct 2-dyads of the original tetrachord: G-A-B♭-C/*E-D*-C♯-B) (Ex. 23). The cello-bass-bassoon passage at mm. 13–15, which "extends" the violin sweep, is a "scale-degree 3rd"-partitioning of the hexachord centering on the (G A B♭ C) tetrachord (Ex. 24).

Ex. 21a

Ex. 21 b–e

Ex. 22

Ex. 23

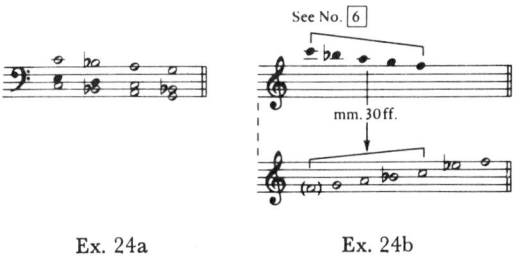

Ex. 24a   Ex. 24b

Now the time-division mm. 1.0–6.33, 6.33–11.67, 11.67–17.0 is an evident presentational symmetry that also, it appears, corresponds to a configuration of pitch-collection change. The $((5^1/_3 + 5^1/_3 + 5^1/_3) \times 3\,\text{♩})$-identity is thus articulative of what might be a significant time-functional relationship. The kind of presentational "intercutting" involved here and throughout the example is, moreover, similar to the phenomena noted in Cone [11], and the notion there of a Stravinskyan "method" in this domain seems even more firmly supported when pitch-content structure can be regarded as generative *for* the most conspicuous articulative boundaries rather than the other way around.

Thus it is particularly interesting to note the immediate restatement of the whole succession: first (D E G A) alone, then (B C♯ D E), then (G A B♭ C); this time, however, the whole succession is stated in just one $5^1/_3$ measure (17–22.33) span; and the (D E G A B♭ C) hexachord is unfolded for an overlapping $5^1/_3$ (21.67–27.0) measures (an interpretation yielded by the 1947 version only, by its omission of the F from the harp glissando; the 1911 version suggests the initiation of a pitch-collectional event at m. 23),[5] and is then extended through the superposition of *two* hexachords inversionally related (at mm. 27.0ff.) and producing the "diatonic collection" *as their union* (Ex. 25).

The "infiltration" of both this new "harmonic" function (the *superposed* hexachords) and the new "duple" meter (at mm. 30–31, 34, 36, 39–40) is realized at the upbeat to m. 42 by a

---

[5]The (C B♭ A G F) here, after rehearsal No. 5, and after No. 6, associates the "central" hexachord-inversion complex with its T5 form (presented at No. 6).

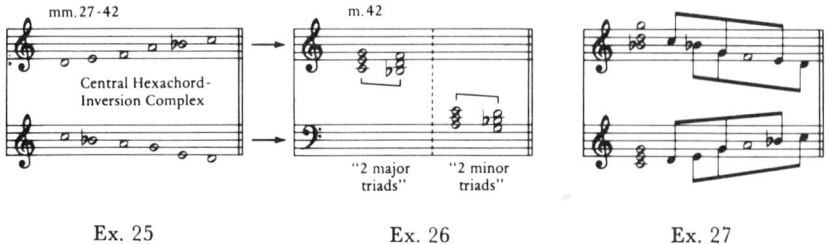

Ex. 25 Ex. 26 Ex. 27

simultaneous assertion of the "chords" (C E G) and (G B♭ D); the lower-voice succession in triads then juxtaposes triad-pairs ((C E G/B♭ D F); (A C E/G B♭ D)) each of which pairs determines one of the two concurrent hexachords, and presents them now in a *trichordal* partitioning (Ex. 26). The simultaneity at the upbeat to m. 42 superimposes the only two "triads" the two complementary hexachords contain in common (Ex. 27). Here, the articulative "beat-divisions" are interesting: in quarters, the pattern is 4+4+4+8+6+14, in which the relationships 4+4+4+8 and 6+14 both partition 20 (associating with the "around 5" of the opening), but the whole succession incorporates the internal isomorphism of (8+6)+(14) as well, the latter encompassing a pitch-functionally *distinct* field (see Ex. 28). The chord on the downbeat of m. 49,

Ex. 28

etc., is the conjunction of the inversionally derived (D F) and (A C), the F and A of which are the mutually exclusive members of the hexachords (D E G A B♭ C) and (D E F G B♭ C). It is this chord, and the "contrary motion", that isolate the 8+6+14 from the initial 4+4+4. Note that the close of the entire succession is on (G B♭ D), one of the "shared" triads, and the section so initiated (No. 6) concludes with (C E G), the other of the two shared triads; these

Ex. 29

boundaries enclose a 5-transposition of the whole 2-hexachord complex of mm. 42–60 (Ex. 29). (N.B. that this (G B♭ D) is also the "unison" trichord at the lower limit of the first 4-beat succession *from* (C E G) *to* (G B♭ D) at the upbeat to mm. 42ff.) And there is a time span of just 20 quarter-notes *between* the (G B♭ D) at No. 6 and the (C E G) that ends the passage. E♭, too, appears for the first time in the piece in this passage (as the 10th pitch class to appear: first (D E G A), then (B C♯), then (B♭ C), then F, then E♭; of course, T8 (D E G A) is (B♭ C E♭ F) and T4 (D E G A) is (F♯ G♯ B C♯)); and every pair of consecutively introduced pitches determines a 2-dyad). The appearance of F♯ is imminent by this point, and that of G♯ (which forms a 2-dyad with F♯) is delayed until later, but is remarkably strategic when it does happen.

The tritone bass sweep (E-D-C-B♭) at No. 7 exposes a segment of the hexachord not previously unfolded as a melodic succession, but which is registrally articulated in the harp, celesta, and piano from No. 3 on, and which is an "inner voice" of the triad succession at mm. 42ff. The transpositions involved at No. 7, however, represent a new relationship: after the *succession* of (D E G A)-tetrachord-centered hexachord pairs, then the *superposition* of such pairs within the same time spans, there occurs here a superposition of hexachord pairs related through their intersection on one *pitch* (D) that appeared at an "extreme" of our representation of the hexachords of the preceding span (Ex. 30). F♯ appears in this new transposition, a "form" which preserves the (D E G A) of the opening as its intersection with the "referential" (D E G A B♭ C) hexachord. The span of thirty quarters is divided 20+10 by reiteration.

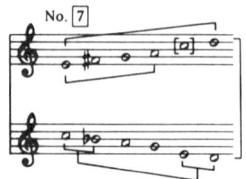

Ex. 30

At No. 8 a new trichordal juxtaposition that exposes (A D) as in the opening flute solo as the upper line, and (D G) as a lower—together an inverse of the initial flute line—of a succession that alternates a "minor triad" and a "major triad" (a *kind* of alternation familiar from the "*stepwise*" version at m. 42, etc.) whose relation to one another is identical to that of the two elements of the simultaneity before m. 42 (C E G) and (G B♭ D); in other words, the intersection of inverse hexachords with 5 pitch-classes in common (Ex. 31).

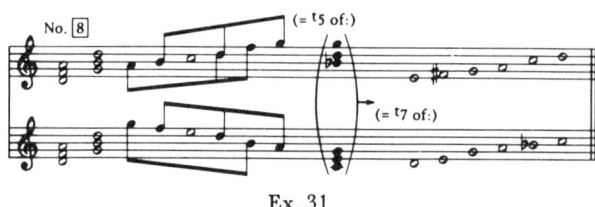

Ex. 31

The hexachord forms here are "midway" between the two superimposed in No. 7, the "lower" of which recurs as the "opening" hexachord of mm. 6–10, this time drawn out of the opening tetrachord (D E G A), of mm. 1ff., before No. 9 by the "tritone tetrachord" (E D C B♭) of No. 7 (thus "skipping" the intervening C♯-B of the *actual* opening—but see the 1947 version's piano part, which mystifyingly adds B♮ to the piano's sweep). The collections at No. 9 (Ex. 32) duplicate those at No. 7, but the (B♭ D F) of the "central" collection is more explicitly articulated as a "stratum of the texture" that "emerges" 3 measures after No. 9 (in the 1911 version, the $^2/_3$-speed tempo marking produces the rough equivalent of 20 quarters of the old tempo here, but all these proportional niceties are altered in the 1947 edition with no evident substitute time-span rationales). Also, the rather striking "scale-degree inversion" of the (E-D-C-B♭) spanning of the tritone "into" (B♭-A-G-F-E) in the 1911 edition is altered to omit the B♭ in the 1947 revision, although the F

Ex. 32

is not also altered to F♯ to "weight" the collection, so the net result is a somewhat less determinate succession. But the triad-superposition that "harmonized" the flute's A-D at No. 8 is here (No. 10) extended to include the (E A) of the original (whose "lower line" is, in fact (A D)). The resultant "minor-major"/"major-minor" sequence invokes a complex of 4 different collections (Ex. 33). The notes of these collections "missing" in the 2-triad successions

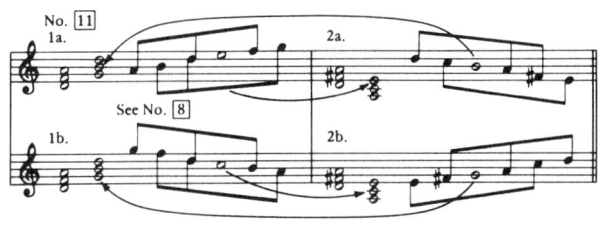

Ex. 33

((C E) in the (D F A/G B D) alternation and (G B) in the (D F♯ A/A C E) alternation) are supplied in the neighboring passage. And the (A D E A) of the "triads" is conjoined with its "referent" by the reprise of the opening flute line six measures after No. 11.

The 20-quarter-note-long tune at No. 13 extends the 5-transposed inversional hexachord pair (as at No. 6), but the interesting development here is the "chromatic" passage in the bassoons and violas, which adds E and F♯ to the complex; what this does is to articulate as *simultaneous* the relation between the two hexachords presented at the beginning of the piece as *successive*. Here the (E F♯) so relates to the (E♭ F) of the T5 hexachord (see Ex. 34). (The 1947 edition considerably clarifies this relationship in the passage, now assigned only to the 2nd violins, by replacing the E♭ with E, exchanging the "coloristic chromaticism" for sharper dyad (hexachord) identification.) The last remaining unpresented

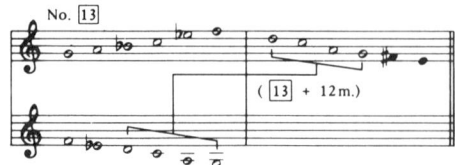

Ex. 34

pitch class, G♯, appears at the corresponding place after No. 16 (+ 3 measures), where its association with F♯ completes a *double* presentation of the opening relation. With, in effect, 4 different hexachord transposition-inversion complexes unfolding simultaneously here, the point of maximum "harmonic" saturation, or simply, of referential complexity, in the first scene, is reached (see Ex. 35), with 11 different pitch classes (all but B) associated with the

Ex. 35

multicollectional conjunction. Everything from this point to 5 measures before the *10*-measure drum-roll transition at the end of the scene, is reprise. And the "chromatics" at that last 5-measure passage in fact duplicate the "chromatic" relationship just cited.

I have not pointed out every "cut"-length in the passage; in fact, what suggests itself is not so much a rhythmic structure in the Brahms sense but a series of intercut "patches" of varying lengths, which produce a "macrodurational contour" of event-to-event continuity. But that, at least in this scene, the diatonic collection is generated (and deployed) in a way quite independent of a "tonal" interpretation, and quite responsive to a hexachordal one, is, I think, assertible. Moreover, this collection is so variably partitioned in different passages as to suggest an interpretation for the piece as "*collection*-centric" at the primary (syntactical) level, with "construct"-partition centricity sustained, if variably, at more local articulative levels; but I do not find much support for a "pitch-centric" interpretation at any level. Perhaps this collection-centricity is itself an analog of "textural-section" events (rather than pitch-to-pitch events) as the virtual atomic elements of continuity in the excerpt, apart from internal partitioning by immediate pitch-collectional reiteration. In any case, the generative status of the hexachord was realized through an initial tentative reification of those $5\frac{1}{3}$-measure "patches" at the beginning and in a rather one-to-one (though not unvaried in *degree* or *type* of change) correlation throughout between *textural* and *pitch-functional* event-boundaries. From this sketch, therefore, a structure in several layers could presumably be realized; I have here given only a set of possible referents against which variabilities in pitch succession, registral counterpoint, instrumental counterpoint, and durational counterpoint may be commensurately described.[6]

---

[6]I claim no extensibility for my "*Petrouchka* hexachord" beyond No. 30 of the 1911 score, although I have tentatively "followed" it through the end of the First Tableau. On the other hand, the "octatonic scale" constructed by Arthur Berger (see his [5]) for the Danse Russe and elsewhere can be construed as a concatenation of two of our "reference tetrachords":

Tetrachords:
    (a) 0 2 3 5 / b) 5 7 8 10) / (c) 0 2 5 7 / d) 3 5 8 10)

Hexachords:
1.   0 2 3 5 8 10 = (a) 0 2 3 5 + d) 3 5 8 10)
     10 8 7 5 2 0 = (b) 5 7 8 10 + c) 0 2 5 7)
2.   0 2 5 7 8 10 = (b) 5 7 8 10 + c) 0 2 5 7)
     7 5 2 0 11 9 = (9 11 0 2 + 0 2 5 7)
3.   0 2 5 7 8 10 = (5 7 8 10 + 0 2 5 7)
     10 0 1 3 6 8 = (10 0 1 3 + 1 3 6 8)

Octatonic Scale:
    0 2 3 5 / + (T6) 6 8 9 11

"*Petrouchka* chord":
    0 2 3   6 8 9   ((0 3 8)/(2 6 9)

    But I have no basis for advancing a claim that this is a *preferable* way to generate the octatonic scale or its P-chord subset.

8. SCHOENBERG: OP. 15, NO. 1, mm. 1–7

Schoenberg's Op. 15 is part of that group of his works from Op. 9 to Op. 24 that has remained analytically inscrutable but still cared about by analysts because of its position in Schoenberg's work as an intervening "literature" between antecedent and subsequent literatures that, however "refractory", are evidently susceptible to analytic rationalization. Analysts have offered varying conceptual and methodological explanations for this transitional literature, but with a low level of enthusiasm that is evidenced by the vague and essentially negative character of the "conceptual" terms employed ("free atonality", "pantonality", "contextuality"—the latter of which simply identifies the absence of evidence of significant intersection among these pieces), and the very partial applicability of the associated "analytic" terms ("basic cell", "chromatic completion", etc.). My suggestion that "motivic" is a conceptually preferable term for this literature derives from a notion that the basis of the compositional approach involved is to be found in the interstitial, non-triadic counterpoint in "extended-tonal" music, where the elaborations between asserted (or inferable) triadic references are so extensive that an "inner" referential basis is essential if one is to account for the structures with a degree of specificity comparable to what is normally available for satisfactorily describabable music. Thus the triadic sonority model for all linear expansion even in such maximized tonality as is observable in Brahms, a model that fundamentally delimits the observation of coherent tonal music, crosses a threshold in some works of Mahler and Schoenberg, where the maximally extended triadicity is further expanded through a non-triadically referential contrapuntal elaboration, one whose "between triad-reference" spans are not restricted to the interiors of discretely articulated events, but sometimes subsume several such articulations in the course of a single "inter-triad" elaboration. Now this counterpoint, in creating such *internal* phraseological articulations (and thus creating a presumption of structural levels *within* them), obviously requires a contextually defined basis for constructing coherent small- and large-scale successions. These are no longer adequately conceivable (by virtue of their extensiveness and the structural weight we would like to attribute to them to correspond to our perceptual sense of their importance) as simple triadic neighbor-note relations. And their description as such, in some analytic discourse, reaches a point of explanatory complexity beyond what is likely to be regarded as descriptive of "coherent music"—especially in the relatively low "interevent influence" such analyses extrude between background triadic-succession motives and actual foreground successions, and in the relatively few levels of explicable tonal generation before the elaborate—and essentially unexplicated—"linear" foreground. Perhaps the most radical instance of this situation is in Schoenberg's Op. 9, where the diatonic collection itself is presented in a "motivic" form (as a 5-cycle) as one of several motivic means of elaboration between the sparsely distributed tonal referents. But the question of whether "tonality" or "motivicity" "is" the best *syntactical* explanation for such music is somewhat ambiguous—for the "tonal" aspects are not any more evidently *subsumable* by the "motivic" ones than vice versa; so the question "Tonal oder Atonal?" may have a special twist with regard to this literature, and may be answerable only with a rather unsatisfactory "Beide". And by this token, one might consider that a "motivic" musical language had "grown up" independently "inside" the tonal superstructure in Mahler and Schoenberg, and that the "atonality" of Op. 11 just realizes the independent-structural implications of this "inner" language, without the superstructure that had actually become a "dichotomous" rather than a "concomitant" aspect. Surely the "sound" of Op. 11—the surface of simultaneity, register, and duration- and pitch-contour configurations—is virtually that of the "interstices" of Opp. 8 and 9 (though pre-Op. 8 Schoenberg seems to proceed more directly from triadicity than does late Mahler). But the "language of interstices"—a way of conceiving it that perhaps underlies the slogan of "emancipation of the dissonance", for it at least suggests some notion of what is being emancipated, and from what—is not necessarily an adequate "language of total structure". And it is evidently not until the works composed after the formulation of the "12-tone method" that a referent inferable from but not necessarily one-to-one with any presented configuration can be ascribed to Schoenberg's music. It was only then, therefore, that a "syntactical" basis for "structural levels" and "structural polyphony" that could be regarded as *distinguishable from* "articulative counterpoint" was regenerated in musical thought.

My last remark concerning *Petrouchka* touches on a curious condition that characterizes Op. 15, No. 1 as well: namely, that individual sections of these "motivic" pieces often exhibit structural coherences of a higher order than seem to result from their concatenations into a "*total* structure". Thus the results obtained below from mm. 1–7 of Op. 15, No. 1 are not claimed to be extensible in any known way to the remainder of the song (for all that tantalizing clues of all kinds abound, from the "11th pitch-class" B that is the first vocal pitch, later followed by A in a succession B-A that "completes the chromatic", to the "harmonic" and textural complexes throughout that appear to create a quite explicitly demarcated "phraseological structure"). What, in a "total-structural" analysis (such as we do *not* undertake anywhere in this essay) is an appropriate response to this "inverted" coherence? Not, I believe, as in much of the analytic literature, merely a concentration on the areas that do exhibit uniformities at the minimal-detail level and a vague nod at the rest, with the hoped-for imputation that, 1) the "same things" function therein, but their discovery is left as an "exercise for the reader", or 2) that their "function" elsewhere is no less to be assumed for being temporarily inscrutable (or permanently "free"). I think the rational response, if our purpose in analysis is to seek truth rather than approval, to construct something coherent rather than to write something "professional", is a systematic "retrenchment": if a "micro-analysis" performable at one level or over one time-span is not conjoinable with that performable at another, either we have several pieces, or we "withdraw" to a more complex "atomic unit", first perhaps trying to use a given *segment* and other, commensurate, segments as minimal units of succession, and, upon failure, retrenching further, until, at the furthest remove, we might have to take the whole piece as "atomic", which simply means that we would be unable to regard it as a coherent *total structure,* no matter what *local* sub-coherences we were able to construct independently. What the cognitive consequences might be for the possibly significant collection of musics to which such strictures concerning piece-identity might apply presage some radically interesting—even perhaps paradigm-shifting—speculative possibilities.

But since I wish here only to raise some provocative analytic questions, and to "analyze" only those sub-pieces that suggest them, I do not undertake to implement the proposed procedure here either. This evasion is especially necessary since, in the case of Op. 15, No. 1 (not to take into account Nos. 1–15 as a single piece!), I have no, even well-retrenched, structural picture to offer. I do, however, notice some intriguing "macro-phraseological" clues to the possible total-structural identity of the song; in particular, that the "unit" of 56 8ths (7 measures) that determines the time-span of the (piano-solo) "introduction" to the song, with *its* characteristic phraseological "temporal-shape" articulation, may be seen as "carried out" in the remainder of the song in terms of different kinds of temporal-shape partitioning of the same time-extent span:

mm. 1.25–8.25	56 ♪	7 × (8/8) = 7 o
mm. 8.25–15.25	56 ♪	7 × (8/8) = 7 o
mm. 15.25–17.0	14 ♪	7 × (2/8) = 7 ♩
mm. 17.0–23.0	56 ♪	7 × (8/8) = 7 o

As noted, the individual partitionings are quite different—a domain of difference which thus becomes a possible "developmental" observation-field; but the "integrity" of each "phraseological unit" is "motivically" quite secure: thus, the "(0 2 5)" and ultimate "cycle-of-fifths" plus "chromatic expansion" clearly joins the two "big" articulative partitions of mm. 8–15, a division that splits that span into 18 ♩ (as 6 ♩ × 3) plus 10 ♩ (as 3 ♪ + 9 ♪ + 8 ♪ , with the latter two "joined" to produce a ((17/8)/2) division (as the "phraseological close" is on the *first* 8th of m. 14, but the *next attack* is on the 3rd 8th)). The "motivic" significance of this multiple division is clinched by the time partitioning of the 56 ♪-span from mm. 17–23 (see below). The "third" unit is the "recitative bridge passage" characterized by a uniquely "sparse" piano texture relative to the voice line; its extent is a "7" also, interpreted as a "diminution" by a factor of 4 of the 7 whole-note spans of the preceding 2 macro-articulations. Finally, the "last section" divides its 56 8th-note span into the "ostinato" of mm. 17–19, the "reprise" of mm. 19–20, the "reiteration" of mm. 21–22, and the "2 chords" of mm. 22–23 essentially (if a little roughly) a 10 ♩ + (6 ♩ × 3) division, which compares with mm. 8–15 as its "time-partitional inverse", creating a symmetrical articulation-structure around the recitative, with mm. 1–7 regarded as "introductory" in explicitly this "structural" sense. What we have thus outlined is a suggested demarcation of areas which might seem to be reasonable ones to expect to be generated by "pitch-structural" functions, yet to be discovered. Hence these areas might be good places to start in looking for such functions. This is the whole extent of the large-scale analytic value of the above observations; the failure of a pitch-function analytic program to give these "7"-articulations some structural meaning would ultimately vitiate them as significant, or useful, or at least satisfactory, ways to slice the pitch-presentational data in constructing the piece. For should another rhythmic structure of *pitch-functions* be found that was out of correspondence with *this* articulative structure, we would then want to regard the latter as "counterpointing" the former at a relatively superficial "foreground" level, in a way quite familiar from reconstructions of tonal and 12-tone pieces.

Aside from the obvious demarcation of mm. 1–7 as a "piano alone" introduction preceding the "first vocal entrance" in m. 8, some of the motivations for its isolation as an articulative unit might be considered. To begin with, at the most immediate level, there is an obvious "closure" by direct restatement, in doubled durations and registers, of the opening 4-note group, a restatement divided such that the originally 4th pitch sounds first, and then sustains through and beyond the succession of the originally first, second, and third pitches. Thus, "as sounded", the original ordering is both preserved *and* permuted, and also, an "overlapped" 3-attack/4-attack interpretation of the passage is enabled. But first, having such a "reasonable" basis for isolating mm. 1–7, we can survey the whole attack-grouping scene therein. What we find is a succession of attack-stretches separated by silences, and distinguished by considerable internal uniformity, which form three (or four) distinct groupings: one of 7 attacks (all ♩, except one ½♩ followed by one double ♩), one of 5 attacks, and one of 9 attacks (or 6+3 attacks, the 3 doubled to balance the 6 in total time-extent). The "dual" aspect of the last group is significant with respect to other aspects of the articulation as well, but here we need to observe only a simple set of symmetries: 7 attacks as a "norm", followed by a 5 and a 9, equally "balanced" about 7; or 7+5, whose "balance" around 6 is confirmed by an asserted 6, followed by a 3 whose "time" equals that of the 6, to produce 7+5+6+6. That both of these alternative groupings are *worth* noticing will be argued in the sequel.

Let us examine the first articulation alone. Here 7 attacks are divided in 5+2 by registral disjunction, an associative link with the "5 in all" of the next group. The pitch symmetries here, too, are relatively immediate: "balanced" on the conjunct midpoint, E, the 7 attacks divide into 2 transpositionally equivalent tetrachords:

(T2) (F♯ D F E) = (A♭ E G F♯)

of which the two pitches of the second tetrachord not shared by the first are just the two pitches isolated in the upper register, the "jump" to which coincides with the durational halving/doubling of the reference quarter-note. But this kind of isomorphism is not extensible over the second group as well. By analogy, this group may be articulated into two conjunct trichords, the one presented first in the song followed by a "new" dyad:

F♯-D-F
F-C♯-A♯

Note again the registral parallelism in the isolation of the 2 pitches not in common between the two equidimensional segments of the attack-group. But the intervallic relationship between the two trichords can be related to a kind of association that, in various contexts, emerges as virtually the one "universal" characteristic observable in Schoenberg's "motivic" music. It consists in an interval-associative technique for generating successions of distinct trichords by an "intervallic" operation that preserves (nontrivially) 2 of the 3 intervals of each trichord, while "inverting" one of the two, in mapping one into the other. This is nontrivial even for 2 trichords having 2 pitches in common, as the absence of this property in the following trichord succession illustrates:

F♯-D-F
 ＼
  D-F-G

In our song the first 4 + 3 (F♯-D-F) is duplicated by the second-phrase (F-C♯-A♯), but the "inversion" of 3 into 9 results in a different kind of "outside" interval, 5 in the second and 1 in the first. (The "outside" relationship is interestingly invoked in the first attack-group as well, in the presentation of E and F♯ as the temporally "outside" pitches of the first tetrachord, and then as the first temporal adjacency of the second tetrachord.) Now this mode of transformation may be generalized just to the extent that the total possible range of such interconnections can be shown. The result of doing so (see below) demonstrates that the (12) trichords divide into the group of 8 that can be linked by a single chain of transformations, and the 4 outside this chain. Within the linked 8, a distinction can be made between those associating at one link's remove with 3 others, and those associating with just one other. Here is a picture of this transformational chain, which seems significantly "motivic" in its generation of *successions,* and in its evident dependence on literally presented succession for its identification as a reference:[7]

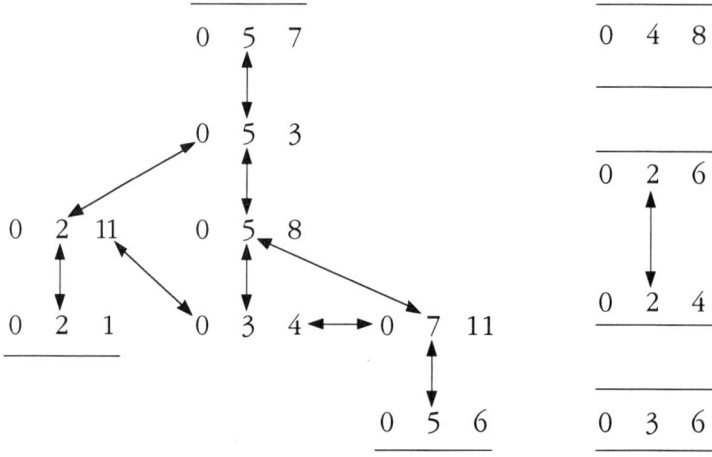

---

[7]For an earlier explanation of this relation as it generates "succession" in *Erwartung,* see Boretz [7]. Note that the "range" of this transformation is quite narrow, and that it is exhausted in relatively few stages. Even in combination with transpositional connections, it seems fully extended after just one page of *Erwartung* (a circumstance especially attendant on the dependence of the *syntactical* reference on a one-to-one relation to the *presented* foreground) . So whether and how the huge further extension of the work is consequent on this motivic evolution remains inscrutable, even though one can discern trichord chains throughout.

The generating "musical operation" for the trichord-chain relation may be considered to be that of complementary partitioning mod-12 of the interval determined by two of the elements of the trichord by the interval determined with respect to one of those two elements by the third element, and by its mod-12 complement. The relation is that defined in Df. 2.13 of Part II (q.v.). The chain, in fact, may be reconstructed just as the set of distinct trichord pairs resulting from such partitioning (each such trichord pair representing one pair of "adjacent" trichords on our chart). Note the exhaustion by the complete set of the relations and content of our chart, and the correspondence of the number of trichords having three distinct pitch-class elements, and the number of distinct trichords, to the number of "adjacent" trichords with respect to each one being partitioned.

Each of the 5-element strings listed below represents one trichord pair, such that the first, third, and fifth elements represent the determinants of the interval being partitioned, as:

$$0\ (\ )\ 3\ (\ )\ 0$$

and the second and fourth elements represent mod-12 complementary partitionings of the mod-12 complementary intervals thus determined, as:

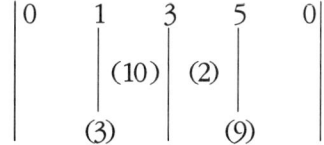

where the p. c. interval from 3 to 1 is the mod-12 complement of that from 3 to 5, such that (0 1 3) and (3 5 0) are complementary partitionings of ((0.3), (3.0)):

(Partitions producing equivalent intervallic results are represented side by side; those producing self-duplication or fewer than three distinct elements are preceded by asterisks.)

"Left-Hand Trichords" Partitions

0 1 3:

        0 1 3 5 0 / 1 0 3 6 1
        3 1 0 11 3 / 1 3 0 9 1
        3 0 1 2 3 / 0 3 1 11 0

0 11 3:

        0 11 3 7 0 / 11 0 3 6 11
        3 11 0 1 3 / 11 3 0 9 11
        3 0 11 10 3 / 0 3 11 7 0

3 5 0:

        3 5 0 7 3 / 5 3 0 9 5
        0 5 3 1 0 / 5 0 3 6 5
        0 3 5 7 0 / 3 0 5 10 3

1 2 3:

   2 3 1 11 2 / 2 1 3 5 2 / 1 2 3 4 1 / 3 2 1 0 3
        *3 1 2 3 3 / 1 3 2 1 1

3 7 0:

        3 7 0 5 3 / 7 3 0 9 7
        0 7 3 11 0 / 7 0 3 6 7
        0 3 7 11 0 / 3 0 7 2 3

11 10 3:

        11 10 3 8 11 / 10 11 3 7 10
        3 10 11 0 3 / 10 3 11 7 10
        3 11 10 9 3 / 11 3 10 5 11

5 7 0:

        *5 7 0 5 5 / 7 5 0 7 7
   0 7 5 3 0 / 0 5 7 9 0 / 5 0 7 2 5 / 7 0 5 10 7

10 3 9:

   *10 3 9 3 10 / 10 9 3 9 10 / 9 10 3 8 9 / 3 10 9 8 3
        3 9 10 11 3 / 9 3 10 5 9

"Right-Hand Trichords"
0 2 4:
  4 2 0 10 4 / 0 2 4 6 0 / 2 0 4 8 2 / 2 4 0 8 2
             *4 0 2 4 4 / 0 4 2 0 0
4 6 0:
  *4 6 0 6 4 / 6 4 0 8 6 / 0 4 6 8 0 / 4 0 6 0 4
           0 6 4 2 0 / 6 0 4 8 6
0 4 8:
  *0 4 8 0 0 / 8 4 0 8 8 / 4 0 8 4 4 / 8 0 4 8 8 / 0 8 4 0 0 / 4 8 0 4 4
0 6 3:
         *0 6 3 0 0 / 6 0 3 6 6
  *3 6 0 6 3 / 3 0 6 0 3 / 0 3 6 9 0 / 6 3 0 9 6

  The trichords in the right-hand column transform only into themselves or one other trichord. Of the linked 8, (0 5 3), (0 2 11), (0 3 4), (0 5 8), and (0 7 11) all transform at one step into any of 3 others, and (0 5 7), (0 2 1), and (0 5 6), the "terminals" of the system, link with just one other each at a single step.

  In Op. 15, No. 1, the characteristic that most obviously invites the invocation of this trichord-transformation concept is the presented interval succession taken as a whole:

F♯-D-F-E-F♯-G♯-G/F♯-D-F-C♯-A♯/E♭-F-D♭-C-E♭-E-F♯-D-F
4 3 1 2 2 1 4 3 4 3 (5) 2 4 1 3 1 2 4 3

If we examine the complete interlock of all specifiable trichords (as overlapping 3-pitch adjacencies) in the entire passage, we find the linkage relation defined above to be extended consistently, and to be broken only at evident articulative points, and then always by the introduction of a "right-hand column" trichord:

   F♯-D-F-E-F♯ (G♯) = (0 3 4) $\rightarrow$ (0 2 3) $\rightarrow$ (0 2 1) $\rightarrow$ ((0 2 4))

which articulates our "tetrachord" group trichordally (cf. the remarks about the "reprise", above). Over the "break" there is a simple T2-transpositional identity relation between the two trichords, corresponding to the T2 aspect of the second tetrachord with respect to the first, and perhaps also "preparing" the 5-attack group following:

$$\underbrace{\text{F-E-}\underbrace{\text{F}\sharp\text{-G}\sharp\text{-G}}}$$

The interlock is complete, in the second attack group, *through* its junction with the third group, a factor to be regarded as significant in the sequel. Note that the chain is carried to the furthest "limit", ultimately, from the "position" of its initiation, and the limit "opposite" to the one arrived at by the first chain:

F♯-D-F-C♯-A♯-E♭-F: (0 3 4) → (0 3 4) → (0 5 8) → (0 5 3) → (0 5 7).

And finally, the next 5+2 attacks form the chain:

$$\underbrace{\text{D}\flat\text{-C-}\underbrace{\text{E}\flat\text{-E-}\overbrace{\text{F}\sharp\text{-D-}}^{(\quad)}\text{F}}}\quad (0\ 2\ 11) \to (0\ 3\ 4) \to (0\ 2\ 11)$$

(Note that the result of marking the trichord-chain-terminations is to produce a timespan structure whose component timespans overlap the spans of the attack-group structure; the trichord-chain structure links groups of 7+7+7 attacks, the later two lapping "over" the 7+5+9 attack-articulative partitions—see the chart on p. 352, and compare "trichord-chain extents/attacks" with "attacks" and "pitches/attacks".) (0 11 7) occurs between the last two links as (F-D♭-C); and only (0 5 6) is missing, but it is supplied immediately by the vocal-entrance B, which is also, as mentioned, a "new pitch class" (the 11th). On the other hand (0 5 6) is formed by the (upper-) registrally isolated (G♯-G-C♯); otherwise this register associates as adjacencies right-hand column-type trichords: (G-C♯-A♯/A♯-C-E). (0 7 11) is of course conspicuous in the song proper.

In each case, we have noted, the (0 2 4) trichord is the articulator of a "break". But in proceeding to this last set of attacks, note that, while the last 4 are identical with the opening 4, and the last 7 form a unit resembling the first 7 (5 linked, then a break, the last conjunct 3 linked to the last of the 5), the last 6 attacks present 6 different pitch classes, and these six pitch classes form a total transposition of the six pitch classes unfolded in the first 7 attacks. And the transpositional interval (2) is just the one which related the two conjunct tetrachords of that first group. All of this makes the "closure" symmetry of this last attack group considerably more complexly "inside" than it might first have appeared:

mm. 1–2: $\left\{\begin{array}{l}\text{D E F F\#}\\\text{E F\# G G\#}\end{array}\right\}$ = D E F F\# G G\#

(T2)

mm. 5–7: (T10): C D E♭ E F F\#

Now this macro-association suggests the possible operation of a "6 pitch-class" reference in conjunction with the "7-attack" reference; thus we discover that the first 7 attacks unfold just 6 different pitch classes, as do also the next 8, and the final 6—creating a "norm" of (6 pitches:7 attacks) as the balancing average of (6:7), (6:8), and (6:6) . This 7:8:6 "averages" to 7 differently from the attack-sequence of 7:5:9, but different aspects of the pitch-association structure are determined by each slicing. And the relation between the outer 6-pitch-class collections and the inner one is of course determined primarily by the interval-transformations of the trichords; but the total content also exhibits a trichord-chain relation:

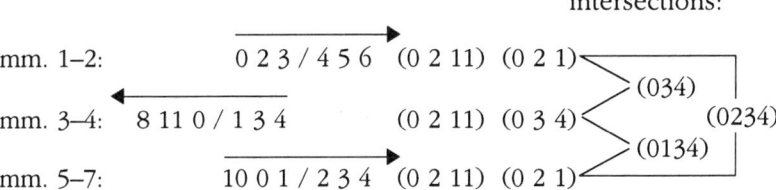

Thus the final group associates with the first group by a pitch-intersection equivalent to the opening tetrachord (obvious by its direct statement), while the trichord (0 3 4) (F\# D F) is common to all three. The last 4 pitches of the lower-register part (E♭ F\# D F) represent the intersection between the second and final groups (0 1 3 4), while the last 5 attacks of the piano introduction represent the union of all the intersection sets of the three groups: (0,1,2,3,4), or (D,E♭,E,F,F\#), which is a 10-transposition of the "chromatic pentachord" that concludes the *first* 7-attack articulation, and "fills in" the interval that *initiates* that articulation (F\#-D) .

Here are some additional interidentities observable in the passage, and a summary of those already noted: the attack-partitioning norm of 7 is, as noted, an aspect of the 7-determined time contours of the whole song. Its being noticed is particularly facilitated by the even-duration contours associated with the entire introduction. Also, in all the relations we have noted concerning attack-groups, trichord-chains, and hexachord-to-attack relations, the "norm" has been inferable from the first articulation (the first 7 attacks). So the last 14 attacks constitute the "field" of simultaneous variability in all dimensions. But on the other hand, the *time* articulation of the three attack groups is precisely divided into 2 × 7 half-notes by the initial 7 + 5, on the one hand, and the final 9 (or 6 × 1 (quarter-note) + 3 × 2 (quarters)) on the other. This produces the attack-to-time relation 12:1 + 9:1, and 12:9 = 4:3 which of course is a partition of 7 (this is nontrivial for partitions of 21; only 3-factorable partitions will produce it: 3+18, 6+15, and the present 9+12, which reduce to 1+6, 2+5, and 3+4, respectively. And 9+12 is the *minimally differentiated* partitioning of these). Such variable partitioning of the same time- and attack-span is a strong associative "micro-macro" link with the variable internal partitionings of equal (and proportional) time-spans that we remarked on above as a strong articulative characteristic of the song as a whole. Here is a table linking these interidentities at different levels:

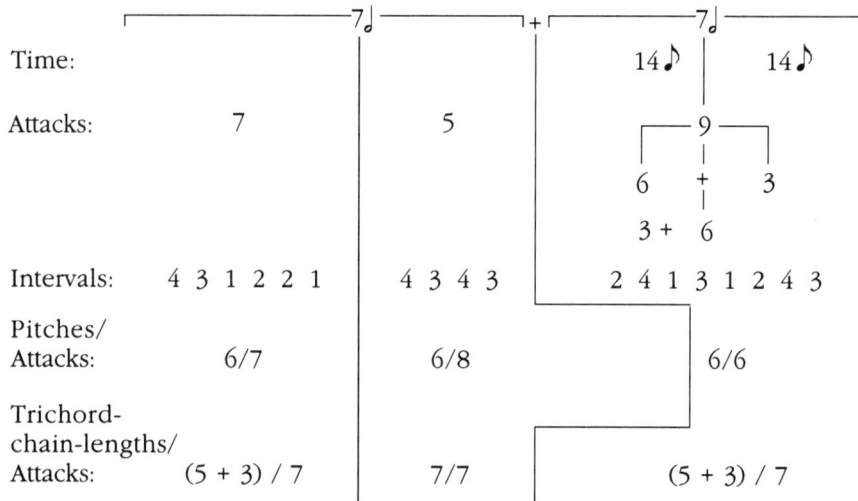

The interlock of 14 half-notes overall, an overall 4:3 attack-time relation, with the internal 7+14 and the variable partitioning of the 14 in different dimensions, surely seem to associate in a rather direct way with the idea of temporal-shape structure observed in connection with the Brahms Fourth Symphony passage examined earlier.

The richness and closeness of this pitch-time-interval web holds a structural promise which cannot be said to be fulfilled by the song proper in any way that I can presently assert, despite trichord-chain relations and a "rationalized" articulation-structure throughout, as we have seen. Some indication that a registral-counterpoint-reading of time-partitioning groups (based on qualities of pitch- and dimension identity to within repetition such as have been employed for the introduction) may yield cognitive results has also appeared. But I have in fact no further claims to make regarding the structure of the song.

9. CONCLUDING REMARKS

Thus, as suggested above, it may appear that a frequent consequence of the "motivic" approach, as we have observed it in Schoenberg's Op. 15, in *Erwartung*, and in *Petrouchka*, is that a more complete and coherent description is possible for a local structure regarded *as* a "piece" in itself than is possible for that same passage when it is regarded as *part* of a larger total structure.

Such a situation is virtually the reverse of that of the tonal music we care about, where local coherence is normally "improved" and clarified by identification with total-structure coherence. But if we were to regard such a different "relative coherence of macro- and microstructure" condition in different pieces as a "degree-of-difference" rather than a "degree-of-coherence" factor at various levels of those pieces, such a relation could play a significant role in generating individual continuity structures for these maverick motivic pieces. Such generation, however conceived, particularly remains to be attempted for virtually all music composed by Stravinsky (of which even its most fervent admirers have yet to produce a single satisfactory total-structure reading of a single instance), that of Schoenberg, Webern, and Berg composed between ca. 1910–1925, and all of Bartók and, as far as I am aware, of Hindemith as well (the list of others is as long as that of the "non-12-tone" pieces anyone cares about, including music by Ruggles, Sessions, Carter, Varèse, Prokofiev among those I still care about). The claim here is just that *no* description of a minimum adequacy reasonably comparable to that which would be normally regarded as satisfactory for tonal or 12-tone music has yet been offered for any of this music, and it is hard to understand, first, why people who do care about it don't construct something out of it worth their concern: or, second, if, having tried so to construct, they couldn't, and have given up on the possibility, then what grounds they retain for caring about it, and, more particularly, just what they suppose themselves to be caring about. The answers to these questions may reveal much about the present state of musical thought, instruction, and awareness, particularly in the domain of composition. For if one acknowledges the purely "conceptual" reality of the musical "object", then the question of the very *survival of* music—past, present, and future—is obviously dependent on the continuance among people of the awareness through which alone (though not necessarily in conjunction with *verbal* expression) "music" as we know it exists.

VIII:
Compositional Postscript: Group Variations*

R.C.: For whom do you compose?
I.S.: For myself and the hypothetical other.

—Igor Stravinsky and Robert Craft,
Memories and Commentaries, p. 85.

Since all of the foregoing has been advertised as the elucidation of a rationale for the composition of a particular piece, a reasonable final question might ask how such a rationale is observably manifest in the piece itself. For methodological, rather than biographical reasons (and certainly not for ideological ones, or to make any assertions regarding the "theory-practice" relation), I might as well mention that among the analytic observations made in the preceding sections, some that can be most intimately related to the particulars of *Group Variations* were actually post-compositional discoveries, the fruit of ideas about possible ways of slicing the data of traditional music according to some notions of pitch-time shape that first occurred to me as potentially significant areas of primary structural determination for the *Variations*. On the grounds that these notions, about the pitch-function-to-time-extent relation, had appeared compositionally realizable mainly by virtue of what was known about traditional musical functions, it seemed reasonable to expect that observations of the traditional literature made in their perspective might yield, not necessarily evidence of primary structural determination by such a rhythmic factor, but rather evidence that the relational data produced by observations derived by its application would at least reinforce (i.e., would probably not contradict or be indifferent—"random"— with respect to) the structures arrived at by more familiar data-slicing procedures. This belief was encouraged by the close connection of the focal relation to some of the factors that we gener-

---

*Group Variations, in its computer-realized version, is available on an OPEN SPACE CD (OPEN SPACE CD 5). The score is available in a University Microfilms facsimile, though the author may be able to supply better-looking copies.

ally choose to regard as conspicuous characteristics of pitch-structural music. That some pieces yielded coherences of a considerably higher degree of particularity through the mediation of such a filter (and sometimes even of a significantly higher order of coherence than had been yielded through more traditional slicing modes) was thus not really a "surprise", but still was more enlivening than had it been trivially predictable *a priori.*

For it is just on a very high degree of motivic determinacy in the relations among times of unfolding of pitch-events, enabled in part through, and in conjunction with, a similar motivic determinateness in the temporal shape of unfoldings *within* pitch events, that *Group Variations* strives to be a particular musical "thing". And since to be a "thing" in music is just to be a determinate structure of determinable differences among observable aspects of elements and events, the extent of *particularity* to which anything is a musical thing depends on the extent to which, and the numbers of levels on which, not only the *fact* of difference, but also the *nature* of difference and the *degree* of difference (in that order) are cognitively determinable through perception. What it means to rely heavily on *any* given dimension to produce the cognitive information regarded as projecting the "ideas" of a piece is— to put it negatively—that a miscalculation about the discrimination-bearing capacities of that dimension or about what constitutes an appropriate utilization of those capacities, are likely to produce a result in which the occurrence of *anything* may not be noticeable, and to which the attribution of *any* structure may thus be made improbable. Or, as is perhaps more likely, the auditory *horror vacui* will produce things to notice and structures to attribute of either a minimal or, to the would-be compositional communicator, a frustratingly inappropriate nature. After all, the denial of intentionality, however desirable in explication, is hardly a becoming social activity for the composer himself with respect to his own work, at least in the privacy of his own thoughts. But such is our music-conceptual world that, where popular "explainers" freely invoke as revelatory the "intentions" of inaccessible or incoherent composers, composers themselves sometimes plead "non-intentionality" in confronting discoveries or inquiries about their works, and refuse to take advantage of "privileged access" to reveal what they consider to be the crucial coherence-gambles taken by them. Indeed, there is even a tendency to criticize those who are willing so to articulate their motives as somehow—to take only the cogent aspect of such objections—likely to *overdetermine* the observer's ascriptions of coherence. But this is a worry whose implementation by reticence hardly bespeaks a decent respect for the critical or discriminative capacities of one's colleagues and auditors, a disrespect that would seem to make even more incomprehensible the apparently simultaneous confidence that, nevertheless, one's work will be appropriately received and understood—or even *more* appropriately received and understood—in the absence of "inside" conceptual or descriptive assistance.

So the question about a compositional rationale is just a question about what has been relied on to make a difference—or differences—on levels of particularity and distinction sufficient for the projection of all the ideas regarded by the composer as essentials of his piece. In *Group Variations*, the relation of pitch function to time extent was considered to have been metricized to the degree that time-proportions of event successions are precisely observable on every dimensionally articulated time-scale in the composition, from the smallest pitch-event complex to the entire "sectional" succession. That this was not unrealistic as a program seemed indicated by the relatively universally assumed capacity among musicians to regard as a precisely observable relation that of the duration of, say, a single sixteenth-note in a classical first movement to the span of the whole movement—or, indeed, of the whole piece. What this suggested about music's resources to precisely project time-proportional relations of a highly complex nature seemed formidable, not only in connection with music already in existence and capacities already developed, but also as it might be projected into new domains out of which still greater amounts of coherent time-structural determinateness could be generated than anything observable in existing music.

Thus the macroformal "variation" notion of the *Group Variations* involves, first, the *concurrent* unfolding of *structurally isomorphic* successions over different timespans, and second, the *successive* unfolding of whole complexes of this type, all structurally isomorphic with one another, over timespans whose proportional differences are also "metric", and, in their aggregate, total-structurally significant. The particular, variable, nature of the "isomorphism" at different levels, in different sections, and with respect to different dimensions, is just the essential "variational" aspect of the composition. The traditional notion of successive restatements of a progressively modified basic succession over an invariant time span is expanded, in *Group Variations*, to time-span variability itself as well, and also to variability in the number and nature of concurrent "time-span levels" on which a basic succession may be considered to be restated. And so, as the piece unfolds, what counts most is the sense of what each successive thing becomes as it merges into the (chronologically and hierarchically) "next" thing.

Obviously, it is only the identity of "something" being unfolded over some specific timespan that makes it possible to experience the relations among the timespans over which it and other things are being unfolded. To put it another way, we may consider that a time structure of this degree of determinacy configures some special ways of cutting paths through a pitch-successional complex to produce "articulative counterpoints" whose totality *is* the piece. So, equally obviously, unfoldings in all of the "activated" contrapuntal domains will contribute, in a typological hierarchy—but one not necessarily identical at all time- or event-levels—to an articulatively interlocked "totality". What is entailed is that, for example, the "completions" of a *registral* counterpoint, if they are regarded as significant, necessarily produce a "rhythm" of the relative times (and time-qualities) of their unfolding. This rhythm, *if* it is regarded as significant, *may* interrelate with other "duration contours" in this dimension or others in other sections, or with other dimensions within one or several unfolding-complexes within a single "section".[1]

The "something" that in *Group Variations* is being unfolded in the most "background" sense—in some way, that is, by every presented dimension and dimensional conjunction—is a pitch-class set, which partitions the pitch-class domain by a hexachord and (trivially) its pitch-class complement, regarded either as a transposition or an inversion—for only the hexachord content, not its order, is syntactically determinate. This hexachord, on the other hand, is actually directly presented only in the central (fourth

---

[1] The specific "weight" of a rhythm, that which counts as its articulative "feel", is a product of the whole complex of qualitative attributes ascribed to it, interpenetrated from whatever domains of sound discrimination as are perceived as functional.

and fifth) sections of the *Variations*; the 8-part hexachordal counterpoint that generates presented successions throughout is, elsewhere in the piece, always determined by superposition of two *different* hexachords having identical *trichord* content whose common derivation from the "basic hexachord" is manifest only in this "center" area. And none of these "structural" hexachords themselves is actually unfolded in any contrapuntal "lines" (in the instrumental version). This complexity of reference-surface relation is accompanied by an appropriate simplicity in the construction and content of the "set" itself, its derived "hexachords", and their "background counterpoint". The unordered source hexachord is the familiar all-combinatorial (0 2 3 4 5 7); its initial derivates are, 1) a "chromatic hexachord" partitioned "all-intervallically" by the (013)/(014) trichords, as ((0 11 9)(2 10 1)), and 2) a (solely) prime-combinatorial hexachord also partitioned "all-intervallically" by the same two trichords, as ((0 1 9) (4 2 5)) . Their "common derivation" is by a cycle-of-fifths transformation performed on the (0 1 3) trichord of each, transforming it into a (0 2 5) trichord—a transformation which is a direct "one-link" association in the "motivic" trichord-chains described in connection with the Schoenberg Op. 15, above:

(0 11 9) / (2 10 1)   (0 1 9) / (4 2 11)
 (×7)   (×1)   (×1)   (×7)
(0 5 3) / (2 10 1)   (0 1 9) / (4 2 5)

And the second "half" of the piece (sections 5–8) counterpoints hexachords generated by a *complete* cycle-of-fifths transformation of the entire "first half" of the piece (sections 1–4), under which the "reference hexachord" (0 2 3 4 5 7) transforms into itself (with different internal trichords): the (0 1 3) trichord transformed in the first operation is "restored", while the previously "retained" (0 3 4) is transformed into (0 3 7):

(0 5 3) / (2 10 1)   (0 1 9) / (4 2 11)
 (×7)   (×7)   (×7)   (×7)
(0 11 9) / (2 10 7)   (0 7 3) / (4 2 5)

The final transformation parallels the first, converting the "chromatic" hexachord to its ×7-equivalent "diatonic" one and reconverting the other into its original shape:

(0 11 9) / (2 10 7)   (0 7 3) / (4 2 5)
(×7)   (×1)   (×7)   (×1)
(0 5 3) / (2 10 7)   (0 1 9) / (4 2 5)

This chain of transformations is one aspect of the "variable isomorphism" of the *Variations,* the most deeply "background" of all (the "set" is presented as a space-location counterpoint in the computer-synthesized version). The "concurrent unfolding over different timespans" is embedded, too, in the "background counterpoint" by the way the latter gives rise to aggregate formation through similar partitionings over variable (dimensional) extents, in a familiar way:

Mosaic 1: Set-voice counterpoint (mm. 1–9)

a:	0	11	9	2	10	1
b:	7	8	10	5	9	6
c:	6	5	3	8	4	7
d:	1	2	4	11	3	0
e:	10	11	7	2	0	3
f:	9	8	0	5	7	4
g:	4	5	1	8	6	9
h:	3	2	6	11	1	10

The disposition of the two different hexachords to produce a high degree of "harmonic" invariance in their conjunction is discernible here; in 8 voices, just 2 distinct "chords" are represented, and their 4-voice components consist of just 3 chords, the same 3 in each 4-voice "block" ((0 7 6 1), (2 5 8 11), (3 4 9 10)). Also observable is the relation of "top" and "bottom" counterpoints as "trichord retrogrades" of each other (the (0 1 3) trichord is followed by the (0 1 4) in the "upper" 4-voice block, and this order is *reversed* by the lower block); the blocks are *initially* distinguished registrally. Aggregates are formed within each 4-voice block at the trichord (3 × 4) level. But the 4 registral voices at the beginning of the piece are formed out of pairs of the 8 set voices, disposed so as to produce aggregates at the "half-trichord" level of the *set* counterpoint (the trichord level of the registral counterpoint), and to create a total "registral pitch-voice retrograde" at the trichord level of the set counterpoint:[2]

Registral counterpoint (top to bottom) (mm. 1ff.)

set		register							
c+d	=	1	1	6	5	/	2	3	4
a+b	=	2	0	7	8	/	11	10	9
e+f	=	3	9	10	11	/	8	7	0
g+h	=	4	4	3	2	/	5	6	1

Here, all of the registral hexachords are 12-tone operationally (content- and order-) equivalent despite the non-equivalence of their generating hexachords (i.e., (0 11 9 2 10 1) and its three derivates, and (0 1 9 4 2 5) and its derivates—this is another aspect of the "variational" properties embedded in the background complex). Note, too, that the 4-part registral subsumption of the 8-part set counterpoint causes the "registral hexachord" to reach completion at a "structural time" equivalent to half of that requisite for a set hexachord's completion (i.e., a registral hexachord = two concurrent set trichords). And, at the other remove, the set-hexachord lines themselves also complete a complex of 4 (12-pitch-class) aggregates in T6-related pairs (a+c, b+d, e+g, and f+h). This level of completion takes the longest timespan in the mosaic. But the instrumental voices are partitioned into 16 parts, so that their hexachord-level completions extend over (as in fact composed, average to) 2 whole 8-voice set-counterpoint mosaics. Their disposition, moreover, is not as "isometric" as that of the other structural counterpoints; some parts are "concentrated" in particular areas, while others are isochronously distributed. These instrumental voices, however, are also pitch-content isomorphic with the registral hexachords, but in the form of their *cycle-of-fifths transformations,* thus further identifying the "variational" notion with that of (transformational) repetition. Thus, e.g., the first flute-voice succession reads:

---

[2] At the beginning of the *Variations,* the "attack-component" of each produced pitch is 1-1 with the "registral line", but articulates in trichordal rather than hexachordal swatches, so that the registral-aggregate times are also articulated by attack-characteristic-change times.

(C = 0):   6 5 10 1 8 3, which is the cycle-of-fifths
transformation
of   6 11 10 7 8 9, which is, e.g., T5 of registral
voice 1, or T6 of registral voice 2.

Another aspect of the structure at this background level is the definition of each macrosection as the conjunction (completion) of three successive transpositions of the same set-counterpoint mosaic. This definition makes it possible to regard changes in the nature of the set counterpoint as the most "background" delineators of "sections" in the piece. Thus, the first section (mm. 1.0–28.5) consists of the (8 × 6) counterpoint shown on p. 362 plus two complementary transpositions thereof (at T11 and T1):

Mosaic 2 (set-counterpoint) Mosaic 3

a:	11	10	8	1	9	0	1	0	10	3	11	2
b:	6	7	9	4	8	5	8	9	11	6	10	7
c:	5	4	2	7	3	6	7	6	4	9	5	8
d:	0	1	3	10	2	11	2	3	5	0	4	1
e:	9	10	6	1	11	2	11	0	8	3	1	4
f:	8	7	11	4	6	3	10	9	1	6	8	5
g:	3	4	0	7	5	8	5	6	2	9	7	10
h:	2	1	5	10	0	9	4	3	7	0	2	11

Mosaic 2 preserves the (0 6) conjunction, and Mosaic 3 the (7 1), of the (0 6 7 1) of Mosaic 1. Similarly, (9 3) of (3 4 9 10) is preserved in Mosaic 2, and (4 10) in Mosaic 3. Also the following dyads that appear "harmonically" in 1 appear "linearly" in 2: (0 1), (6 7), (4 9), (3 10), (8 5), (2 11) in voices a, b, c, and d; and (9 10), (3 4), (0 7), (1 6), (11 2), (5 8) in voices e, f, g, h. This exchange ranges over the entire tetrachord content of Mosaic 1. The following dyads that appear linearly in Mosaic 1 appear harmonically in Mosaic 2: (0 11), (9 2), (10 1), (6 5), (3 8), (4 7)—(i.e., voices a and c of 1, reproduced partly by the a+d counterpoint, partly by the b+c counterpoints, of 2). Further, b and d of Mosaic 1 ((7 8), (10 5), (9 6), (1 2), (4 11), (3 0)) are reproduced as linear adjacencies in Mosaic 2, and as "harmonic adjacencies" in Mosaic 3. On the other hand, the Mosaic-1 dyads of f and h are harmonies of 2, and those of e and g are harmonies of 3. The conjunction of the initial three mosaics produces a pitch-content totality of (12 × 12), whose non-isomorphism as a totality with the internal shape of the 3 (8 × 6) mosaics that generate (—partition—) it makes the completion of the (12 × 12) a uniquely articulative completion-level rather than simply the macro-image of a micro-relation.[3] The "variations" notion most directly observable on the "mosaic" temporal level is, in Mosaic 3 (beginning at m. 21.33), the representation in 2 adjacent registral pairs of each of the initial 4-part registral partitions, thus "spreading" them into an eight-register partitioning that "anticipates" the content-doubling of the (8 × 6) mosaics into (8 × 12) ones that form the background set counterpoint of the second macrosection (from m. 28.5 to m. 56.0). In this section (8 × 12) set-voice blocks are divided into two (4 × 12) blocks identified by their generating hexachords, and the basic block is again "repeated" at 3 distinct transpositional levels.[4]

In the third macrosection (mm. 56.0–121.0), a "variant" (8 × 12) counterpoint is variably deployed over 8 registers. Each mosaic is internally partitioned into two (4 × 6) units; here the 4-voice blocks are regarded as successively juxtaposed rather than superposed as before. The variation in the set counterpoint represents a "harmonic" adjustment that generates, out of two hexachord pairs of *each* of the two different previous 4-voice blocks, the same harmonic constituents as are generated by each of the two previous single-hexachord 4-voice blocks. Correspondingly, the instrumental ensemble is, for the first time, subdivided into sets of internally invariant but variably associated sub-ensembles

---

[3]The three transpositions of the (8 × 6) mosaic also preserve hexachord content of each "set line" maximally.

[4]Here the relation between set and registral hexachords is more complex than in the first section: the set hexachords I-related to those of the first section generate, in registrally adjacent pairs, *temporal* successions in the form of S-related transpositions of first, the *set* hexachords, and, then, the registral hexachords, e.g.:

$$\text{register } 1 \text{ (of 8)} : \quad \begin{matrix} 6 & 1 \\ & \end{matrix} \quad \begin{matrix} 2 & 5 & 4 & 3 \\ & & & \end{matrix}$$
$$2 \quad : \quad 3 \quad 4 \quad\quad 5 \quad 2 \quad\quad 1 \quad 6$$

But the individual registral voices preserve the trichordal partitions (as their principal order-determinate characteristic,) that identify those of the first section as well. Also, in the third mosaic of the second section (mm. 51.0–56.0), the previously invariant identification of the 2 4-voice contrapuntal blocks with "high" and "low" registral layers is now "developed" through an "associative" interpenetration.

(conjoined two at a time, with one group providing just the attack-characteristics and the other the "steady-states" of each pitch event). A sample half-mosaic follows:

Section 3, Mosaic 1 (mm. 56ff.)

	a:	0	11	9	2	10	1	(lower-case letters refer to
	c:	6	5	3	8	4	7	voices of section 1, Mosaic 1)
T9	e:	7	8	4	11	9	6	
T9	g:	1	2	10	5	3	0	
	T9 b:			3	4	6	1	5	2
	T9 d:			9	10	0	7	11	8
	f:			8	7	11	4	6	3
	h:			2	1	5	10	0	9

Here each pair of registral voices (voices of section 2, Mosaic 2) is determined by various partitionings of *single* set voices thus "inverting" the 2-set-voice-to-1-registral-voice relation of the first 2 macrosections. And thus the "time of unfolding" (as well as the texture of unfolding) is also inherently "varied" at this relatively background level. The partition produces four distinct trichords (but the *order* rhythm of partitioning is varied right from the start, as is the registral, distribution; and ultimately, the hexachordal *sources* for the [still invariant] trichords are themselves varied):

Registral Voices, mm. 56ff.
(arrows connect set-hexachord segments)

Registers:
```
3:        9   2  10   |     →6  1  5
4:  0 11          1   |     0  7  11↘
────────────────────────────────────────
5:  6  5        7     |  9  10↗       ↘8
6:        3  8  4     |  3   4↙        2
────────────────────────────────────────
1:  1        3  0     |  2    5  10
2:     2  10 5        |  ↘ ↙  →4  6  9
────────────────────────────────────────
7:  7        9  6     |  1↗        0  3
8:     8  4  11       |  8   7  11
```

(Note the 2-out-of-3 invariance of the 2nd-half trichords.)

As elsewhere, this initial (sectionally) "thematic" statement of a set of relationships undergoes immediate variation; the "degree of variation" is conceived to be proportional to the structural level of the articulation involved. The operation of this notion has already been indicated in the differences between the relations in the first of the two trichord-partitioned examples above among set voices, adjacent registers, and order rhythms, and those in the second. The "over-under" relation of the set presentations in the second complex relates to the presentations in the first complex as an "image" of the relation of that first complex itself to the original "thematic" disposition (in m. 1).

I have restricted the discussion thus far to pitch considerations alone to emphasize the rhythmic-structural dispositions embedded even "predurationally". But the initial "'thematic" complex unfolds a considerably greater degree of pitch-time determinacy by virtue of its actual durational characteristics. These, initially, are framed in a tetrachordally partitioned ordering of attack-time-points, which correspond interval-analogically to those "harmonic" tetrachords of the *pitch* mosaics that are extracted by the initial registral partitioning:

   m. 1: 0 1 4 9 / m. 2: 3 6 7 10 / m. 3: 2 5 8 11

But a still more structurally primary determinant is the pitch-attack relation *per* tetrachord, realized as follows:

   pitches: 1 2 1 1 / 2 2 1 2 / 1 2 1 1 / 2 2 1 2
   attacks: 1 1 1 1 / 1 1 1 1 / 1 1 1 1 / 1 1 1 1
              m. 1   m. 2   m. 3   m. 4

The result is 2 pitch-to-attack relation successions of (5:4) and (7:4), respectively, in which the 12-pitch aggregate completes in 2/3 the span of the 12 attack-point aggregate.[5]

But after 2 such cycles, the relationship "inverts", creating a special, structurally determinate, role for *repeated notes* as "1 pitch in *n* attacks" representations:

---

[5]The presented harmonic structure is determinately involved with this relation; its derived trajectories will be, I believe, evident on even a casual audition.

pitches: 1 1 1 1 / 1 1 1 1 / 1 1 1 1 / 1 1 1 1
attacks: 1 2 1 1 / 2 2 1 2 / 1 2 1 1 / 2 2 1 2
measures: 5———— 6 ——————— 7 ———

At the same time,, the rate of attack-succession also alters, not to a simple 5:4/7:4 relation, but to a 7:4/10:4 relation that preserves the original rate of unfolding of pitch hexachords within the altered pitch-attack relation.

The final pitch-time group of the first mosaic aligns the two cycles by an internally symmetrical "coda":

pitches: 1 1 2 / 2 1 1
attacks: 2 1 1 / 1 1 2
measures: 7   8   9

Thus the first measure of the piece can be regarded as the minimal "theme", but the first 2, first 4, first $6^{5/8}$ or first 9 can also be regarded as a "theme" with respect to their successors on the same (structural) time-extent scale. At m. 10, the second mosaic-"section" (still more "internal" than what I have called a "macro-section") varies the first by, first, unfolding at a total pitch-unfolding tempo 5:4 (i.e., in $^4/_5$ the total duration) of that of mm. 1–9, and second, in this section, tetrachordal pitch-time groups alternate (with appropriate internal tempo shifts) at the one-tetrachord level rather than in 4-tetrachord groups as before:

pitches: 1 2 1 1 / 1 1 1 1 / 2 2 1 2 / 1 1 1 1
attacks: 1 1 1 1 / 2 2 1 2 / 1 1 1 1 / 1 2 1 1
measures: 10–11 /   12   /   13   /   14

Similarly, the third mosaic is unfolded at a total tempo $^7/_4$ faster than (i.e., in $^4/_7$ the total duration of) that of the first.

The second macrosection, beginning at m. $28^{1/2}$, reinterprets the 5:4/7:4 relation as a relation of two distinct attack-voices, unfolding the relations, successively, of 5:4, 7:8, etc., as "5 against 4" attacks, "7 against 8" attacks, etc., with the attack intervals reinterpreted as relations among total times of unfolding for each such group. But the pitch-attack relation within the groups counterpoints independently, producing a still larger completion cycle than before:

attacks: 5   7
attacks: 4   8
pitches/attacks: 5:4   7:4   5:4   (for the "5+7" attack-succession)
pitches/attacks: 4:5   4:7   (for the "4+8" attack-succession)

Another aspect of the macro-time relation—the "largest" one regarded as significative—is reached in the "macrosection" beginning in m. 56: this section is as long as the entire preceding portion of the piece; the same is true of the section from m. 121–226. After the latter "midpoint", the succeeding sections revert by an "inverse" procedure. The ratios are as follows:

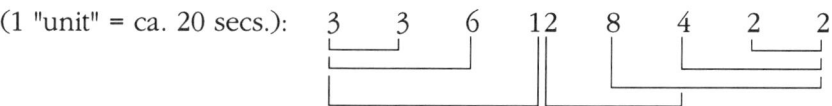

The 2nd section is as long as the preceding, the 3rd section is as long as the 2 preceding combined, the 4th is as long as the 3 preceding, and also as long as the next 2 following: then, the 5th is as long as the remaining 3 following, the 6th as long as the remaining 2 following, and the 7th as long as the remaining single section following. And the pitch-attack relation develops in the third macrosection into an "intervallically" varied attack-point contour relation within the 7-against-4, 5-against-4 time-point groups (and their derivates), which produces a 2-part time-point counterpoint out of 4 attack-point voices. Thus a "7 against 4" produces 10 distinct possible attack-point *locations* per cycle, a "5 against 4" produces 8, etc. Again, the intervals *among* disjunct unfolding groups are modeled on the original presentation.

The fourth macrosection (beginning at m. 121) extends this line of development somewhat complexly by superimposing 3 interlocking groups; one consists of the "original" attack-intervals now extended to a "macrotemporal" level (whose completions are signaled, in part, by some of the tempo changes from ♪ = 125 to ♪ = 156, but not always, for they are not "notational" but "temporal" proportions). Another is a more local "time-of-unit-unfolding" (related to the local attack relations of the third macrosection). And the third is the "local" partitioning, which consists, 1) of a line of evenly spaced attacks interpolated in a succession of differentiated time intervals, and 2) an "intervallically variable" succession; each is associated with a particular group of parts defined in other-dimensional respects. For example, the evenly spaced attack line is initially associated with "legato" articulation, the variable one with staccato, repeated-note articulation, the former "horizontalizing" pitch groups, and the latter "verticalizing" them. The fifth macrosection (mm. 227ff.) is not only varied by its cycle-of-fifth transformations of the set counterpoint of the fourth, but also unfolds its entire pitch mosaic as a simultaneous prime-retrograde superimposition, doubling the number of set voices (from 8 to 16), timepoint voices (from 4 to 8), and timbral voices (from 8 to 16), but not increasing the rate of unfolding except in the overall tempo, as noted above. The mosaics of the fourth and fifth sections are also distinctive in the "background rhythm" with which they generate harmonic-aggregate formation. Here is a sample (8 × 24) half-mosaic:

Measures 121ff.: Section 4, Mosaic 1

3 6 2	7 5 4	9 0 8	1 11 10				
4 1 5	0 2 3	10 7 11	6 8 9				
	10 1 11	6 2 3	4 7 5	0 8 9			
	9 6 8	1 5 4	3 0 2	7 11 10			
			1 4 2	9 5 6	7 10 8	3 11 0	
			6 3 5	10 2 1	0 9 11	4 8 7	
				7 4 8	3 5 6	1 10 2	9 11 0
				0 3 11	4 2 1	6 9 5	10 8 7

A "chordal-linear" distinction, developed in sections 4 and 5 first as a simultaneous subdivision in the texture, then as a series of side-by-side alternations, reaches the macrosection-identifying level in the sixth section (mm. 317ff.), where "chordal" articulation alone is represented, and in the seventh section beginning at m. 365 where "linear" texture alone is represented, contrasting a maximal linear "legato" to the extreme "staccato" into which the sixth section develops at its close. The 16-voice counterpoint of the seventh section produces determinate harmonic complexes of varying (measured) lengths by the overlapped sustaining of pitches to precise release-points.

The final section (mm. 383–395) maps the opening pitch-to-attack contour onto a *hexachord*-to-attack relation; the (presented) hexachords are so composed that pairs of them generate 12-pitch chords with just 8 distinct pitch-classes in each. The tempo is specified to produce a 2/3 total time-relation to that of the opening mosaic, but the *time-point span* is just half (24 time points) of that of mm. 1–9.

The "timed release" final chord (mm. 395–403) is a registrally ordered 12-pitch-class chord (the only one in the piece); the ordering superimposes harmonic units presented in the opening segment; and the order in which the percussion instruments' release-marking attacks peel off pitches reverses the order of their first appearance in the piece.

The shapes in *Group Variations* that surface in dynamic and timbral slices through the pitch data will be left undiscussed here; similarly, the developmental paths based on small-scale time-span relations are far too involuted to encourage any attempt to outline them. Also, the role of octave doubling is quite significant, but again forbidding to brief description because of its multiple interpretations through the course of the *Variations*: in this connection, though, it might be worth mentioning that the role in the structural counterpoint of the attack-component voices in the first two sections is reinterpreted into the octave-doubling and mode-of-articulation characteristics in the later variations.

In any case, any more elaborate exegesis is beside the point here, since my principal intention has been just to indicate, by a few brief excerpts from a rather lengthy score, how the particulars of a complexly articulated pitch-structural composition were derived through a chain of interpretations of some concepts about musical thought and structure in general and about rhythm and continuity in particular. But I have also hoped to suggest how it might be possible to sustain the sense of being engaged in original and exploratory composition while remaining innocent of any concern for "new sounds" or even "new kinds of events". Philosophers and poets, of course, create new language by thinking in language rather than by inventing new words or syntax; and ultimately, even the identification of anything as a particular musical identity, even as a "new sound", depends on the existence of a cognitive musical context, which in turn can be created only by the occurrence of appropriate instances of coherent thinking in music.

And since music, in our sense, is not continuous with any "informal" or "natural" mode of communication, it is only through the occurrence of "compositional" or "analytic" thoughts (whether intersubjectively communicated or not) that "music" may be said to exist at all. And so I am led to the parting speculation that perhaps the only cognitive explication—or at least the only cognitive measure—of what we call originality of musical imagination, profundity of musical conception, and elegance of musical technique, is just in their identification as the degree to which we can regard as maximized the particular coherence attributable to a particular compositional instance.

References

1. MUSIC THEORETICAL LITERATURE

[1] Babbitt, Milton: "Twelve-Tone Invariants as Compositional Determinants". *Musical Quarterly*, April 1960.

[2] Babbitt, Milton: "Set Structure as a Compositional Determinant". *Journal of Music Theory*, April 1961.

[3] Babbitt, Milton: "Twelve-Tone Rhythmic Structure and the Electronic Medium". *Perspectives of New Music*, Fall 1962.

[4] Babbitt, Milton: "Remarks on the Recent Stravinsky". *Perspectives of New Music*, Spring–Summer 1964.

[6] Berger, Arthur: "New Linguistic Modes and the New Theory". *Perspectives of New Music*, Fall–Winter 1964.

[7] Boretz, Benjamin: Review of George Perle: "Serial Composition and Atonality". *Perspectives of New Music,* Spring 1963.

[8] Boretz, Benjamin: "A Note on Discourse". *Perspectives of New Music*, Spring–Summer 1966.

[8a] Boretz, Benjamin: "Nelson Goodman's *Languages of Art*, from a Musical Point of View". *Journal of Philosophy*, LXVII, 16 (1970).

[9] Cone, Edward T.: *Musical Form and Musical Performance*. New York: W. W. Norton, 1968.

[10] Cone, Edward T.: "Analysis Today". *Musical Quarterly*, April 1960.

[11] Cone, Edward T.: "Stravinsky: The Progress of a Method". *Perspectives of New Music*, Fall 1962.

[12] Cone, Edward T.: "A Budding Grove". *Perspectives of New Music*, Spring–Summer 1965.

[13] Cone, Edward T.: "Beyond Analysis". *Perspectives of New Music*, Fall–Winter 1967.

[14] Forte, Allen: "Context and Continuity in an Atonal Work: A Set-theoretic Approach". *Perspectives of New Music*, Spring 1963.

[15] Forte, Allen: "A Theory of Set Complexes". *Journal of Music Theory*, Winter, 1964.

[16] Howe, Jr., Hubert. S.: "Some Combinational Properties of Pitch Structures". *Perspectives of New Music*, Fall–Winter, 1965.

[17] Johnston, Ben: "Scalar Order as a Compositional Resource". *Perspectives of New Music*, Spring–Summer 1964.

[18] Johnston, Ben: "Proportionality and Expanded Musical Pitch Relations". *Perspectives of New Music*, Fall–Winter 1966.

[19] Kassler, Michael: *The Decision of Arnold Schoenberg's Twelve-Note-Class System and Related Systems*. Princeton: Princeton University, 1965.

[20] Kassler, Michael: "Toward a Theory that is the Twelve-Note-Class System". *Perspectives of New Music*, Spring–Summer 1967.

[21] Komar, Arthur: *Theory of Suspensions*. Princeton: Princeton University Press, 1970.

[22] Krenek, Ernst: "Some Current Terms". *Perspectives of New Music*, Spring-Summer 1966.

[23] Lester, Joel: "Pitch-Structure Articulation in the Variations of Schoenberg's Serenade". *Perspectives of New Music*, Spring–Summer 1968.

[24] Lewin, David: "A Theory of Segmental Association in Twelve-Tone Music". *Perspectives of New Music*, Fall 1962.

[25] Lewin, David: "Two Schoenberg Studies". *Perspectives of New Music*, Fall–Winter 1967.

[26] Lewin, David: "Inversional Balance as an Organizing Force in Schoenberg's Music and Thought". *Perspectives of New Music*, Spring–Summer 1968.

[27] Lewin, David: "Behind the Beyond: A Reply to Edward T. Cone". *Perspectives of New Music*, Spring–Summer 1969.

[28] Mitchell, William J.: "The *Tristan* Prelude: Techniques and Structure". *Music Forum*, Volume I, 1967.

[29] Perle, George: *Serial Composition and Atonality*. Second Edition. Berkeley and Los Angeles: University of California Press, 1967.

[30] Randall, J. K.: "Godfrey Winham: Composition for Orchestra." *Perspectives of New Music*, Fall–Winter 1964.

[31] Randall, J. K.: "A Report from Princeton". *Perspectives of New Music*, Spring–Summer 1965.

[32] Randall, J. K.: "Three Lectures to Scientists". *Perspectives of New Music*, Spring–Summer 1967.

[33] Schenker, Heinrich: *Der Freie Satz*. Vienna: Universal Edition, 1935.

[34] Treitler, Leo: "Musical Syntax in the Middle Ages: Background to an Aesthetic Problem". *Perspectives of New Music*, Fall–Winter 1965.

[35] Treitler, Leo: "On Historical Criticism". *Musical Quarterly*, April 1967.

[36] Treitler, Leo: "The Present as History". *Perspectives of New Music*, Spring–Summer 1969.

[37] Westergaard, Peter: "Some Problems of Rhythmic Theory and Analysis". *Perspectives of New Music*, Fall 1962.

[38] Westergaard, Peter: "Webern and 'Total Organization': An Analysis of the Second Movement of the Piano Variations, Op. 272". *Perspectives of New Music*, Spring 1963.

[39] Westergaard, Peter: "Some Problems Raised by the Rhythmic Procedures in Milton Babbitt's Composition for Twelve Instruments". *Perspectives of New Music*, Fall–Winter 1963.

[40] Westergaard, Peter: "Toward a Twelve-Tone Polyphony". *Perspectives of New Music*, Spring–Summer 1966.

[41] Winham, Godfrey: "Henry Weinberg: Three Songs". *Perspectives of New Music*, Spring–Summer 1964.

[41a] Winham, Godfrey: "Composition with Arrays". *Perspectives of New Music*, Fall–Winter, 1970.

2. GENERAL-METHODOLOGICAL LITERATURE

[42] Apostel, Leo: "Towards the Formal Study of Models in the Non-Formal Sciences". In [59].

[43] Bar-Hillel, Yehoshua: "A Prerequisite for Rational Philosophical Discussion". In [60].

[44] Bergmann, Gustav: "Two Types of Linguistic Philosophy". In *The Metaphysics of Logical Positivism*. Madison: University of Wisconsin Press, 1928.

[45] Carnap, Rudolf: *The Logical Structure of the World*. Translated by Rolf A. George. Berkeley and Los Angeles: University of California Press, 1967.

[46] Carnap, Rudolf: *Foundations of Logic and Mathematics*. Chicago: University of Chicago Press, 1939.

[47] Carnap, Rudolf: "Empiricism, Semantics, and Ontology". In *Meaning and Necessity*. Reprinted in [51].

[48] Carnap, Rudolf: "The Methodological Character of Theoretical Terms". In [52].

[49] Carnap, Rudolf: "Replies to Criticism". In [68].

[50] Church, Alonzo: "The Need for Abstract Entities in Semantic Analysis". *American Academy of Arts and Sciences Proceedings*, Vol. 80, 1951.

[51] Copi, I., and J. A. Gould, eds.: *Contemporary Readings in Logical Theory*. New York: Macmillan, 1967.

[52] Feigl, Herbert, and Michael Scriven, eds.: *Minnesota Studies in the Philosophy of Science* (3 vols.). Minneapolis: University of Minnesota Press, 1956.

[53] Goodman, Nelson: *The Structure of Appearance*. Second Edition. New York: Bobbs-Merrill, 1966.

[54] Goodman, Nelson: "On Likeness of Meaning". In [62].

[55] Goodman, Nelson: "A World of Individuals". In [51].

[56] Goodman, Nelson: *Languages of Art*. New York: Bobbs-Merrill, 1968.

[57] Hempel, Carl C.: *Fundamentals of Concept Formation in Empirical Science*. Chicago: University of Chicago Press, 1952.

[58] Hempel, Carl G.: "Aspects of Scientific Explanation". In *Aspects of Scientifc Explanation*. New York: John Wiley, 1965.

[59] Kazemeir and Vuysie, eds.: *The Concept and the Role of the Model in Mathematics and Natural and Social Sciences*. Dordrecht: D. Reidel, 1961.

[60] Kazemeir and Vuysie, eds.: *Logic and Language*. (Studies Dedicated to Professor Rudolf Carnap on the Occasion of his Seventieth Birthday). Dordrecht: D. Reidel, 1962.

[61] Kleene, Stephen Jay: *Mathematical Logic*. New York: John Wiley, 1967.

[62] Linsky, Leonard, ed.: *Semantics and the Philosophy of Language*. Urbana: University of Illinois Press, 1952.

[63] Martin, Richard M.: "On Carnap's Conception of Semantics". In [68].

[64] Morris, Charles W.: *Foundations of the Theory of Signs*. Chicago: University of Chicago Press, 1938.

[65] Myhill, John: "On the Ontological Significance of the Löwenheim-Skolem Theorem". In [51].

[66] Quine, W. V. O.: *Word and Object*. Cambridge: M.I.T. Press, 1960.

[67] Quine, W. V. O.: "Carnap and Logical Truth". In [51] and [60].

[68] Schilpp, Paul A., ed.: *The Philosophy of Rudolf Carnap*. Chicago: Open Court, 1963.

[69] Sellars, Wilfred: "Empiricism and the Philosophy of Mind". In [59].

[70] Suppes, Patrick: "A Comparison of the Meaning and Uses of Models in Mathematics and the Empirical Sciences". In [59].

[71] Suppes, Patrick: "The Desirability of Formalization in Science". *Journal of Philosophy*, LXV, 20 (1968).

[72] Ubbink, J. B.: "Model, Description, and Knowledge". In [59].

[73] Wang, Hao: "On Formalization". In [51].

[74] Weyl, Hermann: *Philosophy of Mathematics and Natural Science*. Princeton: Princeton University Press, 1966.